By Ved Mehta

Face to Face

Walking the Indian Streets

Fly and the Fly-Bottle

The New Theologian

Delinquent Chacha

Portrait of India

John Is Easy to Please

Daddyji

Mahatma Gandhi and His Apostles

The New India

Mamaji

The Photographs of Chachaji

A Family Affair

Vedi

THE LEDGE

BETWEEN

THE STREAMS

Family group, Rawalpindi, 1944.
Top row: Umi, Om. Bottom row: Nimi, Usha, Mamaji,
Daddyji with Ashok, Ved, Pom.

VED MEHTA

THE LEDGE

BETWEEN

THE STREAMS

W. W. Norton & Company

NEW YORK / LONDON

The contents of this book originated in The New Yorker.

The text of this book is composed in Garamond, with
display type set in Garamond 248. Composition and
manufacturing by The Maple-Vail Book Manufacturing Group.
Book design by Guy Fleming.

First Edition

Library of Congress Cataloging in Publication Data

Mehta, Ved, 1934–
The Ledge Between the Streams.

Continues: Daddyji, 1972, Mamaji, 1979, and Vedi, 1982.
1. Mehta, Ved, 1934–   2. Children, Blind—
India—Biography.   3. Children, Blind—Education—
India.   I. Title.
HV2093.M43A34   1984   362.4'1'0924 {B}   83-13101

ISBN 0-393-01828-8

W. W. Norton & Company, Inc.,
500 Fifth Avenue, New York, N.Y. 10110

1 2 3 4 5 6 7 8 9 0

To Om, Usha, and Ashok

For nearly thirty years now, between writing other books, I have been engaged on a large autobiographical work. "The Ledge Between the Streams" is the fourth book in that work—the three others being "Daddyji," "Mamaji," and "Vedi." (There are also two related books—"Face to Face," a sort of outline for the larger work, and "The Photographs of Chachaji," a sidelight on it.) Each of the four books is independent and self-contained, but, of course, each is a volume of one continuing life story. As the famous race between Achilles and the tortoise suggests, no matter how fast I write, the writing of the life can never catch up with the crawl of my day-to-day life ("Vedi" and this book chronicle a span of barely ten years), so, not surprisingly, I sometimes feel I am leading two lives—the life I'm remembering and interpreting and my ordinary, day-to-day life. And I expect to continue this double life, intermittently, for many years.

I wish to express my lively thanks to Sally Ann Brickell, Naomi Grob, Harriet Walden, Martin Baron, Eleanor Gould Packard, and William Shawn, each of whom contributed subtly but mightily to the making of this book.

V.M.

New York
November 1983

CONTENTS

CONTENTS

PHOTOGRAPHS

THE LEDGE

BETWEEN

THE STREAMS

I

THREADS OF LAHORE

T HE REIGN OF THE TOP QUEEN WAS THE
best of all reigns," Bhabiji used to say to us.
"In her reign, people could walk on the streets
wearing a lot of gold and no one would bother
them. Such was the presence and authority of
Queen Victoria." Bhabiji was our paternal
grandmother, and she used to say that in any good
city she'd heard of, the best road and the best walk
always led up to the statue of the Top Queen, and the
Top Queen always had the best-kept gardens surrounding her. Every day, morning and evening, Bhabiji used to go for a walk to the statue of the Top
Queen in Lahore. Whichever of us grandchildren happened to be around would go with her—often six, eight,
or twelve of us. Two of us would take her hands, and

the rest of us would hold one another's hands and troop behind her. As often as not, in the course of the stroll each of us would get a turn walking with her. I remember that she always walked straight, without the aid of a cane or umbrella, and, unlike our mothers, she never stopped to look in shopwindows or to engage in long conversations with shopkeepers or friends. If along the way we whistled or swung our arms or put our fingers in our mouths or pinched each other, Bhabiji would say, "Your daddies have big hands," but it was an empty threat, and she knew it, because our fathers hardly ever slapped us.

"How nicely your white clothes go with your white hair, Bhabiji, and how nicely your gold goes with your white clothes!" Sister Umi once said as we were going along the Mall Road. Daddyji had told me that, as long as anyone could remember, Bhabiji had always worn a white shirt with a collar and gold studs, white pajama trousers, and, when it was cold, a white shawl over her shoulders. "But, Bhabiji, what are those black hairpins doing on your head?" Sister Umi went on. Sister Umi stopped us and took up a collection of our pocket money and bought Bhabiji a silver hair clip from a shop we were passing. She put the hair clip in Bhabiji's hair in place of the black hairpins.

Bhabiji couldn't bless us enough. "God give you long life," she kept saying, over and over.

Sometimes, on the way to the Top Queen, we would visit the Bird House—actually a zoo. Near the gate, there was a skunk. We would all hold our noses and exclaim "Chhichhi!" Bhabiji couldn't understand why we were making such a fuss—she had no sense of smell—but she would hurry us along to a vender who was roasting peanuts, and buy us some peanuts in their shells, fresh off the fire. We would race up to the monkey cage. We would put our hands through the bars. A monkey would come down and take all the peanuts in one swoop. I could never get over the feel of a monkey's hand—it felt exactly like a person's hand.

We would always finish our walk at the statue of the Top Queen. I never knew what the statue looked like. (When I was almost four, I had been left totally blind as a result of an attack of meningitis.) It was cordoned off with chains, and a sentry was posted by it. No one was allowed to go near the chains, let alone touch the statue. I always imagined that the statue was tall and stately, had a crown on its head, and was made out of marble. I imagined, too, that it was cold to touch but very nice to climb on, with lots of hills and dales for footholds and handholds.

"Are all these your children?" the Top Queen sentry would sometimes ask Bhabiji.

"They're all God's bounty," Bhabiji would say evasively. Bhabiji didn't want to admit to the Top Queen sentry that we were all her grandchildren and part of the Mehta clan, because she was afraid of the curse of the evil eye.

❧

BHABIJI LIVED IN Mehta Gulli, a small cul-de-sac in Lahore where Daddyji's brothers and their paternal uncle, Bhaji Ganga Ram, had got together and built houses with common walls and terraced roofs—all designed by Daddyji's architect brother, Romesh Chacha. ("Chacha" is a form of address for a paternal uncle.) Bhabiji had given him all her savings and told him, "Make me a little room. I want to have a corner of my own in Mehta Gulli. I don't want to be dependent on any of my sons or interfere in their lives." He built her a room, with its own entrance, on the ground floor of his house. Bhabiji's room, as it came to be called, had only one window, which opened out onto the *gulli,* or alleyway. The window was so low that we were often tempted to jump through it into the room, but we wanted Bhabiji to think well of us, so we always used the entrance. While all our relatives in Mehta Gulli lived simply, Bhabiji lived the most simply of all. Her room was small and square. By the window was a cot, and in one corner was a *chulah,* a makeshift oven of a couple of bricks and a few iron rods, on which she did her cooking, over charcoal. Aside from these and a steel trunk, an old spinning wheel, and a few pots and pans, the room was bare.

More often than not, we would find Bhabiji sitting cross-legged on a plank, the spinning wheel in front of her on the floor. She would be rotating the wheel with one hand and holding the cotton with the other. As she spun, we would gather around her on the cement floor or else we would sit on her cot, being very careful not to swing our legs. She said she preferred sitting with us children to sitting with the grownups. We asked her once why that was, and she said, "My sons belong to their wives now, and mothers-in-law should be like children, seen and not heard." We would busy ourselves with rolling raw cotton into strands. Whenever she finished spinning one strand, each of us would try to be the first to hand her a new one.

Over the undulating buzz of the spinning wheel, Bhabiji would tell us about village life. She had spent many years of her married life in our ancestral village, which our fathers had left as children to come to Lahore for their education. In time, they had all married women from city families, and we Mehta cousins were all city children.

"Mehta Gulli looks a little bit like our ancestral village, except that the houses here are made of brick and cement and are permanent," she once told us. "The huts in the village were made of mud and clay. Nowadays, you touch a switch and there is light, but in those days you needed oil and a wick." We were fascinated. When we were with her, we thought we preferred simple village life to showy city life. Many of our women relatives made a great to-do about being very religious, going to temples and consulting pandits; Bhabiji never did. She did, however, own a string of wooden beads, and when she tired of spinning she would now and again quietly pick it up and murmur the names of gods. She was the only woman among our women relatives who never raised her voice, hardly ever cursed. "I had never heard a woman raise her voice until I came to the city," she once told us. "A village woman did not have the boldness to speak like that."

Whether she was spinning or praying, cooking or washing, she would listen to our quarrels and complaints and often tell a story bearing on them. She seemed to have a story to illustrate any situation.

I remember that once she heard Sister Umi and me

quarrelling about which one of us should hand her the next strand. "Two sheep reached a bridge," she told us. "The bridge was so narrow that they couldn't both cross it at once. They started quarrelling about who would go first, and both tried to cross the bridge at the same time. Both fell into the river and drowned. Then two other sheep reached the bridge. One said, 'Let me be the first to cross.' The other acquiesced and lay down to rest. The first one got across safely, and then the other. So to what one says the other agrees, and in agreement they are both wise."

Cousin Leil once borrowed some money from Sister Umi. She didn't pay it back, and Sister Umi threatened to charge interest. Cousin Leil complained to Bhabiji, and Bhabiji said, "Once there was a man who went to his neighbor's house. The man said, 'Mother, an unexpected guest has arrived. May I borrow a quilt?' The woman lent him a quilt. The next day, the man returned the quilt, with a pillow. 'How is it that you are bringing me a pillow when I lent you only a quilt?' the woman asked. 'In the night, the quilt gave birth to the pillow,' the man said. 'It's yours.' The woman was very pleased. The next day, the man came back and asked to borrow a pot. The woman gladly lent him one. The day after, he returned it, with a bowl. The man came back another day and asked to borrow some jewelry. The woman lent him the biggest and best gold necklace she had. But the man never brought it back. When the woman asked for her necklace, the man said, 'The necklace has died.' She exclaimed, 'Died! How can that be?' He said, 'Mother, if your quilt and pot can have children, then the necklace can die.' "

Bhabiji paused to let the whining buzz of the spinning wheel die down, and then concluded, "So, children, you should never borrow and never lend—especially for profit."

Another time, Sister Umi complained about how often her classmate Fatty ate at our house, particularly when we were having chicken or fried fish. "I don't know how she gets to know of it, Bhabiji, but she can smell it from a mile away. She's really a leech."

"Leech!" Bhabiji exclaimed. "Umi Daughter, such a word doesn't suit your mouth." She continued, "Once there was a tiger. Every day, a friend would arrive at the tiger's house for dinner. Every day, the tiger's wife would cook the best meal she could for the tiger's friend. One day when the friend arrived at the door for his dinner, he heard the tiger and his wife quarrelling inside. 'Every day, your friend invites himself here for dinner!' the wife was shouting. 'He has not invited us back even once!' The friend walked into the house and handed the tiger's wife a sword. 'Sister, take this sword and put a cut on my forehead,' he said to her. The tiger's wife said, 'Why do you ask me to do such a terrible thing?' The friend said, 'Just do what I tell you.' So the tiger's wife did as she was told. The friend ate his dinner and went away. He didn't come back for a week or ten days. When he did, he said to the tiger's wife, 'See, Sister, the cut is gone, healed. A wound from a sword gets erased, but a wound from a mouth—that is never erased.' " Bhabiji finished, "That's why, children, you should always weigh what you're going to say before you speak."

The stories followed one another, and they became

so familiar that sometimes it was only when we heard the moral that we were aware that one had ended and another was about to begin. "Once there were two *gulli* cats," she told us when two of us were arguing over dividing a slab of Cadbury's chocolate. "They found a loaf of bread and started quarrelling about it. A monkey dropped down from a rooftop and addressed them, asking, 'Auntie Cat and Auntie Cat, what are you quarrelling about?' 'We can't divide this loaf equally,' they said. 'Here, let me do it for you,' the monkey said. He broke the loaf in two, but the cats said that one half seemed bigger than the other. So he broke off a little piece from the bigger half and ate it. But then the other half seemed bigger to the cats, so he broke off a little piece from that half and ate it. But then the first half seemed bigger. While the cats sat watching him, he kept breaking off little pieces and eating them, until he had gobbled up the whole loaf, and then he jumped back onto the roof. So you see, children, be content with what you get. But if you fight you should settle the fight among yourselves."

I remember that one of our favorite stories was about a mother and a pencil: "Once a mother was tidying up her son's schoolbag, and she noticed that he had two pencils instead of his usual one," the story went. "He must have lifted it from another boy, she thought, but she said nothing to her son. Another day, she noticed a pocketknife in her son's schoolbag. She still said nothing to him. All small boys do a little bit of lifting now and then, she thought. So it was that the small boy continued to lift things and grew up to be a big thief. He was sentenced to be hanged. The superintendent of the jail asked him for his last wish, and the thief asked to see his mother. His mother came running to him, weeping because he was going to be hanged but happy because his last wish was to see her. The thief took out a pocketknife and cut off his mother's nose and then cut off one of her ears. 'What have you done?' his mother cried. He said, 'If you had stopped me from lifting that first pencil and then the pocketknife, I would not have grown up to be such a big thief.' The moral is: It's very important for us mothers to give our children good training. That's why we tell you that if you see a pencil, although it may be lying on the table and may not seem to belong to anybody, you shouldn't lift it."

We never tired of her stories, and if she paused to draw breath when she had finished one we would say, "Tell us another, Bhabiji."

"That's enough for today," she would say, finally.

"Just one more, Bhabiji. The last, the very last, for today."

Without hesitation, she would begin again.

"Once there was a cow," she told us on one occasion. "Every day, she used to go to a jungle to graze. One day, a tiger happened upon her. 'How dare you graze in my jungle?' the tiger said. 'I am going to eat you up.' The cow said, 'Tiger, please don't eat me now. Eat me in the evening. My calf is waiting at home for me to give him his milk. I will run home, give him his milk, and then come back.' The tiger said, 'You lie. You won't come back. You'll run away.' The cow said, 'I give you my lasting promise that I will come back in the evening.' The tiger let her go.

She went home, fed the milk to her calf, and then started crying. 'Why are you crying, Ma?' her calf asked. 'This evening, the tiger is going to eat me up,' she said, and she told him about her lasting promise. 'Don't go back,' her calf said. 'Let's run away. The tiger will never find you then.' The cow said, 'But I've given the tiger my lasting promise.' It was growing dark. The tiger was getting more and more angry, pacing around the jungle. I have been tricked, he thought. Just as I expected, the cow has given me the slip. Then he saw her. She was coming toward him slowly. 'You've come!' the tiger said. 'Did your calf not say anything to you?' 'He said that we should run away, but I told him that I couldn't break my lasting promise.' The tiger said, 'Are you *that* faithful to your lasting promise? Cow, you can graze in my jungle for the rest of your life. No one will bother you.' So, children, you should all be as faithful to your word as the cow was.''

We had often heard Bhaji Ganga Ram, who was the oldest Mehta in Mehta Gulli and the first university graduate in the family's history, say to Bhabiji, "You can neither read nor write, but you know all the stories of the world." We used to ask her how she came to know so many things.

"I never studied, but I married Lalaji," she would say. "Everything I know, I know because he taught it to me."

❦

IN THE COURSE of a day, if the weather was right, one or another of my boy cousins—"cousin-brothers," they are called—was sure to climb to the terraced roof of his house and send up a kite. As soon as the kite was spotted, my other cousin-brothers and boys living near Mehta Gulli would race up to the terraced roofs of their houses and send up their own kites. In no time, kites would be tangling in the air, and the kite fliers would be trying to cut one another's kite strings.

Brother Om had no interest in kites, but as soon as I heard that a kite battle was on I would shout for my sister Usha and my cousin Ravi—they were both younger than I was, and were therefore at my command—and we would run to whichever roof was the center of the noise and activity. On the roof, Ravi, Usha, and I would run around, playing tag or hide-and-seek. Our cousin-brothers would often scold us for getting in their way and generally making a nuisance of ourselves, but whenever I asked for a kite and a ball of string of my own they would say, "You're too small, Vedi." (At the time, I was eight.) And they might add, "Besides, you have to be able to see to fly a kite." Once in a while, though, one of them would let me hold the string of the kite he was flying, but just as I was enjoying feeling the strong pull he would take the string back.

One day, Cousin Yog, Ravi's older brother, who was the oldest Mehta son, and therefore the leader in Mehta Gulli, took me to a vender around the corner on Mozang Road and bought me a hydrogen balloon. "There. Now you can fly your balloon while we fly our kites," he said.

"But who will I tangle with?" I asked. "There are no balloon battles."

"You can tangle with Ravi and Usha," he said, and he bought two more hydrogen balloons, for me to give to them.

At Mehta Gulli, I gave Ravi and Usha their balloons, and we went up to the roof of Ravi's house. We chased one another around the roof, holding our balloons as high as our arms and the balloon strings would permit, and tried to tangle them. But while a kite string was fortified with glass and resin, was as sharp as a knife, and seemed endlessly long, the balloon string was only a short ordinary thread; moreover, while a kite in the air sometimes generated so much pull that when I held its string I felt I would be carried aloft, the balloon had hardly any tension. Then, too, kites flew at an angle, but the balloons flew straight up and wouldn't tangle. I seized the thread of Ravi's balloon and forcibly tangled it with mine, but, of course, we couldn't cut the strings of each other's balloons.

"Look!" Ravi cried. "The balloons are going soft on us. The gas must be leaking out."

I felt my balloon. Its tautness was gone, and it had dropped down and was floating in front of my face. Even as I was feeling it, it fell at my feet like a collapsed pocket of air.

I complained to Cousin Yog. He offered to buy us new, bigger hydrogen balloons, with long threads, but I knew that balloons had as little to do with kites as Bhabiji's strands of raw cotton had to do with Cousin Yog's ball of kite string, and I would have no part of the balloons.

❧

ONE MORNING, I found myself alone with Cousin
Yog on the roof. "I'm going to fly this big *patang,*" he
told me. A *patang* was a heavy, many-cornered kite,
and had the status of royalty among *guddis,* which were
lighter, square kites. He continued, almost to himself,
"If I am lucky, maybe my *patang* can bring the tangle
right down onto this roof. But you can never tell. Some
measly little *guddi* can appear at the last minute, from
nowhere, and make the booty fall into the *gulli.*" He
walked this way and that way, muttering about wanting a stringwallah. He suddenly asked me, "Do you
know how to be a stringwallah?"

"Of course I know," I said.

From being around kite fliers, I knew that the ball
of string rolled about on the roof as the kite flier ran
around, letting in and hauling out the kite. The string
had a tendency to get tangled, especially if the kite
was hauled in quickly, or if the resin was fresh, or if
the ball had not been wound symmetrically. There was
an art to winding the string. One end of it had to be
made into a skein and the skein into the core of a ball,
and the rest of the string had to be wound carefully
onto the core, a few strands going in one direction and
a few strands at right angles to them, so that the groups
of strands alternated and lay tightly next to one another.
A properly wound ball felt like a series of symmetrical
rises and depressions. It was a stringwallah's task to
keep the ball of string from getting stuck and knotted,
and so allow the kite flier to concentrate his entire
attention on manipulating and watching his kite. I
was very excited at being Cousin Yog's stringwallah.

Cousin Yog was moving from parapet to parapet

in search of some breeze to launch his kite. It was summer, and although it was the early morning the air seemed close and it was already getting hot. I felt a stirring of the wind to my right, and I called to Cousin Yog. He ran over. I heard the rustle of the *patang* as he threw it over the parapet.

"There she goes!" he exclaimed. "She's caught the wind. She's climbing. Quick, more string!"

I crawled all over the roof with the ball, ducking under Cousin Yog's hands and arms as they almost bicycled in the air. One minute, I was yanking string off the ball as Cousin Yog needed more string; the next minute, I was winding string back onto the ball as it became heaped in bunches around his feet. I had never worked with the string in that way before, and it was so highly resined that it felt alive, fresh, and dangerous.

"Hey, your fingers are bleeding!" Cousin Surinder said, joining us on the roof and taking the ball of string away from me. He was Cousin Yog's younger brother, a year older than I.

I tried to hide my hands in my pockets, but Cousin Yog saw the blood, too. "What if your daddy saw that?" he cried.

"You see with your fingers. Leave kite flying to your ruffian cousin-brothers," Cousin Surinder said.

"But I want to fly kites like you!" I cried.

Neither paid me any attention, though, for a battle had been joined. From roofs all around were coming battle cries.

"Look! My kite has hooked them!"

"Pull! Pull!"

"Bo-kata!" ("There, it's cut!")

Up and down Mehta Gulli and beyond, on Temple Road, boys were shouting *"Bo-kata! . . . Bo-kata!"* and I could hear them running toward the spot where they thought the kites were going to fall. The best way of acquiring a cache of good kites was to capture a booty of fallen ones, because a good ready-made kite from the bazaar was expensive, and a homemade kite, no matter how carefully it was put together, fell apart in battle. We small boys, when we had nothing else to do, would try to serve as scouts for falling kites. I had good hearing, and I had trained myself to tell the direction of the cries of *"Bo-kata!"*

"At the Mehta Gulli gate, Cousin Yog!" I now shouted.

Cousins Yog and Surinder started running in that direction.

Ordinarily, Ravi and Usha would be at my side and I would alternately propel and lead them toward the sounds of the chase. It used to be that as we were running from roof to roof and from house to house they would call out to me, "Take a long step. . . . Climb down. . . . Jump. . . . Not that side—there's a table in the way," but after a while they noticed that I could somehow tell by myself what to do, and for the most part they left off warning and helping me. At the time, I could not have explained any more than Ravi and Usha could how I knew by myself when to take a long step or how to avoid crashing into a table, but I later learned that the explanation had to do not only with memory but also with what is called "facial vision"— an ability that the blind develop to sense objects and terrain by the feel of the air and by differences in sound.

The air at the edge of a roof feels lighter than the air near a table, and sounds echo differently in different rooms, depending on the size of the room, the number of its open and shut windows, and so on. Those who lose their sight in childhood develop this ability naturally and fearlessly, and therefore to a higher degree than those who lose their sight in later life. So, without knowing it, during the kite chases I was learning how to get around—by sensing the currents of air and by listening to the patter of feet on a roof, to the scrapes of shoes along a wall, to the rattle of a drainpipe as boys clambered down it. I was helped in this attempt by the fact that Ravi and Usha were too small and my cousin-brothers too busy with the kite chase to worry much about me.

Now here I was on the roof without Ravi and Usha, and Cousins Yog and Surinder were running to be the first to get to the fallen kites. I heard them leap over the parapet and jump down onto the eaves of the next house. I followed; I leaped over the parapet, but I missed my foothold on the eaves. My heart skipped a beat. I was so terrified that I could scarcely breathe. I thought I was going to fall straight down to the *gulli* two stories below, like a deadweight. I frantically reached for something to hold on to that would break my fall. I hit my chin on the edge of the eaves, caught hold of it even though it seemed to have been sloped expressly to precipitate a fall, and pulled myself up with such force that it seemed that I hit my knees on the bottom of the eaves and my forehead on the top at the same time. Without stopping to take stock of my injuries, I balanced myself on the eaves and listened. Cousins

Yog and Surinder were clambering down the drainpipe ahead. I inched along the eaves sidewise, clutching the parapet above, found the drainpipe, and slipped down it. Cousins Yog and Surinder had already jumped from the drainpipe into an open window opposite and were thundering down a staircase inside the house. I tried to reach out and find the open window but discovered that my arms were too short. I threw myself across, almost flying through the air, like a football. I took the stairs two or three at a time, heedless of the turns where the steps narrowed to points.

At the Mehta Gulli gate, so many boys were shouting and threatening that I could scarcely tell the voices of Cousins Yog and Surinder from the others. I slipped through the knot of legs, caught hold of two small kites fluttering under a big one that was being dragged through the mud, got them free, and started running away. Suddenly, I myself was the object of a chase. Someone with a long arm reached over my shoulder and made a grab for the kites. As I was about to resist, I heard Cousin Yog's voice behind me and realized that it was his arm. I immediately let the booty go. He was the tallest among us and had the longest legs, and he ran with the kites into Mehta Gulli.

❧

I REMEMBER THAT once during a kite chase I had to get from the parapet of one house to the parapet of another. As I pushed off, using my left foot to gain leverage in flight, I heard my big sisters exclaiming from far below, "Look! He's falling!" "Oh, my God!"

I missed the parapet and started hurtling through the air. But, as I had on so many other occasions, I saved myself from a fall—this time by catching hold of a brick projection.

When Mamaji came to hear about the incident, she forbade me to have anything more to do with kite flying. "You are to stay with your big sisters and let them watch you," she said.

I complained to Daddyji, but he wouldn't listen.

For many days, Mamaji and my big sisters did not let me out of their sight. But then, one day, they began letting me do what I liked. Years later, Daddyji explained, "You grew irritable and sullen. You would throw a tantrum at the smallest thing, like not getting your meal on time. I noticed the change and decided that yours was one case where an ounce of prevention was not better than a pound of cure. I told everyone to let you do whatever you wished."

I remember that after Daddyji's decision I ran around with my cousin-brothers from morning to night, and even flew my own kites. There was hardly a day when I didn't get bumps or bruises, but my cousins began treating me as if I were really one of them—with, as Cousin Yog once put it, "two good eyes."

❧

I DON'T REMEMBER how I heard that Brother Krishan was dead or exactly where I was when I heard the news. All I remember is that there was a news bulletin in English that had come over a Japanese radio station, and that everyone seemed to be repeating it in a hushed voice: "Captain G. K. Mehta has been killed fighting for a cause which he did not know." There was no mistaking the name, because the bulletin had apparently come through the shortwave radio as clear as a bell. I didn't understand the phrase "a cause which he did not know," and in the stunned atmosphere I didn't dare ask, but the phrase kept repeating itself in my head.

I remembered that once, when the subject of my blindness came up, I had heard Brother Krishan say to Daddyji, "Vedi will be my responsibility."

There had been a long silence. "As long as I am alive, he is my responsibility," Daddyji had said, his voice quavering as if he were talking outside during a dust storm. "I have broad shoulders. But thanks all the same." I didn't know what "responsibility" meant, exactly, but I remembered thinking that if anything happened to Daddyji I would go and live with Brother Krishan.

Brother Krishan was actually Daddyji's brother, the youngest, and was eight when their father, Lalaji, died. At the time, Daddyji was twenty-eight (a year older than Brother Krishan was when he died). Daddyji was the eldest surviving son, and, as a matter of course, Krishan had come to live with him. When Daddyji married, Brother Krishan was ten, and he had become Daddyji and Mamaji's first "child." Though he was our *chacha*, we called him not Krishan Chachaji but Brother Krishan. Of all our *chachas*, we felt closest to Brother Krishan. "Your other *chachas* can be wily," Mamaji would tell us. "They can be obstreperous, rowdy, and inconsiderate. But your Brother Krishan is a good, straight person. I know him well. I brought him up myself, with buttermilk churned by my own hands."

I remembered that Brother Krishan had liked to play a game with me. He would cradle me in his arms and then toss me again and again toward the ceiling. He would toss me higher and higher and let me fall farther and farther before catching me. I would shriek with fear and delight.

I remembered that Brother Krishan had always been after my big sisters to do their homework, and if they got their sums wrong he would visit hand-torture on them—insert a pencil between their fingers and twist it. My big sisters would beg to be let off and would promise to do their homework over. I used to feel sad that I didn't have any homework to do or sums to get wrong, and that I couldn't be punished with the pencil.

One day when I was about four, I ran into the house and let the screen door bang behind me.

"Go out, and let me see you come in without banging the door," Brother Krishan said.

"I won't."

He caught hold of me, raised me high over his head, and put me down on top of a tall cupboard.

"Get me down!" I cried.

"Not until you say 'Sorry' and promise to let me see you come into the room without banging the door."

I ranted, kicked my heels against the cupboard, screamed, but in the end he got his way.

"Why are you so strict with the children?" Bhabiji once asked him. "You're going off to the war. Don't you want to be well remembered?"

"I have to make something of these children," he replied. "It doesn't matter how they remember me."

But Brother Krishan wasn't as much of a taskmaster as he sometimes seemed. True, when we children used to sing along with gramophone records of film songs about love Brother Krishan would burst into the room, lift up the needle, and say, "They have dirty lyrics. Put on some hymns." Still, because he was very musical and had a good memory, if he heard a film song he never forgot the lyrics. I remember that when we were at the singsong part of Auntie Dharam's wedding festivities my aunties and big sisters could not recall the lyrics of a song about a Punjabi girl. They asked Brother Krishan, and after a lot of hemming and hawing he sang out:

Don't become chums with a lass from the Punjab,
Be she covered with a hundred thousand weights of gold.

There was an explosion of clapping and laughter the like of which I had never heard. "More, more!" everyone shouted. "Now the 'boyfriend' song!"

Brother Krishan hesitated, and then sang:

I call my boyfriend out of shyness;
I hide my breasts out of shyness.

Everything about Brother Krishan was first class, I felt. He had a first-class voice, first-class shirts with military appliqués, a first-class military cap with a visor, and first-class ways. I remembered that he had come back on leave from the Army and brought me a mouth organ. I didn't know what it was, and he showed me how to put it against my mouth and breathe into the openings. I was thrilled to discover that every opening made a different sound. All the notes of the harmonium seemed to be fitted into a little box.

On that visit, Brother Krishan was home only a few days, and then he went off to the war. Somehow, Bhabiji seemed to sense that he wouldn't come back.

"So many people go off to the war, Bhabiji," Daddyji said. "You will see—Krishan will come back decorated. He'll be a war hero. He'll be paraded around the city, on shoulders, and shown off to the children." But when Daddyji was away from Bhabiji he would sound uneasy and sad whenever the subject of Brother Krishan came up. "I should never have let him go into the military," he would say. "I don't know why I weakened. I don't know what came over me. He was such a good boy—the best of us brothers. Golf, tennis, painting, music, photography, dancing—my God, what couldn't he do? Handsome, open, loving—and, if something had happened to me, such broad shoulders. He could have taken on the responsibility of finding husbands for Pom, Nimi, and Umi, and of educating Vedi."

I would stand next to Daddyji's chair as he talked, and secretly wish that I might grow up to be like Brother Krishan. I would be carried along by the wish until I remembered about the golf and tennis and painting and photography and dancing.

In the meantime, Bhabiji had taken to sitting by the window of her room in Mehta Gulli and waiting for the postman. "Has the postman come?" she would ask. "What time is it?" She dictated her letters for

Brother Krishan, generally to Sister Pom. Then Bhabiji started saying that she wanted to write letters with her own hand, and every evening Sister Pom sat beside her with a primer of Hindi and taught her script and grammar. But then Brother Krishan died.

After the news bulletin, Sister Pom continued to teach Bhabiji reading and writing and to take down letters to Brother Krishan, because somehow it had been decided—and all of us were aware of it without being told—that Bhabiji was not to know about Brother Krishan's death. She was told only that he was "missing in action." Even that news so shocked her that she took to her bed and was extremely sick for several weeks. She rallied only when she was told that he was a prisoner of war and might be permitted to receive letters.

For a long time, I used to walk around the house thinking about Brother Krishan. My every footfall sounded like a gunshot. I used to walk over to the cupboard on which Brother Krishan had set me down. I would touch it; I would open the door and close it; I would drag over a chair and stand on it to see if I could reach the top—I never could.

❧

AT THE TIME of Brother Krishan's death, I was only eight, but I felt that it was wrong to lie to Bhabiji. I think that all of us who liked to listen to her stories felt that. One evening or another, someone was sure to ask Bhabiji to tell the story about the honest cow, either because someone had brought along a new friend or simply because we found the story affecting, no matter how often we heard it. Bhabiji never tired of repeating the moral of the tiger's-guest story, "Think before you speak." But when Bhabiji told the story of the honest cow after Krishan's death we would all start chattering thoughtlessly, as if we were eager to change the subject, didn't want to remember the moral.

Sometimes when we were away from Bhabiji, we talked among ourselves about whether we could tell Bhabiji the truth about Brother Krishan, but dread that she might die from the shock kept us quiet.

I once asked Daddyji, "Do you really think Bhabiji would die from the shock?"

"I don't know," he said. "She is seventy-two, and four years ago she did almost die from the shock of Romesh marrying a Christian." After Romesh Chachaji secretly married a Christian, Bhabiji had been sick for some months.

Even when the war was over—when the soldiers had come home, when the prisoners of war had been released, and when the missing persons were accounted for—our elders continued to keep the truth from Bhabiji. They met her inquiries after Brother Krishan with answers like "Bhabiji, there are many soldiers who have not come home yet," and "Bhabiji, the Japanese are keeping many secret prisoners of war," and "Bhabiji, there are so many missing persons that even the government doesn't know about them."

In the last years of her life—she died in 1956, at the age of eighty-six—she was totally blind. Sometimes if she heard a footstep she didn't recognize, she would say, almost to herself, "My Krishan has come home." Yet her inquiries about Krishan were infrequent and perfunctory, and were easily satisfied. Everyone felt that she had long since guessed the truth but was keeping up the pretense for everyone else's sake.

I I

THE FRESH WOODS
OF RAWALPINDI

•

I N FEBRUARY, 1942, DADDYJI WAS PERMA-
nently posted in Lahore, and at last we came to
live in our own house, at 11 Temple Road, just
across from Mehta Gulli. As we all followed
Mamaji from room to room, opening up bedrolls
and unpacking suitcases, we were struck by the
fact that she kept calling the rooms after our *chachas*.

"There isn't a single room in this house named
after us," Sister Umi complained.

"That's because your *chachas* lived with us in this
house when they were getting on their feet, and none
of you have lived here," Mamaji said.

We had always thought of Lahore as our home.
Mamaji's family was from Lahore. Daddyji and his

brothers had come to Lahore, the capital and the most important city of our Punjab, long before we were born. We and all our cousin-brothers and cousin-sisters felt we were Lahoris. Daddyji, as the eldest Mehta brother, had been the first one to build a house of his own, at 11 Temple Road. Much of the time that we were growing up, however, we had hardly known the inside of our house, because Daddyji was then posted in various cities outside Lahore. When we came to Lahore, either because he was briefly transferred there or because we wanted to be with our relatives, our house had almost always been rented out to pay off the mortgage; Mamaji used to say, "Your daddy's hair is tied up in debt." When we were in Lahore, we would stay with Babuji and Mataji, our maternal grandfather and grandmother, at 16 Mozang Road, because it was spacious and Mehta Gulli was cramped. By chance, Mehta Gulli and 16 Mozang Road were separated only by an easily scalable wall, so we spent quite a lot of our time in Mehta Gulli.

Now, within days, our house was swarming with bricklayers, electricians, painters. They set about converting the garage into a stable for a couple of buffaloes, so that we could drink fresh milk instead of diluted or contaminated bazaar milk; enlarging the driveway, so that Daddyji could park his car there instead of in the garage; building a whole new room above the garage, with a separate staircase, for my oldest sister, Pom, who was fifteen and was about to enter college. (In those days, people generally started college when they were fourteen or fifteen.) In the drawing room, they were installing a ceiling fan; in the bathroom, laying marble chips on the floor; in Mamaji's bedroom, painting the walls green.

I rushed around from room to room, touching everything and asking the laborers how they secured the hook for the ceiling fan, how they mixed cement and water, what the difference was between oil paint and whitewash.

I don't think we had been in the refurbished house for more than a few weeks when Daddyji returned home from the office and said, "Dr. Harnath Singh has done his dirty work. I have been transferred again. I have been posted to Rawalpindi."

We all started sniffling.

"I can't pack again," Mamaji said. "I can't leave this house again. I can't leave Lahore again. I can't leave Babuji and Mataji again."

"How will we all study medicine in Rawalpindi?" Sister Pom asked. "There is no medical college there, and I've just bought all these expensive science books." All three of my big sisters had decided to follow in Daddyji's footsteps and become doctors.

"I myself don't know what to do," Daddyji said. "Dr. Harnath Singh has done his dirty work really well. I will probably have to be in Rawalpindi for three years."

A couple of days later, he left for Rawalpindi, saying that he would send for us as soon as he had seen to the accommodations and settled in, and quoting Shakespeare to us in Punjabi: "Sweet are the uses of adversity, Which, like the toad, ugly and venomous, Wears yet a precious jewel in his head."

Years later, Daddyji explained to me what Dr. Harnath Singh's dirty work had been. "When I was posted to Lahore, I felt on top of the world. I was the most senior assistant director in the Punjab Public Health Department and was in line to succeed Dr. A. H. Butt, the director. I therefore assumed that I was in Lahore for keeps. One fine morning in late August, I got a letter from Dr. Butt asking me to take on additional duties—those of the district medical officer for Lahore—in place of Dr. Harnath Singh, who had been selected to go to Rawalpindi as an assistant director of public health. Imagine my surprise when, the very next morning, I got a second letter from Dr. Butt, saying that I should immediately proceed to Rawalpindi in place of Dr. Harnath Singh. I was flabbergasted. I made inquiries at the office and was told that Dr. Harnath Singh had been selected as the assistant director in Lahore in my place. I walked into Dr. Butt's office and protested my transfer. 'I had no hand in it, Dr. Mehta,' he said. 'I myself was flabbergasted. The orders came from the ministry, from the secretary of our department. How could I withstand such pressure?'

"The secretary was an Englishman, Henry John Bosanquet Taylor, and I knew him from the Gymkhana Club, where we used to play tennis together. I called on him at his office and protested. He seemed to be put out. 'You have not taken any active part in the publicity and propaganda on behalf of the Allies in the war,' he said. 'But Dr. Harnath Singh has been actively associated with this work—he even had a poster made showing Japan as a cobra when Hirohito joined Hitler. Besides, Dr. Harnath Singh has declared himself a Sikh.' For some time, Dr. Harnath Singh had been putting it about that while I was preoccupied with clubs and society in my spare time he was spending his spare time doing great propaganda work for the War Publicity Department. He was now also using his newfound Sikh religion to press his position as a member of the minority Sikh community, in order to get preferential treatment from the British secretary. I pleaded with Mr. Taylor to rescind my transfer order, and told him that a couple of days earlier we had heard that Krishan, who was like a son to me, had been killed in the war, that my mother, Bhabiji, was old, that she lived in Lahore, and that she needed me. I told him that we had told Bhabiji only that Krishan was missing in action, but even so she had taken ill, and the doctors didn't hold out much hope. The British considered us all part of the official family and made exceptions on compassionate grounds, but Mr. Taylor refused to rescind the order. I subsequently learned that, despite what Dr. Butt had said to me, Dr. Butt, who was a Muslim and a member of the other minority community, had made common cause with Dr. Harnath Singh to do me down with Mr. Taylor, because I was a Hindu. This was my first whiff of the religious intrigue that later on took such a toll of all our lives."

❧

IN SEPTEMBER, 1942, a few days after Daddyji left for Rawalpindi, we received a letter in English from him. It was passed around, read aloud, and translated into Punjabi for Mamaji, Usha, and me, since we couldn't understand much English. Daddyji wrote:

Shanti, you should rent out the house and come to Rawalpindi with the children early in the year. Pom, I have made inquiries, and there is a very nice Presentation Convent here. It was recently upgraded from a school and now has a college of its own called St. Anne's. The college is affiliated with Punjab University. You can study at St. Anne's for your B.A., and Nimi and Umi can study in the school. For the time being, you three sisters will have to give up sciences and the thought of studying medicine, because St. Anne's is strong only in arts subjects. I've told the Mother Superior about Usha, and she can be admitted into the first standard. In the higher standards, the convent is only for girls, but I understand from the Mother Superior that nearby is a boys' school called St. Denys' which is every bit as good as the convent and where Om can go should he decide to leave Bishop Cotton School in Simla and come and live with us.

I've always felt that the Lahore *gullis* are bad places for children to grow up in. They make for a narrow, often mean-spirited outlook. In contrast, Rawalpindi is a very pleasant place for children to grow up in. It has open, wide roads and a country atmosphere with all the advantages of a good city. It is only a hundred and sixty miles north of Lahore, but is at the foot of the Himalayas, at an elevation of seventeen hundred feet. It is not far from Kashmir, and, in fact, is known as a gateway to that heaven on earth—the only metalled road to it goes from here. The winter here is invigorating; the cold winds come down from the Himalayas. I'm sure that here you children will all gain weight and your color will improve.

I have revived many of my old associations with Rawal-

33

pindi. It was here that I got my princely first job, with a horse allowance so ample that I could keep not only a horse but also a carriage and a syce.

Now, finally, about the office-residence that the government gives me with my post here, deducting a mere ten per cent of my salary *per mensem* for rent. It is something that has to be seen to be believed. The house has a couple of rooms at one end which serve as my office. I can go to work or leave off work, take my lunch or rest at any time in the day I like—just by walking through a door. The house has a big compound. In the compound are many low-roofed hutments. One is the kitchen, a couple are quarters for our private house-servants, and the rest are quarters for servants allotted to the assistant director by the government. I have here two peons, a watchman, a gardener, a washerman, and some sweepers. Best of all, our compound is right next to the Rawal Club. I just have to walk through the hedge to be on the club grounds. The Rawal Club has very nice tennis courts, so that the children will be able to play tennis regularly, and, with such a start, who knows? They may be able to play one day in Wimbledon.

The office-residence and the club buildings are situated in the Civil Lines, a lane reserved for government officers and set apart from the city proper. They look as if they were put up quickly by English officers. They are quite run down. Although our compound is a holding comparable to that of any other officer in the government, the whole place has a feeling of a little, decaying palace for an Englishman—a decrepit outpost of the Empire.

To quote Milton: At last he rose, and twitched his mantle blue: Tomorrow to fresh woods and pastures new.

Ved, Bombay, 1942.

Nothing was said in the letter about what I would do in Rawalpindi, because I was to go back to Dadar School for the Blind, in Bombay, thirteen hundred miles away, to which I had first been sent when I was just short of five years old. I did go back, but within a few months the principal of the school, Mr. Ras Mohun, informed Daddyji that though I'd studied only up to the fourth standard I had learned all I could at his school, and should return home, especially in view of the war conditions.

Daddyji says he was distressed to get the letter, because Mr. Ras Mohun's school was one of the best schools for the blind in the country, and, for all he knew, an interruption in my education could disqualify me from studying further. But he felt he had little choice, and reconciled himself to my leaving school with the thought that, after all, it was wartime and little was normal anywhere.

I arrived in Rawalpindi to live with my family in May, 1943, a month or so after my ninth birthday. I couldn't get over how spacious the house seemed in comparison with the cramped school building or with the well-like *gullis* of Lahore—how high the ceilings were, how big the doors were, how open the rooms were. The rooms seemed to flow into wide verandas, and the verandas into the compound. My facial vision was little help in such open spaces.

I missed our old servant Sher Singh, who used to take me out for walks and let me help him bake biscuits whenever I was home from Bombay. I asked at the dinner table what had happened to him.

"Oh, your Auntie Pushpa has taken him with her

to Kanpur," Mamaji said. Auntie Pushpa was one of Mamaji's younger sisters. "When Pushpa got married, last year, she didn't know anything about running a house—how to cook, how to shop, how to lock cupboards to keep servants from stealing flour, ghi, and lentils. She wanted a trustworthy servant, and I lent her Sher Singh. I don't think he'll ever come back to us now. But you wouldn't like Sher Singh anymore anyway. Pushpa has thoroughly spoiled him. He spends all his time going to the cinema or sitting around in the bazaar smoking *biris*."

"We have Gian Chand now," Daddyji said. "He's every bit as good as Sher Singh."

"Hardly," Sister Umi said, with a laugh. "Whenever he milks Mamaji's buffalo, he aims one stream of milk into his mouth for every stream he aims into the milk bucket, and he milks the buffalo twice a day."

Everyone laughed.

"Umi always exaggerates," Mamaji said.

"But Mamaji hasn't seen the number of biscuits he puts away for himself every night," Sister Umi went on. "I once surprised him and saw him putting one batch aside for himself for every batch he put in the biscuit tin for us. No wonder he bakes them only after dark, when the other servants have gone to sleep. Then he has the cheek to say that it's because he doesn't want them to pinch his recipes. Mamaji, you've got to admit that every day he looks a pound or two heavier than the day before."

"Don't exaggerate," Mamaji said, slapping Sister Umi on the arm. "He's so young and hardworking. If he drinks a little milk and eats some biscuits, what's the harm? He needs to build up his strength. He never stops, and he's so punctual. He gets you children off to school on time, he doesn't pinch money when he is sent out to the bazaar, he always has fresh carrot *halwah* for you children to eat, he always has breakfast, lunch, tiffin, and dinner on the table on time."

"Mamaji won't admit it, but Gian Chand has become a real favorite of hers," Sister Umi said.

However Mamaji praised Gian Chand, I never took to him the way I had taken to Sher Singh. Gian Chand seemed to be always bustling about—scouring the pots and pans, fanning the kitchen fire with a hand fan or blowing on it to keep it going. He made me feel that I was in the way. Also, he was at once effusive and quarrelsome. He hardly ever addressed me as "Vedi Sahib," the way Sher Singh had, but instead as "Little Commander Sahib," "Little General Sahib," "Little Admiral Sahib," "Little Marshal Sahib." And if I got hungry, went to the kitchen, and asked to have my tiffin a few minutes earlier than four—the usual time— he would get angry.

"I will report you to Mistress!" he would bellow. "I will tell her that you are harassing me, making me late for tiffin."

"I'm not harassing you, I'm hungry. Give me a biscuit."

He would ignore me, knowing full well that I didn't know where he had put the biscuits. If I started feeling around for them, he would shout, "I will report you to Mistress! You are making me late!"

"I order you to give me a biscuit!" I would shout back.

He would march off to the house to tell on me to
Mamaji. Then I would get a scolding from her.
"Why do you have to get in Gian Chand's way?"
she would ask. "Why can't you wait a few minutes for
tiffin to be ready? Why don't you go and play with
Lakshman Singh or Raj Kumari?"

Lakshman Singh and Raj Kumari were new servants, and I didn't get on with them any better than I
did with Gian Chand. Lakshman Singh was sixteen or
seventeen but gave himself the airs of an old retainer.
He wouldn't answer to his name—only to his title,
"Bearer." He had somehow taken it into his head that
bearers, who worked in the house, were more important than cooks, like Gian Chand, who worked in the
kitchen, a separate little building behind the house.
Yet he had such a nervous disposition that he could
scarcely carry a tray without making the plates on it
rattle and dance. Sister Nimi used to make fun of him
by calling him Charlie, after a butler she had seen in
an English picture. " 'Bearer,' Memsahib," he would
correct her.

Raj Kumari, a young maid, was stuck up in her
own way. She had got the job of maid by claiming
that she was a Christian and could speak English, and
so could help my big sisters practice their convent
English. Mamaji had naturally interviewed her in
Punjabi and then had hired her. It had turned out that
she knew scarcely any English, but by then it was hard
to dismiss her. Her favorite topic of conversation was
her name—*raj kumari* means "princess." She claimed
that she was a real princess, who had been engaged to
a real prince. As proof, she would show us a necklace
of "precious" stones which she said the prince had given

her. "The prince died, Sahib-people," she would say. "But I have his necklace for always. I am only working as an ayah temporarily, until another prince comes and takes me away."

The subject of her name and her engagement was always a source of great mirth and could be depended upon to help us pass the time. I remember that Sisters Nimi and Umi used to serenade her with a popular film tune: "Go to sleep, Raj Kumari, go to sleep."

I used to feel sorry for both Lakshman Singh and Raj Kumari, and would sometimes take their side, only to be serenaded by Sisters Nimi and Umi in my turn: "Go to sleep, little brother, go to sleep. Or you'll grow up to be Charlie in Princess Raj Kumari's court."

❧

MY VISITS HOME for holidays from Dadar School had been brief, and I remembered that during them my big sisters used to indulge me; they would buy me sweets and Carry Home ice cream with their pocket money. Now I was home for good, and I had to buy my own sweets and ice cream, with my own pocket money. Hardly anybody paid special attention to me or cared what I did during the day. My big sisters didn't seem to like my company anymore. Usha, however, was always at my side. She was now almost six, and was a good playmate. If she heard the bicycle bell of the ice-cream man at the gate, she would come running for me and catch hold of my hand, and we would race out to the ice-cream man. If someone mentioned that our buffaloes were grazing outside, I would call for Usha, and she would take me to them and show me how the buffaloes stood around chomping on the grass. We were inseparable. We did everything together: spun tops; swung from the gate; climbed trees; played hide-and-seek or high-and-low, a version of tag.

One morning, Sister Pom took Usha to the Presentation Convent, where my big sisters were studying, and got her admitted into kindergarten. The next morning, Usha began attending the convent with my big sisters, riding in the hired tonga that took them there and brought them back daily. (The convent was about two miles from the house.)

I remember that I cried a lot that first day. Now I had no one to play with, and I walked around the house saying Usha's name to myself and waiting for her to come back. The moment I heard her feet on the front veranda, I ran to greet her. She was crying, and I thought that that was because she had missed me.

"Why are you crying?" I asked her.

"I've lost my goggles," she said. Daddyji had bought her goggles, or sunglasses, for going to school.

"Never mind," I told her. "I'll buy you new goggles with my pocket money."

"I don't want you to," she said. "Daddyji wouldn't buy you goggles, because you couldn't go to school."

"No, Daddyji wouldn't buy me goggles, but he said that it was because I might hit against something and cut my face with the glass," I said.

She stopped crying.

"What is school like?" I asked.

"I am in the English section," she said.

"What's that?"

"The girls in the Indian section stop after the fourth standard. The girls in the English section go on to higher standards. You have to know English to study after the fourth standard."

I felt a pang. Mamaji had stopped after the fourth standard. I had stopped after the fourth standard. Usha was three years younger than I was, but she was going to surpass me. "Then who goes to the Indian section?" I asked, as if I didn't care.

"Oh, I think they are called charity children. I think they are probably from the city. They are certainly not from the Civil Lines or from the cantonment."

Later, at the dinner table, Sister Pom told Daddyji, "At first, the nuns put her in the Indian section. Then I went to the Mother Superior. She said, 'Well, Promila, since she is your sister she should certainly be in the English section.' "

"There are some advantages to being the Mother Superior's favorite," Sister Umi said.

"Usha's so fair-skinned that she's already called Mem by her section-mates," Sister Nimi said. ("Mem" is short for "Memsahib.")

After Usha started going to school, any time we spoke to her in Punjabi she would answer in English. She started playing English games. She spent hours doing something on the ground—throwing a stone, hopping and skipping, and counting to herself.

"What are the rules of the game?" I once asked her.

"There are no rules. You just skip from one box to another."

"Where are the boxes?"

"They are drawn on the ground. You can't feel them."

I wanted her to play a game that we could play together, but I couldn't think of any game. In fact, I couldn't even remember how she and I had played together before she was entered in the Presentation Convent.

❧

I TOOK TO spending much of the day playing in Daddyji's private office, or in his outer office, in which his head clerk, his stenographer, and his assistant clerk sat in chairs, or on the veranda just beyond the outer office, where Qasim Ali and Ram Saran, the two peons, sat on their haunches, behind a chick, or bamboo screen, ever ready to run errands. Once in a while, a clerk would hit the desk bell and shout "Qasim *Ali!*" or "Ram *Saran!*"

"Huzoor!" one or the other of them would reply, jumping up, lifting the chick, and running in. More often than not, the summons was for tea or lemonade and required the peon to run no farther than the kitchen.

The clerks and the peons, like me, seemed to have little to do all day. I would sit around with them, touching and exploring things I had never felt before—typewriters, desk bells, hand blotters, paperweights, metal seals, sticks of sealing wax. If the head clerk needed to telephone anyone (we had a telephone for the first time), I would dial the number for him. I would sit in the stenographer's chair when he was with

43

Daddyji taking dictation, and idly peck at the typewriter. I would take the paper to the head clerk, get
him to sign it, get the assistant clerk to seal it properly—glue it shut, tie it with a string, affix the seal to
it with sealing wax. I would then strike the desk bell
and summon Qasim Ali. I would order him to deliver
the envelope to Ram Saran, then I would go out on
the veranda and hold a conference with Ram Saran,
pretending that I was Daddyji and that Ram Saran was
my subordinate.

There were many other official servants to get to
know and to play with. They seemed to have no names.

"What's your name?" I once asked the gardener.

"Gardener."

"What were you called as a boy?"

"Gardener's Boy. My father was a gardener in this
compound."

"What do you call your wife?"

"Gardener Woman."

There was an unused trough on the far side of the
kitchen garden, and so on the near side of the henhouse
and the buffalo stable. I filled it with water, using a
garden hose. I then got Gardener to get me a dozen or
so goldfish from the bazaar, and put them in the trough.
Every day, I would go into the trough, catch the slippery fish one by one, and drop them into a bucket of
water. Then I would let the water out of the trough,
scrub the trough, and refill it. I would feed the goldfish bread crumbs in the bucket and return them to the
trough. As I counted and re-counted the goldfish in
transferring them to and from the bucket—bringing

them quivering up in the air and identifying them by
their sizes—and as I fed them with my fingers, I imagined that I had my own little family, who were my
complete responsibility.

III

DINNER-TABLE SCHOOL

E COMPLAINED TO MAMAJI THAT WE NEVER
saw Daddyji. Often, he was out on tour, and
the rest of the time he wasn't around much,
even though he had only to walk through the
door of his office to come in for a cup of tea or
a bit of lunch. In the morning, he would get
up, shave, have a quick breakfast, and go into the
office. What little time he had at home in the morning
was taken up by visitors who came to see him on some
business or other. He would work through the lunch
hour, come back for a nap, and then, at four-thirty or
so, start getting ready to go to the Pindi Club for tennis and bridge; he preferred the facilities of the Pindi
Club to those of the Rawal Club, next door. No one
would yet be home from school, and I would have him

46

to myself for a few minutes as he was changing his clothes and putting on his shoes, while Mamaji rushed around packing his tennis clothes in his tennis bag. He would come home from the club long after we had gone to sleep, having sometimes dined there and played bridge until midnight. On Saturday, he worked until lunch and then went straight to the club. Sundays he had off, but then he sometimes went to the club even before lunch. Whether he played tennis or not, cards were a must with him, day in and day out. If he had friends to dinner at home, they sat down to play cards in the drawing room. Of course, whenever he was needed he was there, because he could be fetched from either the office or the club at a moment's notice. But we all began to feel that we didn't see enough of him. I remember that when I used to come home to Lahore on holidays Daddyji would also be away all the time, at one or another of his clubs. But there we somehow weren't as much aware of his absence, perhaps because we were surrounded by our relatives. In Rawalpindi, there was no Mehta Gulli for us to go to after dark and nothing for us to do.

"Why do you complain to me?" Mamaji said. "What can I do? I'm only his wife. I don't have the nerve to open my mouth in front of him."

One night when we were all in our night suits, in our cots, and Sister Pom had turned off the light, Sister Umi said, "I know what. We should go on a hunger strike, like Gandhiji, and refuse to eat dinner without Daddyji."

Sister Nimi burst out laughing. "My foot! The biggest eater in the Mehta family wanting to go on a hunger strike! What next? You and Gandhiji have as much in common as Vedi and Mother Superior."

"Hunger strike for what?" I asked, raising myself on my elbow.

"Hunger strike to make Daddyji come home for dinner," Sister Umi said. "Otherwise, we will never get to see him."

"Daddyji will beat us," Brother Om said. He had left Bishop Cotton School and joined St. Denys'. He was about the only one whom Daddyji ever slapped.

"I think disobedient children grow up to be bad people," Sister Pom said.

Usha began to cry.

Sister Nimi eventually agreed with Sister Umi's plan, and it was decided that Sister Umi would be the strike leader.

"Just don't look to me for moral support," Sister Pom said. "If Daddyji so much as frowns at me, I will start crying."

The next day was Sunday, and over breakfast Sister Umi boldly announced the hunger plan to Daddyji.

"I can't leave in the middle of a bridge game and come home," he said.

"Then you have to give up cards," Sister Umi said. "We are just not going to eat dinner without you."

Daddyji laughed. "I don't play cards for fun," he said. "I play to win, so that I can give all of you everything you need and want. I am farsighted, like Lalaji, and I know what's in your best interests."

"You may say what you like, but we won't eat dinner until you come and sit with us," we all said.

After that, for some time Daddyji would come home

at nine, just as we were sitting down to dinner, but within an hour or so—the moment we had finished—he would get into his car and drive away. We hit upon the strategy of detaining him by lingering at the dinner table long after the servants had cleared away the plates.

All three of my big sisters were now doing their B.A. courses in the Presentation Convent's college, and they were full of talk—of concerns and impressions. They would talk about playing mysterious games called volleyball and basketball, and about how the nuns encouraged them to eat sweets from a tuck shop nearby, rather than Punjabi snacks from a street vender. "Today, Mother Lourdes caught me eating *ambpappar*," Sister Umi once told us. *Ambpappar,* a leathery, waferlike mango confection, was a favorite with all of us, and the blacker and more awful-looking my big sisters said it was, the better it tasted. " *'Chhichhi,* that's black skin you're eating!' Mother Lourdes said. 'Go rinse your mouth and get some Cadbury's chocolate from the tuck shop.' "

It seemed that at the convent Sister Nimi was always getting into trouble. "What can I do?" she said one evening. "When Sister Bernadette is writing something on the blackboard, the girls will whisper something to me and make me laugh. They laugh, too, but they stop the moment Sister Bernadette turns around. Then I'm the only one left laughing."

"If the other girls can stop, why can't you?" Sister Pom asked.

"I just can't. I can't be bothered," Sister Nimi said. She never bothered about what people thought of her.

Another evening, just as Daddyji was getting up to go back to the club Sister Pom said, "Why is it, Daddyji, that when you go to a Hindu temple there is no pattern or order to anything, no peace and quiet in any corner to think about God? People wander in and out as if the temple were a railway station. Beggars, loafers, children crowd everywhere, and everyone pushes and elbows. Here someone is eating *halwah* from a banana leaf, there someone is spitting. There are flies; there are soiled banana leaves and rice grains underfoot. At one end, a pandit is sitting on the floor, eating and burping and licking his lips right in front of the worshippers, while someone is clapping fire tongs together, or clashing bells, or beating a drum. Now, when you walk into our convent chapel everything is clean and orderly. It's so quiet that you can hear the Mother Superior shift in her pew. When the nuns kneel and pray, they look like angels. You really feel that you're in the presence of something awesome. And the nuns have such discipline. Even when they are not in the chapel, they speak so softly."

"Every week, they keep a day of silence to think about God, and on that day, no matter what happens, no matter what the emergency, they will not utter a word," Sister Umi said.

"Christianity is an organized religion," Daddyji said, settling back in his chair. "They have one book, one God, and all kinds of dogmas and doctrines about the coming of the Messiah. We Hindus have no book as such, and many gods and goddesses, and no dogmas, no doctrines to speak of, no messiah."

There seemed to be no Punjabi words for "chapel,"

"dogma," "doctrine," "messiah," and the discussions were often carried on in "pink English"—English colored with Punjabi words. Even when English words were explained to me with the greatest care, I often felt that I was on the verge of understanding them without actually doing so. It was like listening to endless discussions among my big sisters and Mamaji about the colors of their clothes—thinking, for instance, that I understood what royal blue was until Sister Umi confused me by saying that she didn't think the color suited her. Just when I thought that I had understood a word, it would fly out of my reach, like a kite, and be lost in the confusion of conversation.

Even when Daddyji was speaking pink English, I enjoyed hearing his easy, confident, reassuring voice, interrupted by an occasional question, though sometimes whole courses would pass by without my catching any more than the few English words I had learned at Dadar School. But I would also feel sad, because each time I was reminded that I was falling behind my big sisters and my big brother. I would get impatient to go to the Perkins school, in America, where Daddyji intended to send me after the war was over—to have my own nuns and Mother Superior and fathers, my own chapel to go to, my own pew to kneel in. Then I would interrupt.

"What is a 'messiah'? The leader of all the leaders?" I once asked.

Daddyji laughed. "Not all leaders accept him as that."

"Then he's not the leader of all the leaders."

"That's right."

"But you said that he was the Son of God."

"Christians say that."

"But either I'm your son or I'm not, and why did God have only one son?"

"Ask me another," Daddyji said, laughing. "Anyway, that's what Christians believe. I don't believe it. We Hindus don't believe it."

"Who's better? Who's right—Hindus or Christians?"

"No one is better. They're both right. Christianity is orderly but perhaps constricted. Hinduism is chaotic but perhaps freer."

"I hate pandits. I like the sound of nuns," I said.

"I don't like my fathers," Brother Om said. "What right do they have to call themselves fathers? They are not even married."

"Shut up, both of you," Sister Umi said. "Neither one of you knows what he's talking about."

"I'll take an Indian temple over a chapel any day," Sister Nimi said. "I like my licks of *halwah,* and there is more God in our crowds than there is in a chapel. What is a chapel? Just a sterile room."

"I prefer the convent chapel," I said. I felt sad that I could never go to the convent chapel. I knew I didn't like going to the Hindu temple, where Mamaji would sometimes drag me simply because during the day she and I were home alone and she wanted company.

"By the way," Daddyji said, "there are some churches in America which are quite rowdy."

"But did you miss temples when you were in America?" I asked. Daddyji had been in America as a young man, in the early twenties, on a Rockefeller Foundation Fellowship.

"Not at all. I followed the principle 'When in Rome, do as the Romans do.' "

Brother Om started singing his favorite Hindustani song:

> Best in all the world is India of ours.
> We are its nightingales—this is our garden.

"I'm sure that best in all the world is England of theirs," I said.

"What nonsense!" Sister Umi said. "I'd like to see you, Vedi, keep the nuns' day of silence."

And so it would go. I never did really find out what "messiah" meant.

❦

EVERY NIGHT at the dinner table, my big sisters would all talk at once, telling the latest pieces of news about their friends and teachers, games and escapades. They would talk about English prayers and English songs and about classmates and their expensive clothes. They would talk about the strange customs of the nuns—how they always wore black habits, black head coverings, black shoes, and black rosaries, except that in the summer they would dress all in white. The nuns sounded mysterious and elegant. And there was something exciting about thinking of a whole convent with only unmarried girls and women.

"Can nuns ever have children?" I asked.

"Silly," Sister Umi said. "They've taken vows. They're married to the Son of God."

I wanted to know more but was too shy to ask. "What about the Mother Superior, then?"

"Mother Lourdes is an only daughter," Sister Pom said. "Her parents were looking forward to getting her married, but she decided to marry Christ instead."

"How do you marry Christ?" I asked Daddyji.

"It's a manner of speaking," Daddyji said.

"I don't understand," I said.

"You do things like observe a whole day of silence every Monday and say lots of 'Hail Mary's to your mother-in-law," Sister Umi said.

"We have a new Muslim history teacher," Sister Pom said, irritatingly changing the subject.

"I thought all the teachers at the convent were nuns," I said.

"Convents often hire local Indian teachers for subjects their nuns don't know, like vernaculars or Indian history," Daddyji said.

"How do you know she's a Muslim?" I asked.

"She arrived at the convent dressed in very high heels, and covered from head to toe in a black cloak," Sister Pom said. "The cloak had only two slits, for her eyes."

"She looked so awful with those high heels and slits," Sister Umi said.

"Then she took off her cloak," Sister Pom continued, "and she had one of the prettiest faces I've ever seen."

"She has such a proper, forbidding manner that she's unapproachable," Sister Nimi said.

"But she lives in Lal Kurti," Sister Umi said. "Everyone asks her when she is going to get married. She blushes and she won't answer, and yet she lives in Lal Kurti."

Lal kurti means "red shirt." Gian Chand had told me that it was the Muslim section of the city and that in one part of it lived dancing and singing girls who did dirty things. For years afterward, I imagined that all prostitutes wore red shirts. I thought of the color red as being as forbidding as the Muslim teacher, and Lal Kurti as a forbidden area, to which I could never go. Brother Om could simply bicycle over there and see the women dancing and singing in their red shirts, but I imagined that even if I were an old man I would have to be taken there; the very thought seemed forbidden. I nicknamed the teacher in the cloak "the forbidden lady," and every day when my big sisters returned from the convent I would ask them for news of the forbidden lady. One day, they told me that they were all trying to get her married off and had placed a marriage advertisement for her in the newspaper; another day, that they and their school friends had pored over the answers and had selected a man from Lahore and written to him; still another day, that they had heard from the man.

"What did he say?" I asked.

"It's none of your business," Sister Umi said, "but he said that he was coming to see the girl, and was taking the next train and arriving in Rawalpindi in the evening. He said that he expected the girl's closest male relatives to meet him at the railway station. We were just able to telegraph him in the nick of time to say that it was a hoax. Now, don't go and tattle on us, or I'll never tell you anything else."

❦

I REMEMBER THAT Sister Umi once asked at the dinner table for new, satin clothes. "Satta comes to the convent every day dressed in a different satin shirt and different velvet pajama trousers," she said. "We feel so drab next to her."

Sister Umi had always taken a great interest in clothes. One evening, Daddyji had come home from the club and asked about her pajama trousers: "Umi, why does your salwar have such wide cuffs, and why is it so long? It's dragging on the ground, picking up all the dirt—it's very unhygienic. Besides, you'll trip and fall."

"But, Daddyji, these cuffs are the latest fashion," Sister Umi had said.

"Going out with loose hair is also the latest fashion," Mamaji had said. "But you don't do it. The daughters of good families don't do it."

The next day, when my big sisters went out for a walk they had made a point of hitching up their salwars about six inches off the ground and parading past Daddyji. As soon as they reached the street, they put them down.

In contrast, Sister Pom showed little interest in clothes, Sister Nimi none. Sister Nimi was something of a tomboy. Whatever she took up—volleyball, field hockey, or tennis—she was completely absorbed in it. She would go out for a game of tennis in old clothes and old shoes, for instance, and without even a thought for her appearance.

"But Satta's father is a rich contractor," Daddyji now said, at the table. "He has made a lot of money from the war. Showing off is part of a businessman's stock-in-trade. But you are the daughters of a Class One government officer, and you don't need to impress anybody with your clothes. There is a respect and a special status that go with government service which no amount of money can buy. Anyway, nobody ever notices clothes. I wear the same coat and tie to the club every day for a month, and no one notices or cares. People simply don't remember what you were wearing yesterday."

"You're so good-looking that whatever clothes you wear look marvellous on you," Sister Umi said. "Naturally, no one notices. But Nimi and I have acne. Besides, Auntie Pushpa and Auntie Vimla wear satin clothes."

"They don't need to," Daddyji said. "They are spoiled. You must have noticed how badly they did in their studies. Your model should be not your aunties but your Cousin Vidya."

Cousin Vidya, who was the daughter of Parmeshwari Devi, Daddyji's only sister and our *bhua,* or paternal aunt, had deformed hands, and as a result, it was said, she had not been able to get married. She was religious and nationalistic, and had become active in Arya Samaj, a movement to reform Hinduism. Her clothes were of homespun cloth, like Gandhiji's. She used to tell us Gandhiji's views on the cloth—that it was a badge of national pride, purity, and equality, because every poor person could make his own cloth and cover himself, and that machine-made cloth was a badge of slavery, because it came from Britain or from Indian businessmen who were interested only in making money off the backs of the poor. She used to say that girls who studied in convents became "mems," and preferred slacks to salwars, coats to Indian shawls, walking shoes to sandals, factory chocolates to freshly made *halwah*—that they polished their nails, wore rouge, bobbed their hair, and ended up choosing their own husbands. In part because of her influence, all our Mehta cousin-sisters had gone to Indian schools. Although Daddyji was sending my big sisters to convent school, they usually wore clothes made of homespun material, and this was because of Cousin Vidya. Their pajama trousers and shirts were made by a tailor who came regularly to the house, but they always knitted their own sweaters; and their shirts and sweaters, though they might be bright-colored, had long sleeves. Their veils were white, but they did give them a touch of color by crocheting edgings on them. When they went out, they covered their heads, and they didn't wear makeup—not even lipstick.

There was a strong family resemblance among the three oldest sisters, which came to be well known. When they were walking on the Mall, they would often be stopped and asked if they were Dr. Mehta's daughters.

If Mamaji was with them, she would be taken for another daughter. I asked Daddyji once why that was, and he said, "She naturally looks young. And she's an asthmatic. I don't know why it is, but asthmatics generally look young."

Daddyji always insisted that the three sisters go everywhere together. Once, Sister Pom was invited to the house of her friend Pushpa Chopra. She took Sisters Nimi and Umi with her but left them sitting outside the house, saying, "Just wait here. I'll go inside to the party and come out quickly." She didn't emerge for an hour.

Whatever the sisters' family resemblance, I felt closest to Sister Nimi, because Sister Pom ordered me about and Sister Umi found fault and tried to get the last word. Sister Nimi had the most free time and was always laughing. She had lots of friends, who were often in the house, and who seemed to be as relaxed as she was. And when they weren't around she would talk about them—Satish said this, Santosh did that, Satish didn't like so-and-so, Santosh was coming over.

Once, Daddyji explained to us at the dinner table, "Because Pom is the firstborn, she is the most responsible, the most like Mamaji. Because Umi is the third child, she has had to push a bit to call attention to herself. But Nimi is the second child, and second children seem always to have an easier time of it."

❧

WHAT I LIKED best about our "dinner-table school" was hearing Daddyji tell of his experiences in the West. I remember that at one time Sister Pom was studying about ancient Rome. "Why did the Roman Empire fall?" she asked. "Why didn't the Romans discover the steam engine and start the industrial revolution?"

"Who knows?" Daddyji said. "But Christianity is an otherworldly religion, just like Hinduism, and once it came it probably turned the Romans away from empire and from science."

"Do you like the Romans?" I asked. "Are they better than the British?"

"In my travels, I found the Italians to be more like us Indians than like the British," Daddyji said. "They seemed to me to be rather lazy and quarrelsome, disorganized, and interested in food. They love to eat spaghetti and macaroni, which I've never seen in India, but which are very tasty." I never got a good description of spaghetti and macaroni, but just the mention of them made me hungry for the food that Daddyji had eaten in Europe. "The Italians are easygoing and the British are not, probably because Italy, like India, is hot most of the time, and Britain is cold."

"I think I'd like the cold of England," I said.

"Like father, like son," Daddyji said, laughing.

"What is England like, Daddyji?" Brother Om asked. It was one of our favorite questions—we asked it again and again.

"Oh, marvellous. I remember that one of the first days I was in England I walked along Gower Street to buy a newspaper. I came to a bus stop, and I saw a pile of newspapers sitting there but no vender. 'Hello,' I said. 'This is odd. Someone could walk off with the whole lot of them.' Then I noticed that Englishmen were picking up their newspapers, dropping some change in a hat, and going along. I stopped a man and said, 'Good morning, sir. Where is the vender?' He pointed to the hat and went away. In London, they have no newspaper venders as such; venders just leave their hats in the morning and pick them up in the evening, and trust in the honesty of their fellow-countrymen. Not only that but the milkmen leave sealed milk bottles in front of the doors of houses and no one pinches them."

We'd heard this story many times, but we never tired of it. We never quite understood how an Englishman could be a mere newspaper vender in the first place, since all Englishmen spoke beautiful English—something that Indians had to spend years in school and college learning. We also never quite understood how all Englishmen could be so honest. We were impressed each time.

"Who does the sweepers' job over there?" I asked.

"People of low caste, stupid," Sister Umi said.

"Low class," Daddyji corrected her. "In England, they don't have a caste system as such. In America, however, they do have Negroes, who used to be slaves. Still today, they are not allowed to travel in the same railway coaches as whites. I myself once almost got into a coach marked 'Black'—until the conductor set me right."

Sometimes Daddyji would tell us about a night club he had visited in Paris, about races he had been to in Deauville, about jazz bands he had heard in New York. As we listened to the accounts of his travels, we would all be fired up with the wish to go to the West, too—to visit the places he had visited.

I don't know when our dinner-table school turned

into an imaginary journey and then into the planning of an actual tour of the West. We were too many and Daddyji's government salary was too small for us to buy passage on a ship or to stay in hotels and inns. We would therefore have to go overland in a specially made lorry, which could be ferried for a nominal fee over any lesser body of water we might have to cross. In fact, we would have to live in the lorry, and earn and pay our way.

"Westerners are naïve about Indian—indeed, about all Asian—life," Daddyji said. "That's not for lack of curiosity—they simply don't have any way of getting at the information. The truth is that even though the British have ruled us for almost a hundred years they have not been able to feel our heartbeat. Probably we are as much at fault as they; the poorest among us are proud and reserved, and we don't take to foreigners, any more than they take to us."

"But I am a proud girl, and I take to foreigners," Sister Umi said, "I get on better with your foreign friends and our Irish sisters at the convent than I do with some of our relatives."

"You are not as good an example of what I am talking about as, for instance, Gian Chand would be," Daddyji said. "Have you noticed how he skulks away when an Englishman enters our house? That's because he associates white skin with authority, and he fears authority. You may have also noticed how he argues freely with your mother but the moment I come into the house he skulks away. To him, I am like an Englishman—a man of authority. When I go on tours, peasants in villages also at first shy away from me, like

Gian Chand. That's why I always make it a point to speak Punjabi in their hearing. You should see what a difference that makes."

Before we went to the West in the lorry, Daddyji told us, we would have to spend some time in India travelling and getting to know the country, taking and collecting pictures, obtaining various kinds of clothes and costumes, and developing skits, with a view to conveying Indian life to Westerners—its history, its people, its dances, its music. We would bill ourselves as the Mehta Family Troupe, and go from lecture hall to lecture hall, instructing and entertaining. Daddyji would speak and comment; Mamaji would demonstrate Indian cooking; my big sisters would do skits portraying Indian women in different parts of the country and from different social backgrounds.

"Pom can wear a peasant woman's simple dhoti with cheap glass bangles and talk about the life of a peasant," Daddyji said. "Umi can dress like a princess, in a rich Benares sari and a gold necklace, and talk about Indian princely states."

"What about Nimi and me?" Brother Om asked.

"Nimi will no doubt insist on dressing like herself, and she would portray a nice, middle-class Hindu girl very well, and talk about arranged marriages. You can talk about boarding-school life in India. Vedi can sing, and maybe Usha and he can play some Indian games— hit a peg around with a stick, as on an Indian street. Maybe we could even open a restaurant in London, and call it the Mehta Family Group. When I was last in London, in 1937, I helped the three daughters of my old teacher, Professor Sambon, open a restaurant. I named it the Three Smart Sisters, and it did very well until Hitler started bombarding London. Maybe we will become as well known as the Indian dancer Uday Shankar and his troupe, who have toured all over America, to great acclaim."

"These dreams of travel are all very well," Mamaji said. "But where are we going to get the money to go around the world?"

"Industrious people with imagination don't have to worry about money," Daddyji said. "I have already accumulated six months of paid leave to be used just for our tour, but we have to wait for the war to end."

While we waited, we spent many evenings discussing the lorry and making drawings of it: where the beds would be placed, and how they would fold into the walls; what kind of stove would be required, and how and where we would cook; how much water we would have to carry in a water tank on the roof for journeys across the deserts. We had to provide for every need, economize on every inch of space. The idea that we might live and eat and sleep in a running lorry constantly excited us. Since our kitchen in Rawalpindi was a separate building, the noise and smoke were kept away from us. Gian Chand used to have to get up at five o'clock—at least two hours before any of us got up—simply to light the coal fire. During the day, I had sat with him often when he was trying to get the fire going again—coughing and complaining of his eyes smarting from the smoke. When the food was cooked, the servants had to run with it from the kitchen to the bungalow, so that it wouldn't get cold. Here we were designing a stove that would run on kerosene. We would, of course, have to eat simple things, but no servants or coal fires would be necessary. We would be completely self-sufficient, all together as one happy family, under the roof of the lorry.

We called in our carpenter, discussed the plans with him. He said that the lorry would have to be long and big—at least two stories high. The wood and the labor for the body would cost about fifteen thousand rupees (four thousand dollars at the time). We went to the local Chevrolet dealer and asked him to get us an estimate for a complete Chevrolet chassis from America.

One day, the carpenter arrived with a small wooden model of the lorry, and it was set on the mantelpiece of the drawing room. There, as it were, the matter rested while we all waited for the war to end.

IV

IN THE COMPOUND AND OUT ON TOUR

D ADDYJI WAS REQUIRED TO SPEND AT LEAST twelve nights a month away from Rawalpindi, on tour. Even though I had been sent off to school before I was five, and had stayed there for the greater part of four years, still, in Rawalpindi, every time I heard the wheels of his car disturb the gravel as he drove away for his tours I would cry. I think we all felt a little sad and a little frightened without Daddyji around, for we thought of him as educated, reasonable, and compliant, and of Mamaji as uneducated, capricious, and stubborn.

Mamaji disagreed with our view of him as much as

she did with our view of her. "You children see little of your daddy—he's always in his office or at his club or on tour—so you glorify him," she would say. "You see me all day long, washing, cleaning, and picking up after you, so you denigrate me. He gets all the credit, but I bring you up. When he's around, you are all coöperative and agreeable. You behave like angels. When he's not around, you are all contentious and disagreeable. You behave like the Mehta demons you really are. You children think that just because I'm not educated I don't have good sense. But I have eyes in my head. Your daddy says he wanted an educated wife. I would like to see an educated woman who could have lasted in this demon Mehta household. She would long since have waved her hand, and said, 'Ta-ta, nice to know you,' and walked out."

"Sister Pom and Brother Om are demons, too?" I would ask. Mamaji had a special weakness for them, because, she said, they had taken after her side of the family.

"Well, they're the exceptions," she would answer.

Whatever Mamaji said, the atmosphere when Daddyji was around and in charge was noticeably different from the atmosphere when he was not. If we asked Daddyji for a rupee for sweets, he would give us five, and say grandly, "I don't have anything smaller," or "When we were little, Bhabiji used to say, 'Your pockets should never be empty.' " If we asked Mamaji for a rupee for sweets, she would say, "We don't have money to waste." If we told Daddyji that we needed a pair of shoes, he would immediately drive us to Bata's, the best Western-type shop, which had fixed prices, and buy us the best shoes there, saying that they might be expensive but they would last longer. If we asked Mamaji for them, she would stall and ask for many explanations, and when she did finally get around to buying the shoes she would march us to several little shoeshops that did not have fixed prices, haggle and bargain with the shopkeepers, and buy us the shoes on which she could get the best price, saying that all shoes were more or less alike. At the same time, she might lecture us on the inadequacy of a government salary and on the expenses of a large family—school fees and schoolbooks, fruits and ghi, clothes and servants. She could be really expansive on the subject. "You children are all like your father. You have no head for money. He would mortgage away our house and my jewelry to pay his card debts. Pinch-and-save is all left up to me."

At the dinner table when Daddyji was not there, voice levels would rise. Mamaji would forcibly spoon into my mouth butter or vegetables I didn't like. Also, she and my big sisters would often talk among themselves and ignore Usha and me. After dinner, she would closet herself with them in her bedroom and wouldn't allow us in. She would tell us to go to bed before the usual hour. During the day, she would sometimes forbid me to go and play in the chicken coop, without giving a good reason. If I disobeyed her, and went and played there anyway, she was not beyond catching hold of me and slapping me. Her slaps never hurt very much. More often than not, she struck us on a hand or an arm, and we would wriggle out of her hold, duck, run across the room, jump up on a chair. Sometimes I even provoked her to slap me more. The slaps made me feel that I was being treated like others—like a normal child. I much preferred them to the stinging eyedrops that she used to put in my eyes after faith healers told her that they would enable me to see.

Once, I didn't eat my lunch. Mamaji scolded me, and then she gave me a banana.

"I'll eat it in a minute," I said.

Mamaji left the dining room.

I turned around and fed the banana to the neighbor's dog, who was panting next to my chair. She choked and spat some of it on the carpet.

Mamaji happened to come in just then, and she slapped me.

"Beat me!" I cried. "More!"

She obliged.

Sometimes, however, the slaps were unprovoked and undeserved. Mamaji would hear Usha cry, assume I had hit her, and slap me, when actually Usha had fallen down.

When we complained to Daddyji about Mamaji, he would chide us for carrying tales and at the same time would try to explain her to us. "She came from a house of plenty," he once told us. "Babuji was in private legal practice and had a lot of money, but, like many city types, he was tight with it, and certainly did not give any of it to the women of the house. For all they knew, he had no reserves. So your dear mother grew up with the fear of not having money—maybe even the fear of finding herself in the *gullis* without an anna. Lalaji had much less money than Babuji, but, like many village types, he had a very casual way with it, so I grew up with, as your mother says, 'no head for money.' " Another time, when my big sisters were complaining, he told them, "Your mother doesn't keep in good health, and the more education you girls get, the more inadequate she feels—that's why she has a quick temper." I felt a pang. Like her, I was uneducated. "Anyway, in her house they believed in slapping, and she's only taking out on you children what she suffered herself. She doesn't understand that slapping may have an effect opposite to what she intends."

Mamaji didn't like Daddyji to talk this way. "It's because you run down my family and me that the children don't respect me," she said. "When the servants see that, *they* don't respect me."

"Everyone respects you," Daddyji said.

We set up a cry that we all loved her.

I remember that when Daddyji was away the house felt lonely and a little dangerous, for reasons I could not then have named. I would dream about thieves in the night, about temperamental ghosts, about women who spoke only in hand gestures that I couldn't see or understand, about dogs that would suddenly bite when I was petting them, about cars colliding with furniture in the drawing room.

❧

MAMAJI FELT that my blindness was a curse on her for something she had done in a previous incarnation, and that if only she found the right penance, the right faith healer, she could remove the curse. I felt that blindness was a terrible impediment, and that if only I exerted myself, and did everything my big sisters and big brother did, I could somehow become exactly like them.

I never sat still. I never walked. I always ran. My facial vision was often useless, because of all the noise and activity in the house. Everywhere, there seemed to be booby traps, and every day I seemed to get a new lump on my forehead or on a cheek or lip, or a new bruise on a hand, knee, or shin.

I would bump into the most familiar objects, because they had been placed in an awkward spot. In my mind, a standing lamp was in a corner, but it had been pulled next to an armchair for reading; I would get up suddenly from the chair and be clobbered by the lamp. Servants were constantly moving furniture to sweep under it, or, when we slept outside in the hot weather, standing cots on their ends with their legs sticking out, and stacking them here and there. Friends, official guests, out-of-town relatives were constantly arriving for a stay. They would leave a steel trunk in a passageway, or leave a tea tray sticking out over the edge of a table, or leave a dresser drawer open. Even the elements were always taking me by surprise. A wind would have blown a door or a window half open or shifted the position of the wicker furniture on the veranda.

Everyone in my family frequently had lapses and left things lying around. Wherever Mamaji was, for instance, she was surrounded with paraphernalia—for knitting, for sewing, for embroidering, for cleaning, for washing clothes, for peeling vegetables. She was constantly jumping up, moving around, calling to the servants in the kitchen or in the servants' quarters,

wheezing, coughing. The combination of the paraphernalia and the distracting movements and sounds
insured that whenever I went near her I hurt myself.

Mamaji would see me bleeding, and she would
immediately get an asthmatic attack. She would
scream, "You'll kill yourself! Why don't you ever stay
put in one place? Why do you always have to run
around? Why don't you ever call for me or a servant
when you have to go somewhere? Who told you to run
in the house like that?"

I would scream back, "Why can't you be like Daddyji? He doesn't leave things lying around! He's not
noisy. What do you want me to do, become an invalid?
I can't wait around for someone to help me! This is my
house, too. Send me back to Dadar School!"

She would cry; I would cry. Then we would embrace
each other and laugh.

Daddyji would buy me padded shin guards (the
kind that hockey players wore on a hockey field) and a
sola topi (the kind that Englishmen wore in the sun),
but I felt silly wearing them around, especially inside
the house, and before the day was out I would get rid
of them. I also gave up screaming for silence, because
screaming only drew attention to my blindness, which
I wanted to forget and to make others forget.

❧

ONE AFTERNOON when Daddyji was away on tour,
I was alone in the house and I heard the distinctive
sound of his car horn. I heard it as a distant chord way
off somewhere—a C and a G sounded together—like

the sound of an approaching cavalcade. There was first a long, definite statement, then a short, tentative afterthought, as if he had meant to sound two long honks but had changed his mind, because he didn't want to make too much noise. I wondered if I was hearing things, but the sound was unmistakable.

I was usually the first to hear the horn, but we all found the sound especially thrilling, because we never knew when we might hear it. Daddyji sometimes arrived home from a tour a day earlier than we had expected him, because he liked to surprise us, and also because he didn't want to worry us in case he was delayed. Whatever time of day or night it was, I would shout, "Daddyji has come!" rousing everyone for a welcome. Neighbors who had witnessed our welcomes used to laugh at us. "Someone would think your daddy had come back from the war," they might say. But nothing they said ever diminished our excitement at his return.

I now ran out to greet Daddyji. From long practice in listening to the sound of the tires on the gravel, I knew when it was safe to put my hand on the door and run alongside the car as it came to a stop.

"I have brought you some quails," Daddyji said, getting out of the car.

"To eat?" I asked, somewhat disappointed. They had very little meat on them and were very hard to eat.

"No, to play with—they're alive," he said. "Ram Saran will get them out for you." Ram Saran had accompanied Daddyji on his tour.

I couldn't contain my excitement. I had heard that

quails appeared when the wheat ripened in the fields, and that though they were almost as small as chicks they could fight like cocks.

I shouted for Ram Saran to get them for me immediately.

"In a few minutes," he said.

"At once!" I ordered him.

"They're somewhere in the boot."

"Idiot!" I cried. "At once!"

Before I knew what had happened, Daddyji's big hand had slapped me across the face. "Is that any way to speak to another person?"

I was stunned. Daddyji had never slapped me before, and he had slapped me in front of a servant. My cheek felt as if there were a burning coal on it.

I cried quietly, and Daddyji took me inside and dried my eyes with his handkerchief.

Daddyji went into the bathroom to wash, and Ram Saran handed me a basket with netting over it and fell at my feet.

"Sahib, pardon, forgive, pardon," he said. "I should have kept the bag on the top, at the ready. I talked back. I made Big Sahib lose his temper. I am only a poor peon. Pardon, forgive, pardon."

Ram Saran had me by the legs and wouldn't let go until I said I forgave him.

I slipped my hand under the netting. Inside the basket were half a dozen wriggling, vibrant creatures. They felt naked and unprotected, and pecked at my fingers as if they were hungry. I got busy arranging a cage for them, and clay cups for water and grain. But that day, the day after, the day after that, whenever I thought of the quails or the slap the burning on my cheek would return.

Then, one evening, I was aimlessly wandering and decided to pay a visit to Ram Saran, who I knew lived in the servants' quarters, in the back of the compound. I strolled over there and called his name.

"This way, Little Sahib," he called back. "What is your command?" He was in the doorway of his quarters, and he bent down to touch my feet.

I sat down on the ground and started unlacing my shoes. (Although we always wore our shoes in and out of our house, Ram Saran, as a servant, always left his shoes at our door, so as not to track the filth of the street into our house; and I felt I should be as respectful of his dwelling as he was of ours.)

"Little Sahib wants to see my quarters? Little Sahib can bring his shoes."

I wouldn't hear of it. I removed my shoes and went in. The quarters were just a small room, filled with smoke, and the floor was covered with a patina of dried cow dung—cows are holy—which gave it the texture of rag paper. One side of the room was taken up by a cot, the other side by some utensils, and at the back there was a makeshift *chulah,* like Bhabiji's, on which, Ram Saran told me, he did all his cooking, over charcoal.

The ceiling of the room was so low and the cot so small that I blurted out, "What would you have done if you had been a tall Sikh?"

He laughed. "All good servants come from the Kangara District, Sahib," he said. "I am from Kangara. And, like the mules in our part of the country, we are short of stature." I remembered that Sher Singh was from Kangara, and remembered how proud he was of coming from there. I missed him terribly and resented Auntie Pushpa's having appropriated him, but now I thought that perhaps Ram Saran could in some way take his place.

Ram Saran had a little board raised off the ground by a couple of strips of wood—the kind of board we used in the bathroom so that we wouldn't slip when we were bathing. He said he sat on it when he cooked. He put it in the doorway and insisted that I sit on it; he squatted on the floor.

"I like my quails very much," I said. "They are better than chickens. They don't make a lot of mess."

"Big Sahib thinks of everything."

"What were you doing when I called for you?"

"Cooking lentils for my meal, Little Sahib."

I insisted that he go on with his cooking, but he wouldn't until I had agreed to move the board a little way out, away from the smoke.

❧

I OFTEN VISITED Ram Saran in the early evening, when he was usually starting a fire, getting it going, cooking, and eating. He ate only two meals a day, and had his evening meal a couple of hours before we did, and although it consisted of only lentils and a paratha (fried unleavened wheat bread) it took him a good couple of hours to prepare it. I couldn't have explained why I spent so much time at his quarters. At first, I thought I went there because he was religious. He daily basted the floor of his quarters with cow dung and daily chanted verses from the Ramayana; the story of the good Ram triumphing over the evil Ravana never failed to stir me. Then, one day, I cajoled Ram Saran into letting me have a piece of his paratha. It was hard and tough, like the maize bread that the poor boys at Dadar School ate, and eating it made me realize that he reminded me of my poor orphan friends at school. That made me feel close to him.

One evening, I discovered that Ram Saran read a newspaper. I had never heard of a servant who could read; not even Sher Singh had been able to read. Anyway, no one else in the compound except Daddyji read a newspaper. Afterward, when I went to his quarters, in addition to reciting the Ramayana he would summarize the newspaper and tell me what he and it thought. He could read only a word at a time to himself.

"Mahatma Gandhi is not our great leader," he once told me, putting down the paper and stoking the *chulah* with the fire tongs. "Our great leader is Subhas Chandra Bose. Mahatma Gandhi is sitting in prison here, but Subhas Chandra Bose has escaped to Germany and is now fighting alongside the Japanese to win us our freedom from the bad British." Daddyji's paper was in English and was very pro-British, but Ram Saran's paper was in Urdu and was very pro-Japanese.

"The British are not bad," I said. "Daddyji likes them, and I am going to go and study in England and America."

"Little Sahib, the British are very bad," Ram Saran said. "They drink. They are slave masters. I was once a peon for a British officer. He came home from the club and he couldn't open the cupboard with his key. The British officer would not wipe his boots on the doormat, and sometimes he would go to bed with his boots on—the filth of the streets right on his bed. I had to stay on duty all the time, because he was likely to shout for me at any time, day or night."

"But Mahatma Gandhi doesn't drink," I said. "And he goes everywhere barefoot."

"In the newspaper, it says that the British have become so powerful in the universe because they know how to kick," Ram Saran said. "Almost before a peon can disobey, a British officer will let fly his boot, without caring exactly where the boot lands. Mahatma Gandhi says, 'Let him kick.' If a British officer kicks me in the stomach, Mahatma Gandhi says I should show him my chest and let him kick me there, too. Now, Little Sahib, we are poor people. The most well off among us have only slippers, and they have boots. How can we fight back? Subhas Chandra Bose has found a way—with the Japanese, who have bigger boots than the British. He says, 'We must kick back, and kick back with big boots.' Subhas Chandra Bose is building a big Indian army with Japanese boots, and if Subhas Chandra Bose is on that side the Japanese and the Germans will win. Little Sahib will see."

"The Japanese killed Brother Krishan, and I heard at Dadar School that the Germans will kill the blind, the deaf, and the dumb. The Germans allow only healthy, fit people to live."

"Hitler loves Aryans, and we Hindus are Aryans. Anyway, if any German raises his hand against you,

Little Sahib, Subhas Chandra Bose will kill him. He's a very good man."

When I reported to Daddyji what Ram Saran and his newspaper said, he told me, "Ram Saran had a bad experience with a British officer. I tell you from my experience that Englishmen are thorough gentlemen. They are decent and civilized as no other people are. Subhas Chandra Bose is little better than Hitler."

"But Ram Saran says we are the slaves of the British."

"Before the British came, we Indians were all fighting amongst ourselves and killing each other. They brought us law and order. If they leave tomorrow, we Indians will probably again be at one another's throats."

Each day, I would get ammunition from Ram Saran to debate Daddyji, and ammunition from Daddyji to debate Ram Saran. But I was convinced that Daddyji was right.

❦

OUR NEIGHBOR Divan Hukam Chand, who was the local magistrate, started coming to our house. He would arrive in the morning with Daddyji's newspaper just as Daddyji was settling down to shave with a towel around his neck.

"When I come here on weekends, Doctor Sahib, your children are lying down," Divan Hukam Chand said one day, drawing up a chair. "Whenever I arrive home, my children stand up. If you don't discipline your children from the start, they will not be good for anything—not for housekeeping, not for earning a livelihood." He had a booming voice, so whatever he said sounded emphatic.

"They may be lying down," Daddyji said, "but they are lying down, as you notice, with a book."

"A book, a book! What book? A storybook—'Kim,' 'A Pair of Blue Eyes,' 'Gone with the Wind.' Have you ever known anyone to become a magistrate or a doctor by reading that kind of book? I tell you, Doctor Sahib, you should teach your children discipline and get them to stand up when you walk into the room."

Daddyji laughed, and Divan Hukam Chand launched into a familiar theme, attacking British-educated Indians. "Indian gentle-men!" he said contemptuously. "Which of them has ever gone to prison, like Gandhiji or Subhas Chandra Bose? They can play tennis at the club, but can they pray in a prison cell or escape to Germany? Can they have the vision of Gandhiji, Subhas Chandra Bose, and Hitler?" Like many nationalists, he was a Hitler sympathizer, because he wanted the Germans to win.

"Magistrate Sahib, I think Gandhiji would be the first one to disown any comparison with Hitler," Daddyji said, and he called for Gian Chand to bring him more hot water.

"Hitler would liberate India and make Gandhiji the king and Subhas Chandra Bose his Prime Minister!" Divan Hukam Chand cried. "Germans and Indians, Japanese and Italians will begin a new civilization based on Aryan principles."

Daddyji laughed, and answered a question from Mamaji about what he wanted for breakfast.

"You can laugh, Doctor Sahib, all you want to, but our day is coming."

"Which day?" Daddyji asked in a muffled voice, from behind the towel.

"The new day of Hitler, Subhas Chandra Bose, and Gandhiji," Divan Hukam Chand boomed. Daddyji often lost the thread of what he was saying, but Divan Hukam Chand boomed along as if nothing could divert him, as if Daddyji's distractions were British-type laxities that Hitler would put an end to along with the British Empire.

Daddyji became serious. "Magistrate Sahib, what is the comparison between Gandhiji, with his nonviolent message, and Subhas Chandra Bose and Hitler, with their *violent* message? Besides, who says Japanese are Aryans?"

"You can make your petty distinctions," Divan Hukam Chand said. "But history marches, and I march with it. You, Doctor Sahib, belong to another, pre-Gandhi, pre-Hitler era."

I didn't always follow their discussions, and, with Divan Hukam Chand sitting there, it was hard to interrupt for explanations, but as I listened to them argue, day after day, I imagined that the purpose of my arguments with Ram Saran in his quarters was to set right another misguided Divan Hukam Chand. Every evening, I would arrive at Ram Saran's quarters with new determination and with new ammunition for the British side.

One evening, Ram Saran and I made a bet of ten rupees—one-third of his monthly pay and five months of my pocket money—on who would win the war. After that, every evening we would size up the war effort in terms of which of us would collect the ten rupees.

❧

A FEW STEPS AWAY from Ram Saran's quarters lived the washerman, with his wife and seven children. Sometimes when Ram Saran was not in, I would go across to the washerman's. I especially enjoyed talking to his two saucy daughters, who were two or three years older than I was, and were always laughing and chattering. They were usually ironing with a charcoal-heated iron, and the quarters—a little more than twice the size of Ram Saran's—felt close and stuffy with the smells of damp cloth, steam, and charcoal. One day, I was surprised to find Meena, the older of the two daughters, crying.

"What's the matter?" I asked. "Why are you crying?"

Her mother, who was stirring something on the *chulah* and breathing hard, like Mamaji, said, "For four years, we have lived at the compound. We have washed and ironed the clothes of many white sahibs and Indian sahibs." Since the washerman occupied quarters in our compound, his primary responsibility was to us, but his family took in the clothes of other officers. "In the four years, we have never had any complaints. But yesterday Meena burned a sari. I made her take it to the mistress of the sari and show her the burn."

"The mistress is demanding a hundred and fifty rupees," Meena said, still in tears.

"Where will we get that kind of money?" the washerman's wife asked. "We don't make a hundred and fifty rupees in two months' time, and that with all of us working." The washerman's wife started crying.

Every day, I heard stories in the compound which clutched at me. The sister of the boy who tended our buffaloes had lost her husband in a smallpox epidemic in their village; the gardener's mother was dying, and had no money for medicines. Every day, it seemed, I had another sad story to tell Mamaji and Daddyji. Every day, it seemed, I was asking them to help this person or that person.

"How is it that they never tell me such stories—that they only tell them to you?" Sister Umi once asked.

Daddyji said, "They know that Vedi has a soft heart—that he went to school with poor children."

Mamaji said, "It's only because Vedi's blind."

I left the washerman's quarters hurriedly. I went over and told the story of the burned sari to Ram Saran, who had returned to his quarters, and asked him what I should do. But, however much I coaxed him, I couldn't get him to say anything. He just sat in front of his *chulah,* carefully stoking the coals. He seemed to have only a few coals in it, and he kept shifting them with the fire tongs.

"Why don't you speak?" I stamped my foot—boot and all—outside his door, but he wouldn't say anything.

I went back to the house and asked Sister Pom for my savings from my pocket money. She kept all the money we had saved, and, according to the rules, gave it to me without asking questions. It was only five rupees. I knew that Meena wouldn't accept it from me, so I tried to give it to Ram Saran to give to her.

"Big Sahib and Mistress will get to hear of it," Ram Saran said. "They will hold me responsible."

I finally put the money in an envelope and gave it to the washerman's youngest child, who was five, and asked him to give it to Meena. But the next day the envelope was returned to Mamaji, and there were many questions at the dinner table. Mamaji said that she would speak to the lady with the sari, and Daddyji told us not to worry—he would look after the matter.

That evening, when I saw the washerman's family again, Meena, who had always had a lively word to say, wouldn't speak. The washerman's wife thanked me stiffly. Later, Ram Saran gave me a big piece of his paratha and sang a longer than usual verse from the Ramáyana.

✿

RAM SARAN ONCE EXPLAINED to me, "Big Sahib has a very important job. He is assistant director for the divisions of both Rawalpindi and Multan. He has to fight armies of mosquitoes and flies and rats in two divisions. Even the white sahibs' guns and bombs are helpless against them."

I had no school to go to—no daily commitment of any kind—so when Daddyji went on tour he sometimes took me along. On tour, Daddyji would often be busy with his work, and I would be left in the care of either Ram Saran or Qasim Ali—Daddyji alternated in taking them, so that each could have a chance to earn the "t.a." (the per-diem travelling allowance). I liked it better when it was Ram Saran's turn, because he was young and easygoing and hardly ever wore the government uniform of a peon—a long woollen coat with gold braid and brass buttons, and a big red turban—while Qasim Ali, an elderly man, seemed always to stand on his official dignity as a peon, and always wore his uniform, even when the weather was very hot and sticky. Also, Ram Saran, being a Hindu, ate the food we ate, while Qasim Ali, who was a Muslim, would disappear for long stretches in search of a Muslim cook shop. Also, Ram Saran would let me walk alongside him, sometimes with our hands barely touching, while Qasim Ali would hold my hand in a tight grip. Also, Ram Saran would show me things and let me mix with people, while Qasim Ali would try to keep me back at the government rest houses, where we would stay, and away from people, for fear of my catching an infection. I remember that Ram Saran showed me how a plow's blade was sunk into the earth and then pulled along by bullocks, what a cotton plant felt like, how villagers drew water from an open, shallow well with a series of buckets tied to a rope and hoisted over a pulley, how women molded cow dung into cakes and left them out in the sun to dry, so as to have fuel for the fire.

Once, we happened upon a line of children being inoculated, and Ram Saran let me talk to the compounder—as a Health Department aide is called—and to the children waiting patiently in the hot sun, their arms outstretched for a "prick."

"Ram Saran, why do they put out their arms before

the compounder is ready for them? And why does the compounder take so long to get to them?"

"The compounder has to do many injections a day, Little Sahib, and he has to boil his needle on the kerosene lamp. Every minute saved means one more prick against fever."

"But when the doctor comes to give us injections at home he just calls for us when he's ready."

"That's because you are well-to-do. The Sahib-people did good deeds in their last incarnation. Whatever bad deeds Little Sahib did in his last incarnation, God has already punished him enough by taking away his eyes."

Whatever Ram Saran said, I would remember my friends at Dadar School and would feel that I might well have been one of those children, waiting with my arm outstretched, perhaps for hours, never to get my turn, and never to be saved from the epidemic. Then I would imagine Daddyji pulling a plow with the help of a team of bullocks and planting cotton in the hot sun, Mamaji drawing water and molding cow dung. I would feel very sad.

❧

ONCE, THREE OF US—Cousin Yog, who was visiting us from Lahore; Sister Nimi, who decided to miss school for a couple of days; and I—went on a tour with Daddyji to an annual *mela* (fair or festival). We set out for the *mela* at dawn. It was being held seventy miles from Rawalpindi. Cousin Yog sat in the front with Daddyji, and Sister Nimi and I sat in the back of the car with Qasim Ali, whose turn it was to go on tour, and who sat stiffly on his bedroll among the baskets of food supplies on the floor, and refused to join Sister Nimi and me on the back seat. Just as Qasim Ali lorded it over common people because of his official position, he was overdeferential toward us. Irritatingly, he shifted on his bedroll, audibly adjusting his peon's coat under him and shining his brass buttons with his coat sleeve.

"Memsahib and Little Sahib, you must stay close to me at the *mela*," Qasim Ali said in a low, officious monotone—he didn't want Daddyji to overhear him. "I have accompanied officers to the *mela* for ten years, and I can tell you that the *mela* is very crowded and you can't be too careful. I have seen children bigger than you, Memsahib, separated from their all-important father, never to be found again. I have seen children the size of Little Sahib crushed underfoot."

"Qasim Ali, you will keep the crowds away from us, but who will keep Yog Sahib away from the crowds?" Sister Nimi asked, laughing.

"And another thing, Memsahib and Little Sahib," Qasim Ali went on, as if he hadn't heard the question. "You mustn't buy anything from venders or hawkers. You can catch the plague that way."

"Not the plague, Qasim Ali!" I cried.

"Cholera, then, or typhoid, or whatever," he said. "And if you catch something, who will be hanged in the police station, like a common thief, but me?"

We laughed.

"You can laugh," he went on gravely, "but I have to discharge my duty as a peon of the assistant director of public health."

"What happens at the *mela?*" I asked Daddyji,

leaning forward. "Why do people go?"

"Nothing very much happens," he said. "It's an excuse for an annual outing—for people from many villages in the area to eat and mill about in a crowd. The *mela* is about the only holiday most villagers get all year."

"Another thing, Memsahib and Little Sahib." Qasim Ali was beginning again, and Sister Nimi asked Daddyji in very rapid English if she could switch places with Cousin Yog.

Daddyji laughed—he guessed the reason—and pulled the car to the side of the road, and Sister Nimi and Cousin Yog changed places.

"Qasim Ali, have you ever been to Kurekshetra Mela?" Cousin Yog asked challengingly.

"I've never heard of it, Yog Sahib," he said. "I don't think that that *mela* is in Big Sahib's two divisions."

"Kurekshetra Mela has hundreds, maybe thousands, of times the crowds of the *melas* in your divisions," Cousin Yog said boastfully.

"If the sahib says so," Qasim Ali said.

"Once, at Kurekshetra Mela, I borrowed a cobra from a snake charmer and wrapped it around my neck."

Qasim Ali shifted on his bedroll.

"As soon as people in the crowd saw the cobra, they made way for me. I could go anywhere I liked, eat anything I liked and not pay for it. Venders and hawkers were eager to have me move along."

After a while, the car slowed down. Daddyji rolled down his window and asked, "Sentry, is this the turning to the *mela*?"

"Yes, Sahib. Two miles ahead."

At the *mela* grounds, another sentry directed us to a special tent pitched for us. While our bedrolls and suitcases were still being unloaded, Daddyji was surrounded by a staff of sanitary inspectors and started out on his inspection. All of us accompanied him.

It was still early in the morning, and the lane leading to the *mela* thoroughfare was deserted. All around were tents for the villagers, and I could hear the sounds of children scurrying about as they were got ready, of women chattering as they waited to get water from a common tap, of people washing in the open—of people preparing for the *mela.*

"The arrangements look really good," Sister Nimi said.

"It's like creating a whole separate town for two days, water and all," Cousin Yog said.

Daddyji, who was walking a little ahead, turned and said, "Vedi, many of the villagers are wearing torn and shabby clothes, but they're all freshly dyed. The poorest of them has tried to give some color to his clothes, because he is at a *mela.* Ours is a land of color; rich and poor, all love color."

Daddyji inspected the washing arrangements for the villagers, and the supplies of vaccine.

A sanitary inspector said there was a case of illness, and Daddyji went into a tent. He soon came out and said that it did not indicate the onset of an epidemic.

The thoroughfare was alive with the sounds of hawkers and venders setting up their wheelbarrows and stands, hoisting canopies, rinsing pans and platters with water from buckets, shouting directions to their assistants for hanging balloons and streamers. Here was someone slapping a ladle around a pot to get a batter ready. There was someone snapping a hand fan to get a fire going. As we walked up and down the thorough-fare, Daddyji exchanged a word or two with each of the hawkers and venders while the sanitary inspectors examined the milk, the supplies for cooking, and the cloths and other coverings to protect the food from flies.

The villagers started arriving all in a rush. We left Daddyji to carry on with his work, and struck out on our own. Cousin Yog led, and I followed, holding Sister Nimi's hand, with Qasim Ali close behind, muttering, "Memsahib of good sense and Yog Sahib, go slow."

Cousin Yog—agile, as ever—didn't break his stride. The crowd grew thick. We were pushed and jostled from all directions, by people using their elbows and their pungent breath to make a little room for themselves and for the children in their train.

We easily shook off Qasim Ali, and went from wheelbarrow to wheelbarrow, from stand to stand, eating little delicacies with abandon and buying *mela* souvenirs—clay vessels and pitchers, and clay likenesses of women in peasant dress and of the monkey-god. The sun was very hot, and we were almost swept along. There was something at once exciting and revolting about being taken over by the crowd—mothers shouting for children, men scolding women, hawkers trying to make their cries heard.

In the evening when it was beginning to get dark, we started back toward our tent, weary but happy, and now feeling a little lost without Qasim Ali. Then Sister Nimi spotted a landmark—the cottage of a sanitary inspector—and we knew we had reached a path leading to our tent. Ahead, Cousin Yog caught sight of an orchard of trees bearing ripe loquats.

"Let's eat some loquats before Qasim Ali finds us," Cousin Yog said.

Sister Nimi held back, reading out a sign: "No Trespassing, Rs. 150 Fine."

"Only people like Qasim Ali pay attention to such signs," Cousin Yog said. He dashed into the cottage of the sanitary inspector and returned with a basket and a couple of electric torches. He gave one torch to Sister Nimi and asked her to be the lookout, and gave me the basket and posted me under a tree. Then he quickly climbed the tree. He used the other torch to find the branch with the most loquats, and called down to me to move under it. "Hold the basket up!" he called. "Otherwise, we'll have loquat pudding."

I raised the basket as high over my head as I could. I listened to the plop-plop of the loquats dropping into the basket and felt it sag under their weight.

Finally, Cousin Yog came down, and led us to a patch of grass hidden by the trees. We sat down with the loquats, and, abandoning all caution, we ate and laughed and talked as if we owned the orchard. Once, Cousin Yog spat a stone to see how far he could make it fly, and managed to knock a loquat off a tree. He hooted with delight.

"Who trespasses? Who eats?" we heard. "Police! Police!"

A rough-sounding man appeared in our midst, and

he set about kicking all the stones into a pile, as if he planned to use them as evidence against us.

"As a watchman, I have to file a full report," he muttered.

I heard behind him the voice of Qasim Ali calling our names. As a rule, Qasim Ali was slow, but now he quickly grasped the situation, and demanded of the watchman, "Don't you know they're children of the assistant director of public health of two divisions?"

"I had no idea," the watchman stammered. Before he could summon his employer and consult with him, Qasim Ali hurried us away.

"I have been looking for you all day long," Qasim Ali scolded us. "For all I knew, Vedi Sahib had been trampled by the crowd and Nimi Memsahib kidnapped. Who would have been hanged at the police station? Yog Sahib, don't you have any thought for your poor servants? Where have you been all day? Where did you eat? Where did you wash those loquats, Yog Sahib?"

"Why, Qasim Ali, it rained only yesterday," Cousin Yog said. But Qasim Ali was not amused.

We reached our tent, and, luckily, Daddyji was there, so Qasim Ali withdrew. Cousin Yog later told us that when he went back to pick up the basket and the torches, which in our haste we had not returned to the sanitary inspector, he saw Qasim Ali sitting on the ground, uniform and all, feasting on loquats.

❧

THE SECOND DAY at the *mela,* we again shook free of Qasim Ali and wandered by ourselves. The thoroughfare was a little less thronged by villagers than the first day, and the hawkers were a little more hoarse.

"Look, there is a *puriwallah!*" Cousin Yog cried. (*Puris* are light fried wheat cakes.)

"Quick, Vedi!" Sister Nimi said. "Before Qasim Ali catches up with us!"

We pushed our way through the crowd to a little clearing where there was a vender. We each ordered a big portion of potatoes and chickpeas in a pungent sauce with a lot of whole chilis and slices of onions, which were served to us in banana leaves with pickled mango skins and pickled lemons and *puris*. We finished off with some carrot *halwah*.

From somewhere behind us, a pilgrim struck up a melancholy tune on an Indian bagpipe—the kind of tune usually played at weddings and festivals to remind everyone that happiness and sadness go together.

As we stood licking our fingers, Sister Nimi noticed a little family standing next to us—a wan little woman who had in tow a healthy-looking boy and four wan little girls, ranging in age from five to ten. The boy was eating a huge serving of potatoes, chickpeas, and *puris,* like us, while the four girls stood to one side of him, all gazing fixedly at his food. The girls had thin, knobby legs and looked so weak and so unsteady that Sister Nimi thought that at any moment they might be thrown and crushed by the crowd. The girls' hands were joined, their mouths were half open, and their eyes looked hungry. (I gathered the visual particulars later. They helped me to imagine the world around me, which was, after all, in many ways, mostly visual. I sometimes even thought that they awakened my early memories, put to sleep by the meningitis.)

Sister Nimi pounced on the boy. "How dare you eat by yourself! Hasn't anyone taught you to share?" Sister Nimi, who generally had the most happy-go-lucky temperament of anyone we knew, could sound really fierce when she was aroused.

The boy started wailing.

Sister Nimi turned on the woman. "Is he your son? Are they your daughters? How dare you treat the girls in this way?" She sounded so fierce that the crowd pulled back even as it collected to watch what was going on.

"Some have to starve, Memsahib," the woman said, raising tired eyes to Sister Nimi. And, pointing to the frail little girls, she added, "My daughters will have to go first."

We were stunned. Before any of us could do anything for the girls, there was an onrush of more people, and we were separated from the little family.

In the tent, we told Daddyji about the family. "What a terrible mother!" Sister Nimi said. "I had a good mind to catch hold of her and thrash her."

"Try to see it from the parents' point of view," Daddyji said. "A girl is a heavy responsibility, especially for poor people. If they don't find her a husband, she becomes a burden to them and can sink them all, and whether they can get the girl married off or not depends almost solely on the size of the dowry they can offer. Poor people must often borrow money for the dowry from the village usurer at killing rates of interest. A dowry for just one daughter can put a poor family in debt for life, and yet by custom they cannot ever accept even a morsel of food or a glass of water from her in-laws, because a daughter is born and reared only to be given away. A son, on the other hand, can be relied upon to work from the time he is ten and to be their security in sickness and old age."

"But settling a girl is a problem for anybody, whether he's poor or well-to-do," Cousin Yog said.

"Still, the problem is much worse for poor people," Daddyji said.

"What rubbish!" Sister Nimi said. When Sister Nimi was worked up, she didn't care what she said in front of anybody. "I'm jolly well happy to be a girl. I'll never get married. I'll take a job, and you'll see, Daddyji, I'll look after you and the whole family."

"Nimi, not being married is a fate worse than death," Cousin Yog said.

I agreed with Cousin Yog. I had often heard that people—whether they were boys or girls—who had something wrong with their limbs or their eyes, and the like, could never get married. And Cousin Vidya, with her deformed hands, was the only person among our scores of relatives who hadn't got married. She had been condemned to the fate of a spinster. But here was Sister Nimi, with normal hands, deciding to be a spinster, and, knowing her as I did, I was afraid that once she had made up her mind about being a spinster she wouldn't change it.

Inexplicably, Daddyji laughed, and I couldn't get him to argue with Sister Nimi.

V

TO

MURREE HILLS

"MURREE IS MUCH LIKE SIMLA, WHERE YOU children spent such happy summers before the war, except that Simla is over three hundred miles from here and Murree is only twenty-seven miles," Daddyji said. "As a hill station, Murree is every bit as good as Simla."

"Why is it called a hill station?" I asked.

"The British established hill stations to escape from the heat of our plains," Daddyji explained.

"Was I in Simla?" Usha asked, trying to climb the slope of the mudguard of the car.

"Born in 1937—sure," Daddyji said.

It was the dawn of a hot summer day, and we were getting ready to leave for Murree for a few weeks. Ram Saran and Qasim Ali were strapping half a dozen

bedrolls—bulging with quilts, pallets, and pillows—
onto the roof racks; fitting suitcases and crates of crockery
and utensils into the boot, which was so full that its
door had to be left half open and tied down; and stow-
ing inside the car baskets of picnic food and thermoses
of boiled water for the journey.

Usha and I fastened the Union Jack to the little
stick on the hood—flying the flag was a privilege granted
only to important travelling government officers—and
we all piled in: Mamaji and Usha, with Sister Pom,
who complained of headaches in the car, in the front
seat with Daddyji; the rest of us in the back seat; and
Gian Chand, the only servant we were taking with us,
on the floor, among the legs, baskets, and thermoses.
(The other servants were to stay behind and look after
the house.) Then we set off, the car creaking and sway-
ing under the weight of our travelling household. As
Daddyji drove on, we sang songs, told stories, and quietly pinched each other to get a little bit more room.

I fell asleep. I heard the sound of rushing water.
"We are drowning!" I cried, and abruptly woke up.
My ears popped. We were all dry and safe, but there
was actually a deafening sound of water coming from
one side of the car.

"Where are we?" I asked.

"We are at Chharra Pani—it's a hill runoff," Daddyji said. "It's our last chance to stretch our legs, wash,
and eat and drink something before we begin the
winding climb to Murree."

"How far is Murree now?" I asked.

"It's only fourteen miles, but the climb has a lot
of bad turns. The traffic is regulated—cars can go only

one way, up the hill or down the hill, in any three-hour period—and, luckily, we have arrived at the foot of the hill in good time for the climb." We walked off the shoulder of the road to a miry patch and took turns washing our hands and faces in the icy runoff, and then took turns walking up the hillside to find a secluded spot for a bathroom. Mamaji had brought along potato parathas, and scrambled eggs cooked with a lot of onions and tomatoes, and we ate our picnic lunch standing around the car, with the waterfall and the stirrings of the mountain wind in the background. We washed our hands and faces in the runoff again and got back in the car.

Although Daddyji drove very slowly around the bad turns, one or another of us got carsick practically each time, and he had to pull over so that we could get out. Mamaji was always ready with a towel and a lemon drop.

At Murree, Daddyji parked the car at the motor stand—cars were not permitted in the hill station—and we proceeded on foot, some baggage coolies following us with our belongings on their heads and backs. The coolies all seemed to have racking coughs, and breathed heavily, as if they were gasping for air.

"They make me feel sad," I said to Sister Pom. I was walking beside her. She had her hands thrust in her coat pockets, and I had my arm looped through hers. Daddyji and the others were walking ahead, because the road was narrow.

"Who—the coolies?" Sister Pom asked. Then she pulled me to one side. There was the sharp, rhythmic sound of many bare feet slapping on the road as some people hurried past us, with someone saying in a brusque voice, "Faster—I must keep an appointment."

"Who are they?" I asked. "What is it?"

"They are rickshaw coolies rushing someone to an appointment. You must remember rickshaws from Simla. We used to ride in them. They are hooded two-wheelers pulled by two coolies and pushed by two coolies."

I felt a pang. Ahead, I could hear the front coolies calling to the back coolies, "Don't push! We are dying!" Their voices came out small and close to the ground, as if the coolies were doubled over with the burden of the rickshaw. Also, now that I listened carefully, I realized that the baggage coolies, like the rickshaw coolies, were barefoot. They all reminded me of the students and teachers at Dadar School, none of whom could afford a pair of shoes.

"We should never ride in rickshaws. We should carry our own luggage," I said.

"Coolies need work," Daddyji said. He had dropped back and fallen into step with us. "Otherwise, they would starve. None of us could lift a single bedroll, but you wouldn't believe how much these coolies can carry on their heads and backs, how they can haul and push." He added reflectively, "I know from my medical experience that coolies don't survive more than ten or fifteen summers of steady rickshaw work. Few live beyond their thirties. God knows how they survive the snows and storms of the winter, with their scant clothes and scant rations and no work."

"You're contradicting yourself," I said.

"In a way, I suppose I am," Daddyji said.

"How pleasant it is here," Sister Umi said, joining us. The hills smelled of pine and fir, and though it was the middle of the day the air felt light, cool, and fresh.

Our cottage was at the bottom of a ravine and felt small, dank, and empty. It consisted only of a main room and two bedrooms, but it had a glazed veranda. As soon as we walked out on it, we felt at home. It was flooded with warm sun.

❧

I REMEMBER that, one of the first days we were in Murree, Daddyji left to do some work and then Mamaji and my big sisters prepared to leave, too.

"I want to go with you," I said.

"We are all going to meet our friends," Sister Umi said. "They are grownups. You stay with Usha—she'll take you wherever you want to go."

I protested, but they all left.

After Usha started school, I hadn't spent much time with her. In any case, she was only six—three years younger than I was—and I had had my own daily activities. In Murree, there was no Ram Saran to talk to, no resident clerks, no washerman, no gardener. The cottage had no compound, no office, no servants' quarters. Gian Chand slept in the kitchen, and he was busy from morning to night cooking and cleaning, serving and clearing up, going to the bazaar. I couldn't go anywhere by myself, because there were ledges, rocks, gorges, and ravines everywhere. In Murree, I spent more and more time with Usha—constantly calling her to play with me, to go outside with me, to come with me for a walk. I had only to shout for her, and she was at my side. She was easy to walk with. She was a few inches shorter than I was, but when we walked our hands were at the same level. We would run or skip along, our hands just touching, I trying to match her step and her speed. When we were negotiating bad slopes, I would follow her with one hand on her shoulder, trying to place my foot directly behind hers. In the beginning, passersby would cluck and make comments on my blindness and her devotion. They would surround us and ask how I had lost my sight, why she wasn't holding on to me, why our parents weren't with us. I had grown up mostly behind walls—of Dadar School, of 11 Temple Road, of Mehta Gulli, of 16 Mozang Road, of 10 Civil Lines. People I came in contact with were friends and relatives, who were used to me and knew what I could do. I usually went out with grownups, who often shielded me from the pity and curiosity of strangers. But in Murree we were two children out on the road by ourselves. I didn't know how to deal with the nosy passersby, and wanted to kick them, but Usha seemed to know how to stop their questioning, and they would send us on our way with blessings and good wishes.

"How do you do it?" I once asked her.

"I don't know myself," she said. "They look at me and stop."

"She has the piteous face of a cocker spaniel—she'd make a good Seeing Eye dog," said a family friend who happened to overhear our conversation.

I felt angry, but Usha only laughed.

Luckily, Murree was a small place, and everyone soon knew us and got used to us.

❧

In Bombay, Lahore, and Rawalpindi, I had known only a neighborhood, but Murree was so small that I soon knew all of it—indeed, walked around almost all of it with Usha every day. Yet the hill station never felt quite familiar. There was something foreign about it, although I couldn't have said what that was. We used to cover the Mall daily. It was a gentle two-mile incline starting from near our cottage and ending in a quarter-mile level stretch known as the Upper Mall. There were several points along the Mall where coolies with ponies for hire congregated and sold rides to Pindi Point and Kashmir Point. Their din, especially by the Upper Mall, seemed constant. No sooner did a pony or a donkey set out with its coolie shuffling or running alongside than a new ponywallah or donkeywallah materialized. Whenever Usha and I passed them, they would call after us and beg us to take their ponies and donkeys.

"Big, dangerous climb, excellent for good rider!" the ponywallahs would shout.

"Little, safe climb, excellent for children!" the donkeywallahs would shout.

We would walk briskly on, because we didn't like the idea of being lugged by a pony or a donkey any more than we liked the idea of being lugged by coolies in a rickshaw.

For a long time, I wasn't clear what Pindi Point and Kashmir Point were, and thought that one was a bridle path for horses, the other a road for donkeys. Then I learned that Pindi Point was actually the top of

a hill that afforded a view of the entire valley of Rawalpindi, and Kashmir Point the top of another hill, which
afforded a view of the mountains of Kashmir. After
that, Usha and I would often walk up to Pindi Point
and Kashmir Point. The two hill roads, each about a
mile long, were at opposite ends of the Mall, and were
popular walks.

All along the roads were weather-beaten wooden
railings for protection against falling into the gorges
and ravines. Here and there were breaks in the railings
for paths leading down to cottages like ours, perched
on the slopes of the gorges. I would walk with a hand
on the railing and count the breaks in order to tell
where I was. I would kick stones into the gorge in
order to try to guess how deep it was. I would climb
onto the railings and swing on them like a monkey,
sometimes dangling over the gorge.

"Don't! It's all shaky! You'll fall!" Usha would cry,
clutching me.

"How far down is it?" I would shout, leaning into
the gorge.

"I don't know. I'm afraid to look."

At least once a day, we would walk along the Upper
Mall. It had Western-style shops and Western-style
restaurants, and was full of strollers window-shopping
and taking the air. Usha would call out to me its few
landmarks—the post office, the first Chinese shoeshop,
the second Chinese shoeshop, the chemist's, the first
Chinese restaurant, the second Chinese restaurant, Uncle
Kirpa Ram's cloth shop. (Like good Punjabi children,
we called all Mamaji's and Daddyji's friends, like Mr.
and Mrs. Kirpa Ram, "Uncle" and "Auntie;" they called

us "Son" and "Daughter.") I got to know where each landmark was, and took pride in calling them out for Usha. We would walk into every shop and restaurant, but would sometimes do no more than go in and wish the manager good morning or good evening, laugh, and walk out. Sometimes we would stroll into the cemetery nearby and sit on cold marble tombstones. Usha would read out to me the names inscribed on them—generally names of Englishmen and English ladies. Saying them aloud would fill us with awe. Something would dart or rustle, disturbing the still air, and we would fear we had awakened the ghosts. We would race away. We would always stop in at Lintot's to see Mamaji and our big sisters. (We called Lintot's, a sort of Anglo-Indian restaurant, by its proper name, perhaps because it served Indian and English savories and pastries, and the name somehow sounded grand and British.) Mamaji and my big sisters would be sitting on the veranda with their friends, at a table that commanded a good view of the Upper Mall, knitting, eating, and talking. We would go up to them and pester them, and to get rid of us they would sometimes give us money. We would run out and buy sweets from the chemist's, or a ribbon for Usha's hair from Uncle Kirpa Ram's cloth shop, or some stamps at the post office. I don't know why we wanted the stamps, but I remember that neither of us was tall enough to reach the counter, and I would have to lift Usha up. If we had enough money, we would go to the first Chinese restaurant, which was up a flight of stairs, and, like grownups, get a table by a window with a good view of the Upper Mall. We would order what we imagined was Chinese fare—fried rice and slices of bread with tomato sauce on them. They were served to us by a Chinese who understood little Punjabi. He had to speak in a mixture of Punjabi and English, which sounded particularly funny because he invariably said "r" for "l" and "l" for "r."

Until we came to Murree, we had not met a Chinese, and at first Usha would correct him. She was proud of the progress she had made in English at the convent; she had been able to say "thought" and "healthy" right off the bat when the others in her first standard were going around saying "tought" and "healty." But the Chinese would only mutter something and go away. Then we decided that that must be the way all Chinese talked, and Usha stopped correcting him. In fact, we came to enjoy him—the more so because he seemed to have no name. Everyone in the restaurant just addressed him as "Chinaman." But we couldn't get him to talk much.

I once asked him, "Chinaman, what are your ladies called?"

"Chinaman," he said, with a laugh.

"Are you all called 'Chinaman' because you make china?" Usha asked.

"Yes, maybe," he said.

We might go from the first Chinese restaurant to the unfashionable, bad-smelling Lower Mall, a narrow, cobbled *gulli* that sloped off from one side of the Upper Mall. It was an ordinary bazaar, with hawkers, coolies, and servants haggling over fruits, vegetables, grains, ghi, and curios. Usha and I would make a bee-line for a particular vender, who sold carved sandalwood boxes. The scent of sandalwood in his stall was so strong that we forgot the smells of the bazaar all around us.

I remember that I became enamored of one sandalwood box. It was long and squat, and was carved with what felt like a hill-and-dale pattern.

"How much is it?" I asked the vender.

"Twenty rupees. A special price for Sahib," he said, in pink English.

"Twenty rupees!" I cried. "I'll give you five."

"Sahib, sandalwood boxes very expensive, very special. Sandalwood very hard to come by. Snakes liking the scent of sandalwood trees and wrapping themselves around. When you go to cutting the trees, snakes bite you. Sandalwood boxes only available in hill station. The scent keeping away termites. English sahib and memsahib liking sandalwood because it reminding them of clean homes. Nineteen rupees—very special price for Sahib."

"Five rupees, not an anna more," I said, in the manner of Mamaji.

Every day, we would return to the sandalwood vender. In a week or so, I had the price down to ten rupees. I bought the box and gave it to Usha. Although I liked the sandalwood scent, if Usha and I got a whiff of it when we were out for a walk we would run, for fear of snakes.

Usha and I and everyone else were always at home before it got dark. Gian Chand would be struggling with the fire in the main room. The fuel was the anthracite variety of coal, which was equally hard to

get burning and to keep burning. Whenever Gian
Chand added a bucket of fresh coal, the fire would
almost die out. He alternately fanned the fire and—in
order to prevent it from smoking—covered up the fireplace with a sheet of tin. We would all sit around the
fireplace, drawing our chairs as close as we could and
rubbing our faces and ears to rid them of the evening
hill-station chill. As the coals caught, the fire would
hiss and crackle behind the tin, making it rattle fero-
ciously. When Gian Chand finally removed the tin,
the fire would practically leap into the room, making
us push back our chairs. We would eat dinner sitting
in front of the fire.

No matter how good the fire was, it heated only
part of the main room. The rest of the cottage remained
cold and damp. Mamaji took the only hot-water bottle
to bed, and I remember I used to get between my
sheets in stages. I would start with my knees close to
my chin and, as the bed warmed up, move my feet
slowly toward the bottom. I would fall asleep listening
to someone playing a flute in the distance, its notes
fading in and out with the rush of the mountain wind.
The melody was always wistful, and was made somehow more wistful because it was simple and repeti-
tious, like a hill chant, and because it was played on a
primitive bamboo flute with a limited range. Sometimes the flute was accompanied by the dolorous chant
of a man, his hill song also swelling and receding with
the wind.

❧

USHA AND I liked stopping in the first Chinese shoeshop on the Upper Mall and talking to the Chinese there. He talked exactly like the restaurant Chinese.

The shoeshop Chinese was always glad to see us. "Ah, Doctor's children," he would call out as we entered. His English sounded so funny that we would burst out laughing. He would join in our laughter without ever asking why we were laughing.

He would let us stay at the shop as long as we wanted, and would talk to us between working behind the counter and taking measurements for the occasional customer who dropped in. I liked to breathe in the pervasive smell of leather, rubber, glue, and polish in the shop and listen to the sound of the Chinese cutting and sewing leather and hammering nails.

In contrast to the restaurant Chinese, the shoeshop Chinese talked a lot. "What does gentleman want to do when he grows up?" he once asked me.

"Be a Chinaman," I said.

"Oh!" He laughed. "And little lady?" It amused us that he called me "gentleman" and Usha "little lady."

"I'm going to be my big brother's helper," Usha said.

"Very nice, very nice," he said. "Little lady has true spirit. What kind of shoe would gentleman like?"

"I don't know what you have," I said.

He let me touch all the shoes in his shop. I had touched only the few shoes that people wore at home, and I was surprised at how many kinds of shoes there could be. Here were shoes with buckles, buttons, laces. Some had rubber soles and heels, with treads; others had leather soles with pointed high heels. Some had uppers of smooth, squeaky leather, others of grainy leather. Some had bows on top, others had punched-out tops.

"You have so many different shoes!" I exlaimed.

"The Chinese two doors up has more," he said. "Which shoes would you like?"

I told him that I had taken a fancy to one particular pair, because they had crêpe soles and smooth but not polished uppers.

"Good choice. Crêpe soles very good for hills. They don't slip, but they're most expensive. I have to hand-make them for you. I hand-make all shoes. Little gentleman should come with Madame and give special order. Perhaps little lady would like the same."

Usha said she would, and we insisted that he take our measurements right there and then. He sat me down on the only chair in the shop and made me take off my right shoe. He put my foot on a piece of paper and started tracing it with a pencil. I had trouble holding my foot still, because the pencil tickled me. After he finished with me, he took a tracing of Usha's foot.

Usha and I ran out of the shoeshop very excited about having crêpe soles to walk around in on the hills. But when we asked Mamaji for the money to buy them she said, "You both have a perfectly good pair of shoes. When they wear out, we will see."

"But they're leather and they slip on the hills!" we cried.

"I've told you your shoes are perfectly good. Go and play," she said firmly.

We appealed to Daddyji, but once she had said no we couldn't get him to say yes—in this case, perhaps because our shoes were indeed perfectly good.

The next time we stopped in at the shoeshop, we told the Chinese that we were going to save our pocket money so that we could order his crêpe soles.

"How much pocket money do you get?"

"Two rupees each a month," Usha said.

"Oh, it will take you a year. Maybe next summer when you come to Murree I will make you crêpe soles."

"Maybe we should get cheaper shoes," Usha said.

"I want the best," I said.

"Crêpe soles are the best," the Chinese said. "Very light. Very comfortable. Perfect for gentleman and lady at a hill station. Maybe your mummy will change her mind." He abruptly asked, "Would you like crêpe soles with two eyelets for laces, or five?"

"Which are better for a hill station?" I asked.

"Oh, two eyelets," he said. "Less pressure on the top of the foot."

After that, I couldn't bear to walk in my old shoes, because they had five eyelets and I felt the pressure of the laces. The leather felt hard and unyielding. Every time I took a step, I felt I was going to slip and fall.

One day, I came home from a walk, pulled a chair to the sideboard, and took down a big bread knife. I took one of my shoes off and quickly sliced its toe and then took one of Usha's shoes and sliced its toe. When Mamaji and Daddyji returned home, I held up the shoes. "A mosquito did it," I said.

Mamaji began to scold me severely, but Daddyji laughed, and the next day they took Usha and me to the shoeshop and gave an order for crêpe soles with dull, soft uppers for each of us. Until the new shoes were ready, we had to thump around in our sliced-up shoes.

When we got the crêpe soles, I wasn't sure I liked them. The crêpe soles were soundless, and I began bumping into things oftener. I realized that I had relied on the sound of my leather soles to orient myself—to tell whether I was near an obstacle, whether I was near a drop, whether I was nearing steps, even how big a room was. But I soon trained myself to kick and scuff when I walked and to orient myself by that sound.

Having realized that there was a variety of shoes, I began taking an interest in what I wore and how I looked.

❧

ONE EVENING, Usha and I were walking in our crêpe soles up to Kashmir Point, and she was calling out the cottages in the ravines by the side of the road: "The cottage of Uncle Basheshwar Nath Khanna. . . . The cottage of Uncle Devi Chand. . . . That's the house of Uncle Mehr Chand Khanna." Then Usha cried, "There are our big sisters!"

We raced up to them. They were walking very slowly, with their friends Chinta, Sheila, Satish, and Satta. Satta was very religious. It was prayer time, and as they walked Satta said a prayer aloud and they recited it with her. We heard some boisterous voices ahead.

"Soldiers! Soldiers!" Sister Pom cried.

"Yankees! Yankees!" Sister Umi exclaimed. "They do dirty things to Hindu women."

We all started running back down the hill in panic.

The "Yankees" started running after us, like dogs who sense the fright of strangers.

I got a terrible stitch in my side, but I kept up.

Sister Umi called, "Down!" I didn't know exactly where she was. Usha's hand was gone. But I heard everyone scrambling in the ravine by the road, and I jumped. I banged my chin on a branch, somersaulted, bumped my head, and landed on top of someone. I cried out.

Sister Pom shushed me, whispering, "The Yankees!"

We sat crouched, hardly daring to breathe.

The "Yankees" stopped and stood just above us. They idly kicked some stones down the slope, but we didn't so much as stir.

"Come on," one of them said. "Let's go. They are not girls. They're a family." They passed on, singing and laughing.

"That was a near miss," Sister Pom said after they were out of earshot. "We should never come to Kashmir Point again when it's getting dark."

❧

OFTEN, MY BIG SISTERS would meet their friends and go on long hikes. I once cornered them and insisted that I be taken along. "Where do you go? What trails do you take? I want to come."

"On some very dangerous trails," Sister Umi said. "They are no trails for you."

"It's because I can't see that you're not taking me,"
I said.

"Even if you could see, we wouldn't take you with
us," Sister Umi said.

"They are no trails for children," Sister Pom said.

I knew from long experience that Sister Pom was
too responsible and Sister Umi too dismissive for my
appeals to them to do any good. But Sister Nimi had
a soft heart—she cried as easily as she laughed. She
was also the most daring and the most athletic of the
three. I took her aside and appealed to her.

"O.K., O.K., Vedi," she said to me. "I will take
you on a hike tomorrow. But don't tell Pom. If she
gets to hear of it, she will eat my head."

The next morning, the two of us sauntered out of
the house as if we were going for a stroll. We walked
on familiar roads, passed through a break in the railing, scrambled along some paths, and were finally on
a sheer mountain trail. It was little more than a ledge
with stumps and rocks and overhanging bushes. Sister
Nimi always stayed in front, and called back to me to
put my foot on this or that rock and duck under this
or that branch and grab the stump of this tree or that
wild bush ahead. I stayed close behind her, holding on
to her shoulder or waist, or sometimes only to the cuff
of her pajama trousers, and feeling at once frightened
and exhilarated. A wind came up, and it started mist-
ing threateningly.

"Oof, these hills look really beautiful," Sister Nimi
said. "Mountaineers all over the world would give anything to come here and climb our Himalayas. Many of

them dream about these mountains for years and never get here. Some of those who do get here die trying to climb them."

I had to let go of Sister Nimi, because the trail had come to an end and we were now climbing up the mountainside. I had to use my hands to grip the rocks. Now and again, a stone would come loose in our hands or give way under our weight and roll and crash down the mountainside, taking with it mud and debris.

She was saying, "Vedi, it's really beautiful, the sweep of mountains in the mist." Abruptly, she added, "Be careful. This cliff is really bad."

A rock came loose from above my head. I caught my breath. It rolled down the side of the hill frighteningly close and then fell over the cliff and was gone without a sound.

Now we were walking along a mountain that seemed to shoot straight up. I could tell by my facial vision that it was a towering wall. The wind began to roar. The mist turned into a steady, hill-station rain, drumming all around us deafeningly. My facial vision became utterly useless. I completely lost my bearings. I put each foot down cautiously, testing the ground with my toe at every step. I hung on to Sister Nimi with both hands.

"Not so tight!" she cried, her words almost swallowed up by the wind and the rain. "We'll both fall."

The rain let up as abruptly as it had started.

"Oof! The mountains are really looking magni—"

"Stop it!" I cried.

Sister Nimi broke off.

I felt terrible about my outburst.

"Let's start back," she said.

"Let's," I said, feeling tired all at once.

❧

"THE BEST FUN in a hill station is riding a pony," Sister Umi said. "Every time I get into a saddle and put my foot in a stirrup, I feel the thrill all over again."

"I didn't know you went riding," I said.

"I started yesterday."

"How much does it cost?"

"Eight annas for the Kashmir Point round. Why do you want to know?"

I didn't answer, but after that all I could think about was riding a pony.

"It's no different from being carried around on someone's shoulders," Usha said when I told her what I wanted to do.

"I'm sure it's not like that at all," I said. "You can fall off a pony and kill yourself, and they have leather saddles, and they run."

She got excited, and we went to the Mall to hire two ponies.

The coolies surrounded us while their ponies shifted all around us. They set up a clamor, each shouting that we should hire his pony.

"Sahib, Memsahib, my pony!"

"No, my pony much better! Feel, touch, look, Sahib, Memsahib!"

"Sahib will fall off a pony," a new coolie said, shouldering his way into our midst. "Only six annas for two donkeys. Five annas both on one donkey."

"We don't want donkeys," I said. "We want two ponies—two good, reliable ponies."

"How will we get on a pony?" Usha asked me. "They're very tall."

"Blind Sahib never ridden before?" a coolie asked.

"Never," we said.

The new coolie whipped and prodded his donkey, shouting, "Forward, you ass!" He tugged at my hand, asking me to feel the lush coat and tail of his donkey.

"Not donkeys!" I yelled. "We want ponies!"

Before I knew what was happening, he had picked up both Usha and me and set us down on his donkey. The donkey had no leather saddle. There was just a folded burlap bag and a chest-high criblike structure in the shape of a ring tied on to it. Touching the encircling structure made me remember being in Simla some years earlier. There Mamaji used to go for walks and take me along. I was too small to walk very far but too big for her to put me in a pram or carry me, so she would hire a donkey for me. I didn't like being on it. It was so slow that it couldn't even keep up with Mamaji's step, and I remembered complaining that I couldn't talk to her. Also, it was so stupid that it didn't know to get out of the way of a rickshaw coming at it; the donkeywallah would have to beat it and pull it to the side of the road. "Hurry up! We'll lose Mamaji!" I would cry to the donkeywallah, but he was as slow as his donkey, and sometimes we wouldn't catch up with Mamaji until the walk was over.

"Get me down off this horrible donkey!" I now cried. "We want ponies!"

"A ponywallah won't take blind Sahib," the donkeywallah said. "If Sahib falls off, the government will hang him."

Both Usha and I struggled to get down from the donkey. The donkeywallah finally lifted us and put us on the ground.

"The government will hang us in the police station!" the ponywallahs cried. They had retreated to the side of the road.

"Let's not go on a pony," Usha said, pulling me away.

"Sahib doesn't have riding breeches," a ponywallah shouted from the back. The others laughed uncertainly.

"Two rupees for two ponies for the Kashmir Point round," I said, offering them twice what Sister Umi had said it would cost.

Two ponies were led up to us, and Usha and I were lifted onto them.

I was very happy. The saddle creaked and felt like real leather.

The pony snorted, sending ripples down its sides. "Help, I'm going to fall off!" I cried.

The ponywallah showed me how to hold on to the pommel and how to fit my feet into the stirrups. The ponywallah clicked his tongue and we set out, with Usha in the lead and me close behind, and the ponywallahs walking alongside and holding the reins. Halfway up the climb to Pindi Point, I got my ponywallah to let me hold the reins for a time, and though he continued to walk at my side I felt I was in command.

In the following days, Usha and I got Mamaji to have riding breeches sewn for us. They had snug-fitting cuffs and a row of buttons along the outside of the legs. Every morning, Usha and I would get into our breeches, hire a couple of ponies and ponywallahs, and make the rounds of Pindi Point and Kashmir Point. In due course, I learned how to dig my heels into the sides of the pony and make it canter or gallop. As I rushed along—clicking my tongue and prodding the pony with my heels or with a whip, like a ponywallah; bouncing up and down in the saddle, my teeth rattling; clutching the pommel with one hand and the reins with the other; travelling sometimes against the wind, up to Pindi Point, down from Pindi Point, up to Kashmir Point, down from Kashmir Point; listening for other riders, so that I could rein in and pull my pony to one side; sometimes overtaking Usha, sometimes racing ahead to prevent her from overtaking me, the ponywallahs always running at our side, breathless and mindful—I forgot all about my blindness.

VI

CIVIL LINES
GHOST

S OON AFTER WE RETURNED TO RAWALPINDI
from Murree, Daddyji bought Brother Om a
cricket set. "You're already twelve," he said.
"But then I was just your age when I began,
and I was a good cricketeer in my day."
Brother Om hardly looked at the cricket
set and afterward did not so much as pick up a
cricket bat. Then Daddyji decided that perhaps he was
meant for hockey, and got him a hockey stick and a
ball. "I was a good hockey player in my day," Daddyji
said. "Sport is in our blood."

But Brother Om hardly played with his hockey
stick and ball.

"Do you want to go in for some other sport?" Daddyji asked him.

"No, I'll play cricket and hockey," he said.

Behind Daddyji's back, however, he announced to us, "I wish he'd leave me alone. I have no interest in sports."

I thought that Brother Om was just being obstinate, and I resented it. I wished I could play cricket and hockey, but I could play only simple games, like hide-and-seek, with Usha.

Then Daddyji decided to teach Brother Om how to read and write Urdu; Brother Om didn't know Urdu, because at Bishop Cotton School and St. Denys' School they taught only in English.

"Lalaji was known for his Urdu penmanship," Daddyji told him. "Throughout primary school, I was taught all subjects in Urdu. Urdu has a great tradition behind it. At least a third of its vocabulary is Persian, and Persian was the language of our high Mogul culture and was used in the Mogul courts before the British came. The wisdom of the ages is distilled in Urdu poetry. I was reciting verses in Urdu before I was your age."

We had all grown up hearing Daddyji recite Urdu verses and couplets when he wanted to console or cheer himself, to express a thought or feeling, to philosophize or entertain, to cap a conversation or an occasion. They came to him spontaneously, and he seemed to have a limitless store of them. Because Urdu was a difficult language, with lots of Persian words, and none of us had a head for poetry, we all had trouble memorizing it. But we all knew at least one or two couplets by heart—all, that is, except Brother Om. However often Daddyji recited a couplet, Brother Om was never able to repeat it later.

"How can you forget it?" Daddyji would ask, in Punjabi. "They are so beautiful. Listen." And he would recite, in Urdu:

> In dark times, who stays with you?
> Even your own shadow runs away from you.

Or

> The nightingale's destiny is to cry,
> The moth's is to burn,
> But the grief that we were given
> Seems the most difficult thing in sight.

Or

> The day for death is fixed.
> Why, then, can't I sleep at night?

"I don't know—I just forget," Brother Om would reply, in English.

Whenever Daddyji found a little time, he would give Brother Om dictation in Urdu, which he would take down on a slate. When Daddyji looked at the slate, he would complain that Brother Om's handwriting was careless, that his spelling was careless, that he'd left out words. Daddyji himself was meticulous, and he couldn't understand how a son of his could be so careless. But the more he kept after Brother Om, the more careless Brother Om's Urdu became.

Then Brother Om started falling behind in his schoolwork and getting bad marks. He claimed that this was because he couldn't see well. Mamaji bought him a pair of spectacles.

One afternoon, he came home crying. "My spectacles! A boy knocked them off my face."

"But they're not broken," Mamaji said.

"But they almost broke!" Brother Om said. He wouldn't stop crying until Mamaji had admitted that he had a point.

When Daddyji came to know about it, he told Brother Om that when Mehta boys were roughed up they fought back—they didn't run to their mothers.

"They will beat me!"

"You beat them back."

"They gang up on me!"

"You should start your own gang."

"I can't!"

" 'Can't' is not in the Mehta vocabulary."

Whatever Daddyji said, Brother Om would neither study nor fight. I felt that if I could go to school I would study and fight.

Then, although Brother Om started doing better in Urdu, he told Daddyji one day that he was interested only in acting, singing, and dancing, because he was going to grow up to become a film star.

"I was hoping that you would become a doctor," Daddyji said. "I can't believe that you are so foolish as to think that as an actor you could earn a livelihood. I can't believe that a Mehta boy—and a son of mine— thinks that one can get along in life without a profession. You should be like Winston Churchill, who paints on the side."

"I'm not interested in medicine," Brother Om said.

"What about engineering, then? That's what I myself always wanted to do."

"I can't do mathematics."

"You will become good at it if you apply yourself. Application is the royal road to everything."

In front of Daddyji, Brother Om agreed, but behind his back he said, "I have application only in acting."

Brother Om would refuse to eat, and if ever Mamaji slapped him he would point to a knife and say, "Stab me! Kill me! Cut my throat!"

Daddyji considered me a good child and Om a bad child. But next to Brother Om I felt entirely inadequate—I could never even aspire to learn to read and write Urdu, for instance, to say nothing of developing beautiful Urdu penmanship. There wasn't even a Braille system for writing Urdu. Yet though I felt jealous of him I sympathized with him. He was the only one of us who got an occasional slap from Daddyji, generally because he was careless—for instance, he misspelled the commonest English words. I, too, was careless— for instance, I was always knocking into things and getting injuries—yet Daddyji hardly ever slapped me.

"Daddyji favors you because you're blind, Vedi," Brother Om used to say to me. "He doesn't bother about the sisters, because they are girls and will get married. I have to carry the burden of all his ambitions on my back. He makes me the scapegoat. You have Usha. Our big sisters have one another. I have no one. I am the black sheep of the family."

❧

ALL OF US children slept in one long, narrow room, called "the gallery," right next to our parents' bedroom. Our cots were placed so close to one another that there was hardly any space between them; we usually got in and out of bed from the foot. We all slept in a row, from the oldest to the youngest—Sister Pom, Sister Nimi, Sister Umi, Brother Om, then me, and then Usha.

One night, when everyone else was asleep I quietly got up, took a five-rupee note from Brother Om's knickers, which were lying at the foot of his bed, and crept back into my bed, praying all the time that the Civil Lines ghost, who seemed to walk around the restricted government lane in which we lived as if it were his private road, hadn't seen me. I hated to steal, but I needed the money urgently. Gian Chand was going to the bazaar in the morning, and he had promised to buy me some more goldfish if I could give him the money; my goldfish had died while we were away in Murree.

The next morning, at the breakfast table, Brother Om reported the loss, and Mamaji scolded him roundly for being careless with money. The pulse in my forehead raced furiously, and I was sure that it would give me away as the thief. But I kept mum. That day, I got my goldfish, and Brother Om got yet another bad mark against him.

A few nights later, I woke up with my cot shaking, rocking from side to side. I stiffened, and hugged the covers; I was sure that the Civil Lines ghost had come to punish me. He was going to tip the cot over me and trample me. I tried to scream, but no voice would come out—he must have me by the throat, I thought.

The Civil Lines ghost floated over Brother Om's pillow and then floated down to the foot of his cot. Then he lifted off Brother Om's blanket, making a stirring sound in the air.

He is going to suffocate me with the blanket, I thought. I buried my face in my pillow.

I heard the Civil Lines ghost wrap the blanket around his shoulders, the way we did in the winter; there was no heat in the house, and when we were in our night suits we used to wrap ourselves in our blankets. The Civil Lines ghost wandered up and down at the foot of our cots, as if he couldn't decide how to punish me.

I lay very still.

"The nightingale is the shadow. The moth burns and is happy." The voice reciting in Urdu was thick and slurry, but it sounded like Brother Om's, and it was coming not from his cot but from the foot of our cots, as if the ghost were mimicking Brother Om. Now it hovered at the foot of Sister Pom's cot, now at the foot of my cot.

The regular breathing of my big sisters stopped. The door to our parents' bedroom opened.

"It's Om!" Sister Pom exclaimed.

"Sh-h-h," Daddyji whispered. "You mustn't wake him up."

Daddyji tiptoed over and escorted the ghost to Brother Om's bed. I was afraid to open my mouth for fear the ghost would tattle about my stealing.

After that, the ghost would come every week or two, and walk along the foot of our cots. Mamaji or Daddyji or one or another of our big sisters would wake up and put him quietly to bed with Brother Om. No one would ever speak about it, as if everyone, including Daddyji and Mamaji, were afraid of the ghost.

❧

DADDYJI WAS AWAY on tour, and Mamaji had to go to Lahore to attend the *chautha* (the fourth, and last, day of mourning) for her maternal grandmother, Manji. She arranged to have a family friend, Usha Malhotra, stay with us and to have Gian Chand sleep in the house until she got back. The first night without her, I woke up and was petrified. There was a rustling noise in the bushes outside the window.

"Sister Pom, there's someone in the bushes," I whispered from my cot.

"Mmm," she said drowsily, as if she were deep in sleep, dreaming.

"Umi," Sister Nimi whispered. "Do you hear that?"

Suddenly, we were all shouting together.

"Thief!"

"Gian Chand!"

"Robbers!"

Usha Malhotra shouted from our parents' bedroom, "The bushes! We are going to be killed!"

Gian Chand came running with a stick, but he wouldn't go out to the bushes.

"Out! Out!" Sister Umi shouted.

"I'll report you to Daddyji!" Brother Om yelled. "You'll be dismissed."

"Come on, Gian Chand, be a good sport. We are all alone," Sister Pom said.

Finally, Gian Chand climbed out the window.

The thief seemed undaunted. He continued to rustle in the bushes even as Gian Chand cursed and beat them with his stick.

"I'm going to kill you!" Gian Chand shouted, suddenly sounding bold, and cracking the stick across the intruder's back.

We all became bold, too, and jumped out of our cots and ran out to see whom Gian Chand had caught, only to discover that the intruder was the washerman's straying jackass.

VII

MUSIC MASTERS

ONCE, THE WHOLE FAMILY WENT TO LAHORE for a few days and stayed with Babuji and Mataji, at 16 Mozang Road. One afternoon, while we were all sitting on the veranda, Auntie Pushpa, who was also staying there at the time, sighed and clicked her tongue and said, "Look, girls, that's Master Kohli going home after giving Vimla her tuition. See how nicely he walks— with just one hand on his boy-servant's shoulder. He has a tonga of his own. He uses it when he has to go far. You should see how he sits in it, with his stomach out—like a real tycoon."

"Which tuition? Master of what?" I asked.

"Master of music, Master Sahib," Auntie Pushpa said, using my aunties' nickname for me. "He's totally blind, but he gives tuition in singing. He comes daily to teach Vimla, and he goes to several other big houses to give tuition. If only you could grow up to be a real Master Sahib, like him, and give tuition in singing to daughters of good families! Then you could keep a private tonga, too."

For some reason, I didn't like the idea of Master Kohli, but when Daddyji came to hear of him he told me, "I think it would be a good idea for you to take some tuition in singing. I don't know when the war will be over—when you'll be able to go to the West and study at the Perkins Institution. Like Master Kohli, you could teach singing. It would give you a good livelihood. You wouldn't need anyone to support you."

I tried to get accustomed to the idea. We had a His Master's Voice gramophone, and I used to like to wind it again and again and listen for hours to the same record of Saigal, the famous singer, singing a *ghazal* (love song). It was in difficult Urdu, and I didn't understand more than a word of two, but listening to it filled me with longing and sadness. I wouldn't have minded growing up to be another Saigal. But then I heard that Master Kohli didn't speak English, that he sat on the floor, like a girl, and that he wore a collarless shirt and pajama trousers, like a servant. Although I enjoyed the company of servants—unlike my sisters and brother, I had no friends of my own—what I really wanted was to grow up to be like Daddyji: to speak English, to sit in a chair, and to wear a collar and tie. I told Daddyji that I didn't want to become a music master.

"You could live upstairs at 11 Temple Road and rent out the downstairs and have enough to eat and be independent, but you would still need to have something to do," Daddyji said. "If you could supplement the rent with some music tuition, like Master Kohli, you could live in style."

"I don't want to learn singing," I said. "If I must learn music, I think I'd like to learn the violin and play in your Gymkhana band."

Daddyji had taken me to the Gymkhana Club, which had mostly English members, and had let me sit with the band musicians and feel the instruments. The musicians wore collars and ties, sat in chairs, and played Western music while people ate or danced. It was all festive and English.

"But singing may be about the only thing that can provide a respectable livelihood for a blind person," Daddyji said. "You certainly can't play a violin. Its strings would ruin your fingers, and then you wouldn't be able to read Braille." Years later, I learned that he was mistaken about this. Unlike many Indian stringed instruments, the violin does not lead to calluses—its strings are not particularly sharp, and, in any case, their pressure on the fingers is slight, because of the little distance between them and the fingerboard.

"But I don't want to go around in a private tonga, like Master Kohli," I said. "I want a car, like you."

"You can surpass Master Kohli and keep a car and driver."

"But I have just had my tonsils out."

"You can learn singing in your own good time. There's no hurry."

The next time Master Kohli came to give Auntie Vimla a lesson, I went into the drawing room and sat with them on the floor. Master Kohli was playing the harmonium and singing "aah" up and down the scale, and Auntie Vimla was singing along.

Auntie Vimla stopped and complained that her throat hurt, that the exertion was bringing tears to her eyes.

"These are good signs," Master Kohli said, in rustic Punjabi. "That means your throat is standing up. If you don't sing out, the throat sits down, and then you can't get your full voice out of it. Tears help to bring out the soul in your voice."

Auntie Vimla said she wanted to rest, and Master Kohli asked me to sing "aah" with him. I strained to get my full voice out and bring tears to my eyes.

A couple of tears trickled down my face. I licked them and imagined I was eating ice cream. (For a time after my tonsillectomy, I could scarcely swallow, and about the only thing I enjoyed eating was ice cream— the kind we made in a hand-cranked machine in our own back courtyard. No matter how tightly the cylinder containing the mixture was sealed, some salt from the ice would seep into it, and the ice cream would have a slightly salty taste, like tears.)

I began enjoying the music lesson. I liked the sound of the harmonium and the sound of Master Kohli's "aah"s. There was something jerky in his voice, and as he sang "aah" he drummed his fingers on the side of the harmonium, making me think that we were in his private tonga, bumping along a road, singing and having a good time.

❧

ONE AFTERNOON when we had returned to Rawalpindi, I heard a thin sound, distant and haunting, like
the opening bars of the ghosts' songs I used to hear at
Dadar School. But instead of being frightening, like
the barks and noises of the ghosts, the new sound was
sweet and alluring. I followed it to the drawing room.

"This is my little brother," Sister Pom said, introducing me to someone. She and the stranger were
standing in the middle of the room.

I spoke to the stranger in Punjabi, but he replied
in English.

"Englishman!" I cried, touching his coat.

"Not English—only English schooling," he said.
"Goanese violin teacher of your big sisters."

"But you don't speak Punjabi!" I cried.

"Father Portuguese, Mother Hindu. But taking after
my father, so not speaking Indian." He laughed.

He showed me his violin—how to put the chin rest
under my chin and how to draw the bow across the
strings. I even squeaked out a few notes. I liked it very
much. The harmonium was large and bulky, but the
violin was almost as light as Daddyji's felt hat.

"You need music to play the violin," the violin
teacher said, and he put the music stand in front of me
and adjusted it to my height.

"But I can't read," I said.

There was a silence, and then the violin teacher
said, "Indian music best for you. You not having to
read it."

As the violin teacher was leaving, I asked him if
he had a private tonga.

"No, little fellow," he said. "As you might say, I
am walking like the Englishmen."

When he was gone, I played with the music stand, making the rod go up and down in its sleeve and twirling the frame at the top of the stand. I readjusted the stand to my height and walked in front of it, singing to myself.

Daddyji came in, and I asked him why the violin teacher didn't come in a private tonga, like Master Kohli.

"He probably can't afford it," Daddyji said.

"Then why doesn't he ride a bicycle?"

"He told me that his most precious things are his hands—he's like you in that. He's afraid that he might be knocked off a bicycle and injure them."

"Does he walk everywhere?"

"I think he relies on lifts from passing cars. In fact, that's how I met him. I was driving home from the Pindi Club, and I saw an elderly man slowly walking along the road. He was dressed in a double-breasted suit and a tie and was carrying a violin case under his arm. I recognized him—he was a member of the Pindi Club's dance band. I offered him a lift. 'Much obliged,' he said, and got in. He told me that things were very bad in Goa, and that he had come to the Punjab in search of better prospects. But he couldn't get any private pupils in Rawalpindi. Englishmen here prefer bridge and clubs to music, and Indians consider it unmanly to learn music—our boys all want to excel in sports. And our girls all learn Indian music, because it helps them find a husband. I immediately told him that he could come and teach Pom, Nimi, and Umi violin after school three or four times a week. 'Dr. Mehta, private tuition to your daughters would be a welcome supplement to my income,' he said. 'But I am not being able to accept.' I couldn't imagine that he was haggling, like a shopkeeper, because it was clear from his face that he was a straight shooter. So I asked him why not. 'Dr. Mehta, I am not having how to play the violin Indian-fashion, without chin rest and music stand— sitting on the floor and holding it upside down.' I laughed right out. 'My daughters will stand up and play violins with chin rests in front of music stands, as you do at the Pindi Club,' I said. He nodded hesitantly, and I told him that when I was a student in England I used to visit the house of my teacher, Professor Sambon. He had three young daughters, and they played their violins for me whenever I visited them. Ever since then, I said, I had been in love with the instrument. When the girls grew up, they had got into financial difficulties, and had toured all of Europe and America, playing the violin and billing themselves 'The Three Smart Sisters.' I told him that lately I had begun dreaming that my three daughters might follow in the footsteps of Professor Sambon's daughters.''

❧

ONE EVENING, Daddyji came home and said that he had found a music master for me. "He's quite young, but he's said to be the best music master in Rawalpindi," Daddyji said. "In fact, he simply goes by the name of Masterji. But he can't read or write. The beauty of our music is that it has no notation, so people who neither read nor write can be great musicians."

"How did Masterji study, then?"

"He must have become a disciple of some guru. He must have advanced by living with his guru—massaging his feet, washing his clothes, cooking his food, submitting to all his whims and wishes. He must have learned from his guru all the secrets—of course, one at a time, over a long period. Years must have gone by before the poor boy learned anything."

"I would rather die than go and live with this Masterji," I said.

"You don't have to. He is reconciled to modern times. He will teach you the secrets—of course, one at a time—for three rupees a session."

"What are these secrets, exactly?"

"I don't precisely know myself, but they have to do with voice training, with ragas—which scale pattern is suited to which time of day, to which mood, to which season. No doubt each guru adds his own spices and condiments to the secrets. It's like the flavoring known only to those who cook the dish."

"I'll write down the secrets in Braille and publish them. That will be the end of all the gurus."

"So far, there is no system for writing the secrets down. Singers and players mostly improvise within the rules of the ragas."

"Then it's just like Hindu medicine. And you say the people who practice that are quacks."

"But music is different."

❦

MASTERJI WAS ENGAGED to come three times a week, from two-thirty to three-thirty—just before my sisters and brother came home from school. He often arrived late and left early.

Some time before he was due, Mamaji would start

shouting for me. "Vedi, hurry up! It's time for Masterji! It's three rupees a lesson!"

I would have to drop whatever I was doing and go into the drawing room, sit on the floor, and wait for him, while Gian Chand brought in the harmonium from under my bed, where it was kept.

Like a servant, Masterji would arrive on a bicycle and leave his slippers at the door. But once he was in the drawing room he would call to Gian Chand to bring him a glass of buttermilk and any little refreshments, as if he were a member of the family. Although we would sit down cross-legged on the carpet, side by side, near the harmonium, he would be in no hurry to get started. "Let the milk come, Vedi," he would say, and then he would ask me what I had had for lunch or what was being prepared for dinner.

"What, no buttermilk for Vedji!" he would ask Gian Chand when he returned.

Each time, I would have to explain to him all over again that I hated the smell of buttermilk, that in our family only girls drank it.

"Vedi, I've never heard of a singer who got along without buttermilk," he would say. "A bicycle needs air in the tires, a car needs petrol in the tank, a voice needs milk from mother cow. If you want to be a first-class singer, you will have to learn to drink buttermilk."

After Masterji had drunk down his buttermilk, he would burp, but still would not open the harmonium. To hurry Masterji along, I would ask him what time it was getting to be.

"I'm a poor man," he would say. "I have no watch."

"But the clock." On the mantelpiece was the only clock in the house—an old square alarm clock that Daddyji had bought when he was a student in England.

"Oh, I forgot. Why do you worry? That's only the clock time. Musicians live by God's time. Our minds stand still like the trees and grow like the trees. You must develop the spirit, and that can be done only with a guru."

For days, practically every lesson was taken up with Masterji playing the first tone of the scale on the harmonium and singing "sa." If I didn't immediately join him, he would intone, all on the same note, "Now with me. Sa."

"Sa," I would sing.

"Louder. Clear and strong. Saaa."

"Sa!"

"Too sharp," he would sing. "Listen to the harmonium—to me. Saaa."

"Saaa!"

"More throat force. Saaa."

"Saaa." I would try to imitate his tone.

"Aaah—just like when you're showing your throat to a doctor. Aaah."

"Aaah."

"Now—saa."

"Saa."

"Too loud." His voice would become gentle and soft. "Saaa."

"Saaa."

"That's too flat. Again. Saaa."

"Saaa."

"Saaa—together now, one 'sa,' with one voice.

Saaa—God is one, the universe is one—again one 'sa.' ''

Masterji's voice was rich and full. Mine was light and thin. The note of the harmonium was shrill and insistent. When the three "sa"s were sounded together, no matter what Masterji or I did they sounded like separate "sa"s. Still, I tried to merge my "sa" with his and the harmonium's "sa"s.

"Too much stomach. The stomach is for the wind, the throat is for song. The voice must come only from your throat. Saaa."

"Saaa."

"Without the harmonium, sa." He would snap the bellows shut, but as soon as I met his "sa" he would shift it a fraction up or down, as if without the pitch from the harmonium he weren't sure where to rest the "sa." Then we sounded like a bee and a mosquito buzzing together, now higher, now lower, now faster, now slower.

I knew all the tones of the scale—sa, re, ga, ma, pa, dha, ni, sa—but for days, no matter what I said, I couldn't get Masterji to move up even to "re."

" 'Sa' must be perfected first," he would say. "It's the heart of the scale, the soul of the voice."

When we did eventually move up to "re," for days we were doing "sa, re, re, sa; sa, sa, re, re, re, sa; re, re, re, re, re, sa; sa, re, sa."

He would frequently stop to discourse on how superior the old system of guru and disciple was to the new system of tuition. "I come to teach you because I am a hired man. Your daddy pays me, so I have to discharge my duty. But it is not how a guru teaches a disciple, not how a disciple serves his guru, how *I* served *my* guru—not at all."

At the end of each lesson, I would be left feeling breathless and bewildered. But I was careful never to cross Masterji, because he had a terrible temper and, as Sister Umi used to say, "your Masterji is the head-master of a one-man school."

His temper was likely to flare up at the most unexpected moments. We would be singing "sa," and he would suddenly let go of the note on the harmonium and violently pump the bellows without pressing down a note—the very thing he had told me would cause the bellows to split or the reeds to break.

"Anything the matter?" I would ask.

"Matter? Matter? You know what's the matter. Don't pretend with me."

"Masterji, I don't know."

"Now you're going to lie to me? Lie to your Masterji? Wait till I tell that to Mistress." Like the servants, he called Mamaji "Mistress."

I would try to hold back my laugh.

"So. Now you want to insult. Lie, insult—what next? You think these are modern times. Did you practice your 'sa' today? Tell me!" He would have me there, because I didn't know what there was to practice. He would push the harmonium over to me. "So you think you have become a master of 'sa' already? Then you play the harmonium. You be the masterji."

However much he ranted, I never felt afraid of him, because I was in my own house and I knew he couldn't do anything to me. Besides, he had the speech and manner of a servant. Still, I didn't like it when he was angry, because then he would sulk, and the whole tuition hour would be wasted—there was no singing even "sa" with him unless he was well disposed toward me. So I always tried to please him.

But I remember that, compared with my sisters' and brother's education, mine seemed dishevelled— exposed and smelly and repugnant. It felt the way I felt in the morning: ashamed of my unkempt hair, the sleep in my eyes, my rumpled-up night suit—separate and blind. I didn't feel part of the family until I had bathed, combed my hair, and got into freshly laundered shirt, knickers, and socks.

❧

THE VIOLIN TEACHER came on foot every second day to give my big sisters their lesson. He arrived punctually. He did not leave his shoes at the door, as the servants did. No matter how strongly he was pressed to take a cup of tea or some sweetmeats, he declined. He was formal in his manner: he called Mamaji "Mrs. Mehta," called my big sisters not by their nicknames but by their given names—Promila, Nirmila, Urmila— and called me "Mr. Ved." He was never familiar with the servants. He never cared whether our clock was fast or slow; he had his own wristwatch and left as punctually as he arrived.

He and my big sisters would stand in front of separate music stands, and he would teach them by playing the violin with them or singing "do, re, mi."

Sisters Nimi and Umi said they had no particular

aptitude for the violin, and dropped out after a few weeks, but Sister Pom continued, and practiced very hard. The violin teacher taught her Indian film tunes, like "Go to Sleep, Raj Kumari," but played in "English style," and what we took to be great English classics, like "Jealousy."

One day, Daddyji, as he was writing the violin teacher a check for the month's tuition, asked him how Sister Pom was doing.

"She is very good, Dr. Mehta. If she continues with the violin, as studious and hardworking as she is, she could going right around the world with her violin, like the three smart sisters you told me about."

"Why don't you go around the world giving concerts?" I asked him.

"I am not from a good family," he said. "I am a mixed-blood from Goa. I have no caste."

When Sister Pom took her lesson, I would sit quietly in a chair and listen, silently humming or repeating "do, re, mi." When she was taking a rest, I would get her bow into shape. I would get it taut, then rub resin on it until the layers of strands on the bow felt like one squeaky smooth surface. If there was a stray hair that was broken, I would snip it off with scissors.

The great classics of the violin teacher sounded much more tuneful and sweet than Masterji's "sa," and I learned by heart the entire repertoire he had taught Sister Pom—"Jealousy," the "Merry Widow Waltz," the "Blue Danube," "Give Me Five Minutes More," and "Greensleeves." Even when the notes came out as screeches, they seemed to me to have a gentle lilt to them.

I told the violin teacher that if he gave me tuition I could learn to play the tunes by ear.

"But you not being able to see the bow," he said. "You having to see the bow to learn to bow straight."

"Let me see how you bow," I said. I felt his right hand holding the bow, and made mental notes about his fingers around the frog, the curve of his wrist, the angle of his elbow, and the bending and straightening of his arm as he bowed. I tried to bow as he did on his violin, but no matter what I did my bowing was crooked.

"You must getting Dr. Mehta to buy you a child's violin with a small bow," he said.

"Daddyji says the violin is bad for my reading Braille."

"Dr. Mehta is thinking well," the violin teacher said, and after that I couldn't get him to let me play with his violin.

When everyone was at school, though, I would practice bowing: I would take out Sister Pom's bow, stand in front of the music stand, hold out my left arm and pretend that it was a violin, balance the bow in my right hand, stick side down, and bow across my left arm. During these sessions, I wore short-sleeved shirts, so I could tell exactly where the bow was on my left arm. In time, I learned to bow more or less straight. Then, one day, I got a stiff metal wire, bent it into a sort of arc, and attached it, pincer fashion, to the sides of the sound box of Sister Pom's violin, so that it stuck up just above the bridge. It helped to keep my bow straight, but the bow would occasionally rub against the wire, and the noise was so grating that I abandoned the device. I decided, however, that the violin teacher bowed straight not because he looked at the bow but because of the angle of his elbow.

"Look, I've learned to bow straight without seeing the bow," I told him when he came next, and showed him that I could bow on Sister Pom's violin, although I had to hold it by the sound box.

"Ah, Mr. Ved!" he exclaimed. "You're so right. I am never looking at my bow after I become violin teacher, but every pupil looking at the bow to perfect bowing. It's one thing to keeping bow straight for a scale and quite another thing to keeping bow straight for the whole melody. But, as you say, Dr. Mehta saying that violin is bad for your fingers. Harmonium and Indian singing best for you."

❧

ONE AFTERNOON, Masterji said to me, "*Shabash, shabash.*" *Shabash* means "Well done." "My training is bearing fruit. The apertures of your throat have opened up like the reeds of a harmonium. Now you can sing alone, without your Masterji's voice."

I didn't enjoy singing by myself. My voice without Masterji's sounded even lighter and thinner than it did when we were singing together. Besides, my voice got lost in the drawing room; it was a large room, and all its doors were left open to circulate the air. But Masterji refused to sing with me any longer.

Aside from accompanying me on the harmonium, which mostly involved just playing the scale, Masterji might as well have been absent from our lessons. He said little, and answered all my questions with the same well-worn phrases.

"Am I doing something wrong?" I once asked him. "How can I improve?"

"Practice makes perfect," he said. "The scale again."

I varied my singing and sometimes introduced a wrong note to make sure that he was really listening. But he said nothing.

"I think I sang a wrong note," I once said.

"People who sing wrong notes end up in cinema," he said, suddenly becoming expansive. "The well-to-do hire masterjis, buy their secrets, and then take a train to Bombay for greater riches in the cinema. They never ask after their masterjis then. They live in palaces and sing in the cinema while their masterjis live in quarters in the bazaars, waiting to scrape a few rupees together to afford a missus."

"There is to be a missus!" I exclaimed. Until then, Masterji had never spoken about where he lived or whether or not he was married, and, for some reason, I had never wondered about it.

"Not yet," he said sternly, and he went on, almost to himself, "The wife comes, produces babies with lusty cries, and there are more mouths to feed."

"Do you need more pupils?" I asked.

"Vedji, there is a famine of pupils everywhere," he said. "They are all going to the cinema. Cinema songs will be the death of music. They are notes put together without gurus or ragas, just so people will have some music to tap their feet and snap their fingers to."

"I will never sing in the cinema," I said.

"They all say that, and they all do," he said. "The scale again."

🌷

ONE DAY, WHEN MASTERJI had been with me only a few minutes and I was concentrating on singing the scale, I heard him get up quietly and tiptoe away.

"Masterji, you are leaving!" I cried.

"He has ears for eyes," he said almost to himself, and then to me, a little belligerently, "Go on singing. I am just stretching my legs."

"What are you doing at the mantelpiece?"

"Looking at the clock. Go on singing."

I heard a whirr and a click.

"What are you doing to the clock?"

"Nothing. It's three-thirty."

"But you just came!"

"That's what the clock says. You can ask Gian Chand." He bellowed, "Gian Chand! Vedji is calling you!"

There were scraping sounds on the veranda as Masterji got into his slippers, and the bounce of the tire on the gravel as he pushed the bicycle off its kickstand. Then he was gone.

"Did Little Commander Sahib want something?" Gian Chand asked, running in.

"What time is it?"

"I am a poor man. I don't have a watch."

"Stop talking like Masterji. The clock on the mantelpiece. What time is it?"

"Oh. Three-thirty."

That evening, when Daddyji came home I asked him whether the clock on the mantelpiece was right; only his watch seemed to keep the correct time.

"It's more than half an hour ahead," he said. "How did you know?"

I told him about Masterji and the whirr and the click.

"He's a very foolish man," Daddyji said. "He must have known that we would find out. But he's the best music master in Rawalpindi. There's no point in antagonizing him. Next time he comes for a lesson, just tell him not to play with the clock, and he will get the hint."

The next time Masterji came, I did just that.

"Who says the clock is a toy?" he said. "Anyway, I don't live by the time of the clock."

In the middle of the lesson, Masterji got up and went to the mantelpiece. There was a whirr and a click, then the scraping of his slippers, the bounce of the tire on the gravel, and he was gone.

Sometimes Masterji set the clock forward ten minutes and sometimes half an hour. No matter how clearly I hinted to him that we knew he was cheating, it made no difference.

"I have met many storytellers, but it sounds as though your Masterji were in a class by himself," Daddyji said. "Let me catch him red-handed one day, and then see the fun."

"So, Masterji," Daddyji said with a smiling voice, striding in one day. "Are those your fingers turning those hands forward?"

"Certainly, Doctorji."

Daddyji sat down on the sofa and tapped the seat next to him, for Masterji to come and sit beside him.

"The sofas and chairs, Doctorji, are for the Englishmen and the government. For us poor Brahmans, God's earth is the best." He returned to his usual place on the floor, and, as if he didn't want to waste the valuable time of the lesson, he pulled the harmonium toward him, pressed a note, and sang "saaa."

"Just a minute, Masterji," Daddyji interrupted. "It seems you've been cheating about the time when you're here. What is it that makes you so uninterested in Vedi? You told me that he has talent—'special talent,' I think you said. Is that really what you think, or were you just fibbing?"

"I was telling the truth about Vedi's special talent, and he has already conquered the world of 'sa,' " Masterji said. " 'Sa' means 'breath,' and breath is to song what breath is to life."

"But putting the clock forward and then saying to Vedi you didn't do it is lying."

"Doctorji, why did God make lies if he didn't expect men to tell them along with the truth?"

"But, Masterji, God made poison as well. Would you by that reasoning drink poison?"

"Ah, Doctorji, I do take poison when I am sick, and a doctor gives it to me. But, however that may be, poison is not an innate attribute, like a lie, without which men could not see the truth. Even you, Doctorji, tell lies to a patient on the verge of death. You tell him that he may get well, instead of the truth—that a black and dismal fate awaits him. You call that a white lie, but, white lies or black lies, they are all lies. So, Doctorji, I tell lies just as often as truth, to give truth more value."

They argued for some time. Finally, Daddyji said, "Masterji, I see that you were trained well in Hindu logic by your guru. But I hope that under this roof the climate may be more conducive to truth than to lies. At least, that is the way we are trying to bring up our children."

When Masterji had left, I asked Daddyji, "Why is he like that?"

"He can't bring himself to share. He's afraid. He fears that if he tells you what little he knows he'll be out of a job. He thinks you will take over his pupils."

I had to laugh. I was now nine. He was older than my big sisters, older than the clerks in Daddyji's office. The thought that I would take over his pupils, some of whom went to school with my big sisters, tickled me.

❦

To EVERYONE'S SURPRISE, Masterji started staying his full time and teaching me with newfound enthusiasm. He taught me to play on the harmonium and sing many ragas. He called out the notes of the *bhairon* raga and sang its prescribed ascending and descending runs, and then taught me many variations. "As you hear, the *bhairon* is a raga in a minor key, good for the sad autumn season," he explained. "It has a sad mood, and is sung in the early, quiet hours of the dawn. A raga is the season and the hour."

Masterji even got a pair of tablas and, when I sang the ragas, accompanied me, alternating the patter of the right drum with the thud of the left. As if he were accompanying a top-notch professional singer on the radio, he would frequently stop and tune the tablas, adjusting with a small hammer now this tabla peg, now that one, to match the tablas to the exact pitch of my voice. "Tablas aren't as good as they used to be," he would say, striking a peg. "The earth is undergoing a change of weather [tap]. Not so good for the tablas [tap]. Too high [tap]. Down you come [tap]. Up you go."

I would start singing. He would crack and flick the right tabla, dancing his fingers over it, and cuff and caress the left tabla, dragging his hand over it. Soon the two tablas were talking to each other, the ripples and bubbles of one being answered by the thumps and murmurs of the other. "Dha dhin dhin dha," he would say, counting out the rhythm over my singing and the tablas. "Indian music is rhythm," he would intone, over the tablas. "Rhythm is tabla. Dha dhin dhin dha. Rhythm is the heartbeat of Indian music. Dha dha." The tablas would pitter and patter, gurgle and coo. "Rhythm is second only to throat training. Dhin dhin dhin dha. Dha dha dha dhin. Dhin dhin dhin dha. One beat out of order and the mood of the raga is broken."

Abruptly, he would stand up. "Three-thirty," he would say. "Time is as inexorable as a raga. To my next tuition—to Usha Malhotra." From the veranda, getting into his slippers, he would add, "Just as well. Knowledge needs time to ripen."

He was gone.

"Well, Masterji, is Vedi making progress?" Daddyji once asked, looking in.

"Big strides," he said. "He will be my star disciple—that is, if he doesn't go in for singing in cinema."

I liked singing along with records of film songs. The tunes were very sad and sweet, and I could sing them as I played or went around the house, without the harmonium or Masterji's tablas. But I joined Masterji in decrying film songs, because it made him happy.

"Doctorji, I knew it!" he exclaimed. "Vedi will be a masterji in his own right."

Masterji! I suddenly hated ragas, tablas, the harmonium, Masterji, and his buttermilk. It irked me that his ragas were in Hindi—the language of Mamaji, of familiarity and the bazaar, of servants and sweepers. I thought of my sisters' and my brother's teachers: elegant; well-dressed; scented; speaking English, the language of deference and degree and of offices and clubs frequented by Daddyji, who was at home in any company at any time. But I recalled that there was no school for me to go to, no alternative to Masterji—that I had to go on singing ragas to his tablas.

"I tell you, Doctorji," Masterji was saying, "Vedi will be singing ragas on the radio, and his name will be on people's lips."

❧

MASTERJI ONCE SAID to Daddyji, "If God gives me life and strength and your son has the devotion and determination, I will teach him every secret I learned from my guru, with the exception of one. It can be taught only to a disciple who studies with a guru in the old way. There are no such disciples in this city anymore, so that secret will go with my ashes to the sacred waters."

Daddyji always wanted his children to be the best at everything. Sister Pom was going to be the best violinist; Sister Nimi was going to be the best hockey player; I was going to be the best singer. So Daddyji, as he told me later, didn't like to hear that Masterji was going to keep back something from me, and wondered if Masterji was making an indirect appeal for more tuition money.

"Surely there must be lots of singers who know that secret," Daddyji said.

"I am the only one," Masterji said, patting his chest. "The only one."

"And you are prepared to take it with you—to let it die?" Daddyji asked, laughing.

"What is the secret about?" I asked.

"I will show you what it is about on Diwali, if the Diwali mood sits well with me."

Diwali, our great festival, was weeks away, but we could not get Masterji to tell us anything about the secret.

❧

A FEW DAYS before Diwali, Masterji started saying, "I am in my Diwali mood. You can ask me for anything. But not about that secret. Not yet." He would ask for extra glasses of buttermilk and give Gian Chand orders for plates of different sweetmeats. If the sweet-meats were not in the house, Gian Chand had to go on a bicycle to the bazaar to get them, or remember to get them the next time he went to the bazaar. Every-one, from Sister Umi to Gian Chand, was eager to please Masterji, because everyone had become curious about the secret.

The day before Diwali, he announced, "Tomorrow is Diwali. I won't be coming for a few days."

"But that secret!" I cried.

"Oh, that. I will show it to you today."

I got up to call everyone. Because it was the eve of Diwali, schools and offices were closed, and everyone was at home.

"Only your family!" he called after me as I ran out of the drawing room. "No servants, no friends!"

We all gathered in the drawing room and sat around as if for a family portrait—Daddyji and Mamaji on the sofa, my big sisters and big brother beside them, by age, in chairs, and Usha and I on the floor with Mas-terji.

"Masterji, how are you going to show what the secret is without letting us know the secret?" Sister Umi asked.

"Shush, Umi," Sister Pom said. "You have no sense."

"We are all waiting, Masterji," Daddyji said.

"The secret!" we all cried, and then felt mortified, because if he once said no he would obstinately stick to it.

"Have a glass of buttermilk," Mamaji said encour-agingly.

"No, no," he protested, like a good guest, and then accepted the buttermilk. He pulled the harmonium toward him and ran his fingers lightly over the keys. He pumped so cautiously at first that the notes came out half formed. Then he started pumping hard, and the notes came out almost as bursts of air. His pumping steadied, and for half an hour or so he played one raga after another, conjuring up different seasons, as if he were considering the year from the perspective of Diwali. With each new raga, he wove and embroidered a more complicated scale pattern, filling the drawing room with a tapestry of sounds.

At one point, he unmistakably lifted his hands off the keyboard. That's it, I thought. He's going to stand up and say the mood doesn't sit well and leave. But he resumed playing.

By turns, Masterji prolonged the flats of one raga to underline its mournful mood; skipped along the naturals of another raga to bring out its gay mood; jangled the sharps of a third raga to give an edge to it. But ragas, I thought, were wordless, ineffable moods that passed like the weather—and who remembered yesterday's weather?—while books were full of substance and knowledge. People studied them and became doctors, engineers, and government servants—positions to which I could never aspire.

I was jolted. From somewhere in the room—it could have been from behind the curtains or from near the skylight or from under the sofa—came a noiseless half whistle, like a whistling teakettle starting to boil. The whistle, now insistent and beckoning, eerily floated around Masterji's head and settled in a spot on the

carpet just beyond the harmonium. The whistle suddenly broke into dozens of little whistles, and the dozens of little whistles into scores of little bells—
ghunghurus, the kind of bells that Indian dancers wear
around their ankles and use to weave and embroider
the rhythmic patterns of their dances. It was as though
a weightless dancer had wafted into the room, taken
form in front of the harmonium, and started dancing,
giving shape to Masterji's ragas. The bells jingled and
fluttered around the ankles of the dancer: *tinkle, tink,
chink; chink, tink, tinkle; chink, chink, chink.* By turns,
the jingling assumed a coy or a bold rhythm, and practically started singing to the accompaniment of the
ragas on the harmonium—a slow introduction, a statement, a recapitulation in double time.

Several times, I reached up and touched the knee
of first one big sister, then another, and asked, "What's
happening? Who is it?" Each time, I was shushed. I
began to think that the dancer's presence in our house
depended on some kind of spell, and that if I persisted
the music and the *ghunghurus* would stop. *If the mood
sits well with me . . .* But the quieter I felt I had to be,
the more impatient I grew.

The *ghunghurus* speeded up, and I thought the raga
and the dance were reaching a climax. But then the
raga, without coming to a definite end, elided into the
introduction of a new raga, and the tempo of the *ghunghurus* changed to almost a crawl.

The *ghunghurus* speeded up again. I listened closely,
my heart racing. An odd thing had happened: the dancer
had flown over the harmonium and was dancing in the
air right in front of Masterji's face. There could be no

mistake: the sound of the *ghunghurus* was coming from that exact spot. I could bear it no longer.

"What is going on?" I cried. "Who is it?"

The *ghunghurus* and the music continued for a few seconds more, to complete a filigree of a run, and then the music and the *ghunghurus* came to an abrupt halt.

Everyone exclaimed.

"*Wahwah!*"

"*Bohut achha!*"

"Marvellous!"

"Who is it? Where is it?" I shouted.

"It's Masterji," Daddyji said. "He makes the *ghunghurus* with his breathing—don't you, Masterji?"

Amid the hubbub—Mamaji calling for buttermilk and Diwali sweetmeats for Masterji, and the others talking simultaneously and congratulating him—Daddyji explained to me that Masterji had somehow imitated the sound of *ghunghurus* in his mouth, or throat, or chest, or somewhere, and had managed to conjure up a real dancer by casting the sound into different parts of the drawing room, a little like a street ventriloquist.

"Masterji, is it from the throat, or chest, or mouth, or what?" I asked.

But Masterji wouldn't reply. He sat unresponsive, noisily munching sweetmeats and drinking down buttermilk.

Sister Nimi swore aloud that it was from the mouth, while Sisters Umi and Pom talked about the larynx and the vocal cords, and how they were like an instrument that one could learn to play on with one's breath. But Masterji refused to be drawn into the discussion, even after he heartily burped once and Sister Nimi took the burp to be an assent to her view, while Sisters Pom and Umi took it to be an assent to theirs.

I remember that Masterji breathed hard for a long time. Then he hastily stood up, got into his slippers on the veranda, and was off on his bicycle. There was a momentary pause, as if we were all listening for him to call out his goodbyes. But he didn't.

"Why does he eat and drink so much, in that greedy way?" Sister Umi asked. "And why is he so rude?"

"He's a poor man," Daddyji said. "But he has grand ideas about his art—and rightly so, I must say. I've never heard anything like those *ghunghurus.*"

Mamaji told all of us to get busy for Diwali, as it would soon be dark, and we ran around placing candles and *diyas* (earthenware lamps) outside the house, feeling that Masterji had got our first Diwali in Rawalpindi off to a magical start.

❦

MASTERJI DID NOT give another performance of the *ghunghurus* until the eve of the next Diwali. He remained determined never to teach the art of the *ghunghurus* to me or anyone else.

"Money is no object," Daddyji once told him. "My son would give anything to learn the *ghunghurus.*"

"No rupees on earth could shake that secret out of me, Doctorji," he said. And nothing we said or did seemed to unbend him.

I, for my part, remained determined that I would not rest until I had learned the art of the *ghunghurus,* and for months I went around making breathing sounds in my throat and whistling sounds in my throat and whistling sounds with my mouth, hoping that I might stumble onto the secret—the way I had once solved the puzzle of a dozen or so looped odd-shaped Persian rings that, when they were properly meshed, became one ring. Daddyji asked Master Kohli, and inquired of all our relatives and all his friends, and they of all their relatives and friends, but no one had heard of anyone else who knew the secret of the *ghunghurus*.

"I prefer the real *ghunghurus* of film stars to the fake *ghunghurus* of your low-class Masterji," Brother Om said.

"What's so important about being able to make *ghunghurus* with your throat, or wherever, when you can go out and buy anklets with real *ghunghurus* for two or three rupees and play with them all you want to?" Sister Umi asked me. "You spend all day dancing and jumping around anyway. And you could dance and jump around with anklets on."

Sister Umi had a point. But whenever I was told I couldn't do something, I wanted more than ever to do it. Anyway, not being able to do it—together with not liking buttermilk, not liking to sit on the floor cross-legged, not liking many things that I couldn't name—dampened my interest in learning ragas, and there were days when I almost wished that Masterji would shorten the lesson by the whirr and the click. But the less eager I was, the more diligent Masterji became, perhaps because, in his way, he, too, was perverse, but also because once he had made up his mind he never wavered in thinking of me as his star disciple—minus, of course, the all-important lustre of the *ghunghurus*.

VIII

TO SCHOOL ON WHEELS

O NE DAY, DADDYJI RETURNED HOME WITH A ladies' bicycle in the back of his car. "It's for you, Promila," he said, lifting it out.

"If people in Lahore hear that our daughter is riding a bicycle, we'll really have trouble getting her married," Mamaji said, coming out of the house.

"We have to put behind us the views of the Lahore *gullis*," Daddyji said. "We are now living in the Civil Lines of Rawalpindi."

"I didn't know that girls could ride bicycles," I said.

"Why not?" Sister Umi said. "Ladies ride bicycles in England, and I believe I was the first Indian girl ever to get on a bicycle. I rode a ladies' bicycle when

Daddyji was posted in Ambala—you were at school in Bombay."

"Umi's a great showoff," Sister Nimi said. "The bicycle she rode was just a little children's bike—not a Raleigh, like this one."

"I think you should get us all bicycles, Daddyji, and let us go to the Presentation Convent on them," Sister Umi said. "Satta is from a very good family. She never wears cosmetics. She always covers her head in front of her elders. But she comes to the Presentation Convent on a bicycle."

"Gandhiji says that women are every bit as good as men," Sister Nimi said. "I'm sure he'd have no objection to our going to the Presentation Convent on our bicycles."

"I don't know what Mahatma Gandhi would have to say about it," Daddyji said. "But I think you three sisters would look very smart going to the Presentation Convent on your bicycles. First, however, you all have to learn to ride."

"One bicycle is enough," Mamaji said. "Let Pom try it out first and see whether she even likes it, before all of you go and spend money for bicycles. You'll never learn to ride them, and they'll just stand around the compound getting rusty."

Daddyji agreed that Sister Pom should try out the bicycle first.

I touched Sister Pom's new bicycle all over. "Why doesn't it have a bar between the seat and the handlebars, like Gian Chand's bicycle?" I asked.

"That's what makes it a ladies' bicycle," Sister Umi said. "Don't be naughty." There was something coy in her tone—as when my big sisters talked about lady matters—which made me not ask any more questions about the bar.

Daddyji started teaching Sister Pom to ride the bicycle, first around the house, in the compound, and then, when she was able to sit on the seat without falling off, out in the Civil Lines. I would catch hold of Usha's hand and run after them into the lane. I remember that Daddyji used to walk on Sister Pom's right, between her and the traffic, constantly calling out to her, "Left! . . . Left! . . . Stay to your left!" She had a tendency to veer toward him.

"Help me!" she would call out to him. "I'm going to fall down! The bicycle won't stop!"

"Left! You're on your own now," he would call to her. "You're doing very well. Be independent. Left, left!"

Every day, Daddyji would take Sister Pom to nearby Topi (Hat) Park. Usha and I would tag along. Daddyji would post himself at a spot and clap, and Sister Pom would race to him, her bicycle whirring as she pedalled or clicking as she coasted. I would run alongside her bicycle, pulling Usha with me (she couldn't run as fast as I could), and listening to the music of the bicycle as if to film songs on the gramophone.

Within a few days, Sister Pom had learned to ride the bicycle by herself on the road, and within a few days of that Daddyji had bought Sisters Nimi and Umi and Brother Om a Raleigh, a Phillips, and a B.S.A., respectively.

"I want a bicycle, too!" I cried.

"That's not suitable for you," Daddyji said. "They're

getting bicycles only so that they can get to school on them. Usha will ride on Om's carrier when he learns to ride his bicycle. We'll buy you something else."

Mamaji complained about the expense of buying the bicycles.

"One month's winnings from the cards," Daddyji said grandly.

In due course, my big sisters and big brother were riding off to school together on their bicycles, making the gravel in the driveway fly up, and leaving me behind feeling like a fallen pebble. I thought, Usha will soon grow up and have a bicycle of her own to go to school on, but I will never have a bicycle, I will never go to school. I will be left behind with Mamaji and the servants, with nothing to do, and be counted, as Mamaji says about herself, "neither among the literate nor among the illiterate—just ignorant."

One morning, in the servants' quarters, I found a discarded bicycle. Its tires were flat; its back mudguard was broken, and scraped against the tire; its hand brakes hung loose; its handgrips were missing, so that the ends of the handlebars were cold and hollow to the touch. It was in complete disrepair. I got hold of some wrenches, a pair of pliers, and a bicycle pump, and, over the next many days, took it apart almost to the last nut. I tried to put it together again. At first, nothing fitted. Even when I eventually managed to put most of it together, it required several new parts. I got Gian Chand to buy me new mudguards and new handgrips. I greased the chain, straightened the brakes, and filled the tires with air. But the tube in the front tire leaked. I had Gian Chand take the bicycle and me to a bicycle-repair shop. I followed the hand of the repairman as he slipped a spanner under the tire, removed the tube, filled it with air, then rotated it in a basin of water to pinpoint the leak by the bubbles, and fixed a postage stamp of a patch over the puncture. Except for the puncture, which required the repairman's special patching machine, there was hardly anything about the bicycle that I didn't, in time, learn to fix myself.

In Lahore, both at 16 Mozang Road and in Mehta Gulli, there had always been aunts or cousins with me or watching me, but in Rawalpindi I was left alone to play in the compound as I liked. The others were either at school or busy with their work or their friends. I used to stand the bicycle up on its kickstand and spend hours turning the pedals with my hands and listening to the sound of the rear wheel whirring as the chain engaged it or clicking as it coasted. I climbed up onto the seat and tried to pedal. But the springs of the seat were broken, and I discovered that my feet scarcely reached the pedals. I fell over and scraped my hands and knees.

Mamaji complained to Daddyji that I would hurt myself badly with the bicycle, but he said, "Let him play. It gives him something to do, and it's just around the house, in the compound."

I got an idea: I undid the clamp under the seat of the old bicycle; worked the seat loose from the frame; dismantled the assembly, separating the pole from the seat; tightened the springs; fitted the leather cap tightly over the springs and had its rivets soldered onto them; put the seat assembly together again; worked the seat back into the frame; fixed the seat as low as it would go; and tightened the clamp. Finally, I was able to sit comfortably astride the stationary bicycle and pedal. Before long, I was pushing the bicycle off its kickstand and walking it around the back of the house—from the left side, as I'd noticed that everyone else did it. I would put one foot on the pedal nearer me and propel the bicycle forward by hopping with the other foot. I remember that once I took the hopping foot off the ground and was carried along by the momentum. The bicycle veered from side to side and almost tipped over on me. But I held fast. I pedalled with one foot, propelled the bicycle forward with the other foot, raised that foot off the ground, touched down, ran, and raised the foot off the ground. I somehow kept the bicycle going.

In time, I discovered that when the bicycle was moving and I put my leg on the other side I could pedal from both sides, standing up. If I kept the handlebars very straight, leaned forward, and pedalled hard, the bicycle would steady itself and stay on course. If I suddenly slowed down, the bicycle would tilt, but I would stop my fall by dragging a foot on the ground. Then I would balance myself again, pedal hard, and gain speed. I discovered that if I was standing on the pedals and the bicycle was going fast I could slide onto the seat and pedal sitting down. I realized then that I knew how to actually bicycle—bicycle like anyone else. The realization made me tingle from head to toe.

The house was sheltered by the compound wall and by hedges, and all around the house was an empty stretch covered with gravel. I would climb onto the seat of my bicycle and ride around the house, pretending that I was on the road, going to school with my big sisters and big brother. I would go around and around, stopping and starting, falling down and getting up, entranced by the sound of the rubber tires on the gravel and the rattle and click-click of the bicycle chain, taking the bends and turns faster and faster. I would locate myself by the way the sound of the tires on the gravel bounced off walls and objects. I had developed my facial vision to a high degree, so that I was able to distinguish a lawn chair from a lawn table by the way the screech of the bicycle tires sounded on the gravel. But an object had to be fairly substantial—and there had to be no distracting sounds, like the washerman's donkey braying, or Gian Chand's rattling of pots and pans—for me to sense and avoid it, especially since on a bicycle I approached objects at great speed. I had to learn to react quickly. Sometimes Daddyji's car would suddenly loom ahead, parked to one side of the veranda rather than in front of it—its usual spot. I had to decide quickly where I was in relation to it and how far I had to veer to get around it. If I hesitated for a moment, I banged into it, possibly denting the bicycle and the car and skinning my knees. Moreover, even if I sensed an object, that was no guarantee that I wouldn't bang into it—I might be going fast or not paying attention, or I might simply be unable to stop quickly enough. Every day, I would ram the bicycle into the walls or up the veranda steps and into the columns. Every day, I would bang into flowerpots, stray watering cans, lawn chairs, tables—whatever happened to be in place or out of place. Every day, I would bang up my bicycle.

Ved, Rawalpindi, 1944.

Every day, I would scrape and bruise my knees and shins, hands and elbows. But, every time, I would pick myself up, ignore my bruises and scratches, fix my bicycle as best I could, and be off again.

There was no hiding my injuries, and everyone—especially Mamaji—regularly scolded me. I recall that several times she forbade me ever to go near the bicycle. But the moment people's backs were turned I was on my bicycle again. I remember repeating to myself, "I will. . . . I won't be stopped. . . . I'll show them. . . . I *will* go to school." When I became exhausted, I would drop the bicycle on the ground wherever I happened to be, and go and lie down on the first cot I came to. It would be a while before my breathing became normal and my heart stopped racing. Then I would get up with renewed energy to do more rounds.

Eventually, my facial vision became so acute and my reaction so quick that I could circle the house dozens of times without hitting anything. I would take slightly different routes, intentionally circle a flowerpot or a watering can, pass a buffalo or the gardener with hardly any room to spare. I grew in self-confidence, and before long I was riding any available bicycle. I would get Usha up onto the bar and pedal fast, sometimes taking my hands off the handlebars. She would scream with fear and delight. "No! . . . Please! . . . Enough! . . . Down!"

❧

"CAN I GO to your school, and just sit in on your classes?" I asked Sister Pom once.

My big sisters laughed.

"We go to a girls' school," Sister Umi said, "and all our teachers are convent sisters. Don't you have enough sisters of your own at home?"

"Can I, then, go to your school and sit in on your classes?" I asked Brother Om.

"You're blind," he said. "And, besides, you can't even speak English properly. How will you understand what the fathers say? We are taught in English."

I had no answer, but the next morning when my big sisters and my big brother set off on their bicycles for their schools I set off after them on my bicycle. Brother Om raced away with Usha, but I could hear my big sisters ahead, riding abreast slowly. I followed them as best I could by the sound of their voices and their laughter, keeping a safe distance between them and me, so as not to be discovered and taken home. The hour was early and the road was empty, with only an occasional car, so riding on the road proved to be no more difficult than riding around the house. The air felt fresh and cool and lively, and the bicycle under me was firm and familiar, responding perfectly to the pressure of the pedals or the brakes. It rolled along almost by itself, making me feel light-headed and carefree. Once or twice, I had difficulty hearing my big sisters. They would turn a corner fast and be out of earshot, and I would fall behind. Then I would become worried, and pedal fast, almost recklessly, for I didn't know how I would find my way to school—or back home—without their voices to guide me. The road hissed under my wheels. Once, there was a bump, and I was almost thrown; but I regained my balance.

For a moment, I had no idea where I was. Then I heard the stream of my sisters' chatter, and fell slightly behind, making it a point to ride directly behind Sister Nimi, who rode in the middle.

"Three smart sisters and their little brother," I kept repeating to myself, pushing down the phrase "blind brother," which kept rising up in my mind like the water in Mamaji's teakettle at the boiling point.

I heard the big sisters slow down and stop. I slowed down and stopped, almost by reflex, taking care to make as little noise as I could.

I heard the ringing of a hand bell and retreating voices and laughter, and then all was quiet. Suddenly, I wasn't sure why I had come, what I was doing there, what I should do next. I shouted for my big sisters, and then felt silly, because I had just heard them go away.

I was standing next to a wall that I could sense was high. I put my bicycle on the ground and sat down beside it on a patch of grass, leaning my back against the wall.

I thought of Dadar School, in Bombay. It had been surrounded by noise and chaos and falling soot, but this school could be a building in Topi Park. My school, too, had had a high outside wall, and when we were behind the wall we had hardly ever thought about what was outside it.

I thought of studying at some sighted school or other, but then the whole idea seemed as impossible as Brother Om had said. The school would have no Braille books, no special arithmetic slate, no teacher who knew Braille, no special draughtboard or chessboard for the blind. Above all, I didn't know enough English—the medium of teaching in all the higher standards. How would I manage? My school friend Deoji had lived at our school and gone to a sighted school, but I had no idea how he had managed, because he had never talked about it. Now I wished that I had badgered him to tell me or that he were in Rawalpindi for me to ask him.

I stood up, picked up my bicycle from the ground, then remembered that I couldn't find my way home, and sat down on the patch of grass again to wait for my big sisters to finish their classes and come out of the school.

The sun was hot, and I put my head down in my arms and dozed. I woke to the ringing of the hand bell and then the distant noise and laughter of girls playing games on the other side of the wall. I was probably the only boy in the vicinity, and I felt odd. I wanted to be back in Bombay, competing in races at our special track for the blind, or playing with our special ball, which clinked like a rattle as it rolled. I dozed again, and was awakened by another ringing of the hand bell. I could no longer feel the sun on my face. It must be time for them to come out, I thought, and I picked my bicycle up off the ground and stood up.

All at once, I was surrounded by girls. "What are you doing here?" I heard my big sisters and their friends cry. "And with your bicycle!"

They overwhelmed me with questions.

"How did you get here?"

"You've been here all day?"

"What have you been doing all these hours?"

"Why didn't you tell us?"

We started on the journey home. This time, Sister Nimi rode alongside me and kept her hand on mine—on the handlebars.

When we reached home, Mamaji gave me a good scolding. "I got hoarse calling you all day. Since you learned to ride a bicycle, you don't care for anybody."

Every Sunday, Daddyji and Mamaji would drive over to Topi Park, and we brothers and sisters would all follow on our bicycles. Usha now had a bicycle, too, and had learned to ride it. At Topi Park, we would have bicycle races, sometimes with our hands off the handlebars, while Daddyji played golf on a green nearby and Mamaji walked around with her knitting bag on her arm and knitted.

Daddyji had bicycled a lot as a boy, but Mamaji had never learned even how to get on a bicycle. "It was too late, in Rawalpindi, for me to get on a bicycle," she says. "I often wished I had learned bicycling as a girl. Later on, I never had the time. It seemed I was always pregnant or nursing a baby." Still, the whole world seemed to me to be on wheels.

IX

THE LEDGE

LL OF US HAD WANTED TO GO TO THE VALE
of Kashmir ever since Sister Umi turned up an
old letter from Daddyji. He had written it on
July 29, 1925, a few months before his marriage. At the time, he was posted in Montgomery and was on holiday in the Vale with a
bachelor friend named Jagmair. The letter was to
Vidyadhar, a grass widower in Montgomery (his wife
and children used to go to Murree) with whom Daddyji shared board and lodging for a time. In the letter,
Daddyji told Vidyadhar that the Kashmir scenery had
reminded him so much of England and Europe that he
was thinking of chucking his job and his responsibility
for educating his brothers and fleeing abroad for the
gypsy life of a bachelor. Sister Umi had read out the
letter—which we immediately dubbed the "gypsy letter"—at the dinner table: "My dear brother: At Srinagar, we lived in a houseboat. It had two bedrooms,

two bathrooms, a sitting room, a dining room, and a
balcony. We had moonlit nights, which doubled the
grandeur of scenic views from the houseboat. Like all
houseboats in Kashmir, it was let with a *doonga,* a small
boat that served as a kitchen and quarters for hired
boatmen, and a *shikara,* a small pleasure boat. Our
houseboat was as clean, neat, and pleasant for us sahibs
to live in as the *doonga* was filthy, cluttered, and nasty
for the boatmen. We kept the *doonga* at a respectable
distance from us. We visited Pahlgam, sixty miles from
Srinagar, a really beautiful spot. Jagmair was in ecstasy
over the place. I sang to him and he sang back. By
Jove, he can sing! Today, we have come up to Gulmarg. It is a beautiful place, too, and more or less flat
at the top. About three hundred Europeans are up here.
I got an introduction to the club. I had a game of
tennis and he his pegs of whiskey! We had dinner at
the club. The dining hall is very nice and reminded
me of England. As a matter of fact, I felt a pang, a
pain—for England—what a life! As the Urdu couplet
says, *'Khabar jo hoti yeh, ibtida se keh yoon javani tamam
hogee, to row ke kehtai yeh ham khuda se shabab ham le kai
kya Karengai?'* ["If I had known from the beginning
that my youth would end like this, I would have wept
before the Almighty and said, 'What will I do with
the youth you give me?' "] Jagmair is awfully keen on
going to England, and I find in him a very sincere
friend. I would not be surprised at myself if I were to
give up my settled life and become a gypsy abroad. My
dear boy, it is worth it. We are scheming, and he has
promised to advance me £1,000 to start a practice there,
and I am sure he would keep his word. Of course, I

have not resigned from the government service yet, and there is still time to consider. But, unfortunately, I am already dreaming of England, and the scenery here at every moment reminds one of Switzerland—of Europe. We are coming back on the third and hope to see the jolly crowd at Montgomery. With love, affectionately yours, Amolak Ram."

One of the main lures of a posting in Rawalpindi was that it was "the gateway to Kashmir." It was on the only motorable road from India to Kashmir, and every high government official there arranged a Kashmir holiday. The first summer we were in Rawalpindi, soon after we came back from Murree, Daddyji had to go on a pre-monsoon inspection of some villages lying between Rawalpindi and Kohala—some forty miles northeast, at the beginning of the long climb to Srinagar. He decided to take us all with him to Kohala and then take us on to Kashmir for a ten-day holiday.

Once again, as when we had set off for our stay in Murree, we were all in the car, travelling with our bedrolls on the roof and our suitcases in the trunk. On the floor of the back seat, there was Ram Saran—as before, we had room for only one servant. At several points, Daddyji stopped to do his tour of inspection. It was late afternoon when we reached the dak bungalow in Kohala, where we were to spend the night.

We all jumped out—it was very hot, and we were tired and out of sorts from having been squashed in the car. We were on a slope, and I could sense that on one side was a looming hill—I felt I could almost reach out and touch it—and on the other side was a drop, with rushing waters.

I asked Daddyji what those waters were.

"Fifty feet or so below us is the Jhelum River, which at this point forms a sort of a natural boundary between the province of Punjab and the princely state of Kashmir," Daddyji told me. "Just ahead of us is a bridge, and the moment we cross it we will be in Kashmir."

"But I hear two rivers flowing, not just one," I said.

"That's right," Daddyji said. "There are two streams flowing below. I thought they were one, they are so close together—just a little ledge separates them. But they're both coming out from under the bridge."

"One is so muddy, the other so clear," Sister Nimi said.

Daddyji called the dak bungalow's watchman over and asked him why the Jhelum River had two such different-looking streams.

"Only one of them, Sahib, is the Jhelum River. The other, Sahib, is just a local river," the watchman said vaguely.

"Where does the local river flow from?" Daddyji asked.

"They say, Sahib, from the 'catchment basin.' "

We all laughed, because the watchman said "catchment basin" in English, as if he didn't understand what it was but assumed that we would.

"Where do they say the catchment basin is?" Daddyji asked the watchman.

"They say it is somewhere up there, in the mountains," the watchman said, and he added, as if to make up for his vagueness, "The local water is slow and warm, is good for bathing, Sahib, but the Kashmir water is fast and ice cold."

"Why would that be?" I asked.

"The Jhelum rises high up in the mountains of Kashmir and is fed by the Himalayan snows," Daddyji said. "No doubt it has a very swift current. The local river is probably just a little stream that comes down from one of these hills and has very little current."

"Oof, Vedi, the rivers really look very different!" Sister Nimi exclaimed.

I said I wanted to see for myself how different they were, and Daddyji immediately started walking down with me into what seemed like a gorge.

Daddyji was always easy to walk with. He walked at an even pace, looking straight ahead, his arms hanging at his sides. I never had any trouble following his movements. Usually, I walked half a step behind him, barely touching his little finger or his arm. If he stepped down or stepped up, or stopped to greet someone, I knew almost as a reflex what to do. How different walking with Mamaji was! She tended to amble, wave her arms, fidget with her bag, pat her hair, tug at the loose end of her sari, which covered her shoulder and her head, or hitch up the end of her sari at her feet. She would often walk clutching my hand, or if, for instance, she was knitting as she walked she would keep my hand firmly tucked under her arm. In either case, it was difficult for me to follow her movements. Sometimes she would abruptly stop to admire something in a shopwindow or to pick up something from the ground. If, say, I asked her what she was admiring, either she would not hear my question or she would reply, "Those are not things of interest to you." No matter how hard I tried, I had difficulty getting her attention or conveying to her that if they were things of interest to her they were probably things of interest to me, too.

As I now walked with Daddyji down the gorge, I thought that in a sense we were already in Kashmir. The gorge had uneven stone steps, broken and eroded, and unexpected steep gradients. If I had been walking with Mamaji, her hand would have tensed up at every step, and that would have made me tense up, too, and stumble over the steps. But Daddyji walked in a relaxed, self-confident way, his little finger steady and straight. Because I thought I wouldn't stumble, I didn't stumble, and his movements and also the erosion and indentation of the steps told me when to step down.

The whole family trooped behind us to see the streams. Yet if we had been driving along the road, and Sister Umi had mentioned the streams we were passing, and I had wanted to know what the streams were like, Sister Umi would have tried to change the subject. If I had persisted, she would have said, "What streams? Who said 'streams'?" (Mamaji was not the only one who ducked the chore of explaining things to me.) I would have appealed to Daddyji, and, no matter how late it was getting or how much of a hurry he was in, he would have immediately stopped the car and walked over to the streams with me. The whole family would have trooped behind us and would have been almost as much interested in the streams—or whatever it was—as I was. But that was always after Daddyji had taken the initiative.

Now Mamaji was impatiently saying something about getting up to the dak bungalow. It was growing dark. Maybe I had to go to the streams and Daddyji had to go with me to show me, she said, but why should the whole family follow, like sheep? She couldn't go up to the dak bungalow and start doing everything herself. She needed my big sisters to come and give her a hand. The bedrolls and the provisions had to be unloaded, the cook at the dak bungalow had to be told what to prepare, the bedrolls had to be unrolled, cots had to be found and set up for all of us. Woollen clothes had to be taken out, because early the next morning we were beginning the climb to Kashmir, and it was said that it got very cold on the road very quickly.

The gorge was extremely dry. The earth was pebbly and flaky, and crunched under our feet. Our footfalls sounded especially loud in the still evening air.

"Why is this gorge so steep?" I asked Daddyji.

"This is a dried-up riverbank," Daddyji said. "As soon as the monsoon comes, it will all be under water. After all, the Jhelum is one of the Punjab's most powerful rivers, and sometimes it must even come out from under the bridge with such great force that it overflows its banks."

We reached the waterside, and I took a long step, following Daddyji. I squatted down on the narrow ledge between the streams and put a hand in each stream. The right stream felt glacial, and I could scarcely keep my hand in it. The left stream was thick and soupy, and felt almost tepid. I remember thinking that, in their way, the two streams were as different as Daddyji and Mamaji.

"How unlike the two streams are, and they're hardly a foot apart!" I called over to the others.

"I want to see!" Usha cried. Daddyji reached across, lifted her up, and put her on the ledge in front of me. She sat exactly as I did, with a hand in each stream.

Soon everyone but Mamaji had joined us on the ledge.

"Look how dark it's suddenly got!" Mamaji remarked over the gurgling waters, walking down to the edge.

"Look at those black monsoon clouds gathering over there across the bridge!" Daddy exclaimed. "I've never seen clouds appear so fast!"

"They are hovering close," Mamaji said. "Let's go back up before we all get drenched."

Usha and I were having fun paddling our left hands in the tepid stream and dipping our right hands in the icy one to see how long we could bear to keep them in. We didn't want to go back, but we obeyed.

We had got hardly halfway up the bank when I heard a terrific roar behind us, like dozens of trains thundering after us.

"Oh, my God!"

"The water!"

"A wall of water!"

"Run, run!"

The voices were overwhelmed by the rushing roar. I could barely make out the words. The roar seemed to be coming straight at us, as if it were determined to run us down. We raced up the hill, stumbling, and dragging each other over the broken steps.

There was a sudden downpour. It was like no monsoon rain I had ever heard. It was heavier and louder and splashier. The noise of water on water—the roars merging—sounded like the end of the world.

We didn't stop until we had run up the steps of the dak bungalow and were on the veranda.

"Look—all the steps in the gorge have disappeared under water," Mamaji said, breathing hard. She clutched my arm. "The water is almost up to the dak bungalow."

"We'll all be drowned—dak bungalow and all!" I cried. The water sounded as if it were rising and coming closer.

"The water won't come up here," Daddyji said. "We are above the bank, and the channel of the Jhelum in the plains is huge. It can take all the water there is."

"A dam must have broken," Sister Umi said.

"No, Memsahib," the watchman said. "It's just the steep mountains of Kashmir."

"I've never seen anything like it," Daddyji said, almost to himself. "I have never seen water rise up with such force so quickly. There must have been a cloudburst, or it must have rained heavily up ahead, in the mountains."

"If we had been a minute longer by the streams, we would all have drowned," Sister Umi said. She added, with a nervous laugh, "It would almost have been as if you, Daddyji, had become a bachelor gypsy in England, and none of us had ever been born."

"Your mother has saved our lives," Daddyji said.

Ram Saran later told me that all the dak-bungalow servants had been standing on the veranda watching us below with fascination. They had never heard of an important officer having a blind child and were struck by how much interest Daddyji was taking in me. When I was on the ledge, they had looked up and seen the wall of water heading toward us. From experience, they knew that within moments the riverbeds would be flooded. But they knew of no way to warn us. We were far out of the reach of their voices, and the fastest legs among them couldn't get to us in time. They closed their eyes and prayed. When they opened their eyes, they saw us slowly climbing up, still unconscious of the wall of water, which even at that moment was coming out from under the bridge. They gave us up for dead. Then they saw us break into a run. They held their breath as they lost sight of us in the blinding rain. "Little Sahib, none of them took a breath till they saw you coming up the dak-bungalow steps," Ram Saran told me. "Your escape is a great miracle."

I remember that when the bedrolls were finally unstrapped from the car their coverings and the bedding inside were drenched, and we spent the night on damp pallets and pillows under damp sheets and blankets. We woke up early in the morning, shivering. The rain had stopped, but the water was high. We packed quickly, crossed the bridge to the Vale, and began the steady climb to Srinagar. At many points, the road ran along the Jhelum River.

Of our holiday in Kashmir itself, I remember little. I recall that we visited Srinagar, Tangmarg, and

Gulmarg, and went to a nameless place to see the per-
petual snow line; that to get to most places we had to
ride on ponies, because that was the only method of
transport; that everywhere the air felt fresh and thin,
and, as a consequence, we felt giddy. Wherever we
went and whatever we did, sooner or later one or another
of us would mention, with wonder bordering on awe,
how we had barely escaped drowning in Kohala. In
fact, the incident subsequently became famous from
Kohala to Rawalpindi as "the time the Mehta family
drowned but for the grace of Ram."

X

TURN OF THE
JUTI

A FTER WE CAME BACK FROM KASHMIR, MAMAJI took to her bed. Occasionally, she would get up and walk around the house, but then she would say, "My head is going round and round," and would go back to bed.

Mamaji had more than her usual trouble breathing: her chest would sometimes rattle and squeak frighteningly. She would be racked by fits of coughing, spitting repeatedly into a basin that was kept by her bed. It would be some time before she was able to catch her breath, and then only after she had smoked a "special cigarette." She had had bad asthma as long as I could remember, and I couldn't understand why she had suddenly got so sick with it.

Doctors came daily and called for the servants to

bring some spirits for "sterilizing the needle," and if I happened to be in the room they sent me out. After they left, the room smelled of burned spirits for a long time.

In those days, Mamaji had on her bed a velvety blanket. It was smooth and had a very firm nap. She would lie under the blanket and groan and wheeze, and say, "I am dying. All these doctors are really going to see me out."

I would lie on top of the blanket and hug her. "Don't go."

"Pom will be a better mummy to you," she would say. "She'll take care of you. She'll take charge of the whole house."

"What's the matter with Mamaji?" I often asked my big sisters.

Every time, there would be an awkward pause, and then they would say, "Go and play."

I would then worry more than ever that Mamaji was on her way out—that is, until I talked to Daddyji. "She'll be all right," he would say. "You will see."

❧

ONE DAY, when a doctor came I stood behind the door curtain and listened, understanding little but fixed to the spot, determined to find out what was really wrong with Mamaji.

"Before we went to Kashmir, I kept on bleeding, and I felt I had contracted some kind of uterine infection," Mamaji was saying. "Doctor Sahib had gone on tour. I sent a message to him, and he came rushing back. We went to Dr. Bakshi, and she said I might be pregnant. After Vedi"—the mention of my name made my heart quicken; for a moment, I thought I had been discovered—"went blind, I didn't want to have a child ever again. But then Anand came. He had a swollen neck, and he died. I think it was a year or two later that I developed a thyroid deficiency. They say that women who have that sometimes give birth to cretins."

"Did the bleeding stop?"

"No. The bleeding was a bad omen. I knew that if I had a child it would be defective. I was afraid."

"Then you went to Kashmir."

"It had all been arranged. The children were so looking forward to it. I rode horses there, hoping I would lose the baby."

"And the bleeding?"

"It continued. When we got back, I went to Dr. Bakshi again. 'My dear, you're at least three months pregnant,' she said. 'There is no doubt about it.' I felt the ground give way under my feet. I pleaded with Dr. Bakshi for an abortion, but she said it was simply too late. Even Doctor Sahib pleaded. 'She has not been keeping well,' he said. 'She had to take several hormones by mouth. The bleeding is a bad sign.' But Dr. Bakshi said, 'Sorry. I will not endanger her life.' We consulted several other doctors, but they said the same thing. I became sad. I'm already over thirty-four years old."

I heard the doctor's bag snap shut. He's coming out, I thought, and I ran away. I ran as fast as I could, my bare feet scarcely touching the gravel or the grass, to Ram Saran's quarters.

"Mamaji has been spitting blood for many months now," I said. "She's going to die."

"Mistress has surely got consumption," he said. "But Big Sahib is an expert on consumption. He'll save her. I will paint the horns of the cow buffalo saffron tonight, and you say 'Ram, Ram' all the time."

Thereafter, I recited "Ram, Ram" whenever I thought of Mamaji, and sometimes woke up saying it.

❧

IT WAS GOOD FRIDAY. I didn't know why it was called that or what Bad Friday was—if there was such a thing—but I was very happy. My big sisters and my big brother and Usha all had holidays from school, and Mamaji was up and about, cooking special carrot *halwah* in the kitchen for our lunch. I was helping her.

Mamaji suddenly said, "Call Ram Saran! Call Ram Saran! Run! Run! Tell him to fetch Doctor Sahib from the tax commissioner's house. I must go to the Holy Family Hospital."

I ran to Ram Saran's quarters, shouting his name all the way. Ram Saran sped off on his bicycle. My big sisters gathered around Mamaji, who had gone into the house. They were packing her suitcase.

"What's going to happen?" I asked, afraid to voice my terrible fears, remembering the terrible words "All these doctors are really going to see me out."

"Get out. Go and play."

"You're in the way."

"Out, out, Vedi, out!" Sister Umi gave me a little push.

I went and sat on the steps of the veranda and held Usha's hand.

There was the sound of Daddyji's car on the gravel. We jumped up and ran to him, but he barely acknowledged us and ran into the house. Then everyone came out. I heard the car turn on the gravel fast. Daddyji and Mamaji were gone.

Sister Pom was audibly sniffling. Usha and I began to bawl.

❧

WE HEARD DADDYJI'S CAR on the gravel and ran out.

"You have a baby brother!" Daddyji called out from the window of the car. "He weighs nine and a half pounds. How do you like the name Ashok?" The car was still moving, and there was a slight breeze. For a moment, I thought Daddyji's voice was coming from the wind.

"Ashok! Ashok!" everyone said.

"It's a lovely name!"

"Ashok Mehta!"

"But Mamaji!" I cried, running alongside the car with my hand on the door as the car was coming to a halt.

"She's doing well," Daddyji said.

"A baby brother!" everyone else cried, and then became awkwardly quiet.

I had no idea where babies came from, but I had a vague notion that there was something dirty in even thinking about the question. (Years later, our Rawalpindi friends would talk about how innocent we all were—about how Sister Pom didn't realize that Mamaji was pregnant until the baby was almost due, even though she was sixteen and a half at the time, and about how embarrassed she felt afterward at having a baby brother at her age.)

"Is he healthy?" Sister Pom asked.

"Very healthy," Daddyji said. "I examined him myself. His left eye is a little watery, but that will stop. I don't think I've ever felt happier. Let's go."

We all piled into the car and rushed over to the Holy Family Hospital, about two miles away from our house. There was a general ward with many babies crying—they all sounded alike.

"Which one is he?" I asked impatiently.

"None of them," Daddyji said. "He's behind the glass."

We all clustered around the glass, and everyone commented on how handsome our brother was. I put my ear tight against the glass to catch his cry or some noise, but I could hear nothing.

"I want to hold him," I said.

"He's too small and has to be protected from infection for a few days," Daddyji said.

Everyone remarked on Ashok's resemblance to me. But he was so small. He was seven years younger than Usha, ten years younger than I, sixteen and a half years younger than Sister Pom. We couldn't understand how he had chosen this time to come.

"Here, let's go and see your mother," Daddyji said. "She's in a private room just behind this curtain."

❦

I REMEMBER the day Mamaji came home from the Holy Family Hospital. It was a very hot day, and Ashok was ten days old. He was crying in the car when he arrived, crying on the veranda as he was carried in, crying as he was taken into Mamaji and Daddyji's bedroom and put in a tall new metal crib beside Mamaji's bed. He had a loud cry that could be heard from one end of the house to the other.

"Why does he cry so much?" I asked.

"It's his way of telling us, 'I have come,' " Sister Umi said.

I stood near the foot of the crib, frightened that he would never stop crying, while Mamaji tended to him.

Mamaji shouted to Raj Kumari to bring Ashok's bottle.

Raj Kumari arrived with the milk in a teacup. She was all atwitter.

"Silly girl, don't you know the difference between a bottle and a teacup?" Mamaji scolded her. Ashok was crying loudly and would not be soothed.

"But, Memsahib, in English households babies drink milk from teacups."

Mamaji threatened her and cajoled her, but Raj Kumari wouldn't bring the bottle. In the end, Mamaji had to call for Lakshman Singh, and Raj Kumari withdrew, grumbling. "Bottle babies grow up to be horse thieves who steal horses from princes," Raj Kumari said.

Everything in the house seemed a little mad and confusing. I couldn't understand why Ashok had to be given formula milk, why it had to be heated, why his bottle had a wide mouth and a nipple, why Mamaji had to feed him every four hours, why there had to be an oilcloth under him, why his hands were always closed.

I ran around the house trying to get answers to my questions, but everyone seemed to be preoccupied with Ashok, and to have no time for me.

"All of you must behave," Sister Pom said. "Mamaji has to stay in for forty days after Ashok's arrival."

"Why can't Mamaji go out?" I asked.

"She was sick, silly," Sister Umi said. "She'll catch cold."

"But it's so hot."

"Well, then, she'll catch something else," Sister Umi said. "Now mind your business."

❧

ONCE, WHEN I WAS very small, I was in Mehta Gulli, and just outside the gate there was a dog straining against its chain, which clanked and rattled as the dog frantically ran this way and that way, barking and yelping. Mamaji was holding my hand, and I tried to pull it free, so that I could rush over to the dog.

"Look out, Vedi!" Mamaji said. "He's mad. He'll bite you. Then you'll get dumb-rabies." She held my hand fast and hurried me along.

"What will happen to that dog?" I asked.

"An animal doctor will put him to sleep," she said. "We are lucky to have escaped him."

I remembered that some months earlier—when we

were living at 16 Mozang Road, just after I went blind—
I had played with a puppy named Kalu.

Mataji, my maternal grandmother, used to get very
angry with me. "A mad brain with bad eyes is all you
need," she would say. "If Kalu bites you, whom will
Doctor Sahib blame?"

"Let it be," Mamaji would say. "Kalu is just a
puppy." My playing with Kalu became a secret that
Mamaji and I kept from Daddyji. Daddyji wouldn't
let me play with a dog or keep my own dog, because,
he said, the dogs in the *gullis* of the city often went
mad, and if a mad dog bit me I would have to have
fourteen injections in my stomach.

"Why can't doctors give dogs injections against
madness, the way they give us injections against
typhoid?" I asked Daddyji when I was a little older.

"They can," Daddyji said. "But when dogs are bitten by a monkey or a jackal the injection does no good.
We used to have a wonderful dog named Susky. She
was bitten by a monkey and died of dumb-rabies."

Although I would scream every time I had to have
an injection in the arm, I sometimes wanted a dog so
badly that I thought I didn't care whether I had to
have fourteen injections in my stomach or not. But
Daddyji said that only when he was transferred to an
open place would he get me a dog.

Still, after we moved to Rawalpindi, an open place,
he kept putting me off, pointing to my goldfish and
my quails, to the chickens in the coop and the buffaloes in the compound as pets enough. Then, one day,
he said, "I will be going to the princely state of Jind
soon, and I will bring you back a first-class cocker spaniel

from there. Cocker spaniels are the best dogs for children—they never bite. And Jind has the best cocker spaniels. I think that the Prince of Jind is England-returned, and that he brought back a pair of pure cocker spaniels, which he has bred in Jind. I'll be able to get the best puppy he has, because I helped to arrange a marriage for the daughter of the Queen of Jind. Besides, Sir Ganga Ram Kaula is Jind's chief minister, and he is a personal friend."

Daddyji returned from Jind and put in my arms a small, bony puppy with a silky head and coat and long, floppy ears. "She has very wistful eyes," he said. "And, as you can tell, a soft head and coat, and very long ears. I was told that the longer the ears, the more aristocratic and purebred the cocker spaniel is."

"Oh, Daddyji, she's horribly black!" Sister Umi exclaimed, joining us.

"She's not black," I said, hugging her. "She's mine. I'm going to call her Top Queen."

"You can ask anyone—she's as black as pitch," Sister Umi said. "She's a pitiful little thing. I thought she'd at least have nice white spots, like Susky."

I felt sad.

"She's black because she's purebred," Daddyji said.

"I know what!" I shouted, feeling happy in a surge. "I will call her Blackie!"

The name stuck.

Blackie arrived in the house when Ashok was just a few weeks old. I used to carry Blackie around in my arms. I couldn't pat her head enough. It had the texture of Mamaji's velvety blanket. When Ashok got a little older, he, Blackie, and I often played on the carpet in the drawing room while everyone else was at school.

One day, Daddyji brought home a dog's collar with a few bells on it, and asked me to put it on Blackie.

"She's too small for a collar!" I cried.

"She's getting big now, and will be running around all the time. If she has this collar on, you will always know where she is."

I put the collar around her neck. It was too big for her, and she tried to shake it off, making the bells jingle all the more. I decided I liked the collar on her.

Many years later, I asked Daddyji why he had finally got me a dog, and he said, "I read somewhere that a dog, especially if it had bells around its neck, was a good companion for a blind child."

❦

IT WAS THE MIDDLE of June, and Rawalpindi was in the grip of the brain-numbing heat of the Punjab plain. One day, when the temperature was already a hundred and six degrees, though it was not yet eleven o'clock, I went out to feed the chickens. The ground underfoot was so hot that I had to run fast. The chicken wire was hot to the touch, and the chickens cowered in a corner, on a pile of cut grass, trying to get away from the blazing heat. I could scarcely get them to eat.

As I was running back to the house, my feet on fire, Gian Chand called after me, "Big Sahib and Mistress have taken Ashok Sahib to the hospital!" Ashok, who was fourteen months old now, had had a high fever for several days. The doctors who came to the house to examine him could not make any sense of his fever.

I ran into the drawing room. It was summer holidays, and everyone was home. Now my sisters and big brother were gathered there as in an emergency—sitting on the sofa and chairs and waiting. "Why has Ashok been taken to the hospital?" I asked. "Have they found out what's wrong with him?"

"He has brain fever," Sister Pom said in a strained voice. "Brain fever" was the popular name for meningitis.

I sat down on the carpet with my head against the side of the sofa. I had been blinded by meningitis. Now there will be two of us, I thought. I wondered if Mamaji would also take Ashok to faith healers and, following their prescriptions, put stinging drops in his eyes to open them, and have him beaten with birch twigs to exorcise the evil eye. Maybe, like me, Ashok would have to go to Dadar School for the Blind. But then I remembered that everyone said I had been lucky to survive the meningitis without brain damage—to survive at all. Few who got meningitis did.

The house felt cold and empty. The tick-tick of the alarm clock on the mantelpiece was such a familiar sound that I was hardly ever aware of hearing it, and when I was it was comforting, for some reason, like the sound of the cooing of the pigeons who nested in the eaves of the veranda. But now every tick of the clock sounded like the beating of a drum—it was as if I myself had a high fever.

Gian Chand called us for lunch. We went to the table and ate very little, trying not to make a clatter with our spoons and plates.

We went back to the drawing room. I returned to my place on the carpet, with my head against the side of the sofa. Several times, I thought I heard the sound of Daddyji's car on the gravel. But there was never any car—just the occasional desultory sounds of everyone else knitting or flipping pages of books. Now and again, the stillness of the heat was broken by the cry, from somewhere in the compound, of the brain-fever bird: "Brain fever . . . brain fever."

❧

ASHOK HAD BEEN in the hospital for two days. Mamaji was staying with him. Daddyji would go to the hospital in the morning and come home in the evening. The only news he gave us was that Ashok's spine was being tapped twice a day. I had been told that when I was sick with meningitis my spine was tapped twice a day for weeks. I myself remembered nothing about it. The sickness had obliterated my memory of that—and of all that had gone before. I had often wondered what my sickness was like; now I thought I knew.

We were all in the drawing room. I was vaguely aware of something missing when I heard the convulsive howls of a dog from somewhere in the heat of the empty compound.

"We must be edgy, to let a dog's howls startle us," Sister Pom said.

I realized that Blackie hadn't been around for some time, and ran out of the house.

"That sounds like Blackie!" Sister Nimi exclaimed. My big sisters had followed me outside.

"It is Blackie!" I cried. "She must be at the back of the house."

We all ran in the heat, our feet making a terrible din on the gravel and almost overwhelming the sound of Blackie's howls, which were now short, subsiding whines.

At the back, near the kitchen, was Daddyji's head clerk, talking to Gian Chand.

"What's the matter, Panditji?" Sister Pom asked the head clerk. He was a Brahman, and out of respect for his high caste we called him Panditji. "Why is Blackie lying like this?"

"Gian Chand, bring some water," Sister Nimi said.

I ran to Blackie and was about to bend down and pick her up when I heard Sister Umi say, "Maybe she's got dumb-rabies. Maybe she should be chained."

I stepped back. I clutched at Sister Nimi's hand.

"Poor Blackie!" Sister Nimi said. "She's too far gone to need a chain."

Blackie gasped and writhed on the gravel between spasms.

"Save her! Save her!" I pleaded. "Someone send for an animal doctor!"

Not caring what might happen to me, I sat down next to Blackie and patted and stroked her, but she didn't respond. She felt at once inert and jerky under my hand.

"Leave her alone," Panditji said. "She may bite."

"She's not going to bite anyone," I said. "She's too sick."

"Do you know when the bitch was born?" Panditji asked.

I didn't like Blackie's being called a bitch, and that by Panditji, and I couldn't imagine why her day of birth mattered to him. But I said, "Daddyji told me that Blackie was born around the time Ashok was born."

"I thought as much," he said. "If two souls are born on the same day, and both are sick, that means one of them has been called to reënter the cycle of birth and death." I felt too sad to listen to all of what he was saying. Then he said, "As God Brahma is my witness, one of them is going to die, and die today."

I stood up, absently wondering whether Blackie was in a fit condition to be moved. None of us had even thought of moving her into the shade. "The sun . . ." I began, but I couldn't go on. I thought of another Panditji, long ago. Soon after I went blind, he came to our house in Lahore. He examined my forehead and the palm of my hand while I sat in Mamaji's lap. "Mistress, there is nothing in his forehead or in his hand about blindness in this cycle of reincarnation," he said. "It's temporary. His hand says he will grow up to ride a blue horse." He suddenly addressed me. "Vedi, do you know what that means?"

"I'll be a rich man," I said.

Mamaji laughed, and hugged me. "Imagine, he already knows what a blue horse means!" She gave him extra money that day.

Now this Panditji asked, "So what time was Ashok Sahib born?"

Blackie was yelping at my feet, and I wanted to shout at Panditji to stop talking, but he was a Brahman and I dared not speak.

"Ashok was born at two o'clock in the afternoon," Sister Pom said.

"And, Gian Chand, what time was the bitch born?"

"Two o'clock in the afternoon, Panditji," Gian Chand said.

I wanted to scream at Gian Chand that he couldn't possibly know the hour of Blackie's birth, because she was born in Jind, but I couldn't find my voice.

Panditji did some rapid calculations, counting off numbers of days and murmuring names of constellations.

We all stood there in the blazing heat, stupefied.

Panditji finally announced, "The bitch has to die an hour from now if Ashok Sahib is to be saved."

Blackie suddenly let out a vigorous cry, and I thought that she was going to live and Ashok was going to die. Then she whimpered and panted, and I thought that Ashok was going to live and Blackie was going to die. She continued to struggle, and though I winced at each of her penetrating whines I felt I should have no pity for her.

Before I knew it, I was praying for Blackie's death, even as I remembered that only the day before she had fetched a ball, run after my bicycle, sat by my chair in the dining room and spoken for food, slept under my bed. Forever, I thought, we would be consulting pandits and faith healers. Even as I put my trust in Panditji to save Ashok's life, I hated him.

"She has to die a natural death," Panditji was saying. "No one can take the law of karma into his own hands and kill her"—as if such a thought had occurred to any of us. Abruptly, he shouted, "Qasim Ali! Come here! Bring me an old *juti!*" A *juti* was a slipperlike Indian shoe that all the servants wore, because custom did not permit them to wear their shoes inside the house of their masters, and they could slip in and out of the *jutis* without touching them. A shoe or *juti* was considered unclean, because it came from the hands of cobblers, who were Untouchables, and because it came in contact with filth in the streets. I couldn't imagine why Panditji was calling for a *juti*.

Qasim Ali came running. "Pandit Sahib," he said stiffly, "where can a peon look for an old *juti?* But you're welcome to mine, even though I own only the pair I have on. You have but to order."

"I so order," Panditji said. "Hurry up, give it to me." I couldn't imagine how Panditji, a Brahman and a head clerk, could consider touching the *juti* of Qasim Ali, a Muslim and a mere office peon.

Qasim Ali squatted down subserviently, his woollen uniform audibly straining with the effort and making me feel still hotter. I thought of feverish Ashok lying in the hospital, in a private room, surrounded by nurses in their cool uniforms.

"Right *juti* or left *juti?*" Qasim Ali asked.

"Right *juti,* of course, idiot," Panditji said petulantly.

There was much ado as Panditji ordered Gian Chand

to bring a long nail and a hammer, and then squatted on the ground and set about slowly hammering the nail into the inside of the heel of Qasim Ali's *juti*. I thought of the long needle used to puncture Ashok's spine and draw out the bad fluid.

Panditji was exclaiming that the *juti* was so old and worn that the heel wouldn't hold the nail, while Qasim Ali was muttering that his only pair of *jutis* was being ruined.

Panditji directed Qasim Ali to squat opposite him, put the tip of his forefinger across from his own, under the head of the nail, and hold the *juti* a few inches off the ground.

"Sisters and brothers," Panditji said to us, with the familiarity permitted by his high caste, "you see the *juti* suspended between our fingertips —"

"Panditji, what is this nonsense?" Sister Nimi said. "Gian Chand, I told you to fetch some water. Poor Blackie is dying."

"Wait, sister, wait," Panditji said. "Don't anyone move. You will upset the concentration of the *juti*. I am going to call out names, and the *juti* will turn right around in a circle at the mention of the soul that is going to be taken today. It will not lie. You will see. Hold your finger steady, Qasim Ali."

"You'll just make it turn at any name you like," Sister Umi said.

"Sister insults my religion," Panditji said sombrely. "God is my witness. A Muslim sits in front of me. We are united not by religion but by truth. The *juti* will tell."

Blackie shifted and pawed the ground.

"You, *juti!* Child of mud and muck!" Panditji shouted, enunciating each syllable as if he were addressing a dense servant. "Defiler of home and hearth! Befouler of temples and kitchens! Hide of a murdered cow, sweat of Untouchable tanners and cobblers! Tell us the truth!" Panditji, a pious man, began to heap curses on the *juti,* accusing it of all kinds of dirty acts— and in front of my big sisters. "Defiler of sisters and mothers! I order you to tell us the truth! Whose soul will be taken today?"

Blackie yelped and heaved, sending a shudder up my spine. I tried to think of what Panditji was saying and of what Sister Nimi had said and at the same time to listen for the sound of Daddyji's car.

"Is it to be Ram Saran?" Panditji was saying. "Is it to be Gian Chand? Is it to be Qasim Ali? The assistant clerk? Is it to be Nimi Memsahib?" The muscles at the back of my neck tightened. "Is it to be Ashok Sahib? The bitch Blackie?"

I heard the *juti* drop, hit the ground. I wanted to cry out, "Did the *juti* turn? At whose name did it turn?"

"You have nothing to worry about," Panditji said, standing up. "Ashok Sahib has been spared. It's the bitch's turn on the wheel of reincarnation."

He walked away, the gravel crunching under his shoes, and left us standing there. As if released from our numbness and from the power of the sun, we all simultaneously knelt down and started feeling Blackie, our hands overlapping and groping. Her body felt heavy and stiff, her legs half spread out and half bent. It seemed she had died in the middle of a spasm.

Desultorily, we all walked into the house, as if away from an uncovered grave, leaving Qasim Ali and Gian Chand to dispose of Blackie.

"That horrible pandit!" Sister Umi exclaimed. "He probably gave her some rat poison beforehand to prove his *juti* nonsense."

"Hold your tongue, Umi," Sister Pom said, "or you will bring bad luck."

Half an hour later, I heard Daddyji's car, and we ran out to meet him. "Ashok is going to be all right," he said. "The spinal taps are working. His eyes are saved."

"Daddyji," I asked, "why should this have happened to both of us?"

"I don't know," he said.

In both Ashok's case and mine, the source of the meningitis was never found—there was no other case of meningitis reported in the vicinity.

XI

TRANSFER

ORDERS

A ROUND TEATIME, ONE DAY IN OCTOBER—THE year was 1945—Daddyji walked through the door that connected the office with the residence and called us all to him. "I have just received my transfer orders," he said. "We are going to Lahore. We must pack everything and vacate this house in ten days for the new assistant director."

Postings were hardly ever for more than three years, and Daddyji had already been in Rawalpindi longer than that. For months, we had known that he might be transferred any day. We had even been looking forward to living in Lahore, in our own house, with all our relatives around us. But now that he was really being transferred none of us could bear the thought of leaving Rawalpindi. We all started protesting at once.

Sister Pom, who cried the most easily of us all, started sniffling. "I can't possibly leave," she said. "My courses won't finish till January, and I have to sit for my B.A. exam in less than six months."

"Well, you can stay back with your school friend Chinta Tandon and come to Lahore in January, and sit for your B.A. examination from there," Daddyji said.

"I can't pack in ten days," Mamaji said, in a shaky voice. "I can't leave without saying goodbye properly to Tara and Jaya. Where will I ever find friends like them?"

"Shanti, you've gone through so many transfers with me—you can do it again," Daddyji said, laughing. "We have to vacate the house in ten days. Those are government orders."

"How will we take the buffaloes?" Usha asked.

"They'll have to be sold," Daddyji said. "We'll get some new ones in Lahore."

"There is not time to sell the buffaloes," Mamaji said.

"Ram Saran can sell the buffaloes after we leave, and give the money to Promila," Daddyji said, and he continued, "Just imagine, we'll finally be in Lahore— that's where I was a student, that's where Shanti and I got married, that's where you children were born. And I am now so senior in the department that we'll never have to move again. Remember how we didn't want to come to Rawalpindi? But it's been a marvellous posting. Shanti, you have really bloomed, away from all our relatives, and made your own friends here. You three sisters have grown up in a free, open atmosphere, and have escaped the narrow outlook of the Lahore *gul-lis*. Om, you have readjusted to family life and are making progress in Urdu. Vedi, you have gained in self-confidence. And in Rawalpindi we got Ashok."

"What about me?" Usha cried. "You've forgotten me!"

Daddyji drew Usha to him and said, "Well, in Rawalpindi you started school. That's no small thing."

XII

THE

TWO LAHORES

I N Lahore, everyone went to the pictures all the time. Daddyji didn't like children
to go to them. "Pictures ruin the eyes and the
mind," he used to say. He restricted my big
sisters and my big brother to one picture a
month. Quite often, the picture they chose was
in English, and it would have been pointless for me to
try to go with them. But sometimes they chose an
Indian picture, and then I would beg to be taken along.
At the cinema, I would frequently lose the thread of
the story and ask whomever I was sitting next to,
"What's happening? . . . What's happening?" Even if
that person was Sister Nimi, she would try to put me
off, saying, "Nothing. . . . Don't talk. . . . We won't
bring you again." I would agitate, and talk louder and

louder—I didn't want to make trouble; it was just that I didn't want to miss any part of the story—until I was told or I caught on. Then the story would often turn out to be really sad, and I would sob and blow my nose. "If you don't stop blubbering, we won't bring you again," Sister Umi would say. But I could no more control my tears than I could control the course of the story, though I was nearly twelve years old. Moreover, before coming I had promised that I would be a good boy—that I wouldn't disturb anyone in the middle of the picture—and so I would try to hold off asking to be taken to the bathroom. But the need would build up and become so urgent that I could scarcely sit still. Yet I would have difficulty rousing even Sister Nimi. No matter how much I tugged at her arm, she would say, "Oof! He's about to die," or "Just a minute," or "Don't be a nuisance," or "Wait, there's a song coming." The song was usually the part I liked best.

In Lahore, I remember, I was once taken to "Zeenat," a picture in Urdu, featuring the Muslim actress called Baby Noor Jehan, the most loved actress of the time. In the picture, Noor Jehan plays a fifteen-year-old Muslim girl, Zeenat. Her parents betroth her to Sharafat, whose parents are dead and who has been brought up by his elder brother, Fajahat. Zeenat is delirious with joy. Sharafat is her first cousin, and they have grown up playing together. (Among Muslims, first cousins can marry.) On the day of the wedding, as Zeenat's parents are receiving Sharafat on his wedding horse, merrymakers set off firecrackers. A firecracker explodes near the horse. The horse rears back.

Sharafat is thrown—he falls on his head. There can be no wedding. But in the middle of the night Zeenat looks in on him. Sharafat insists that she come to his bedside. They rejoice. The next morning, Sharafat's condition worsens, and he dies. He is buried, amid the crying and wailing of women. A few months after his death, it becomes known that Zeenat is pregnant. She insists that it is Sharafat's baby, but Fajahat and his wife accuse her of being a loose woman and turn her out. She goes to her parents, but they don't believe her, either. She is delivered of a daughter, Saeeda. When the taunts are directed against the daughter, too, Zeenat leaves with Saeeda—condemned and penniless. She goes to her only refuge—Sharafat's grave—and pours out her sorrows in song. By a turn of fate, Saeeda is given for adoption to a well-to-do childless couple, and Zeenat becomes a maid in the couple's house. At fifteen, Saeeda falls in love with Akhtar, a son of Fajahat. Their marriage is arranged, and it is now Saeeda's wedding day. In the middle of the ceremony, Saeeda's identity is discovered. Fajahat and his wife immediately call off the wedding. But then Sharafat's younger brother Liakat produces a diary in Sharafat's hand, which he has kept as a memento. The diary leaves no doubt that Saeeda is Sharafat's child. The wedding ceremony goes forward. But the discovery of the diary comes too late for Zeenat. She has taken poison and is violently ill. She is told that she has been vindicated and that Saeeda's wedding has been solemnized. She thanks Allah and dies.

I don't think I ever cried more than I did during "Zeenat." I think everyone cried except Daddyji, who had come along, for once, because the picture was famous for its Urdu poetry and Urdu songs. He was sitting next to me, and tried to make me stop crying by saying, "It's just a set of curtains and backdrops," and "It's just a story," and "Can you imagine anyone turned out by her own parents going to a grave site and singing such a beautiful song?" But I was so involved in the picture that I didn't want him to talk, and once even told him to be quiet. I went to "Zeenat" six times—we children all did—and, after "Zeenat," went to all Noor Jehan's pictures and got all her records. I couldn't play them often enough on our wind-up gramophone. Her voice had the shrill lilt of a bagpipe, and her songs were frequently tragic—so full of longing, sadness, and goodness that I often imagined her as a nightingale without a tree or a nest, crying to the unfeeling sky. I used to go around saying, "She has pathos in her throat." I would sing along with her records. I would wake up thinking about her, I would go to sleep thinking about her. Every time any of my sisters mentioned Noor Jehan's name, I would blush. I would be asked to sing her songs at gatherings of family and friends, and I would sing with tears trickling down my cheeks. My favorite was one from "Zeenat," and when I sang it there was hardly a dry eye in the room. It went:

> Storms of sorrow swept along in such a way
> The garden was left uprooted.
> One who was my prop,
> He, too, was torn away.
> Don't ask me the story of my sorrow,

How I have been uprooted.
The light of the house was put out,
The house itself was uprooted.
Spring had come my way, too,
But for a very short while.
Just on laughing, tears came,
And everything lost its color.

We children thought of Lahore as two distinct cities: one, which we associated with Daddyji, was the new, clearly demarcated British city, with its Mall Road, its Lawrence Gardens, its Queen Victoria statue, its King Edward Medical College; the other, which we associated with Mamaji, was the old, unplanned, chaotic Indian city, with its narrow *gullis* and mean bazaars, its dilapidated Mogul gates and arches, its beehives of cloth peddlers, carters, smiths, ironmongers, cobblers, grain sellers, colliers. In actuality, the two cities had long overlapped—much as Mamaji's family had settled into a British-style bungalow, and Daddyji's family into an Indian *gulli*. Everywhere—whether on the Mall Road or in the *gullis*—we heard dirty words shouted, from shops and stalls, from vehicles, by passersby; the obscenities were graphic and made us burn with shame. Everywhere, there was traffic and noise, ditches and open drains. Technically, we lived in the British city, and yet I couldn't even go out into our *gulli* by myself. Everywhere, the *gullis'* stones seemed waterworn and slippery; the *gullis'* houses were constantly belching coal smoke through their chimneys; the *gullis'* walls seemed to trap the smell of refuse and rubbish. There were no mountain winds to carry away the smells, no Civil Lines that we could escape to. For the first time, I appreciated what Daddyji had meant when he inveighed against the Lahore *gullis* in which Mamaji spent her childhood.

When we were younger and merely visited Lahore, it seemed that the brothers and sisters and cousins had all been more or less one large family group, and had done things together, perhaps because everyone had been on holiday. We boys might go out into Mehta Gulli to play, or climb up to the terraced roofs to wage battles with our kites, and our sisters and cousin-sisters might sit in the shade of the veranda to knit or sew, but we would all come together two or three times a day, to share a meal, or to listen to Bhabiji tell stories, or to walk with her to the statue of Queen Victoria. But now everyone—aside from me—was at school or, if not at school, busy with homework. Everyone, it seemed, had a special group of school friends for playing volleyball, tennis, hockey, or cricket, or even for studying. Indeed, during the day Mehta Gulli and Mozang Road resembled women's quarters or the domain of servants. Moreover, I felt that some of my cousins were too small for me to play with, while other cousins felt that they were too grown-up to play with me.

After the Rawalpindi government office-residence, our house seemed small. It had no grounds, no detached kitchen, no detached quarters for the servants. Instead of occupying an independent compound in a row of compounds, the house was one of a series of houses with common walls, and stood near the bottom of a *gulli* off Temple Road. (Although our address was 11 Temple Road, our house actually faced on a nameless *gulli*—a cul-de-sac, little wider than a driveway, that ran perpendicular to Temple Road—and so did nine other houses.) Instead of being a one-story bungalow with big verandas, it was a typical two-and-a-half-story Lahore house with a terraced roof, built on a small plot of land, with a little garden and a veranda in front, and a smaller veranda, which gave onto an inner courtyard, at the back. The main part of the house consisted of four rooms: a corner room, where Daddyji slept (it had been made by cutting off part of the front veranda); a big bedroom behind it, where Mamaji slept, and which had a bay window that looked out on the driveway and the garage; a drawing room; and a dining room. Along the back of the inner courtyard were a kitchen, a small storeroom, and the servants' quarters, and to the left side of the courtyard were a couple of rooms that Brother Om and I occupied. (To the right side of the courtyard was the wall that we shared with the last house in the *gulli*.) There was a staircase going up from the back veranda to my big sisters' rooms and, above them, to the terraced roof, where we slept in the summer. It had a rain shelter at one end, and whenever it rained in the middle of the night we would scoot our cots into it.

At our Lahore house, there was no place for me to bicycle. I had nothing to do all day. I would go from room to room, sitting now on one cot, now on another, or go round and round the inner courtyard, the way a pet myna I once had used to go round and round her cage.

At first, of course, we were excited and thrilled to be in our own house, and it was pleasant that there was a newly distempered room for each one of us older children, with each room now called after one of us. But for me the new arrangements had their disadvantages. Our night suits no longer hung from one clothes peg, and my little sister Usha and I could no longer have fun burrowing ourselves into a collection of satin and linen pajamas and pajama coats, salwars and kemises, looking for our night suits. Now each one of us was in charge of his or her own night suit. Now that we children no longer all slept in one room, or shared one bathroom, doors to rooms were no longer left open; in fact, the doors to the separate rooms seemed always to be shut and bolted from inside. Friends were no longer entertained by the family as a group in the drawing room or on the veranda. And I was no longer the "baby brother," who could come and go as he pleased; Ashok was nearly two now, and had taken that place.

Brother Om and I shared a bathroom, but he didn't like my coming into his room uninvited. "I have all kinds of friends coming and going," he protested when Daddyji tried to intervene on my behalf. "We talk about all kinds of things."

"Let him sit and listen," Daddyji said. "He'll learn something."

"My friends feel awkward," Brother Om said. "They don't feel free in front of him. He's in the way."

"But he's your brother."

"But they're my friends."

Daddyji acknowledged that Brother Om had a point. After that, I stayed clear of Brother Om's room whether he was in it or not.

Everyone suddenly seemed grown-up and difficult.

I, too, didn't feel like a child anymore—I was now taller than Mamaji—and I became subject to all kinds of new worries. I would continally touch my elbows and get worked up about how rough they seemed under my fingers. I felt that my arms were too long. My knees felt exposed below my knickers. I didn't know what to do with my hands. They felt strange whether they were in or out of my pockets, whether they were behind me or in front of me. I would walk around clasping them behind my head, with my elbows sticking out. Or I would sit down in a chair and clutch one knee, but then my foot would be off the ground, sticking out in midair like a displaced limb. I also began to worry about my eyes—whether they looked closed or open.

Then I woke up one day and found that my voice sounded like a half croak coming out of someone else's throat. I tried to recover my old voice by pitching it higher, only to find that I sounded like a girl. For weeks—or maybe it was for months—my voice would shift unexpectedly, as if I were condemned to groan and squeak. "Commander Sahib, it's the heat of Lahore," Gian Chand told me. "Everything gets cooked here. Your voice is being cooked." But my voice did not improve with the relief in the weather. It continued to crack uncontrollably, going up and down like the hee-haw of a jackass. It grated on everyone's nerves. Yet I had an overwhelming urge to talk non-stop—to interrupt, to shout, to be heard. I became truculent; I would talk back to everyone and pick fights with everyone.

When Mamaji complained to Daddyji about me, he said, "Leave him alone. He'll be all right. His age is the most difficult for boys, Tagore says." I didn't know who Tagore was, but I felt he must understand why I was the way I was. I certainly didn't. Inside, I felt like a child who should obey, but outside I felt like a man—at the edge of another world, which was full of embarrassment and danger but also of adventure and discovery.

Daddyi continued to counsel me to look to music for solace, but with the coming of the hee-haw I had lost my singing voice. Besides, in my view nothing could take the place of studying—of reading and writing and taking examinations, of learning English, of progressing from standard to standard, like my sisters and my big brother and my cousins. I had the helpless feeling of falling behind. Because my health had broken down at Dadar School, Daddyji wouldn't hear of sending me away to another such school.

"I will retire from service in five years, and then we'll all go to America and I'll enter you in Perkins," Daddyji said.

"But Perkins has refused to accept me."

"I'm sure that when the Perkins people meet you and see the whole family they will change their minds and accept you."

"But by that time I'll be an old man."

He laughed. "Don't be silly."

❧

ONE EVENING when Daddyji came home, he told me, "Believe it or not, I've learned that there is a school

for the blind in Lahore. It is named the Emerson Institute for the Blind, after Sir Herbert William Emerson,
an ex-governor of ours. But it's in such a poor locality
that I'm not even sure it can be reached by motorcar.
I've given my clerk tomorrow off to go there and look
at it."

"What did the clerk say?" I asked Daddyji the
moment he got home the next day.

"Just as I feared, it's a wretched place. It's simply
a few rooms in the old city, inside Sheranwala Gate.
They have only boys and men, and mostly teach them
trades, like caning and weaving."

"I'd still like to give it a try."

"But it doesn't even have a teacher or a principal
who's a college graduate," he said, and he continued,
almost to himself, "And yet it seems that it is the best
school for the blind in the whole of the Punjab, and
there are pending petitions for admission there from
all over the province."

"What do you mean?"

"In a village, whenever someone goes blind he
becomes a charge on his relatives. They try to palm
him off onto the government—all government institutions are free. There are apparently so many peti-
tioners for the Emerson Institute that the government
has a strict quota system for the admission of various
communities and religious groups."

I kept asking Daddyji when I could at least go and
visit the school. He kept putting me off with plans for
our going to America, but then one day he told me,
"I've been talking to our finance minister, Sir Manohar Lal, about you and the Emerson Institute, and he's

made a grant that will enable the school to appoint a sighted college graduate as its principal. Let's wait until the principal is selected."

Within a few days, Ram Gopal Khanna, a recent college graduate, was selected, and we drove out to see him. It took us more than half an hour to reach the place, even though we went along modern, paved roads that skirted the old city. Daddyji parked the motorcar on a dirt road, and we got out.

The sun was hot, the air sluggish. The place smelled of rotting refuse. All around were the sounds of crows cawing and kites shrieking.

At the edge of the dirt road, there was a big old tree with a cleft in it, and Daddyji stopped to show it to me. "It looks like two trees, but here, feel the trunk— it's actually one tree," he said.

The trunk was flaky and worm-eaten; jagged slabs of bark seemed to drop off almost at my touch. But there was something magical about the cleft—round and smooth, it was indented like the space between two fingers, reminding me of the V sign I had been taught to make during the war. It had a faint smell of moss and resin. While I was examining the cleft, we were surrounded by Mr. Khanna and his few teachers—all men, and all blind or partially sighted.

"Khanna Sahib, why does the school building face away from the road?" Daddyji asked. "From a sanitation point of view, it's always better for a building to face the road, so that people don't trek filth into it from the surrounding area." He was speaking English, and he sounded as if he were on an official inspection.

Mr. Khanna didn't know the reason, and he asked

the teachers. There was a heated discussion, in a mixture of Punjabi and English, from which it emerged that the reason had to do with the cleft tree. It was a stopping place for the procession celebrating an annual festival called Step by Step, which was based on the notion that good children walk in the footsteps of their fathers. For decades, those taking part had camped under the tree, so when it came time to put up the school building it had had to be constructed around the tree in a sort of half U, with all the doors facing away from the road.

"How old is the school?" I asked.

At first, none of the men seemed to know the answer, but then one of them came forward and gripped my hands between his callused ones and shouted at me, as if I were deaf, "Welcome, Boy Sahib, welcome, with your question! This is the sighted weaving teacher talking. I am the longest resident of the Emerson Institute for the Blind." His fingers were short and thick, like sausages. He had overpowering breath, and I tried to step back, but he held me fast. He had been speaking Punjabi but now he switched to English, and said, "This is one of the oldest blind institutes being in the country. It getting its start in 1933." I reflected that the school was a year older than I was.

Daddyji asked him if there was any written record of the date.

"They must having records in official buildings," the weaving teacher said. "But I'm not able to be learning to be reading. I know Emerson Institute was four years old when I came, and that was two years before the big war."

With all the teachers trooping behind, we walked through the school. It consisted of a half-dozen bare rooms, which were along an open veranda and were screened off with bamboo chicks.

"Where are the students?" I asked. We hadn't met a single boy since we got there.

"We cleared the school for your tour," Mr. Khanna said. "The boys have gone for their food." It seemed that the boys lived in quarters some distance away, like servants.

As we were driving home, Daddyji said, "Khanna looks to be a nice young man." Then he exclaimed, "Oh, my God! I just thought, I didn't see any books there. We should have asked about it."

"I would like to go there," I said.

"You can try it if you like," he said. "It might be a good experience for you."

❧

GETTING TO the Emerson Institute and back every day in a tonga was prohibitively expensive, to say nothing of going by motorcar. Anyway, Daddyji needed his motorcar to get to and from the office, and we couldn't afford to keep a driver. It was arranged, there-fore, that Gian Chand would take me to school on his bicycle in the morning and pick me up in the after-noon. (There was no way, of course, that I could nego-tiate the Lahore streets on a bicycle myself.) It took him a couple of days to work out a short, safe bicycle route. Then a carrier was fitted onto the back of his bicycle for me to sit on. But when I tried it out I discovered that my legs were too long—they touched the ground.

"For years, Sahib has been too big to ride on the bar of my bicycle," Gian Chand said. "Now Sahib is too big to ride on the carrier. What to do?"

Daddyji was consulted, and we improvised a solution. We arranged for a bicycle shop to fit a spindly metal peg on each side of the rear axle as a sort of foot support. The peg had to be specially designed, with treads, so that my foot wouldn't slip off it. When it was finished, I was finally ready to go to school.

The school hours were from eight to four, and on the first morning I set out with Gian Chand at about seven-twenty. I sat straddled behind him with my feet on the pegs, holding on to the seat with one hand and clutching some cucumber-and-tomato sandwiches for lunch with the other. I had to be mindful not to put too much weight on the pegs, and to keep my legs out of the way of the pedals.

The sun was already hot, and the heat seemed to push us down against the road. From every side came the deafening sounds of passing tongas, cars, lorries, and motorcycles, along with the shouts of bicyclists and pedestrians. On the Mall Road, Gian Chand tried to gain some time, pedalling hard and ringing his bell furiously, the seat creaking under him with the effort, and the bicycle swinging from side to side as he wove in and out of the traffic. I kept my legs up and close to the bicycle, out of harm's way, only to discover that this gave me cramps in my calves.

Gian Chand's route was about three miles long. Most of it was in the old city, through a maze of narrow, stifling *gullis* and bazaars. Sometimes the route became so congested that Gian Chand couldn't pedal at all. He had to dismount and walk the bicycle, while I hung on as best I could. But whenever there was a clear stretch he would jump back onto the bicycle and race ahead, sometimes lifting himself off the seat and hunching over the handlebars in order to pedal harder and faster, his back smelling of sweat.

Now we passed a vender hawking cloth, now shops loud with the clatter of metal and tin, now some stalls giving off the stale smell of leather and rubber. In the distance, I heard the beating of carding bows. I had been inside several of the gates and *gullis* of the old city before, but mostly in a tonga with my family—never through so much of it at such close quarters. I thought of Mamaji going to school here, and of how the old city had cut short her education at the fourth standard. For some years now, I had been fighting to break one bond between her and me—the bond of little schooling—and here I was going into the same old city in search of education. I felt nearer to her even as I felt repelled, and therefore happy even as I felt discouraged.

By the time we reached the school, the traffic noise, the kilnlike heat, and the choking bazaars, together with the bumps, jolts, and turns and the grit and grime, had left me feeling dizzy and tired.

My first class was in Braille, English, local history, folklore, and general knowledge, and it was with Mr. Baqir. "Welcome, welcome!" he said, in Punjabi, leading me to a cane-bottomed chair against a long table. Then he told the the class, "We have a new, well-to-do lad—a day scholar."

I remembered that at Dadar School we had once had a day scholar, and how strange his coming and going every day had seemed to us boarders. Mr. Baqir introduced the rest of the class to me—three boys sitting around the table. "This is Roshan Jah, Hindu agri. This is Muhammad Bashir, Muslim agri. This is Semual, Christian non-agri."

I was puzzled by the mention of their religion and couldn't understand what "agri" and "non-agri" were, and said as much.

"The well-to-do day scholar doesn't know the difference between Hindu and Muslim, Muslim and Christian, Christian and Hindu!" Mr. Baqir roared. He had a very loud voice.

"But I do," I said. "I don't know what 'agri' and 'non-agri' are."

"Listen, boys, the well-to-do day scholar doesn't know 'agri' and 'non-agri.' Roshan Jah, tell him."

"Baqir Sahib, 'agri' is agriculture, 'non-agri' is non-agriculture," said a boy across from me, in a very rustic accent.

"Semual, how many kinds of petitions are there for blind schools?"

"Two, Baqir Sahib," a boy at the end of the table said.

"And what are they called?"

"Agri and non-agri, Baqir Sahib," he said.

"Now, well-to-do day scholar, you can tell your doctor father that you've had your first lesson in general knowledge."

The boys laughed and shifted their bare feet under

the table. In spite of myself, I felt at home; at Dadar School, I had been the only one except Mr. Ras Mohun, the principal, who had shoes.

The classroom was perhaps twice the size of a servant's quarters and was stuffy. From the center of the ceiling hung a common variety of manual fan, which I could reach up and touch. It was made out of bamboo strips with a cloth backing, and was worked by a boy posted at the door. He pulled and relaxed the rope in a deliberate manner, making the fan groan and slightly stir the sluggish air over our heads. Mr. Baqir, who sat at the head of the table, facing the doorway, was smoking a *biri,* chewing *pan* and smacking his lips, and tapping a cane on the table. The smell of pungent, cheap tobacco, the noise of his chewing, and the rat-a-tat of his cane gave the place the dissolute atmosphere of a streetside stall.

"We in this room are all totally blind—that is, except for the sleepy fanwallah, and he might as well be blind," Mr. Baqir said. "So be on the alert. Prick up your ears, and the moment you hear the clicking heels of Mr. Khanna clear your throat, for the doorway is Mr. Khanna's eyes."

"What will Mr. Khanna do?" I asked.

"Do?" Mr. Baqir bellowed. "The well-to-do day scholar doesn't know! Mr. Khanna walks up and down the veranda looking into the doorways. He can lift back the chick so silently that even a dog can't hear it. If he sees or hears unseemly things, he will file a bad report on us to the government."

Mr. Baqir didn't explain what unseemly things he had in mind, but I recalled that at Dadar School the sound of Mr. Ras Mohun's shoes would make us straighten ourselves or raise our heads or put our hands under the table. This, too, made me feel at home. It became apparent, however, that Emerson was unlike Dadar School in that there was no bell, no clock, no set hour for doing anything. Roshan Jah, Muhammad Bashir, and Semual stepped out onto the veranda to take the air or smoke a *biri* whenever they liked. All of them were older than I was. Semual was nineteen, Muhammad Bashir was sixteen, and Roshan Jah was fifteen. We had one Braille book among us, which we passed along the table like a basket of sweetmeats, each reading a word or two in English while Mr. Baqir kept up a vague patter in Punjabi about the benefits of being able to read English Braille and knowing at least a few English words. He would stop now and again to shout "A little harder, my boy!" and for a time the irritating noise of the swinging fan would become fast and ragged. Every few minutes, one or another of us would ask the boy what time it was. He alone had a watch. The time at school seemed to pass almost as slowly as the time at home. I felt the walls of the room closing in, crushing my ambition to go to school and to be like others—I longed for four o'clock.

After a couple of hours or so, Mr. Baqir sent Roshan Jah to the weaving class and me to the singing class; he kept back Semual and Muhammad Bashir for more teaching. The singing class was with Mr. Chander, who was so mild-mannered that he could almost have been taken for a servant. Anyway, he couldn't have copied Mr. Baqir's lazy ways if he'd wanted to. "Mr. Khanna doesn't even have to step out of his room at the end of the veranda to know that I'm doing my job," Mr. Chander told me. "He has only to listen for the continuous sound of harmonium and tabla and singing."

Even though I didn't like my singing voice anymore, the music calmed my disturbed spirit.

Then it was lunchtime. The whole school—half a dozen teachers and about fifteen students—milled around the cleft tree, under the hot sun, crunching bark and twigs underfoot and eating parathas with strong-smelling pickles while I tried to swallow a cucumber-and-tomato sandwich. I gave away the rest of my sandwiches to a few boys standing around me. They had never had sandwiches before, and they ate them with exclamations of wonder.

The people around me acted and talked like servants, addressing one another by name but addressing me by honorifics like "sahib" and "huzoor." I imagined that they all regarded me somewhat the way they regarded Mr. Khanna—as a new person who might report on them to the government—for everyone seemed to know that Daddyji was an important official and that it was because of him that Mr. Khanna had been hired in the first place.

When Mamaji became exasperated with my sisters and brother because they gave themselves college airs and were difficult to manage, she would say things like "I know I'm only an unlettered servant in your father's house." When I was a little younger, I would run up to her and embrace her and say, "Don't say things like that. You're our dear mother." At the same time, I felt like a servant myself—in fact, less than a servant, for I had a servant's disability of lack of education but did not have a servant's abilities, such as cooking and shopping, cleaning and serving. Now here I was going to what seemed like a school of blind servants.

I spent the afternoon with the weaving teacher, learning about yarn and a loom. Finally, Gian Chand arrived to collect me. All the way back home on the bicycle, I thought of the sedate nuns who taught my sisters and cousin-sisters in convents in the modern city, and of the sedate monks who taught my big brother and many of my cousin-brothers in monastic schools in the modern city, and I felt ashamed. Later on, at home, I felt too ashamed to relate my school experiences, and no one pressed me. It was as if everyone had guessed what the school was like, and didn't want to know about it any more than I wanted to tell about it.

❧

" 'CONFORM' CAN be written in Braille with only three Braille signs," Mr. Baqir said one morning. "You use the contraction for 'c-o-n,' the contraction for 'f-o-r,' and then letter 'm.' 'Conform' with three Braille signs is easier to read with fingers than 'conform' with seven Braille signs."

I asked, "What is the contraction for 'c-o-n'?"

"Day scholar, do not interrupt," Mr. Baqir said, tapping his cane on the table. "Interruption is one of the failings of Hindus. Hindus will interrupt even a prayer." Mr. Baqir was a Muslim.

I didn't learn that day or the day after or the day after that what the contraction sign for 'c-o-n' was—

or, for that matter, what the contraction sign for any other set of letters was. I stopped asking after a while, however, because I realized that Mr. Baqir was not interested in teaching. Yet if any of us made a mistake in reading Braille or in answering a question he would let fly a torrent of abuse. In my family, we were not allowed to use even ordinary words of abuse, like "idiot." The words of abuse that Mr. Baqir used I had heard only in the bazaars, and then only in bad bazaars.

All the same, I enjoyed being at school. I found the students very friendly. Having my own private world made me feel independent. From seven-twenty in the morning, when I left home, till five, when I got back, I was busy.

❧

MOST OF MR. BAQIR'S class time was spent talking about the Hira Mandi. (*Hira mandi* means "gem market.") As he never tired of repeating, no blind person could ever go there, because its sighted inhabitants imagined that their rubies, emeralds, sapphires, diamonds, pearls were all so many rocks to blind people. Mr. Baqir would add, "In fact, blindness is considered the curse of the place—the darkness that robs the gems of their lustre, the dreaded fate buried in the stones of pleasure, the rank weed in the pleasure garden." He would not explain but would go on, mysteriously, "It's a reminder that disease and death stalk all those who seek pleasure."

"I will slip in there in the cover of night," Muhammad Bashir once said. "If our prophet doesn't deny us the houris, how can Hira Mandi deny us its gems?"

"Ah, you can go, you can go there," Mr. Baqir said. "You can gain entrance, you can be received, under the cloak of darkness. But when, Muhammad Bashir, they find out you are blind they will cast you out like a common stone, for the disease that causes blindness they dread above all." He beat the table with his cane to emphasize his words. "That disease is the fate worse than death."

"What disease?" I asked. "What is it called?"

"Sh-h-h. It's the disease of diseases," he said. He couldn't be coaxed to say more. But after a while he did say, without clearing up matters very much, "Your affliction, our affliction, calls for only pity, not pleasure."

Yet among us we thought that Mr. Baqir himself must once have lived in Hira Mandi, for his talk had the electricity of firsthand experience. "Perhaps he was sighted once, and that's why he was able to go there and enjoy himself," Semual said.

"Go on!" Muhammad Bashir said. "If he had been, he would have told us." He thought for a moment, and then added, "Maybe he caught the dreaded disease there and went blind because of it."

We knew nothing of Mr. Baqir's life—how he went blind, where he was born, where he came from, how he first came to the school, where he went when the school closed in the afternoon. All we knew was that he and the partially sighted weaving teacher left the school together every day. We felt as shut out from his past as he said we were shut out from Hira Mandi.

And Hira Mandi, from his description, sounded so dangerous and alluring that we could scarcely sit still in our chairs. He talked about it the way musicians sing a raga—with plenty of repetition and improvisation. "Hira Mandi is a whole city within the old city," he would say, "with its own bazaars and *gullis,* its own squares and drains, asleep during the day when we are at the Emerson Institute, alive at dusk with courtesans, more various than the jewels in a jeweller's shop, than the fruit in a fruit shop: some of them wandering in their pajamas in the bazaars, hair uncombed, sleep still in their eyes, taking air, looking for sighted men; some lowly pearls among them standing in front of *pan-biri* shops smoking and sucking betel nut, their lips hot, wet, and red; some rubies and sapphires among them walking and shopping with their accompanists—harmonium players, tabla players, sarangi players—buzzing about them like bees, now settling on this flower, now settling on that flower, bantering, making rude remarks and being told off, passing the time until the evening hour arrives to tune up and play. Upstairs, the choicest rubies and emeralds spend a long time getting ready—scrubbing and bathing, sometimes shaving the whole body and making it as smooth as a whistle, applying powder to the neck, rouge to the cheeks, kohl to the eyelids, henna to the hands and feet, combing and plaiting the hair, choosing saris or salwars, kemises, and veils, looking in the mirror, being inspected by the mother, receiving final instructions. As it gets dark, the balconies and windows are lighted up. The choicest rubies and emeralds take their places. Musicians strike up. Nautch girls warm up, little bells jingling around their ankles. Sighted men walk the *gullis,* looking up hungrily. This house is bathed in jasmine and that house in sweet pea. Here and there, there is the scented air of the queen of the night."

Mr. Baqir's talk about Hira Mandi tantalized us, making us feel helpless, as if we were all standing at the gates of Hira Mandi with the sign "Abandon hope all ye blind who enter here."

"From the lighted balconies and windows, they call out in as many tongues as there are sighted men walking below. And the sighted men wonder: Is it to be the Kashmiran with the fair skin in that window? The wheat-complexioned Punjaban in that window? The gray-eyed hill girl standing over there in the corner of that balcony? The blue-eyed Afghani glowering from that doorway? Suddenly, a sighted man darts into a dark doorway and runs up the stairs. He has seen the woman of his heart's desire. He has made up his mind. Upstairs, he sits with her—maybe it's on a divan, maybe it's on a cot, maybe it's on the floor. But they're next to each other, their knees touching. They bargain under the watchful eye of the mother. She asks him for his horoscope. They are superstitious, very superstitious. The best houses shelter the same rubies we blind people hear on the radio and on records. What did you ask? Noor Jehan? Most certainly. Not one Noor Jehan but a hundred Noor Jehans. They are unattainable, like queens. More money than any blind person ever earned is required just to sit with one of them. He leans against a velvet bolster. She makes *pan* with her own hands, and serves it to him on a silver tray with balls of cotton wool dabbed in musky scent. She brings him his own spittoon. She sits at his feet and serenades him with a song, conducting her accompanists with her out-stretched hand. The harmonium sounds a note, the tabla whispers, the sarangi and she begin a lively dia-logue. She and the sarangi float up to the sighted man on a cushion of sound, surround him, caress him, bathe him, tease him. She sets him on fire. For her song is a dream thought, a personal address, a birdcall. The man against the velvet bolster dreams; he goes with his fan-cies, her fancies. The tabla starts up, races after her, catches her. She signals to the sarangi to retreat, and the tabla brings her back to earth. Melody gives way to rhythm, and a new dialogue begins, between the pitter-patter of the tabla and her:

" 'Pitter-pitter.'

" 'No, no.'

" 'Patter-patter.'

" 'Not yet.'

" 'Patter-pitter, pitter-patter.'

" 'Leave be. I'm destined only for the king against the velvet bolster.'

"The king leaning against the velvet bolster hears her song—tremulous, joyous, tripping, beckoning, sweet, adoring. Men materialize from the nooks and crannies, for the song knows no walls and no bounda-ries—except the wall of blindness. She finishes, and the dreamers wake with '*Wahwah!*' on their lips. They make offerings of coins and notes. She sits panting. People around her repeat their favorite lyric, debating and interpreting it. She takes the man against the vel-vet bolster inside and serves him sherbet, cool and misty in a tall colored glass, and a thimble of a delicious liqueur of saffron and spices, pigeon blood and partridge blood. Later on, there are requests for more songs, more ragas. This request and that request and arguments about requests—each sighted man vying to have his song on her lips. All argument comes to an end as she waves her hand. Perhaps the song is an answer to a request, perhaps not. She is the mistress. She can sing what she likes."

I would be transported, imagining that Mr. Baqir went to Hira Mandi every evening—indeed, there were days when it seemed to me that the scent of jasmine or sweet peas emanated from his clothes—and imagining myself in Hira Mandi, roaming, listening, smoking, being serenaded by Noor Jehan, being served sherbet and liqueur by her.

But then Muhammad Bashir would say something like "There is no Hira Mandi on earth. That's our paradise. Hindus are not permitted there."

I had grown up hearing that Muslims were great sensualists, that they made the best cooks, the best butchers, and the best husbands, and that their holy book was full of sensual images. I had grown up hearing Urdu verses by Muslim poets, which extolled the joys of drink and love, of women's lips and hair, of moonlight and sunset. I even preferred my father's Muslim friends to his Hindu friends, because they radiated charm, warmth, and good manners, and were physical. They touched everyone and everything freely. I felt at one with them. Sometimes Muhammad Bashir, too, was persuaded that Hira Mandi was a real place, an earthly mirror of the pleasure garden in Paradise.

Then he couldn't understand why, if houris would receive him up there, their earthly sisters would spurn him. But Muhammad Bashir never discussed the question with Mr. Baqir, a fellow-Muslim, because any time Mr. Baqir was challenged or contradicted the cane in his hand would fidget, its rat-a-tat becoming faster, the swish of its swing shorter, as if he were in a rage at a particularly recalcitrant dog and were whacking it.

We would be lost in the thought of houris and singing girls, but then Mr. Baqir would rudely bring us back to the school—to the cane-bottomed chairs, the sluggish fan overhead, the indolent boy at the door. "The end of pleasure in Hira Mandi is ravaging disease," he would say. "Anywhere on the body, boils break out, the flesh burns, ear, nose, and chin get charred. They crumble and fall off like a burnt coal. Hira Mandi is littered with them, with charred fingers and toes, too, and other things of diseased men and women."

❦

ONE MORNING, Daddyji casually said to me while he was shaving, "Perhaps you can become a teacher at the Emerson Institute one day. You could even become its principal."

I was taken aback. It was one thing to go there because I had nothing better to do, quite another thing to think of making my life there. "It's a disgusting hole," I found myself saying. "They teach you dirty things there."

The even sound of Daddyji's safety razor against his cheek stopped. He hummed to himself and slowly shook his safety razor in the glass of water—the way he often did when he was thinking. "Disgusting hole!" he repeated, and he continued, "I didn't like the atmosphere of the place when I went there, but I had no idea that you felt so strongly against it. Would you like to stop going there?" It was quite common for him to reverse himself in this way at the first sign that we children weren't happy in something we were doing.

I found my cheeks getting prickly and hot. I feared he might find out the kind of things Mr. Baqir talked about, and take me out of the school just when I had begun to feel comfortable there, in a way I no longer did at home. At school, I felt I could look any way I wanted to. I could relax the muscles of my face, look as expressionless and stony as I liked. There was no one to watch and scrutinize. I quickly reversed myself. "It's not disgusting," I said. "I just mean it needs improvements."

"Maybe I can work for some improvements," he said.

After that, I would often ask Daddyji what he had done about the improvements. One evening, he came home from the office and told me, "I spoke to Sir Manohar Lal about you and the institute again, and he has agreed to make an additional forty-five-thousand-rupee grant to it. It's a single-time grant, and it is not much money, but it will enable your institute to add a wing to its building."

❦

ONE DAY, Mr. Khanna summoned me to his room. I wondered what I had done wrong. Had he somehow found out my secret—that Mr. Baqir's talk of Hira Mandi excited me, suffused me with longing even as it filled me with terror?

Mr. Khanna couldn't have been much older than Cousin Yog, who was about eighteen, but I dreamed of him as a giant with eyes the size of windows. The door of his room was open. I went in and sat down in a cane-bottomed chair placed across the table from him. I was exposed to the draft of his gaze and felt small and frightened. I arranged and rearranged my hands under the table and put an interested expression on my face.

"You've been at the Emerson Institute for some time now," he said. "How do you like it, my boy?"

Being called a boy made me feel, if possible, smaller still, and when I answered him my voice cracked even more than usual.

"I like it, sir."

"Do you like your teachers here? Are you learning something?"

I couldn't shake the feeling that we had an audience—that whatever I said would soon be all over the school. For outside there was the sound of someone pacing up and down the veranda, barefoot. Sometimes the footsteps sounded like those of Mr. Baqir, sometimes like those of Mr. Chander. It could have been just a ghost, for the sound was as light as an apparition walking to and fro on its feathered feet.

"I am learning, sir."

"I told your father I wasn't sure that it would be

helpful for you to come here. But he said you were determined. It's a long time since you attended school, isn't it, my boy?"

"Yes, sir. Over three years."

"How did you like Dadar School?"

"I was happy there, sir. But the Bombay climate didn't suit me, so I was sick a lot of the time."

"You were exposed, then, quite young, to what schools for the blind were like, and you still wanted to come to the Emerson Institute?"

"Well, sir, my brother and all my sisters go to school, and I admire my father, who is very well educated and has travelled a lot. He always wanted me to have the same education as my brother and sisters. He even tried to send me to Perkins, in America."

"Your father told me about that. Why didn't Perkins take you?"

"They said, sir, I was too young, and should know more about my country before coming there."

"That's true enough. Well, then, what have you been doing about it—what have you been learning about your country?"

My hands kept circling each other involuntarily under the table, as if I were washing something. "Until we came to Lahore, I had to stay at home, because there was no school for me to go to."

"But didn't you know that if you wanted to go to America you would need a lot of preparation?"

"But, as I said, sir, there was no school for me to go to."

"You could have been tutored at home."

"I was, in music."

"But why not in arithmetic, or English? What good would tuition in Indian music be to you at Perkins?"

"No one at home knew how to teach me—no one knew Braille."

"Teaching a blind child is not so very different from teaching a sighted child. Until I became principal here, I'd never known anyone who was blind. If each of your sisters had helped you an hour a day, you might have learned as much as you would have learned at school."

This was the first time that anyone had ever suggested such an idea, and I couldn't understand why my sisters hadn't thought of it. I couldn't find my voice. Finally, I was able to say, "I don't know why, sir. Perhaps everyone was too busy."

"Too busy to teach you? That's not my impression of your father—of your family."

"I can't think why else, then."

"Maybe they never stopped to consider your special problems."

"My father always said that I would one day go to America and learn everything there."

"But they took your going to America too much for granted. You may never get there. I don't mind telling you that you and your father have left everything to America, and used going there someday as an excuse for not facing up to things here. You've just believed that going there would solve everything for you. You have to prepare yourself here for many years before you can go to America. Even if you should get to America someday, who knows how much they could teach you by then?"

I told him about Daddyji's plan to take me to America in five years, after he retired. "My father says an education is a lifelong asset, like a house or a motorcar."

"So far, you have an education up to the third or fourth standard, which normal children finish by the time they're eight. You're twelve. When your father retires, you'll be seventeen or so. For a boy, seventeen is a big age. Boys of that age go and fight wars."

"I'm going to study in America no matter what."

"I know you and your father, and can sympathize with your ambitions, but I don't think the authorities in America will. Those who don't know you will consider you very foolish."

"I want an education so that I'll be normal—like everyone else."

"Whatever you do, you'll never convince people that you're normal. Anyway, supposing you do get to study in America, what would you like to do in life? Would you be interested in coming back to India and helping the blind people here?"

I knew I didn't want to become a music teacher, like the temperamental Masterji who had taught me in Rawalpindi. I knew I didn't want to teach in a school for the blind, like Mr. Baqir. I knew I didn't want to sit idle and live upstairs off the rent from the downstairs of our house, as Daddyji had sometimes suggested. But I didn't have the slighest idea what I wanted to do—what I could do. "If I could see, I would be a doctor, like my father."

"But you can't see. What else but teaching the blind is there for you to do?"

"What am I to do?" I cried, shivering under the cold draft of his gaze. I wanted to get out and run back to Mr. Baqir's class.

"Maybe I can help you," Mr. Khanna said, suddenly sounding friendly. "You spend two hours with Baqir Sahib, don't you? Say you come into my room instead for one of those hours. Would you like that, my boy?"

I wasn't sure, but I said, "Yes, sir." Then—feeling hopeful in a surge—"I'd like it very much, sir."

"Well, you do just that." For the first time, he fumbled for words. "Well, we'll see. You can go now."

❧

MR. KHANNA started taking me for an hour a day. I had hoped that he would teach me more arithmetic, for instance, but instead he whiled away the hour talking about the British suppression of India, about the bitter differences between Hindus and Muslims, about the lack of facilities for the blind in India. Once or twice a week, however, he did give me a few English words to memorize. Then, one day, he gave me some knitting needles and a ball of yarn, and said, "While we talk, you can knit. That way, you will know at least one handicraft, and knitting is one handicraft that won't ruin your fingers for reading Braille."

I protested. I associated the clicking sound of knitting needles and the bounce of a ball of yarn with Mamaji and my sisters, aunts, and cousin-sisters. I didn't like sitting across from his desk clicking my needles, feeling the ball of yarn dance in my lap. Every day, I decided to tell him right out that I wasn't going to knit anymore, but every day, in his presence, I was tongue-tied. For days, purposely, I would not hold the knitting needles the way he showed me, would drop stitches, and would get knots in the yarn.

One morning, as I walked to his room for my hour I kept repeating to myself, "I'm not going to knit, I'm not going to knit, I'm not going to knit," and the moment I walked into his room I blurted out, "I'm not going to knit."

"Oh, why not?" he asked, with some surprise. "People from good families knit."

"I'd rather cane chairs and weave than knit."

"Those are low-caste occupations."

I objected, I tried to argue, I sulked, but he kept me at knitting. I was careful to leave the knitting, like Mr. Baqir's girl talk, at school. I do remember, however, that I once asked Mr. Khanna to read me something in a book, and he said to me, cryptically, "I have not been able to overcome my dyslexia completely." (It was years before I learned what "dyslexia" meant.)

❦

ONE DAY, I picked up one of Sister Nimi's books from a table beside her pillow, where she kept them. Sister Nimi was always reading a "storybook." The storybook was small and compact compared with a clumsy Braille book, which, when it was open, was almost as large as a pillow and was heavy enough to tip a night table over. Also, Sister Nimi's book had a cloth cover, smooth and satiny, like Mamaji's sari, and

an irresistible smell of fresh ink and new paper. I took
it to Sister Nimi, my heart racing.

"What is it called?" I asked.

" 'Gone with the Wind.' "

I imagined that the book was about a small boy
who had been pulled aloft by a kite and carried all the
way to England, where he joined a Gurkha regiment
and fought Hitler, and that the regiment won and the
small boy was paraded all over London, riding on the
shoulders of Churchill.

"Read me a few sentences," I said.

"It's in English, crazy," she said.

My English was so meagre that I couldn't even
understand an occasional sentence that Daddyji read
from a newspaper to the family gathered around him
in the morning.

"Just a few sentences," I said. "You can translate
them for me."

"That'll take a lot of time," she said. "Besides, this
book is not for children."

That could mean only one thing, I decided—it was
not about war and Churchill but about girls and love.
My heart raced even faster. "Please," I begged.

"Don't be a nuisance," she said. "Be a good boy.
Go and put it back."

That night, when everybody was asleep, I propped
myself on my bed with "Gone with the Wind" in front
of my face and turned its pages fast, the way Sister
Nimi did, imagining a Hira Mandi in America, and
thought how strange it was that both Mamaji and
Daddyji, in their different ways, often tried to stop my
sisters from reading.

Whenever one of my sisters sat down with a book, Mamaji would say, "Put it away. You'll ruin your eyes. Then you'll have to wear spectacles, and no one will marry you. There are lots of girls who wear spectacles, and their prospective husbands are never told about it until the knot is tied. But you are your father's daughter. We can't play such tricks. Remember, Babuji took your Auntie Vimla out of college when it looked as if she would have to wear spectacles." And Daddyji often lectured my sisters about saving their eyes by not reading books with small print, and instructed them to develop good reading habits—to keep the book a foot away from the face, to read in the daylight as much as possible, to sit in such a way that the light fell on the book from the left, in order to avoid any shadow on the page. At night, the lights were turned out at exactly ten-thirty, regardless of how much Sister Nimi protested that she had a few more pages left to finish in her storybook. Here was I, who would have given anything to read—night or day—or, at least, have someone read aloud to me, but, try as I might, that day, the day after, or the day after that, whenever I asked anyone to read something aloud to me there was always some excuse. There wasn't the right light or the right chair, or it wasn't the right time. If the book wasn't in English, it was in Hindi or Urdu, and my sisters and brother, educated in Western schools, had trouble reading those scripts. I soon forgot that it was possible for someone to read aloud to me; after all, the idea was new, having just been planted by Mr. Khanna. I soon forgot even that there were people at home who could read aloud. I was lost. So it was that when I felt glimmerings of a new way of learning, that way was quickly closed.

Years later, I asked my sisters and brother why they hadn't helped to educate me. They gave different answers:

"We always thought you were going to be a music master."

"We took it for granted that you would live upstairs at 11 Temple Road and rent the downstairs and eat and drink and be happy."

"We thought educating you required special training, special equipment."

"Like Daddyji, we pinned all our hopes on Perkins."

"We all remembered what Shambu Pandit had said: 'There is not a shadow in the boy's horoscope. His blindness is only temporary.'"

XIII

PICTURES OF

MARRIAGE

MY SISTERS WERE GROWING BIG, AND EVEN though they protested, and said they would never get married, there was constant talk of finding husbands for them. I could no longer go up to them, squeeze their small breasts, and say "Ponk, ponk," pretending that they were Klaxons on a motorcar. Now even hugging made me shy.

I remember that when I had just gone blind Daddyji put me in his motorcar and we went for a long ride. Then we were in a completely new place. There some cousin-brothers dressed me in a long, heavy coat and tight shoes with curled-up toes. The coat and shoes had thin wire woven in all over and felt shiny. I picked at a bit of the wire on the sleeve. "Don't," they said.

"It's real gold." They put a silk turban on my head, and I pulled at the free end, which hung way down my back, like a veil. "Don't," they said. "The turban will come off."

They carried me into a strange room filled with familiar voices, and everyone clapped. "A perfect child bridegroom!" they cried. "You would think he was getting married instead of Cousin Dharam Bir."

"What's a child bridegroom?" I asked.

Everyone laughed.

We went outside. I was lifted onto a horse jingling with all sorts of things and was made to sit on something still and slippery in front of Cousin Dharam Bir. The horse snorted and shook as if it were getting ready to run.

"Get me down!" I cried.

Many hands reached up and patted me. Cousin Dharam Bir slipped my hand under a little hollow in front of me and told me to hold tight. He put his arms around me. Horns sounded, drums rolled, firecrackers went off, and the horse started walking slowly.

"Where are we going?" I asked.

"To the wedding, child bridegroom," the horse-wallah said. "To get a new lady relative for you. There will be a Brahman, a fire, incense, and ghi." He clicked his tongue and urged the horse forward.

"Will the new lady relative have a horse, too?" I asked, pulling at the coat of the horse with my free hand—the hair was matted but bouncy.

"Oh, no," the horsewallah said. "Only the bridegroom and the child bridegroom ride on the horse. She sits and weeps."

Cousin Dharam Bir said something over my head. The band got really loud. Then I was lifted off the horse, passed from hand to hand, and carried into another strange room. I felt restless and fidgety. A strange lady embraced me and said, "You think you're going to get married. Marriage is not for you." I slept.

When I awoke, my turban had fallen off, and unfamiliar hands were taking off my coat and shoes. Once more, I was in the motorcar. There were the familiar voices of Daddyji beside me in the driver's seat and Cousin Dharam Bir in the back. The voices were droning over the murmur of the motor. Someone rustled in the back seat. "Who's that?" I asked.

"She's your cousin-brother's wife, Satya," Daddyji said.

She leaned forward and put her arms around me. "Come to me," she said, her voice jingling like the things on the wedding horse. I climbed over the back of the front seat and sat with her and Cousin Dharam Bir.

When I was about eight, a cousin-sister from Mehta Gulli came to stay with us in Rawalpindi. She brought us the news that Daulat Ram Chachaji had broken off Cousin Sheila's engagement. "You all heard that Sheila was marrying a very rich boy," she said. "On the day of the engagement, he arrived with some coolies carrying his engagement present. And what a present it was! A teakwood dressing table complete with a stool, a mirror, a cosmetic box, and hairbrushes. The hairbrushes had silver backs with Sheila's initials on them. Daulat Ram Chachaji liked the dressing table, but later he began worrying about the young man's big girth.

He said, "A rich son-in-law is all well and good, but from the health point of view his being fat is a distinct handicap, especially since he could not be a hair taller than five feet four.' Subhadran Chachiji"—Cousin Sheila's mother—"who has recently become very plump herself, tried to minimize the issue. She said that to her the fellow looked just healthy. The two argued for some days. Then Daulat Ram Chachaji had a brilliant idea. He knew that every morning the young man walked past the door of the chemist's on the Mall Road. He posted himself there. When he caught sight of the young man coming along, he stepped on the weighing machine that, you remember, stands just outside the chemist's, and quickly inserted an anna. He was studying the card giving his weight and fortune when the young man came abreast. Before the fellow knew what was happening, Daulat Ram Chachaji had maneuvered him onto the weighing machine. And practically before the card dropped out of the slot Daulat Ram Chachaji had read the weight—fourteen stone. They looked at each other, and both knew that the engagement was off. The dressing table, hairbrushes and all, had to be returned. Sheila has now been engaged to a boy from a professional family, and that means no showy, extravagant presents but probably a healthy, long-lived husband."

A year or so later, when we went to Kashmir, we stayed with some relatives in Srinagar for a couple of days. For long stretches, Daddyji would disappear into the house across the road. "We don't see any more of you here than we did in Rawalpindi!" we children complained. "What's the point of being on a holiday in Kashmir?"

Daddyji wouldn't explain.

"It must be either a card game or a girl for Cousin Prakash," Sister Umi said. Prakash Anand was Dharam Bir's younger brother, and Daddyji's nephew. Since Daddyji was the most successful member of the family and was considered to have the best eye for feminine beauty, Prakash looked to Daddyji to help him find a wife.

Daddyji laughed, and admitted that he was indeed looking over a girl for Cousin Prakash. "She has large eyes and long, thick hair. Her height is good, and she has a very fair complexion. Her father assures me that she doesn't wear lipstick or fingernail polish. Her family is here from Lahore on holiday. She is affectionately called Rani."

Then, a few months later, when we were visiting Lahore, Cousin Prakash came to Daddyji while I was playing within earshot.

"She wears slacks!" he said.

"Who does?"

"Rani!"

"So? When? Where—on the Mall Road?"

"No, no, in her father's house. Sister Vidya went to visit, and Rani was sitting in the garden in slacks. That's worse than wearing rouge. She's too fashionable, too Westernized, to fit into our family pattern."

There was silence, and then Daddyji asked, "What would you like me to do?"

"Tell them that the engagement is off."

"It will be done."

For a long time, I thought about Rani's slacks and about Cousin Vidya. Daddyji used to say that he really admired Cousin Vidya for wearing homespun clothes and living simply on her small salary, and for being one of the first women in the Punjab to do an M.A. in economics and to make a career of teaching in a college—for living by her principles and being self-reliant. Yet it was clear to us children that while people respected her and made a fuss over her they also pitied her, because she had missed out on love and marriage.

"Why is Cousin Vidya a spinster?" I asked Mamaji one day.

"Why? No one would marry a girl with misshapen hands. Poor Vidya—her marriage train pulled out of the station before she was twelve, when she got the sickness in her wrists. After that, she never had a chance to wear good clothes, to have a man and a house, to bear children. Marriage was not in her karma. Her dharma was to live alone, wear spectacles, and strain her eyes at the books."

Cousin Vidya, when she spoke, had a way of pausing and breathing out hesitantly through her nose, doing a sort of reverse sniff. It made her sound very wise and thoughtful. Whenever she came to see us, I would try to copy the way she talked, with pauses and sniffs, and long after she had left, people would say to me, "Stop talking like Vidya." Without my knowing exactly why, people used to think there was a bond between her and me. I now asked Mamaji, "Will I end up a spinster?"

"Not a spinster—a bachelor," she said, without a moment's hesitation.

I remember that Sister Pom had a friend in Rawalpindi named Chinta. She was a year older than Sister Pom and, we thought, the loveliest of all her friends. Once, when I was about ten, Cousin Vidya came to stay with us. She saw Chinta, and the moment Chinta left she quizzed Sister Pom about her.

"She has been studying at Kinnaird College, in Lahore, and is the daughter of Uncle Tandon," Sister Pom said, and she explained that R. R. M. Tandon, divisional engineer of the railway, belonged to the small family of government officials in Rawalpindi.

Cousin Vidya suggested Chinta to Daddyji for her youngest brother, Dev. We children couldn't imagine how Cousin Dev could possibly do for Chinta. He was famous with us for lecturing, for scrimping, for joking. Bhua Parmeshwari Devi—his mother, and our paternal aunt—used to say that when he was eight years old he had climbed up onto a mantelpiece and started lecturing, and that he had never stopped. Whenever we met him, he sang the same film song, "I'm Off to Meet My Beloved." But none of us had the pluck to say anything against the match in front of Cousin Vidya.

"Whatever you say goes with me, Vidya," Daddyji said.

"Chinta's very fair, but she looks to me to be a little bit on the short side," Cousin Vidya said.

"I think she's my height," Sister Pom said.

Everybody in the room started debating about Chinta's height.

"If you can't tell, what difference does it make?" I asked.

"It makes a lot of difference. Be quiet," Mamaji said.

"Why don't we just ring her up and ask her how tall she is?" I asked.

"That would be very rude," Cousin Vidya said.

It was decided that Cousin Vidya must settle the question for herself, and Sister Pom was deputed to invite Chinta to the Rawal Club for tea. As had been arranged, Sister Pom, who was the tallest of my big sisters, took Chinta for a turn around the club gardens, and the rest of us sat with Cousin Vidya on the club veranda as she compared the heights of the two girls. Cousin Vidya was satisfied that Chinta was only two or three inches shorter than Sister Pom. In subsequent days, Cousin Vidya closely observed Chinta talking, eating, sewing, knitting, and studying, and satisfied herself that she had good eyes, that she did not secretly wear spectacles, and that she was not a "modern butterfly type" who would polish her nails, use rouge, or wear slacks. Finally, she told Daddyji to make the proposal, and she left, confident that Chinta's parents would say yes, even though they had not yet met Cousin Dev.

"We don't know the young man," Daddyji reported Uncle Tandon as saying. "We've never seen him. But if he's your nephew he must be a chip off the old block—isn't he?"

"How unfair!" Sister Umi said. "Because of you, Daddyji, Chinta's parents have said yes without even seeing Cousin Dev. But Chinta will not be marrying you—she'll be marrying Cousin Dev."

"Umi, your tongue will get us all into trouble," Mamaji said.

"You don't only marry a man, you marry into a family," Daddyji said. "In the West, things are done differently—there women work and earn and are independent. But we live in India."

I remember that Cousin Dev came to see Chinta,

and that Chinta's family and our family met at the Rawal Club for tiffin. As we were all sitting around, Chinta's younger sister Sheila said to me in a loud aside, "Why are our parents torturing poor, fair Chinta into marrying Blackie-Black? He's the color of an eggplant!" Cousin Dev was known to have a dark complexion. "Haven't there been enough unhappy marriages between Beauty and the Beast in the world already?" People often addressed me as if I were a lamppost, and told me things intended for someone else.

Auntie Tandon stirred her tea very loudly, but everybody had heard Sheila's remark.

Cousin Dev said good-humoredly, "Bridegrooms can be dark—Lord Krishna was dark. Only brides have to be fair and beautiful. Besides, what is there in color when I can recite Urdu verses and set water on fire with them?"

❧

ONE EVENING, in Lahore, as we were finishing our sweet at the dinner table, Mamaji said, "Thank God, Prakash is reëngaged and everything is settled between Dev and Chinta. Now let them get married, and be happy or sad in their own houses and not trouble your daddy." She was outspoken because Daddyji was away at a club.

"What would happen if Chinta was miserable with Cousin Dev?" Sister Umi asked rhetorically. "He's completely unsuitable for Chinta. Cousin Vidya has already let it be known that once Chinta gets married even her name will be changed—she'll be called Nishchint." Cousin Vidya objected to the name Chinta because it meant "worry;" Nishchint meant "without worry." "It's no wonder that when a daughter is born in our country the whole house becomes as silent as a mausoleum. How different it would be if we girls could work and be independent, find our own husbands without any dowry and without relatives getting into it. I think I'll go and live in the West."

"What nonsense you talk," Mamaji said.

"Umi, you'll have to live here, like the rest of us," Sister Pom said. "Wait till your turn comes. Then you'll sing a different raga."

"If I must live here, I'm never going to get married," Sister Umi said. "I'll have a boyfriend. I certainly won't come home crying for a dowry. If I ever did decide to get married, I'd just get married in the salwar and kemise I had on. If he didn't like that—didn't take me as I was—I would show him the door and say, 'Ta-ta, goodbye, nice to have known you.' "

"I'll never forget the four girls I saw starving at the annual fair while their brother gorged himself," Sister Nimi said. "I almost cry whenever I think of them. If parents didn't have to worry about dowries, maybe those girls would have been eating with their brother."

"I think the dowry system is detestable, just as you do, Nimi," Sister Pom said. "But some would starve anyway. You can't blame all that just on the dowry system and arranged marriages, because there still wouldn't be enough food to go around, and there would be just as many children dying from poverty."

"Yes, some must suffer and sacrifice," Mamaji said. "And it has to be women. It's in their nature. Otherwise, there's no happiness for anyone."

"But the suffering here is carried to such an extreme," Sister Nimi said. "It's all very well for us to talk like this, but we sisters haven't had to go hungry. Mamaji has never been beaten by Daddyji. If we were poor women, we would know what suffering and sacrifice really are—how deplorable the poverty is that forces mothers to take food out of their own daughters' mouths and give it to their sons, how deplorable the poverty is that drives husbands to beat their wives."

"But, Nimi, that's just the way of life in our crowded, poor country," Sister Pom said.

"I would like the man to suffer and sacrifice for me," Sister Umi said. "What happiness is there in suffering and sacrifice anyway?"

"The happiness in suffering and sacrifice is the same as the pleasure we get from giving without expecting anything in return," Sister Pom said. "We women may do all the suffering and sacrificing, but because of that we can also endure more."

"If that's marriage, Pom, I would rather go without, thank you very much," Sister Umi said.

"I think Umi is right," Sister Nimi said. "We shouldn't make our parents responsible for our marriage. That's where the trouble starts. The man says, 'If you don't give me a big dowry, I won't take your girl.' Then, when he gets her, he says, 'If she doesn't serve me hand and foot, I won't keep her.' The result: the parents suffer and sacrifice, the girl suffers and sacrifices, and what does the man do? Sits back and enjoys it all. This is fair? This is equality? This is freedom?"

"We don't have freedom and equality," Mamaji

said. "We have only responsibility. I was the oldest in my family, and I took care of my brothers and sisters, just as Pom takes care of you when I'm away. Responsibility was all I ever knew."

"For myself, I think that if girls found their own husbands, boyfriends, or whatever, it would be better all around," Sister Umi said.

"You should do what Mamaji and Daddyji tell you to do, or you'll be very unhappy," I said.

"Who asked you for your opinion, Mister?" Sister Umi said.

"Umi, I don't see how you could make a better choice than Mamaji and Daddyji can," Sister Pom said. "Their experience is so much greater than yours. I wouldn't even know where to begin."

Sister Umi persisted. "If the customs were changed, we would know where to begin," she said. She continued, half laughing, "Pom, you have to admit that this is a man's world, especially in our country. I don't know why that should be. I'm just as good as Om, Yog, or any of them."

"Are you prepared to go and work like a man?" Sister Pom asked. "Bob your hair, give up your sari, and start wearing those horrible practical clothes—horrible slacks—that you have to wear to work in factories in the West?"

"If all of us, men and women, worked, perhaps there wouldn't be so much poverty in our country," Sister Umi said, undaunted. "I am prepared to bob my hair, wear slacks, and work like any mister."

"But can you imagine what our society would really be like if all the women started leading independent lives?" Sister Pom asked. "Who would have children? Who would look after them?"

"I believe in Russia they manage," Sister Nimi said. "Children are just brought up on a collective."

"That will suit me fine," Sister Umi said. "Society is bound to change after our country becomes independent. Whether we like it or not, women will become less subservient to men, and more independent. There will be less useless misery in Indian homes. Whatever Pom's theories, people will change, and change of their own accord. I can hardly wait for that day to come."

"If I'd acted the way Umi talks, I would have said 'Ta-ta, goodbye' in the first few weeks of our marriage," Mamaji said. "Then none of you would have been here. I know of only two ways of pleasing a man: quiet suffering and sacrifice, and saying yes to his every yes, and no to his every no. If your daddy pulled me up, even if I was completely in the right I bit my tongue and said 'Just as you say.' If the sun was shining and your daddy said that it was a beautiful moonlit night, I said it was a beautiful moonlit night."

"It might have been just as well if you had walked out," Sister Umi said. "You might have been happier."

"The kind of happiness you talk about is not for us Indian women," Mamaji said. "I was brought up in the Indian way, and it is all that upbringing that has kept me going all these years. However our customs may be at fault, you girls will have to admit that ultimately our marriages work out very well."

❦

BEFORE WE MOVED to Lahore, Daddyji had gone to Mussoorie, a hill station in the United Provinces, without telling us why he was going out of the Punjab. Now, several months after he made that trip, he gathered us around him in the drawing room at 11 Temple Road while Mamaji mysteriously hurried Sister Pom upstairs. He started talking as if we were all very small and he were conducting one of our "dinner-table-school" discussions. He said that by right and tradition the oldest daughter had to be given in marriage first, and that the ripe age for marriage was nineteen. He said that when a girl approached that age her parents, who had to take the initiative, made many inquiries and followed many leads. They investigated each young man and his family background, his relatives, his friends, his classmates, because it was important to know what kind of family the girl would be marrying into, what kind of company she would be expected to keep. If the girl's parents decided that a particular young man was suitable, then his people also had to make their investigations, but, however favorable their findings, their decision was unpredictable, because good, well-settled boys were in great demand and could afford to be choosy. All this took a lot of time. "That's why I said nothing to you children about why I went to Mussoorie," he concluded. "I went to see a young man for Pom. She's already nineteen."

We were stunned. We have never really faced the idea that Sister Pom might get married and suddenly leave, I thought.

"We won't lose Pom, we'll get a new family member," Daddyji said, as if reading my thoughts.

Then all of us started talking at once. We wanted to know if Sister Pom had been told; if she'd agreed; whom she'd be marrying.

"Your mother has just taken Pom up to tell her," Daddyji said. "But she's a good girl. She will agree." He added, "The young man in question is twenty-eight years old. He's a dentist, and so has a profession."

"Did you get a dentist because Sister Pom has bad teeth?" Usha asked. Sister Pom had always been held up to us as an example of someone who, as a child, had spurned greens and had therefore grown up with a mouthful of poor teeth.

Daddyji laughed. "I confess I didn't think of anyone's teeth when I chose the young man in question."

"What is he like?" I asked. "What are we to call him?"

"He's a little bit on the short side, but he has a happy-go-lucky nature, like Nimi's. He doesn't drink, but, unfortunately, he does smoke. His father died at an early age of a heart attack, but he has a nice mother, who will not give Pom any trouble. It seems that everyone calls him Kakaji."

We all laughed. Kakaji, or "youngster," was what very small boys were called.

"That's what he must have been called when he was small, and the name stuck," Daddyji said.

In spite of myself, I pictured a boy smaller than I was and imagined him taking Sister Pom away, and then I imagined her having to keep his pocket money, to arrange his clothes in the cupboards, to comb his hair. My mouth felt dry.

"What will Kakaji call Sister Pom?" I asked.

"Pom, silly—what else?" Sister Umi said.

Mamaji and Sister Pom walked into the room. Daddyji made a place for Sister Pom next to him and said, "Now, now, now, no reason to cry. Is it to be yes?"

"Whatever you say," Sister Pom said in a small voice, between sobs.

"Pom, how can you say that? You've never seen him," Sister Umi said.

"Kakaji's uncle, Dr. Prakash Mehrotra, himself a dentist, has known our family from his student days in Lahore," Daddyji said. "As a student dentist, he used to be welcomed in Babuji's Shahalmi Gate house. He would come and go as he pleased. He has known for a long time what kind of people we are. He remembered seeing you, Pom, when we went to Mussoorie on holiday. He said yes immediately, and his approval seemed to be enough for Kakaji."

"You promised me you wouldn't cry again," Mamaji said to Sister Pom, patting her on the back, and then, to Daddyji, "She's agreed."

Daddyji said much else, sometimes talking just for the sake of talking, sometimes laughing at us because we were sniffling, and all the time trying to make us believe that this was a happy occasion. First, Sister Umi took issue with him: parents had no business arranging marriages; if she were Pom she would run away. Then Sister Nimi: all her life she had heard him say to us children, "Think for yourself—be independent," and here he was not allowing Pom to think for herself. Brother Om took Daddyji's part: girls who didn't get married became a burden on their parents, and Daddyji had four daughters to marry off, and would be retiring in a few years. Sisters Nimi and Umi retorted: they hadn't gone to college to get married off, to have some young man following them around like a leech. Daddyji just laughed. I thought he was so wise, and right.

"Go and bless your big sister," Mamaji said, pushing me in the direction of Sister Pom.

"I don't want to," I said. "I don't know him."

"What'll happen to Sister Pom's room?" Usha asked. She and Ashok didn't have rooms of their own. They slept in Mamaji's room.

"Pom's room will remain empty, so that any time she likes she can come and stay in her room with Kakaji," Daddyji said.

The thought that a man I never met would sleep in Pom's room with Sister Pom there made my heart race. A sob shook me. I ran outside.

❧

THE WHOLE HOUSE seemed to be in an uproar. Mamaji was shouting at Gian Chand, Gian Chand was shouting at the bearer, the bearer was shouting at the sweeper. There were the sounds of the kitchen fire being stoked, of the drain being washed out, of water running in bathrooms. From behind whichever door I passed came the rustle of saris, salwars, and kemises. The house smelled of fresh flowers, but it had a ghostly chill. I would climb to the landing of Sister Pom's room and thump down the stairs two at a time. Brother Om would shout up at me, "Stop it!" Sister Umi would shout down at me, "Don't you have anything better to do?" Sister Nimi would call to me from somewhere, "You're giving Pom a headache." I wouldn't heed any of them. As soon as I had thumped down, I would clatter to the top and thump my way down again.

Daddyji went past on the back veranda. "Who's coming with Kakaji?" I asked. Kakaji was in Lahore to buy some dental equipment, and in a few minutes he was expected for tea, to meet Sister Pom and the family.

"He's coming alone," Daddyji said, over his shoulder. "He's come from very far away." I had somehow imagined that Kakaji would come with at least as many people as we had in our family, because I had started thinking of the tea as a kind of cricket match—the elevens facing off.

I followed Daddyji into the drawing room. "Will he come alone for his wedding, too?"

"No. Then he'll come with the bridegroom's party."

We were joined by everyone except Mamaji and Sister Pom, who from the moment we got the news of Sister Pom's marriage had become inseparable.

Gian Chand came in, the tea things rattling on his tray.

Later, I couldn't remember exactly how Kakaji had arrived, but I remember noticing that his footfall was heavy, that his greeting was affectionate, and that his voice seemed to float up with laughter. I don't know what I'd expected, but I imagined that if I had been in his place I would have skulked in the *gulli,* and perhaps changed my mind and not entered at all.

"Better to have ventured and lost than never to have ventured at all," Daddyji was saying to Kakaji about life's battles.

"Yes, Daddyji, just so," he said, with a little laugh. I had never heard anybody outside our family call my father Daddyji. It sounded odd.

Sister Pom was sent for, and she came in with Mamaji. Her footsteps were shy, and the rustle of her sari around her feet was slow, as if she felt too conscious of the noise she was making just in walking. Daddyji made some complimentary remark about the silver border on her sari, and told her to sit next to Kakaji. Kakaji and Sister Pom exchanged a few words about a family group photograph on the mantelpiece, and about her studies. There was the clink of china as Sister Pom served Kakaji tea.

"Won't you have some tea yourself?" Kakaji asked Sister Pom.

Sister Pom's sari rustled over her shoulder as she turned to Daddyji.

"Kakaji, none of my children have ever tasted tea or coffee," Daddyji said. "We consider both to be bad habits. My children have been brought up on hot milk, and lately Pom has been taking a little ghi in her milk at bedtime, for health reasons."

We all protested at Daddyji's broadcasting family matters.

Kakaji tactfully turned the conversation to a visit to Mussoorie that our family was planning.

Mamaji offered him onion, potato, and cauliflower pakoras. He accepted, remarking how hot and crisp they were.

"Where will Sister Pom live?" Usha asked.

"In the summer, my practice is in Mussoorie," Kakaji said, "but in the winter it's in Dehra Dun."

It struck me for the first time that after Sister Pom got married people we didn't know, people she didn't know, would become more important to her than we were.

❦

KAKAJI HAD LEFT without formally committing himself. Then, four days later, when we were all sitting in the drawing room, a servant brought a letter to Mamaji. She told us that it was from Kakaji's mother, and that it asked if Sister Pom might be engaged to Kakaji. "She even wants to know if Pom can be married in April or May," Mamaji said excitedly. "How propitious! That'll be the fifth wedding in the family in those two months." Cousins Prakash and Dev, Cousin Pushpa (Bhaji Ganga Ram's adopted daughter), and Auntie Vimla were all due to be married in Lahore then.

"You still have time to change your mind," Daddyji said to Sister Pom. "What do you really think of him?"

Sister Pom wouldn't say anything.

"How do you expect her to know what her mind is when all that the two talked about was a picture and her bachelor's exam in May?" Sister Umi demanded. "Could she have fallen in love already?"

"Love, Umi, means something very different from 'falling in love,' " Daddyji said. "It's not an act but a lifelong process. The best we can do as Pom's parents is to give her love every opportunity to grow."

"But doesn't your 'every opportunity' include knowing the person better than over a cup of tea, or whatever?" Sister Umi persisted.

"Yes, of course it does. But what we are discussing here is a simple matter of choice—not love," Daddyji said. "To know a person, to love a person, takes years of living together."

"Do you mean, then, that knowing a person and loving a person are the same thing?" Sister Umi asked.

"Not quite, but understanding and respect are essential to love, and that cannot come from talking together, even over a period of days or months. That can come only in good time, through years of experience. It is only when Pom and Kakaji learn to consider each other's problems as one and the same that they will find love."

"But, Daddyji, look at the risk you're taking, the risk you're making Pom take," Sister Nimi said.

"We are trying to minimize the risk as much as we can by finding Pom a family that is like ours," Daddyji said. "Kakaji is a dentist, I am a doctor. His life and way of thinking will be similar to mine. We are from the same caste, and Kakaji's family originally came from the Punjab. They eat meat and eggs, and they take religion in their stride, and don't pray every day and go to temples, like Brahmans. Kakaji knows how I walk into a club and how I am greeted there. The atmosphere in Pom's new home will be very much the same as the atmosphere here. Now, if I were to give Pom in marriage to a Brahman he'd expect Pom to live as he did. That would really be gambling."

"Then what you're doing is perpetuating the caste system," Sister Nimi said. She was the political rebel in the family. "You seem to presuppose that a Kshatriya should marry only a Kshatriya, that a Brahman should marry only a Brahman. I would just as soon marry a shopkeeper from the Bania caste or an Untouchable, and help to break down caste barriers."

"That day might come," Daddyji said. "But you will admit, Nimi, that by doing that you'd be increasing the odds."

"But for a cause I believe in," Sister Nimi said.

"Yes, but that's a whole other issue," Daddyji said.

"Daddyji, you say that understanding and respect are necessary for love," Sister Umi said. "I don't see why you would respect a person more because you lived with him and shared his problems."

"In our society, we think of understanding and respect as coming only through sacrifice," Daddyji said.

"Then you're advocating the subservience of women," Sister Nimi said, "because it's not Kakaji who will be expected to sacrifice—it's Pom. That's not fair."

"And why do you think that Pom will learn to respect Kakaji because she sacrifices for him?" Sister Umi said, pressing her point.

"No, Umi, it is the other way around," Daddyji said. "It is Kakaji who will respect Pom because she sacrifices for him."

"But that doesn't mean that Pom will respect Kakaji," Sister Umi persisted.

"But if Kakaji is moved by Pom's sacrifices he will

show more consideration for her. He will grow to love her. I know in my own case I was moved to the depths to see Shanti suffer so because she was so ill-prepared to be my wife. It took me long enough—too long, I believe—to reach that understanding, perhaps because I had broken away from the old traditions and had given in to Western influences."

"So you admit that Pom will have to suffer for years," Sister Umi said.

"Perhaps," Daddyji said. "But all that time she will be striving for ultimate happiness and love. Those are precious gifts that can only be cultivated in time."

"You haven't told us what this ultimate happiness is," Sister Umi said. "I don't really understand it."

"It is a uniting of ideals and purposes, and a merging of them. This is the tradition of our society, and it is the means we have adopted to make our marriages successful and beautiful. It works because we believe in the goodness of the individuals going into the marriage and rely on the strength of the sacred bond."

"But my ideal is to be independent," Sister Nimi said. "As you say, 'Think for yourself.' "

"But often you have to choose among ideals," Daddyji said. "You may have to choose between being independent and being married."

"But aren't you struck by the fact that all the suffering is going to be on Pom's part? Shouldn't Kakaji be required to sacrifice for their happiness, too?" Sister Nimi said, reverting to the old theme.

"There has to be a start," Daddyji said. "Remember, in our tradition it's her life that is joined with his; it is she who will forsake her past to build a new future with him. If both Pom and Kakaji were to be obstinate, were to compete with each other about who would sacrifice first, who would sacrifice more, what hope would there be of their ever getting on together, of their ever finding love?"

"Daddyji, you're evading the issue," Sister Nimi said. "Why shouldn't he take the initiative in this business of sacrifice?"

"He would perhaps be expected to if Pom were working, too, as in the West, and, though married, leading a whole different life from his. I suppose more than this I really can't say, and there may be some injustice in our system, at that. In the West, they go in for romantic love, which is unknown among us. I'm not sure that that method works any better than our method does."

Then Daddyji said to Sister Pom, "I have done my best. Even after you marry Kakaji, my responsibility for you will not be over. I will always be there in the background if you should need me."

"I respect your judgment, Daddyji," Sister Pom said obediently. "I'll do what you say."

❦

MAMAJI CONSULTED Shambu Pandit. He compared the horoscopes of Sister Pom and Kakaji and set the date of the marriage for the eleventh of May—the year was 1946—between the wedding of Cousin Pushpa and the wedding of Auntie Vimla. "That's just three days after she finishes her B.A. finals!" we cried. "When will she study? You are sacrificing her education to some silly superstition."

But Shambu Pandit would not be budged from the date. "I am only going by the horoscopes of the couple," he said. "You might as well protest to the stars."

We appealed to Daddyji, but he said that he didn't want to interfere, because such matters were up to Mamaji. That was as much as to say that Shambu Pandit's date was a settled thing.

I recall that at about that time there was an engagement ceremony. We all—Daddyji, Mamaji, Sister Pom, many of our Mehta and Mehra relatives— sat cross-legged on the floor of the front veranda around Shambu Pandit. He recited the Gayatri Mantra, the simple prayer he used to tell us to say before we went to sleep, and made a thank offering of incense and ghi to a fire in a brazier, much as Mamaji did—behind Daddyji's back—when one of us was going on a trip or had recovered from a bout of illness. Servants passed around a platter heaped up with crumbly sweet balls. I heard Kakaji's sister, Billo, saying something to Sister Pom; she had just come from Dehra Dun bearing a sari, a veil, and the engagement ring for Sister Pom, after Romesh Chachaji, one of Daddyji's brothers, had gone to Dehra Dun bearing some money, a silver platter and silver bowls, and sweetmeats for Kakaji. It was the first time that I was able to think of Kakaji both as a remote and frightening dentist who was going to take Sister Pom away and as someone ordinary like us, who had his own family. At some point, Mamaji prodded me, and I scooted forward, crab fashion, to embrace

Sister Pom. I felt her hand on my neck. It had something cold and metallic on it, which sent a shiver
through me. I realized that she was wearing her
engagement ring, and that until then Mamaji was the
only one in our family who had worn a ring.

In the evening, the women relatives closeted
themselves in the drawing room with Sister Pom for
the engagement singsong. I crouched outside with my
ear to the door. The door pulsated with the beat of a
barrel drum. The pulse in my forehead throbbed in
sympathy with the beat as I caught snatches of songs
about bedsheets and henna, along with explosions of
laughter, the songs themselves rising and falling like
the cooing of the doves that nested under the eaves of
the veranda. I thought that a couple of years earlier I
would have been playing somewhere outside on such
an occasion, without knowing what I was missing, or
been in the drawing room clapping and singing, but
now I was crouching by the door like a thief, and was
feeling ashamed even as I was captivated.

❦

THE WHOLE HOUSE, it seemed, was turned into
women's quarters, dividing the family right down the
middle, like a parting in one's hair. The sisters preferred to keep their own company or to be with Mamaji.
They spoke in whispers and gestures, or in what seemed
like riddles. The dowry had to contain twenty-one saris
and twenty-one blouses, because twenty-one was a lucky
number; at the same time, it had to contain twelve
gold bangles, twelve bedsheets, and twelve table-

cloths, because the quantity "a dozen" sounded more impressive than the number "twenty-one." The dowry had to be lavish—in fact, had to include everything to start a home with except a house and a motorcar— because it might determine the kind of offers the other sisters received; at the same time, it had to be modest, because the dowries of the other sisters would be expected to match it. Since nothing ready-made was available, two tailors were engaged. They sat on the front veranda from morning to night cutting and stitching. Friends and relatives came at all hours with something they had knitted, sewn, or embroidered. Jewellers, cloth merchants, or quilt-makers called daily with samples or for fittings. Once, I found Mamaji bargaining with the family jeweller for some gold bangles and gold chains. "Why haggle, Mistress?" the jeweller asked sombrely. "They're your daughter's inheritance, her *istri dhan.* As our great lawgiver Manu has said, 'Ornaments which may have been worn by women during their husbands' lifetime, their heirs shall not divide; those who divide them become outcasts.' "

For weeks, it seemed, the wedding preparations blew through the house like a storm, displacing the furniture and familiar objects. I could scarcely move about the house without falling over trunks, crates, bedrolls, bundles, packages, baskets, sacks piled up everywhere helter-skelter. I sometimes felt that I was not in my own house but in a crowded, chaotic train compartment. ("Her marriage train pulled out of the station.") When I hurt myself, tradesmen and deliverymen would click their tongues with pity, ask questions about my eyes, and then bless themselves for having been spared my misfortune.

No one in the family seemed to have much time for me, so I spent most of my days and evenings standing around in the kitchen talking to the servants. They were a constant source of news and opinion: Kakaji was coming in a train with fifty male relatives and friends. He could have brought four times as many, but since the Second World War and the Great Bengal Famine the government had restricted the bridegroom's party to a mere fifty. The Big Sahib could easily circumvent the restriction, but he was a government servant, correct to a fault. Just as well, because this way the Big Sahib would be able to save money. The bridegroom's relatives and friends would pay their train fare, of course, but their maintenance and feasting during the wedding would be on the shoulders of the bride's father, and weddings, even in these hard times, lasted at least three days. And to feed fifty healthy men was no joke. Only healthy men came, because the bride had to be protected and guarded—the world was full of bride thieves. Besides, the train journey back to Dehra Dun was more than two hundred miles long, and the route was infested with dacoits—tribes of gypsy thieves who roamed the countryside and who were known to jump on trains in the middle of nowhere and abscond with the dowry and God knew what else. Police? They were good in their way, but they couldn't take the place of blood relatives.

In Mehta Gulli, people were arranging to double up to make room for Kakaji and his force. They were engaging barbers to come and shave the men and cut their hair, washermen to wash and starch their clothes, boy servants to keep their boots polished, cooks to produce Dehra Dun-type fare at a moment's notice, a twenty-piece band to accompany them for the wedding. Tradesmen had already delivered countless tins of ghi and bags of flour. It had definitely been decided to have five weddings, one after another: first Cousin Prakash was going to get married, and then Cousin Dev (although their weddings were to take place in the brides' houses, there were to be many related festivities in Mehta Gulli); then Cousin Pushpa; then Sister Pom; then Auntie Vimla. For days, there would be only wedding preparations at 11 Temple Road, in Mehta Gulli, and at 16 Mozang Road. The whole city was in turmoil.

❧

IT WAS THE MORNING of Sister Pom's wedding. Nearly two hundred of our own relatives and friends who lived at a distance had already arrived, and practically every spare inch of floor in Mehta Gulli and at 16 Mozang Road and in our house was taken up with cots and bedding. The train with Kakaji and the bridegroom's party was due in a few minutes, and many of our male relatives had driven off to the station to receive them. Daddyji and Brother Om and I could not go: we had to wait and meet them in the evening at the *milni,* the formal meeting ceremony. All day, servants ran in from Mehta Gulli with snatches of news: Kakaji and the bridegroom's party had arrived at dawn. They looked bright but tired. Three of them were having a haircut. Kakaji had finished his breakfast, and two barbers were vying for the honor of shaving him. Some of the party had gone out for sightseeing. They had finished their lunch, and the cooks were gratified because they had eaten heartily. Kakaji was having his tiffin and had eaten three pastries.

I ran around the house like a top, touching everything, greeting everyone, trying to find out what was happening. In the back part of the inner courtyard, where the confectioners were stoking makeshift fires, patting dough for *puris,* stirring something in vats, I breathed lungfuls to savor the cooking. They must be getting ready to make a *puri* a second, I thought, and I remembered the Great Bengal Famine. In the center of the inner courtyard, I paced around the *vedi*—four banana trunks firmly set in the ground under a canopy, and forming a biggish square. I helped hang branches and twigs with lots of leaves between them, to form arches, and, on the arches, fruits, flowers, balloons, and strings of lights. I barged into Mamaji's bedroom, and was chased out, because Sister Pom was being dressed there. I wandered into the drawing room, where women were looking over the articles of the dowry, counting them, exclaiming at them. They, too, shooed me away. I went upstairs and downstairs, into the garden and out to the gate, feeling the strings of lights on walls and bushes, eaves and pillars, to see if the bulbs were warm, only to have other people shout at me that I would electrocute myself, that I was spoiling the decorations, that I should get out of the way, that I should go and sit down quietly somewhere. But there was no place to sit. The whole house was restless and hot. Everywhere were rotating table fans and whirring

Pom's wedding, Lahore, 1946.
Left to right: Pushpa (an aunt), Sureshta, Nishchint, Umi,
Pom, Usha, Nimi, Bawa (a cousin), Satta, Vimla.

ceiling fans, and smells of frying, incense, marigolds, powder, kohl, pulling me this way and that way.

A band of trumpets, clarinets, drums, and cymbals struck up from the direction of Mehta Gulli, with a Noor Jehan song from "Zeenat"—"Dance, O Stars, Dance!" "Kakaji is about to get on his mare and ride over here!" Cousin Yog shouted, rushing in. "All his party is gathering behind his mare. They will be here for the *milni* any moment." Suddenly, the steps of our front veranda were thronged with our close male relatives. Sister Umi shouted from somewhere for the servants to bring out the buckets of flower petals and to put more bottles of lemonade on ice.

I slipped into my long coat woven all over with gold wire and ran into Daddyji's room with my turban, gathered, pleated, and starched like a long rope. Daddyji was busy tying his own turban, and I danced around him, impatient for him to tie mine, the long coat rustling behind me like a sari.

"I don't think I've ever worn a long coat before," I said.

"You did, too, at Dharam Bir's marriage," Daddyji said from over my head as he wound my turban.

I followed Daddyji, touching his coat, out to the veranda. The band music became a little distant, as if the band had turned back.

"What's happening? What's happening?" I asked.

"They have probably taken a detour to show off Kakaji," Brother Om said, coming up behind me.

Daddyji and Shambu Pandit arranged and rearranged us, sometimes by age, it seemed, and other

times by our relationship to Sister Pom, and gave each
of us a garland and an odd number of rupees for the
milni. The band moved closer and closer, each medley
sounding a little louder than the last, as if Kakaji and
his people were now coming very slowly along our *gulli*.

I collared my younger cousin Ravi. "What's happening?"

"It's a young mare he's riding," he whispered, tit-
tering. "But he has a sword at his side. I think he used
the sword to get Cousin Pom to say yes."

We both laughed, and felt very smug and knowing.

Kakaji's mare halted right in front of the gate,
between us and the wedding guests. The band stopped
playing, and the absence of its sound made the place
seem quieter than it really was. Shambu Pandit recited
Vedic hymns in a soft, melancholy voice. Then he called
Daddyji to step forward for his *milni* and embrace
Kakaji's uncle, Dr. Prakash Mehrotra. I wondered what
it was like to be fatherless, like Kakaji, and to have an
uncle stand in the father's place. Then Shambu Pandit
called Brother Om and me to meet our counterparts.
Brother Om met one of Kakaji's relatives, but Kakaji
had no younger brother or stand-in for my *milni,* so I
thrust the money back into my pocket and let the garland drop from my hand.

Brother Om and I helped Kakaji to alight from the
mare, and we were surrounded by girls, who teased
Kakaji and threw buckets of flower petals at him.

We all escorted Kakaji to the steps of the veranda,
where my big sisters and Mamaji were now gathered.

Servants ran around spraying everybody with scented water. Shambu Pandit announced, "Time for *jaimala, jaimala.*"

Sister Pom, who was dressed in a filmy dark-red wedding sari with a rich gold border and gold decorations wonderful to touch, shyly garlanded Kakaji. (Shambu Pandit later insisted that, technically, until the *jaimala*—or victory garland—Sister Pom had the choice of refusing Kakaji.)

The band struck up again, and Brother Om and I led Kakaji to Daddyji's room. He joked with us about the elaborate arrangements and about his warm woollen coat with its closed collar. Sisters Nimi and Umi came in and took him upstairs to the terraced roof for his dinner. Servants ran to and fro serving the band in the *gulli.* Our *chachas* led the bridegroom's party upstairs for its dinner.

As I moved about, everyone commented on my glittering coat, and I felt at once like a wedding ornament with legs on and like a walking coat watched by all eyes. Wedding guests were milling about as they waited for the bridegroom's party and the band to finish eating, so that they could eat. At one point, I carried some bottles of lemonade to the band. The drummer proudly showed me the heavy ornamental buckle on his uniform belt, while clucking to his neighbors, "What a pity the little fellow cannot see all these beautiful clothes and lights."

"I've been looking for you," Brother Om shouted over the din, coming up to me. "Daddyji wants you upstairs for a photograph."

❦

THE FEASTING was over by midnight. The band
and most of the wedding guests had eaten and left.
Only close relatives and a few of the bridegroom's party
remained. I remember that there was much confusion
as people went around the house calling, *"Vedi! Vedi!*
. . . Time for the ancient vows from the Vedas. . . .
Come to the *vedi."* Ravi thought that it was a perfect
wedding joke—my nickname was Vedi, and I had been
named after the Vedas. I wasn't so sure: the journey to
the *vedi* seemed long and treacherous—a mere pair of
slacks or a deficiency of an inch or two in height could
end it. I thought that I'd never felt so blind.

We sat on the ground around the *vedi,* I next to
Sister Nimi. Now and then, she whispered to me.
"Kakaji and Pom are sitting on low stools next to
Mamaji and Daddyji. . . . Shambu Pandit is sitting
under the *vedi.* . . . Shambu Pandit is lighting the
sacred fire."

There was the sizzle and aroma of ghi and sandalwood chips in the fire. A huge platter of perfumed salts
was passed around, and I took a fistful.

"A pinch will do," Sister Nimi whispered.

I aimed my fistful at the fire. It crackled, and wafted
scented smoke.

Shambu Pandit chanted the Vedic hymns over the
fire, and then he asked Kakaji and Sister Pom to repeat
the marriage vows after him, and paused now and then
to translate the Sanskrit into Punjabi, so that they would
know what they were promising: to live according to

the Hindu creed, to be true to each other, to share each other's burdens, to propagate the race, to beget sons, to remain rock firm and faithful. Kakaji and Sister Pom sounded odd as a duet—like a parrot and a sparrow chirping alternately in the distance, he sharp, she barely audible in the still night.

"Now they are putting their feet side by side on a stone. . . . Now they are circling the *vedi*. . . . That's one time around. . . . That's two. . . . That's . . ."

"Become thou my partner," Shambu Pandit sang out.

"Become thou my partner," Kakaji repeated after him.

"As thou hast paced all the seven steps with me."

"As thou hast paced all the seven steps with me."

"Apart from thee I cannot live."

"Apart from thee I cannot live."

"Apart from me do thou not live."

"Apart from me do thou not live."

"We shall share alike all goods and power combined."

"We shall share alike all goods and power combined."

"Over my house you shall bear full sway."

"Over my house you shall bear full sway."

Shambu Pandit said the benediction. Then all around there were the sounds of people standing up and stretching. Before I knew what was happening, Kakaji and Sister Pom had left the courtyard.

"Why is he taking her away?" I asked. "Where are they going?"

"He's telling her that he's the master, and that she

now belongs to him," Mamaji said, through tears.

"He's just taking her to Mehta Gulli for a few minutes," Daddyji said, "to show her off to the members of his party who were not invited to the *vedi*. She'll be back. There are still two more days of feasting."

❦

ALL OF SISTER POM'S dowry and belongings were packed up and sent ahead to the station. With many of our close relatives, we silently escorted Sister Pom and Kakaji out of the house, out of the gate, to a borrowed motorcar waiting in the *gulli,* our footfalls like little firecrackers going off haphazardly one after another. Still silent, we showered Kakaji and Sister Pom with handfuls of flower petals, and the motorcar pulled away. Kakaji's party quickly got into other borrowed motorcars, which then formed a line behind Kakaji's. Daddyji, Mamaji, and we children followed in our motorcar. It was almost the first time since the start of the wedding that our family had been alone, and our motorcar seemed suddenly very roomy. There was no need to lean forward or to sit with our shoulders firmly against the back of the seat. Yet the motorcar felt extremely hot, as if the *vedi* fire itself were burning at our feet. I wiped streams of sweat off my face and struck out at a fly buzzing around my ear.

"All our loving relatives must be discussing the dowry and its worth in real gold," Sister Umi said, breaking the silence. "After a wedding like that for your first daughter, Daddyji, you'll never have to worry about proposals for any of us."

"What'll happen to Sister Pom now?" I asked.

"She'll go to her new home in Dehra Dun, to more receptions and feasts," Daddyji said.

"I'm giving everyone fair warning that I'm going to get married in a chapel, as Westerners do, with no crowds of loving relatives around," Sister Umi said.

I waited for Mamaji to contradict or to argue, but she said nothing.

The station was noisy and hot. Daddyji hailed a coolie, took down his badge number, and told him to take the luggage to the coupé near the end of the train. I didn't know what a coupé was, and I remember that Daddyji later took me inside and showed it to me: a small, two-berth compartment with a little fan in the ceiling and blocks of ice placed in the corners to keep it cool. The berths were covered with grainy leather and smelled of saddle soap and polish. The coolie brought in Kakaji's luggage and wanted to undo the bedrolls. There wasn't room enough, and Daddyji and I got out onto the platform. Abruptly, Daddyji's hand wasn't there to guide me. I couldn't take a step forward, for fear of the gap between the track and the train, or take a step back, for fear of the handcarts that were clattering past at great speed. Though I stood on a crowded platform, I felt alone. I remembered the frightening train that had taken me far, far away and deposited me in a strange city, in a strange school, among terrifying strangers, and remembered how, no matter how much I cried and begged, there had been no way to get back home.

The guard trilled his whistle very near my ear. Train-compartment doors slammed shut. The engine let out a deafening burst of steam. The train screeched, jolted, and began pulling out, shaking the platform with a roar.

"Goodbye! Ta-ta!" I cried, with the full force of my lungs, but I didn't hear my voice.

As if in a dream, I heard Daddyji's voice, through the clatter and thunder, the sounds of finality itself: "Kakaji, take the journey gently. . . . She's very innocent."

"Yes, Dad—" The rest of the word was lost in the forlorn, retreating clackety-clack.

XIV

INTIMATIONS OF

PARTITION

B OYS," MR. BAQIR SAID ONE DAY AT THE
Emerson Institute, "tell me, what is the Hindu
religion? Do Hindus have one god, like Allah?
Do they have a prophet, like Muhammad? Do
they have a holy book, like the Koran? No,
there are as many gods, as many prophets, as
many holy books as there are Hindus, which is to say"—
he tapped his cane on the table, rat-a-tat—"Hindus
have no gods [rat-a-tat], no prophets [rat-a-tat-tat], no
holy books. They will worship anything—a cow, a
monkey, a stone. It's not a religion at all but a jungle
of lowly superstitions. Hindus have always eaten grass
and have always been meek and servile, while we Muslims have always eaten beef and have always been bold
and domineering."

I didn't like Mr. Baqir's attacks on Hindus, and several times I cried out "I don't eat grass!" and "I may not eat beef, but I eat mutton!" But then I stopped interrupting, because I didn't like the nervous sound of his cane; it was kept wet and supple, and any time we interrupted Mr. Baqir—or neglected to warn him of the approaching steps of Mr. Khanna—he was not above using it on us. He aimed his blows at our hands or arms. He did not have very good aim, and more often than not he missed. When he did score a hit, however, the skin would sting and burn, and lately he had redoubled the caning of us Hindu boys. His blows did make me feel meek and servile.

"We Muslims are natural rulers," he was saying. "We ruled the Hindus for hundreds of years under the Moguls. We have always trounced them, and we will trounce them now. But beware of the cunning, caste-ridden lot [rat-a-tat-tat-*tat*-tat-tat]. Beware of the infidel. He skulks like a jackal, but he's a dog with a fox's nature."

Mr. Baqir shouted at the fanwallah "A little harder, boy!" and puffed at his *biri* while apparently listening for the faster movement of the fan. The fanwallah pulled and relaxed the rope a bit more quickly, but he barely managed to stir the smoke-filled air.

"Semual, how many Muslims originally came here as conquerors?" Mr. Baqir asked.

Semual didn't know the answer, and Mr. Baqir went around the room. None of us had any idea.

"A handful," Mr. Baqir announced triumphantly. "But today there are ninety million Muslims in India—almost one-fourth of the population. And it has all been done by conversion—by the strength of the meat-eating faith of Allah. The jackals, the dogs!" Mr. Baqir's cane fidgeted in his hand as he inveighed against the Hindus.

❧

I FIRST MET Sohan at a family gathering in Mehta Gulli. He was five years older than I was, and was an acquaintance of one of my cousin-brothers. He had a meek voice, like a boy servant, but his words were bold. Every time someone spoke to him in English, he replied in Punjabi. Yet he announced that he was studying medicine at Sir Ganga Ram Medical College.

"You must know English, if you're studying medicine," Sister Umi said.

"It's not that I don't know the foreigners' tongue," Sohan said. "I choose to speak my mother tongue."

"Let's hear what your English sounds like!" someone cried.

"You'll have to speak good English to practice medicine," someone else said.

Sohan was not bothered. He asked Sister Umi where she went to school.

She told him.

"You go to a convent school," he said in Punjabi, slowly, as if he were explaining a difficult point to her. "You are taught there always to speak in English. They tell you practice makes perfect, or some such thing. Yet when you come to your mother, who doesn't know English, and she asks you in Punjabi 'Would you like some milk?' you say in English 'Yes, please.' " He said

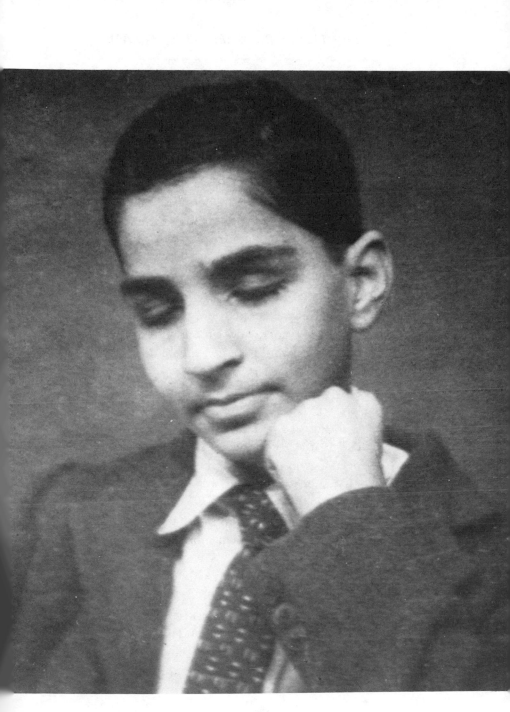

Ved, Lahore, 1946.

"Yes, please" in English, but in a shaky voice, like someone who had not had much practice. "You're ashamed to ask your own mother for some milk in your mother tongue, because you've been taught in your convent school that Punjabi is only good for servants and mothers. Well, the English are going to leave soon, and we'll be independent. Then you'll have to give your mother and your mother tongue the respect that is due them."

There was a little uncertain laughter around the room. Like Daddyji, I admired everything British, but still I liked what Sohan was saying. I felt that in our house Punjabi was spoken only as a concession to Mamaji, the servants, and me. I didn't like that. I wished everyone would speak Punjabi all the time, so that I could follow everything.

"When you become a doctor, I'd like to see you write prescriptions in Punjabi and consult with other doctors in Punjabi," Sister Umi said.

"The British brought us science and medicine," Cousin Leil, who planned to become a doctor herself, said. "It's only natural that we should use English for science and medicine."

"It is unnatural," Sohan said flatly. "We are Indians. We should use our own mother tongue for everything."

"Where are we going to find the vocabulary?" Cousin Leil asked.

"We can create it from Sanskrit," Sohan said.

"I would like to know which language your medical books, your lectures, your laboratories are in," Cousin Surinder said. He was planning to go to America right after he finished school, without going to college in India at all—something that was unheard of.

Sohan admitted that the books, the lectures, the laboratories were all in English, but said that English would be thrown out with the British.

As we were leaving, Sohan took me aside and asked, "You go to a blind school?"

"To the Emerson Institute for the Blind."

"Where do you live?"

"At 11 Temple Road."

"What time do you get home?"

"About five. Why?"

"Because I would like to take you to a special secret place."

The mention of a secret place made me think that maybe Sohan intended to take me to Hira Mandi—maybe introduce me to Noor Jehan. But then I wasn't sure. Still, I wondered why he'd singled me out—my sisters' and older brother's Lahore friends generally tended to ignore me.

"Would you like to come to the secret place with me?" Sohan asked.

I nodded.

"I'll call for you at six tomorrow."

❦

I WAITED for Sohan, my hands and face washed after the bicycle ride home from school, my hair combed, my shirt tucked into my knickers. He arrived at six, just as he had said he would, and we walked along Temple Road and the Mall Road. He didn't talk about

Noor Jehan or anything like that—only about the Hindus and the Muslims. "Hindus and Muslims are both Indians," he said at one point. "We used to pull together like brothers. It's the British who have set us against each other. Don't you agree?"

I was happy that he wanted my opinion, even though I was confused about what to say. "The British are nice, but they kick their peons in the chest," I finally replied.

"Then they are not nice."

I waited for him to bring up the subject of Hira Mandi, but he didn't.

After a few minutes, he abruptly turned off the road, saying, "Here we are at the parade ground." All around me were the voices of grown-up boys, as at a hockey or a cricket match.

Someone blew a police whistle, and we all formed lines for exercises, I next to Sohan, who showed me what to do. One exercise involved squatting and standing up; another, slapping our thighs, then jumping up and clapping our hands in the air; a third, running around the parade ground. I was unfamiliar with the exercises, and it seemed I was either squatting too early or standing too late, or clapping when I should have been hitting my thighs, or being a nuisance for Sohan—I ran holding his hand. But no one seemed to mind.

When we were tired and breathless, we all sat cross-legged on the grass and were addressed in Punjabi by a man. His voice came out of two loudspeakers mounted at opposite ends of the parade ground, one sounding a

little after the other; this created the odd sensation of
two men talking.

"The day of independence is fast approaching," the
echoing voices said. "Boys, unite! Boys, show your elders
the way! Gandhiji is teaching you passivity and nonviolence. His message is as old as Buddha, and as outdated as Buddha. We became slaves of the British
because we were passive and nonviolent. Before that,
we became slaves of the Moguls because we were passive and nonviolent. We will again become slaves of
the Muslims—the new Moguls—if we remain passive
and nonviolent. The British are strong because they
fight. The Muslims are strong because *they* fight. There
are only four million Sikhs in the world, but they are
strong because *they* fight. We Hindus have been weak
for a thousand years or more because we listened to
Buddha. Throw off your slavery. Defend your motherland. Even as I speak"—the echo repeated, "Even as
I speak"—"there are Indians right outside this parade
ground who want to kill the mother cow, who want to
take the precious gift of the gods and make a meal of
it. A meal of the mother cow! For pleasure! Hare Ram!
Hare Ram! God save us from such Muslim breath. Rise,
Hindus, rise! Guard your supply of milk and yogurt.
Guard your supply of dung and fuel. Guard your mother
cow, whose look is love."

I hated milk and yogurt. Gian Chand cooked on
coals, not on horrible dung. Mamaji kept a buffalo
instead of a cow, because she considered buffalo milk
more healthful. But, sitting in the open air, shoulder
to shoulder with the other boys, listening to the echo-

ing words, I felt like embracing a cow and calling her Mother.

The resounding man concluded by leading us in some Hindi prayers and hymns.

For a time, we all continued to sit on the grass.

"The Muslim League is out to ruin our independence," a boy behind me was saying. "Muslims are the Fifth Column in our midst. They will snatch the best part of India from us. They will snatch Lahore from us. They are fanatics. They will kill us, and grind our remains to fertilize the grass for fattening their cows, so that they will have more beef to eat." I thought in a rush of Mr. Baqir. I was sure that his breath was freighted with beef, that his cane smelled of it. I forgot how much, until then, I had always liked Muslims. "Unless we smash the Muslim League, and keep India one, a dark age will come. Divided, we won't be able to govern ourselves. Some other power will come and enslave us after the British leave."

As we were walking home, Sohan explained to me that we had attended a meeting of the Rashtriya Swayamsevak Sangh (National Voluntary Service Society), or R.S.S., whose purpose was to stop the Muslims from spoiling our independence. "When the day of independence comes," he said, "thanks to the R.S.S. our motherland—united and one—will start on a path of glory equal to that of England, America, or Germany."

After that, at school, I scarcely listened to what Mr. Baqir said, or heard what raga Mr. Chander beat his drum to. I only waited for the evening, for Sohan and the R.S.S. meeting.

"Maybe, when India gets independence, we could get a place together," Sohan once said to me as we were walking to the R.S.S. meeting. "I could practice medicine, and you could go into politics."

"I'm not educated," I said.

"In politics, you don't need education. You just need courage, like a good soldier."

I felt that I was in the middle of a war—a twelve-year-old soldier who had been called to battle for my religion and my country.

XV

JANUARY, 1947

O NE EVENING, A SERVANT ANNOUNCED, "Jhanda is on the veranda, but he doesn't have his fruit basket."

We were all surprised. We associated Jhanda only with the morning routine. As far back as we could remember, when we were in Lahore there was hardly a morning without Jhanda's call coming along the *gulli* promptly at ten: "Mangoes! Pomegranates! Litchis!"—or whatever fruit was in season. Mamaji and whichever aunties were around would rush out and select the choice fruit for the day. Sometimes, around the time of Muslim festivals, Jhanda would distribute free fruit to us children. But aside from his Muslim religion we knew nothing about him—where he lived, how many children he had, where he got his fruit. He was mostly a voice—nasal, kindly, and pitched just high enough to be heard above the street noises. "Mangoes! Pomegranates! Litchis!"

Now Mamaji went out onto the veranda, and we followed.

"Mistress, I have come under the cover of darkness," Jhanda said, falling at her feet. "I can no longer come to Hindu houses, or I and my loved ones will be denied burial rights."

Mamaji scolded him for thinking bad thoughts.

"It's the bad times, Mistress," he said.

Mamaji started wheezing, as she always did when she was upset. She walked with him to the gate as if he were a guest or a family member. We heard Jhanda's call no more.

❧

GIAN CHAND BROUGHT me home from school on the bicycle, as usual, and as I was running through the drawing room to go and wash, Daddyji called to me. He patted a seat next to him on the sofa and told me to sit down. "We are living through dangerous times," he said. "Things are happening that I wouldn't have thought possible, and there are things I have to do that I wouldn't have imagined. I'm afraid you'll have to stop going to school."

I burst out crying.

Daddyji made me drink some water, and continued, "It's not safe for you to go there, it's not safe for Gian Chand to take you there. The bicycle route goes through many Muslim sections. Last night, I heard in the club that a Hindu was stabbed to death in the Sheranwala Gate. That couldn't be more than a furlong from your school."

I thought of the stories about Hira Mandi, of my music lessons, of my knitting classes. I thought of the cleft in the tree, and its scent of moss and resin. I heard in my head the slow, rocking sound of the fan in Mr. Baqir's class. The school suddenly seemed like a calming, restful, intimate place. I pleaded and argued, but Daddyji's mind was made up, and I couldn't change it.

So it was that after barely eight months of going to school I again had nothing to do. Being idle was even harder now than it had been before: I felt I had nowhere to go, no life of my own, nothing to look forward to but months, perhaps years, of sitting at home, and I was growing older every day—I was two months short of turning thirteen.

❦

ONE EVENING, Daddyji came home from the office and said to me, "I've been procrastinating for days about telling you something, but I am afraid you won't be able to go to the R.S.S. meetings anymore."

"What!" I cried. "How can you say that!"

"The organization has got a very bad name for being anti-British and anti-Muslim. Children of government servants are not allowed to join political organizations. There are many Muslims in my department—my superior is a Muslim, my subordinates are Muslims. They have their knives out for me, and they have begun talking about my son's being in the R.S.S."

Again I pleaded and argued, but I had to stop going to the R.S.S. meetings.

A few days later, I happened to tell Daddyji as he was sitting and reading his newspaper that Sohan and I were planning a picnic on the bank of the Ravi River when the weather got warm.

He put down the paper. "I meant to tell you—Sohan's activities have been noted in the papers," he said. "I don't think you should see him anymore. The Muslim League leaders have lists of all houses with R.S.S. connections, and those houses are slated for mob action."

"But he's the only sighted friend I've ever had!" I cried. "He's like a brother to me. We've been planning this picnic for days."

We talked for a long time, but I was not allowed to see Sohan, and he was sent word accordingly.

XVI

FEBRUARY

I N THE EVENING, WHEN WE WERE SITTING
down to dinner or getting ready to go to bed,
we started hearing from the direction of Mozang Chowk the roar of a mob fading in and
out, like a bad signal on a radio. Sometimes
the roar would become a chant, and we could
make out slogans: "Death to Hindustan!" and "Death
to the infidels!" and "Allah is great!" and "Long live
Pakistan!" Then we knew that the mob had formed
itself into a procession and was getting ready to march.
If the sound of the slogans became more distinct, we
knew that the procession was moving toward our *gulli,*
and we would silently rush around, turning off the
outdoor light, bolting doors and windows, drawing
curtains. Then we would try to go about our business
as usual. Our actions were instinctive, but they were
also deliberate and methodical, as if we had never known
any other conditions.

Sometimes during the day, we would get reports of anti-Muslim mobs and anti-Muslim slogans, but the only mobs and slogans we ourselves ever heard were anti-Hindu; that was because we and our relatives all lived in a very well-to-do, essentially Hindu area that was in the shadow of Mozang Chowk and Mozang Bazaar, an extremely poor Muslim area. The government daily gave assurances that law and order would be maintained at all costs, and, indeed, at first we rarely heard of a mob's burning down a house or looting it. Then it turned out that government assurances were beside the point as far as we Hindus were concerned, because most of the Lahore police were Muslim, and Muslim policemen would fire shots or use tear gas or make a charge with sticks to disperse Hindu mobs but not Muslim mobs, regardless of government orders. When they were called on to disperse a Muslim mob, they would arrest a few leaders, drive them to a spot a few miles away, and release them. By prior understanding, Muslim League cars would be waiting at the spot to drive the leaders back. Soon the Muslim mob would be remobilized and regrouped. We heard reports that on occasion police even joined the mobs. As Hindus, we felt helpless, and every day we heard stories that one Muslim mob had abducted a Hindu woman and another Muslim mob had killed a Hindu child. Then Daddyji received assurances from several Muslim neighbors in our *gulli* that they would take responsibility for our safety and our property. In the daytime, we believed them, but at night, with the sounds of the Muslim mobs in our ears, we were not so sure.

One night when Daddyji was late in getting home,

we heard a procession shouting Muslim slogans headed toward our *gulli*. We shut up the house, as usual, and ran upstairs to the terraced roof. We stood by the brick parapet overlooking the *gulli,* holding hands. As it happened, the procession passed our *gulli* by, and Daddyji got home safely, but, standing under the open sky, we all realized how defenseless we were, and that we would have to take steps to protect ourselves.

❦

IN OUR HOUSE and in Mehta Gulli, and also at 16 Mozang Road, we all liked the British, but we put the blame for what was happening on their perfidy. We imagined that for centuries India had been a tolerant place, where Muslims and Hindus lived together like brothers, toiling together shoulder to shoulder in the fields and celebrating each other's religious feasts. Then the British rulers had come and, we thought, had estranged us brothers by a policy of divide and rule. We all liked to quote one statement, made by Mountstuart Elphinstone, who had served as lieutenant-governor of Bombay and twice refused the offer of the governor-generalship of India: *"Divide et impera* was the old Roman motto and it should be ours." This statement seemed especially significant to us because it had been made by a very famous Englishman. We imagined that Elphinstone's colleagues and successors had kept to the course he recommended. Because the British blamed the Muslims for the mutiny of 1857, they favored Hindus over Muslims for nearly the first fifty years of the raj, by giving them special opportunities for education and for gaining government positions. When, as a result, Hindus—always enterprising and adaptable anyhow—prospered, and left Muslims politically and economically far behind, the British reversed themselves and favored Muslims over Hindus; they portrayed "domineering Hindus" as a threat to the Muslim minority and Muslim culture, and encouraged the Muslims to found the Muslim League, in 1906, to advance Muslim interests. We recalled that at about the same time one particular Britisher, W. A. J. Archbold, who was the principal of the Muhammadan Anglo-Oriental College at Aligarh, urged a few suggestible Muslims to ask for a separate electorate to elect their own representatives to the government. When the Muslims did ask this, the government hailed the request as typical of Muslim sentiment; and in 1909, when it introduced reforms permitting Indians to elect members to the Central Legislative Council, which was to advise the Viceroy, it granted separate electorates to Muslims, thus drawing an overt political distinction between them and Hindus for the first time. Meanwhile, the Muhammadan College at Aligarh was becoming a training ground for Muslim leaders who preached the doctrine of a separate Muslim identity. We felt that the British could not have asked for better spokesmen for their divide-and-rule policy, since these Muslim leaders spoke the tongue of their people, had their people's ear, and could make the appeal in the name of Muhammadanism. In due course, these leaders, propelled by personal ambition as much as anything, became luminaries in the affairs of the Muslim League and helped to make it into an important divisive force in Indian politics. To us, nothing seemed to prove more conclusively that the Muslims were pawns of the British than the fact that the most important leader of the Muslim League was the England-returned barrister Muhammad Ali Jinnah, who, in defiance of his religion, avoided the mosque on Friday, the Muslim special day of prayer; hardly ever read the Koran; married outside his religion; ate pork, and drank and smoked—in fact, lived mainly on whiskey and cigarettes. Still, many Muslims did not join the Muslim League but remained loyal to the Indian National Congress, which had as its aim one secular, self-governing India. The more the Congress grew in strength under the Hindu leadership of Gandhiji and Pandit Nehru, however, the more the Muslim League, under Jinnah—as it happened, a Congress turncoat—presented the Congress as an instrument of Hindu domination. The British were then able to pose as the guardians of the rights of the Muslim minority. Thus, even as the Congress was becoming a symbol of the whole country's nonviolent struggle against the British the Muslim League was making inroads into the ranks of the Congress. During the Second World War, Congress leaders were out of commission, because they were— as had so often been the case—in jail on charges of sedition, while the Muslim League leaders were, as always, free; they used the opportunity to promote the demand for a separate state of Pakistan, or "Land of the Pure." The Congress leaders came out of jail at the end of the war to find, to their great surprise, that Jinnah and the Muslim League had acquired considerable influence with the Muslim masses, and that the demand for a separate Muslim state had gathered momentum—that India might finally win its struggle against the British, but only at the expense of partitioning the country. Jinnah was vague about how Pakistan was to be brought into existence—understandably, we thought, because the Muslims, while they did number ninety million to a total of two hundred and fifty-five million Hindus, and did have a substantial majority in the two big provinces of the Punjab and Bengal, were dispersed throughout the country, so that wherever there was a Muslim majority there was also a Hindu minority. We daily heard that Gandhiji and Pandit Nehru had once more appealed to Jinnah and the Muslim League to form a coalition government with them, in preparation for independence, but Jinnah, aware of his newfound power, had rejected their appeals. Indeed, he declared that reason was getting nowhere with the Congress and the British, that direct action alone could convince them that India's Muslims would fight to win Pakistan. He wanted Bengal and the Punjab, at the very least, for his Muslim nation. Accordingly, he had proclaimed August 16, 1946, Direct Action Day in Calcutta, the capital of Bengal, as a sort of dress rehearsal for what he was prepared to do in Lahore, in Rawalpindi, and elsewhere. We were shocked to hear that on the appointed day Calcutta Muslims had emerged from their slums howling slogans and wielding clubs and knives, and had rampaged through the streets in a religious frenzy, killing or forcibly converting Hindu men and boys, abducting and raping Hindu women, and looting Hindu houses and setting fire to them. The Bengal premier, Huseyn Shaheed

Suhrawardy, was Muslim and led a Muslim League government, and he had given the police the day off. We heard that many policemen, anxious to save their own skins, did not reappear on the streets for several days. We heard that in the space of seventy-two hours of direct action five thousand people were killed and twenty thousand injured in Calcutta. (Most of them were Hindus, but some Muslims were killed, too.) We heard that a hundred thousand people were left homeless. Daddyji felt that the "Great Killing" was an epidemic, and that it was only a matter of time before it would spread to the Punjab. Many of us in the Mehta and Mehra families wanted Hindus to retaliate in kind. Instead, we heard that Gandhiji had started a campaign of nonviolence, which alone, he felt, could check the violence. Then we were surer than ever that Gandhiji and the Congress were playing into the hands of Jinnah and the Muslim League.

❦

DAULAT RAM CHACHAJI arrived when we were in the middle of dinner. "I've sold my house," he announced, even before he sat down.

We all cried at once, "Oh, no!"

"A non-relative in Mehta Gulli!"

"Where will you all go?"

"We'll rent a house somewhere nearby," Daulat Ram Chachaji said, and he recited an Urdu verse:

This house is neither yours nor mine.
In the end, only birds will live in it.

He drew up a chair and said to Daddyji, "Brother, I advise you to do the same. In these times, it's best to have money in hand."

We were even more appalled. The idea of moving out of our house only a few months after settling into it!

"The house is my castle," Daddyji said. "Here I am the master of my fate and the captain of my soul, Daulat Ram. I have my friends and relatives all around me. My clubs are hardly a mile away, and when I walk in, a dozen people call to me, 'Doctor Sahib! . . . Doctor Sahib!' I feel that with my own house I'm somebody in a city to which you and I came as poor village boys to study—a city that is known throughout the country as 'the Paris of India.' "

After Daulat Ram Chachaji left, we all made fun of his idea. But Mamaji said, in the quiet, tentative way she often adopted when she thought she was saying something unpopular and would have to do a quick reversal, "Daulat Ram is very shrewd. Among the Mehtas, he's the only one with a head for money."

"You're a fine one, Shanti," Daddyji said. "Just this morning, you were telling me that the house had been standing here for twenty years and we'd scarcely lived in it. And didn't you say the other day that now that we have finally paid off all our house debts you feel like a queen?"

❦

DADDYJI CAME home from the office and said, "Believe it or not, just as I was turning in at our gate, who

303

should stop me but Sheikh Sahib." Sheikh Nur Elahi lived in our *gulli,* right opposite us. "He made me an offer of a lakh of rupees for our house. I had no idea the house was worth that much—especially not in these times, when the prices of Hindu property are falling. In fact, if the Muslims succeed in chasing out us Hindus, as they think they will, Sheikh Sahib stands to get our house free. He could just move in and occupy it."

"Why does he want our house?" I asked. "He has such a big house of his own."

"He says he wants it for one of his sons," Daddyji said.

That evening, Daddyji said as he got up from the dinner table, "I am going over to 16 Mozang Road to talk to Babuji."

I was taken aback. Daddyji hardly ever sought out the company of Babuji, our maternal grandfather. The two men disagreed about almost everything. "I've never heard Babuji so much as sing or hum a note," Daddyji had once told me. "He has never taken part in any sports or games, he's never joined any club. His main relaxation is walking, and whenever he goes anywhere on vacation he finds a friend or relative to stay with instead of staying independently, as we would."

I now asked Daddyji why he was going to Babuji.

"Just like that," he said cryptically, and with uncharacteristic haste.

"Can I come, too?" I asked.

"Yes," he said immediately. In contrast to Mamaji, who often sent me out of the room when she was about to have a talk with an older person, Daddyji often let me sit with him, because he said listening was a good education for me.

We walked out of our *gulli,* crossed Temple Road, went along it, and turned the corner into Mozang Road—a familiar stretch of a couple of hundred yards.

As usual, Babuji was sitting at the near end of the veranda, in his favorite chair. I had sometimes surreptitiously sat in it when he was out for a walk, and I had been surprised that Babuji, who was a small man, should have such a big chair. It was wide and deep, with a caned bottom and a slanting caned back, and it always felt cool and shiny, as if it were constantly kept dusted. Folded under the arms were wooden slabs that could swing out to form a leg rest. On one side of the chair was a folding table, always heaped with newspapers, pads, letters, penholders, and nibs; on the other was a brass spittoon.

"Daulat Ram has sold his house," Daddyji said as we pulled up a couple of wicker chairs next to Babuji. I upset Babuji's walking stick, which had been leaning against his chair, but I quickly picked it up and restored it to its place. "Daulat Ram says that in these times it's best to have money in hand," Daddyji went on.

"What a foolish fellow!" Babuji said.

"He's telling me to do the same," Daddyji said. "As it happens, Sheikh Nur Elahi has just made me an offer of a lakh of rupees for my house. I'm thinking about it seriously." I was astonished to hear him say that, but then I thought that perhaps he was just trying to get a reaction from Babuji.

"What a foolish idea!" Babuji exclaimed, hawking and spitting. "Where will you all go? Where will you live? You'll never get another house like yours, in such a good locality, again. A man without a house in old age—what is he?"

"But, Babuji, a lakh of rupees!" Daddyji said. "How many of us have ever seen such a sum? Besides, there is no telling what violence lies ahead in Lahore. The Muslim League has given a warning by its Direct Action Day in Calcutta."

"Amolak Ram," Babuji said, "Muslims, Hindus, and Sikhs are always quarrelling. It's the terrible, quarrelsome Indian character. But that doesn't mean that Jinnah can get Pakistan. He bears full responsibility for what happened on Direct Action Day."

"But, Babuji, without the British to keep order we might start fighting among ourselves and nothing would remain—houses or property."

"Amolak Ram, Hindus and Muslims have lived together for hundreds of years."

"Babuji, that was before the British policy of divide and rule, before the emergence of nationalism in the world. Also, Muslims have the makings of fanatics. Their faith says that non-Muslims are all *kafirs,* infidels."

"Amolak Ram, I have known Muslims all my life. They are not fanatics. Only their leaders are fanatics."

"Babuji, the leaders wouldn't stay leaders unless they could get the masses to follow."

"No, Amolak Ram, the leaders speak only for themselves. They are greedy idiots, they're greedy for power. And they're preaching idiocy to the Calcutta and Lahore masses." Babuji hawked and spat. "A few Muslim-hooligan leaders in Lahore are telling perfectly

law-abiding, good people, 'Take all the Hindu women
you want, and there will be no punishment.' Can any
society be run like that? Has any society ever func-
tioned like that?"

"Babuji, you are remembering the way Lahore was,
and forgetting what it has become."

"But could the good, sensible Lahoris have changed
since January? Could Lahore have become a different
place in a few weeks? I have never lived anywhere but
in Lahore, and I am seventy-five. Believe me, I know
my Lahoris."

"Babuji, you don't understand the fanaticism of
aroused illiterate Muslim masses. War against the
Hindus is being presented to them as war against the
kafirs—as a jihad, or holy war. I've heard the mullahs
shouting, 'Butcher Hindus like your goats! For each
Hindu goat you butcher, you will be rewarded with a
houri in Heaven!' I am afraid that once the butchery
really begins we Hindus—passive, philosophical people that we are—will run like chickens with a fox loose
in their coop. When that happens, Hindus and Sikhs
in other parts of India may get aroused—whether it's
in their character or not, and no matter what Gandhiji
tells them—and may retaliate, and more Muslims will
hit out against us Hindus here."

"What nonsense the mullahs talk! What idiocy!"

Daddyji said abruptly, as if something had just
occurred to him, "Babuji, in this house there are at
least ten women, and Sureshta is pregnant." Auntie
Sureshta was married to Uncle Lakshman Das, the
younger of Mamaji's two brothers. "You're just a stone's
throw from Mozang Chowk, which is now teeming

with Muslim hotheads. Shouldn't we take some measures for the women's safety in case of an emergency?"

Babuji didn't say anything for a time. He hawked and he spat, and then he said firmly, "Amolak Ram, the women here are my responsibility."

"I didn't mean to deny that."

"Then leave their safety to me, and let me look after them in my own way."

"I have nothing more to say," Daddyji said.

Babuji tapped his walking stick impatiently on the floor of the veranda, and Daddyji said something about the late hour, and we took our leave.

"I feel that I have listened to Babuji long enough," Daddyji said as we were walking home. "I respect him, but he's so ill prepared. Did you understand everything?"

I hesitated.

"What didn't you understand?" he pressed.

"Houris," I said awkwardly. I wasn't sure if houris were Muslim fairies or girls in Hira Mandi.

"Houris are voluptuously beautiful women who are found in Muslim Heaven," he said, in a straightforward way. "Muslims believe that on doomsday only men will arise—mortal women have no place in either their Heaven or their Hell. They are like dust. On doomsday, the men's good deeds will be counted, and each man will be presented with houris accordingly." He recited in beautiful Urdu a letter of condolence that the poet Galib wrote to a friend when the friend's mistress, Chhunna Jan, had died: "A wise man once advised me to eat, drink, and be merry; I repeat the same advice to you—forget Chhunna Jan and find a Munna Jan.

Doubtless, on doomsday, our good deeds will be counted; in spite of being a sinner, I have some good deeds to my credit and am certain of getting at least one houri, if not two. Still, I am appalled at the thought that forever thereafter I will be bound down to the same palace in Heaven, under the same shady tree, and to the same one or two houris. What boredom!" Daddyji laughed. "What a letter of condolence! What imagination poets have!"

I felt light-headed, and found myself thinking, in spite of everything, that it would be nice to be a Muslim and a poet.

※

"FOR SOME TIME, I have been worrying about what we would do in case of a mob attack," Daddyji said, coming home one evening. "We can't run to Mehta Gulli or to 16 Mozang Road, because that would involve crossing Temple Road and walking in full sight of the Muslims in Mozang Chowk. Earlier today, I talked to Dr. Mathura Das. He has a plan: that in case of emergency we should take shelter in his house." Dr. Mathura Das lived just behind us in a compound as deep as our entire *gulli,* so its entrance was on Temple Road.

"Since we can't go out on Temple Road, how will we get there?" I asked. "There's no way to scale the wall between our houses." The side wall of Dr. Mathura Das's compound formed the back walls of all the houses on our side of the *gulli.*

"Dr. Mathura Das is proposing that each of us neighbors install a heavy iron door in our back wall for escape. He has already worked out a system for communicating with torches from our roofs."

We all talked at once. I asked what would stop the mob from following us to Dr. Mathura Das's house.

Daddyji explained that the existence of the iron doors was going to be kept secret, that the doors would be painted to look like part of the walls, and that once we got on Dr. Mathura Das's side we would lock them.

"The women and children could all be in a room inside Dr. Mathura Das's house while we men took positions on the roof," Daddyji said. "There would be a lot of us up there, and we could make a good showing."

We objected that we didn't want to abandon our house—that we couldn't possibly flee, since we couldn't choose what to take and what to leave behind. My big sisters said they would prefer to stay in our house and fight the mob with Daddyji and Brother Om, instead of running like thieves to Dr. Mathura Das's house and being closeted with young children and old ladies. "It's a terrible plan," Sister Umi said. "Only someone who failed to get a degree could have thought it up." Dr. Mathura Das was famous throughout the country for his "ten-minute cataract operations" for the poor, but behind his back the neighbors always made fun of the fact that he had never properly qualified as a doctor and technically had no business calling himself one.

Daddyji ticked off Sister Umi for being a gossip, and explained that the iron-door plan alone offered a quick and safe escape from our house and our *gulli*. "It's true that going to Dr. Mathura Das's may mean abandoning our home to the rampaging mob," Daddyji said. "But the times have changed, and what is at stake now may be not property but life."

"Whatever you say," Mamaji said.

We children, however, were not persuaded until that night, when we again heard the mob. The roar sounded now near, now distant, now near again, like the roar of a hungry tiger pacing to and fro. We tried to guess from the sound which direction the animal might jump from. At any moment, we feared, it might lunge into our *gulli*. We sat in the darkened, shut-up house mesmerized and paralyzed.

THREE DAYS AFTER the government banned all R.S.S. meetings, I was awakened by a soft knock on the door of my room.

"Who is it?"

"Sohan."

I cautiously opened the door for him. "I'm not supposed to see you."

"I know," he said. "I came in around the back, through the servants' entrance. I don't think anyone saw me."

"What is happening to the R.S.S.?" I asked excitedly.

"Wait a minute, boy. Keep a cool head. It's not like you to be so jumpy." But what he said then made me more jumpy. "I'm convinced that the Muslim League has a plan for the destruction of the Hindus in Lahore, and it is going to put the plan into action any day now, with the blessing of the authorities. Mayor Mian Amir-ud-Din has a big cache of firearms in his house, and, like a good Muslim, he's giving them free to Muslim League hooligans."

"What are we Hindus going to do, Sohan?"

"The question is: What *can* we Hindus do? After the Direct Action Day in Calcutta, I told our R.S.S. leaders, 'The Muslim League has sounded the bugle. We should arm ourselves.' They heard me out, but they did nothing about it. In spite of what they claim, they go on believing in the nonviolent methods of Gandhiji and Pandit Nehru. I have thought all along that Gandhiji and Pandit Nehru are outdated, that they are too idealistic to cope with these Muslim League hooligans."

I tried to take the other side. "But Gandhiji and Pandit Nehru say that they have all but driven out the British with nonviolence, and if they can succeed against the powerful British they can surely succeed against the weaker Muslims."

"Their methods were good for the struggle against the British, but they are no good for the struggle against the Muslims and the Muslim League," Sohan said. "Besides, it's not Gandhiji's nonviolence that has all but driven out the British—it's the decency of the British themselves." It was the first time I had ever heard Sohan say anything nice about the British, and I was interested. "When Gandhiji fasted in jail, for instance, if it had been the Germans or the Japanese in charge they would have let him starve to death. Most likely, they wouldn't have put him or any other leaders in jail in the first place—they would have just shot them dead, right at the beginning, before they had built up any political following. Instead, the British gave our leaders plenty of ink and paper in jail to write tracts against them."

"But you said that the British were cunning. Look at their divide-and-rule policy."

"They were cunning and decent at the same time."

Sohan had a copy of the *Tribune*, the Punjab English-language daily, with him, and he told me that on the front page was a statement by Gandhiji exhorting Hindu and Sikh women to prefer suicide to rape or abduction, and all Hindus and Sikhs to prefer death to forcible conversion to Muhammadanism. "Oh, these religious men! Why do they get mixed up in politics?" Sohan said, with exasperation.

"Explain! Explain!"

"Gandhiji is like Buddha. Both of them speak to two parts of the Hindu nature that I think will be the end of our country—the passive, philosophical part and the individualistic, noncoöperative part. You can't get Hindus to fight, and you can't get two Hindus to agree or coöperate on anything. How can such passive, non-coöperative people run a country? Nonviolence and noncoöperation—prayer and strikes and fasts—may be all very well for a resistance movement, but they won't do for governing. We Hindus have to change if we are to survive and rule India—the only language a Muslim understands is that of a knife and a grenade."

"Do you know what you're saying, Sohan? You're talking like a wild fellow."

"I know. But it's only the truth."

Like my family, I could no more bring myself to turn against Buddha and Gandhiji than I could face thinking that we all might die in one fateful moment.

Yet I realized that in dismissing them—and Pandit Nehru as well—Sohan was only voicing the secret feelings of us all. I felt that he had the makings of a great leader. I recalled that whenever he spoke at R.S.S. meetings he would make us feel that we alone were strong, that we alone could stop the Muslim League. We would feel like rushing out of the parade ground there and then and battling Muslim League hooligans. We would feel that if the authorities or the Congress leaders tried to stop us we could fight them, too. Even the R.S.S. members who remained devoted to Gandhiji and Pandit Nehru would catch the fever of Sohan's words, perhaps because the more stirring his speeches were, the calmer his reasoning seemed.

"I agree with you, Sohan!" I cried. "Gandhiji is as outdated as Buddha. You're right, as always."

"I don't know about that, but I know I'm right in thinking that all the Congress leaders, the whole lot of them, are outdated."

Sohan was carried away, and I was carried away, and we sat and derided Gandhiji and his latest statement.

"How silly it is of Gandhiji to make such an issue of conversion to Muhammadanism," I said.

"No doubt he thinks that we shouldn't swell the ranks of the Muslims any further—that we already have so many Muslims in our country as a result of the forcible conversions in Mogul times," Sohan said.

"It's so hypocritical. Anything would be better than death."

"Not to Gandhiji. He's a religious man."

"But the Congress is a political party, and here it

is, dumbly going along. How terrible!"

"The truth is that it is a Hindu-dominated party. That is one of Jinnah's complaints. That's why Jinnah says he left the Congress Party and joined the Muslim League. That's why he says he's asking for Pakistan."

"This nonviolent idea of Buddha and Gandhiji seems completely unrealistic. If somebody attacks me, I want to fight back."

"I think like you," Sohan said. "It was because of Buddha's teachings that the early Moguls were able to come down the mountains and conquer our people. We didn't fight back, so we had hundreds of years of Mogul rule. We can't let something like that happen again. The R.S.S. is trying to make sure it won't. If Jinnah succeeds, Pakistan will be one of the largest Muslim countries in the world, and the Muslim countries will stretch all the way from Pakistan, across Afghanistan, to Iran and then all the way to the Middle East and Africa. There will be a revival of Muhammadanism the like of which hasn't been seen."

I told Sohan that I wished I could get him a glass of buttermilk but that I feared he might then be discovered.

Sohan said that he took the wish for the deed. Then he asked, "Has your daddy made any arrangements for your safety? You can't afford to wait a day longer. I love your family like my own." His own family lived outside the Punjab—outside the "danger zone."

I hesitated. "Daddyji has a plan, but it's a secret."

"I suppose I have to respect that—I'm glad you have a plan. Now, the Mehtas in Mehta Gulli can make a good showing and look after your Bhabiji, but what about your Babuji? Does he have a plan for 16 Mozang Road?"

"No. He doesn't think any mob would dare come near his house, because of his age and position. He's as stubborn as ever."

"I was afraid of that. I wish I were old enough to go and talk to him."

"I'm not sure that even you could make him change his mind. I wish you could have heard him arguing with Daddyji about how Muslims couldn't possibly butcher Hindus just because Hindus are infidels."

"What did he say?"

"He talked about how peacefully Hindus and Muslims have lived together through most of their history."

"Then he's outdated. Why can't he understand that those times are gone? He speaks about the peaceful history of Hindus and Muslims, but he forgets the British role in that history—sowing seeds of division for a hundred years. Does he overlook those hundred years because they don't fit his idealistic picture?"

"Sohan, don't be so hard on him. He doesn't see how a foreign power could have changed hundreds of years of good relations."

"I sometimes wonder if he understands how calculating and cunning the British really are." He abruptly asked, "But what is your daddy's plan? Is it any good? I must know it."

I was surprised at his about-face—at his wanting me to tell him our family's secret. He knew as well as I did that he shouldn't ask me and that I shouldn't tell him, but he and I also knew that if he asked me I

couldn't keep it back from him. (I now know something that I didn't know then—that I had what
amounted to a teen-age crush on him.) "Daddyji is
arranging for all of us to take shelter in Dr. Mathura
Das's house," I found myself telling him.

"You won't have time to do that. The mob will be
in your *gulli* before you can run out. It will seal off
your escape."

"Daddyji intends to install a hidden iron door in
the back wall."

Sohan was really impressed.

"What are you yourself going to do, Sohan? What
about your safety?"

"I'll manage. If the Muslims should try to kill me,
I'll take a few of them along with me."

"Don't talk like that."

"You might as well get used to hearing talk like
that. There's going to be a lot of bloodshed. A lot of
people's friends and relatives are going to be killed.
Well, I must be off, before anyone catches me here."

"Will I see you again, Sohan? I must go on seeing
you. I must find out what is going on outside."

"I'll come in tomorrow morning—the same way."

Sohan left just in time, because Daddyji and Mamaji
got up right afterward, and Sheikh Sahib was
announced. It seemed strange for any Muslim to stop
by. Ever since Sheikh Sahib made an offer for the house,
I had felt that he was a snake in the grass—even though
he had taught English to Daddyji at Government College and had known Daddyji since he was a boy. I was
surprised that he should come calling, and in order to
find out what he was up to I hid behind the curtain in

the inside doorway to the drawing room as Daddyji opened the outside door to receive him.

"Ah, Doctorji, I'm so happy to see you," Sheikh Sahib said, coming in.

"It's a pleasure to see you here, Sheikh Sahib."

It seemed a long time since I had heard a Muslim and a Hindu address one another with such cordiality. Yet Sheikh Sahib's voice sounded to me a little sugary, as if he were trying to get Daddyji to let down his guard. I wished Daddyji had Sohan at his elbow to warn him.

"Doctorji, I'll come right to the point. Your women are not safe in your house. The neighbors to your left are Sikhs, and you know what that means in these times. Sikhs are belligerent people, and they are bait to Muslims, as a goat is to a lion. My wife has a proposal for your women. It must be kept strictly between us. Otherwise, even we wouldn't be safe in our own house."

I didn't really want to overhear a confidence, but I didn't want to retreat, for fear of making a noise; I stood as still as a piece of furniture, scarcely breathing.

"Her proposal is that at the first sign of trouble your women run across to our house and take shelter with us," Sheikh Sahib said.

I was aghast: Sheikh Sahib, having failed to scare us into selling our house to him, was now resorting to dirtier means. He was trying to get Mamaji and our sisters into his clutches.

I was relieved to hear Daddyji say, in a firm way that brooked no contradiction, "I don't think that will be necessary, Sheikh Sahib. We'll make a stand at our house and fight all comers."

"Think again, Doctorji. Your wife and daughters are dear to me, and I'd hate to have anything happen to them. Once your house was attacked, there would be nothing I or any other Muslim could do, but if your women were already in my house . . ."

Could it be that he was so devious that he might even stage an attack to frighten us and get our house on the cheap?

"I'm very grateful to you and your begum, Sheikh Sahib, for your concern," Daddyji was saying.

"I can't say that I blame you for refusing my wife's offer. In these times, no one can afford to trust anybody." Sheikh Sahib was being suspiciously understanding. What a fox.

"I thought, Sheikh Sahib, that you would appreciate my position," Daddyji said. "You're my old professor. I revere you. But you know what women are like."

It seemed that Daddyji was changing his tack. But then there was always a chance that Sheikh Sahib's proposal was an honorable one. If so, Daddyji's spurning it might make him vengeful.

"For thirty-seven years, Doctorji, our families have known each other. I remember when you got married, when you built this house. I've seen your children grow up with mine. Your daughters are my daughters. However that may be—"

"Very kind of you. I myself trust you completely, but—"

"I know what you mean, Doctorji. You don't have to explain. I'm sorry, yes, I'm sorry. I'm an old man. I don't understand these times."

I was almost touched. I thought that even Sohan might have been. But then again I couldn't be sure.

Sheikh Sahib began once more: "I hope you'll permit me to do at least one thing for you. As you know, I have my own tube well and water pump. Why don't you pipe my water into your house?"

What an absurd idea! Was he suggesting that his well water was safer than the municipal water supply we depended on for our water—that the Muslim League was going to contaminate the municipal water supply and that therefore we should use his private supply? How could he expect anyone to believe that? Contaminating the municipal water supply would poison the water of Hindus and Muslims alike. There was only one explanation: he wanted to poison our water supply.

"Why do I need the water from your well, Sheikh Sahib?" Daddyji asked. "I don't understand."

"You know how low the water pressure is in this area—that's why we installed our own well. If your house were set on fire, not only would you have practically no water but you couldn't rely on the fire brigade. It's manned mostly by Muslims, and it would not answer your call for help."

I began shaking with fright in spite of myself. I thought I was making the curtain shake. I'm going to be discovered, I thought, and Sheikh Sahib will know that I've heard his confidences. I'll embarrass Daddyji.

"I suppose not," Daddyji said slowly. "Not to save a Hindu's house."

"If your house were on fire, I couldn't stretch a

hose from my house. If I did, the mob would consider me a traitor, and I might fare no better at its hands than you would. What I'm proposing is that we secretly attach a pipeline to my water main, run it under the *gulli,* and connect it with your water line. The work would be done in a few hours, and no one need be the wiser for it."

"That is very generous of you indeed, Sheikh Sahib. I'd like to talk it over with my wife."

I was so busy thinking about Sheikh Sahib's visit and his latest proposal that I scarcely heard Daddyji show him to the door, or their goodbyes. Before I knew it, Daddyji had come through the doorway where I was standing, and had found me.

"Son, it's not nice to eavesdrop on your elders."

"I'd rather be burned than accept Sheikh Sahib's water."

"I wish you could have seen his face. He looked so earnest."

"I could tell it from his voice. But even so—"

"Even so! That's the question, son, isn't it?"

❧

DADDYJI CALLED everyone into Mamaji's bedroom, reported what Sheikh Sahib had said, and asked, "What do you all think?"

Usha didn't know, and Brother Om was opposed to the plan, even if refusing it meant antagonizing Sheikh Sahib and having a Muslim enemy at our doorstep.

Sister Umi was amused. "If Sheikh Sahib plans to poison us, he's certainly very ingenious—I'll say that much for him."

"But we have to trust someone," Sister Nimi said. "If we lose the ability to trust, what will become of us? Sheikh Sahib's proposal is a test that God has sent us to see how mature we are. Daily, we hear reports of Hindu women preferring suicide to being taken by Muslim hooligans. I would rather die from Sheikh Sahib's water, if that's what he has in mind, than kill myself."

"Sheikh Sahib is a good man," Mamaji said. "But you can never tell about Muslims. They have dirty habits."

"I care about our property," Daddyji said. "I also care about Sheikh Sahib. All of you have known him only as our good neighbor, but to me he is a mentor. He is one of the few Muslims I know in Lahore who still seem to believe in one India. Just the other day, I read a letter of his in the *Civil & Military Gazette* pleading for one nation, for Hindu-Muslim amity. The letter could have been written by Babuji." He went around the room again. We all felt that Sister Nimi had a point, except for Brother Om.

"I'm going over to Sheikh Sahib's to make the arrangements," Daddyji said.

"Take Brother Om with you!" I cried. I suddenly thought that we should never have agreed to the water plan.

"Don't worry about me," Daddyji said, laughing. "I'm as safe at Sheikh Sahib's house as I am here. After all, we're going to be drinking his well water."

❧

THERE WAS a gentle rap on my door the next morning, and I hastened to open it. "Come in, Sohan," I whispered. "Am I glad to see you!" I told him about Sheikh Sahib's visit, about what Sister Nimi had said, about the water decision.

"You're making preparations to escape to Dr. Mathura Das's house, yet you hand over your lives to the mercy of one Muslim," Sohan said. "Your daddy gives lectures to Babuji about how a Muslim would butcher an infidel, yet he calmly walks across to Sheikh Sahib's house and makes him the custodian of your drinking water. Your sister talks about a test of maturity, and you come around to a decision that is absolutely immature. It makes no sense. What irony."

"Stop! I don't want to hear any more. You speak about irony, but what about history?" I wasn't quite sure what irony was, but I didn't want to ask, for fear that Sohan would stop talking to me like a grownup.

"Right you are. History is a tragic irony." He sighed, and went on, "Take the British. Churchill's Conservative government was positive that it had played its divide-and-rule cards well, that we'd kill each other and prove to the world that we were unfit to rule ourselves—that we couldn't get along without the British. And what did the British people do? They turned out Churchill and put in Attlee's Labour government, which said, 'Let the Indians have their independence, even if they kill each other.' You see the irony?"

"I see it all too well."

"Yes, and Churchill was one in a long line of misguided British rulers. The high-and-mighty British turned out to be much more stupid than you or I would have thought possible. I have been thinking about Babuji, and perhaps this morning I understand him better than I did yesterday. He doesn't see the contradictions in history. I don't think your daddy does, either. I think you're all too idealistic."

I was getting confused, so I changed my approach. "But, for all your bold statements about history, I still don't see what's wrong with having ideals."

There was a confident tapping. "It's Daddyji!"

There was no help for it, and I opened the door.

"Well, well, well, Sohan," Daddyji said, coming in. "I thought I might see you here this morning. You were here yesterday, too, weren't you?"

"Yes, Doctor Sahib, I was."

"I thought I saw you from the window."

Daddyji sat down on my bed. "You must have heard, Sohan, that the police have seized the R.S.S. records and have handed them over to Muslim League leaders."

I felt chilled with fright. My name was in the R.S.S. register. On top of that, I was entertaining a well-known R.S.S. member in our house. But Daddyji said— as if he wanted to say "What has happened has happened"—"I'm glad my son has a chance to talk to you. I want all my children to understand these times— then they will be prepared to meet any emergency courageously—and Vedi has a special difficulty in going out and about."

Daddyji and Sohan talked for some time, Sohan airing his views about history and bloodshed, Daddyji for the most part trying to temper Sohan's views. I was surprised that they could talk to each other at all.

"He's a good fellow," Daddyji said, without a word of reproach to me, after Sohan had left. "Very courageous. You have a good friend in him. But he's too much of an extremist for his own good."

XVII

MARCH

M ARCH 1ST: IN THE EVENING, A FEW TRUSTED
laborers, who had helped to remodel our house,
and who often worked on jobs for Daddyji's
architect brother, Romesh Chachaji, arrived
with picks and shovels, pipes and joints. There
was no hiding their presence: they made a lot
of noise in digging a trench in the *gulli,* and the night
turned out to be clear. Neighbors came out of their
houses to inquire what was going on. We let them
think that something had suddenly gone wrong with
our water system and the laborers were fixing it; we
hoped that the strangeness of the enterprise would keep
them from guessing its nature. The laborers connected
our water supply to Sheikh Sahib's well, and the water
pressure in our house became so strong that for a moment
we feared that it would blast the taps off the pipes.

I drank a glass of the new supply of water, almost
relishing the thought that I was risking my life—that
a Muslim had the say of life and death over me.

🌣

MARCH 2ND: A closed van pulled into our driveway with an iron door for us. The door was wrapped up in a tarpaulin, like a new sofa, and it was carried into our inner courtyard. There it was propped up in its tarpaulin shroud and left.

We waited all day for the Hindu laborers to return and install the door, but they didn't come. "They're probably afraid to stir out of their *gullis*," Daddyji explained when he got home from the office. "The whole city seems to be on tenterhooks tonight. Khizar has just resigned—what a pity!" Daddyji explained that Sir Khizar Hayat Khan, the premier of the Punjab, led the moderate Unionist Party and, though a Muslim, was against the Muslim League and Pakistan. Moreover, his resignation had come in a volatile religious atmosphere. In the bazaars, Hindus and Sikhs were shouting "We'll fight before we give up Pakistan!" and Muslims were shouting "We'll take Pakistan by force! Khizar is a dog!" Khizar had promised to put all the fanatics—whether Hindu, Sikh, or Muslim—behind bars in return for the Punjab Congress Party's support. It was in the Punjab Congress Party's interest to keep the moderate Khizar in power, but instead its leader, Bhim Sain Sachar, had helped to precipitate his resignation.

"I think Sachar has made a terrible blunder," Daddyji said. "No doubt he hoped to make the Muslims in the Unionist Party and the Muslims in the Muslim League fight it out among themselves, but actually, by failing to support Khizar, he has turned the Punjab over to the rule of fanatics. The music that we hear from this time on out will be the sad music of Partition. I don't know when we'll be able to get the laborers to install our iron door now."

❧

MARCH 3RD: Rumors about no ministry, no government—no one in charge in the Punjab. The radio reported that the Punjab Congress Party and the smaller Hindu and Sikh parties were holding a strategy meeting in the Assembly chamber but that they could no more form a ministry without the Muslim League than the Muslim League could form a ministry without them. It said that the Muslim League had surrounded the chamber with a huge mob, which had shouted, "We'll take Pakistan by force!"—whereupon Master Tara Singh, the leader of Sikhs and their Akali Party, had come out of the chamber and brandished his dagger and said, "We will kill ourselves and give you our lives but will never concede Pakistan!" Master Tara Singh, like all Sikhs, always carried a dagger, as an emblem of his fierce faith.

Later in the day, Sohan slipped into my room. "Master Tara Singh's words fell on the mob like a match on a powder keg," he said breathlessly. "For once, · though, the police stepped in, and separated Master Tara Singh and his followers from the mob. Otherwise, he would have set the whole city on fire. He has called a public meeting at Kapurthala House this evening to decide how to lick the Muslim League and its dream of Pakistan. You may need your iron door this very night." Kapurthala House was a sort of guest house of the nearby princely Sikh state of Kapurthala.

"Are you going to go to Kapurthala House?" I asked.

"Of course."

I went into Daddyji's room and entreated him to let me go, too.

"The authorities have prohibited all public meetings," he said. "They have outlawed all public speeches and public processions. The meeting at Kapurthala House is illegal on every count, and anything could happen there. Police could charge in swinging sticks. They could open fire. You could be trampled underfoot."

"But Sohan is going. He's not afraid."

"Well, I leave it up to you. Think for yourself—be independent."

In later years, I wondered why he was seldom able to refuse me anything when it really came down to it—even when the refusal would have been in my own interest and for my own safety. I concluded that he felt guilty about my blindness. How often I had heard him say, "If only I had not stayed back in Gujrat for a tennis match but had driven you straightaway to a hospital in Lahore, if only I had backed my hunch that you had meningitis, and insisted on a lumbar puncture right away, your eyes might have been saved."

As Sohan and I were going out, we passed Mamaji at the gate. "Be careful—the roads are dangerous," she said. Then she blessed me portentously, as if I were going far, far away and we might not meet again for a long time.

In later years, I reflected that Mamaji, left to herself, would have locked me up rather than let me go out on the road, never mind to Kapurthala House, but that, as she never tired of repeating when we were growing up, she was only a Hindu wife, and her husband's word or fancy was her destiny and her duty.

The evening air around my face felt revivingly fresh, but Sohan and I walked mostly in foreboding silence, and I started several times at unusual crowd sounds.

Kapurthala House, a big, oldish bungalow, was so packed that we had to stand. Yet still more people kept coming, pressing in on us from all sides.

There was a roar so loud that I thought the roof would fall in. "Master Tara Singh has come!" Sohan said, jumping up and down. "And he's with the Congress leaders. Do you know what that means?"

"Yes! Yes!" We had come to think of the Congress leaders as softies, because the more the Muslim League leaders shouted about taking Pakistan by force, the more the Congress leaders seemed to talk about keeping India one through Gandhiji's nonviolent means of love and persuasion. The more the Muslim League roared like a lion, the more the Congress seemed to bleat like a goat. Now the Congress leaders were appearing on the platform with Master Tara Singh, the most daring anti-Muslim leader in the Punjab—the lion-eater himself—who spoke the language of the dagger, which the Muslim League couldn't mistake: they were doing an about-face, and putting the Muslim League on notice that they would fight. From now on, Master Tara Singh, not Gandhiji, was going to be in command.

Giani Kartar Singh, another Akali leader, was

addressing us from the platform in an enraged shout: "Let the Muslims start something! The Hindus and Sikhs will retaliate!"

The crowd roared, the crowd cheered, the crowd shouted ferocious slogans, the voices clashing against the walls and echoing thunderously around me, like those of a thousand and one R.S.S. members. I felt uplifted, as if I had been borne to the platform on the shoulders of the crowd.

The crowd abruptly became silent. "What's happening? What's happening?" I asked Sohan.

"Sh-h-h," he hissed. "Master Tara Singh is about to speak."

The air around me felt hot and thick. I could hear Sikhs here and there scratching their beards and adjusting their turbans. Everywhere were the sounds of heavy, expectant breathing.

"O Hindus and Sikhs! Be ready for self-destruction, like the Japanese and the Nazis," Tara Singh began. His voice had fire and grit. He was a former schoolmaster, and he had a commanding presence. "Our motherland is calling for blood, and we shall slake the thirst of our mother with blood. By crushing Mogulistan, we shall trample Pakistan. I have been feeling for many a day now that mischief has been brewing in the province, and for that reason I started reorganizing the Akali Party. If we can snatch the government from the Britishers, no one can stop us from snatching the government from the Muslims. We have in our hold the arms and legs of the Muslim League, and we shall break them. Disperse from here, on the solemn affirmation that we shall not allow the League to exist. The world has always been ruled by minorities. The Muslims snatched the kingdom from the Hindus, and the Sikhs grabbed it from the hands of the Muslims, and the Sikhs ruled over the Muslims with their might, and the Sikhs shall even now rule over them. We shall rule over them and shall get the government, fighting. I have sounded the bugle. Finish the Muslim League!"

I felt exhilarated, and thought that we were all leaders—that if we just went out of Kapurthala House we could rally all the Hindu and Sikh masses and show the Muslim League that we were not meek and servile but strong and powerful. I curled my fingers and clenched my fists tightly. My hand touched Sohan's. His hand was clenched in a fist, like mine. I felt that we could march down any street and defy any force.

After the meeting, Sohan rushed me home. I told Daddyji what Master Tara Singh had said.

"I'm afraid that the Hindus and Sikhs have woken up too late," he said. "The Muslim League has a long head start. It has thoroughly indoctrinated the masses and supplied them with arms."

"But every Sikh has a dagger at his side."

"Their daggers are little better than table knives. Master Tara Singh is a hothead. I fear he is making a tragic mistake. Everywhere he goes, he's inflaming the emotions of the crowds, but hotheads without arms are helpless. Besides, whatever Master Tara Singh and his company do or don't do may make little difference. The slaughter may come anyway."

❧

MARCH 4TH–5TH: Evening. Still no sign of laborers to install the iron door. We felt the need to be with our relatives, and all of us walked over to 16 Mozang Road. Babuji was not at home. Mataji said that he was probably out at a meeting of the Arya Samaj, a Hindu reform movement. We waited. It got dark suddenly. The mob was already raising a cry in Mozang Chowk, just one house away, and Daddyji said it wasn't safe to walk back. The men went upstairs to the terraced roof to watch, but the women and we children were shunted into Mataji's bedroom. We all lay or sat on the beds without saying very much, as if there were someone sick in the room. We waited—I wasn't sure for what. For Babuji to arrive? For the mob to go away, so that we could go back home? For Daddyji to give the word that we were going to sleep over? My heart thumped, and sounded to my ears as loud as the clock on the wall.

Mozang Chowk and Mozang Bazaar, which lay behind it, were thick with grain merchants and *dal* merchants and little stalls selling rice and wheat flour, ghi and vegetables. People lived above their shops or in tenements behind them. Our servants went there daily to buy supplies and groceries. They knew everyone in the bazaar, and everyone in the bazaar knew them, but the wretched sellers couldn't forget that they were all Muslims and we were all Hindus. They lived in choked little *gullis* with their animals and baskets, we on well-to-do Mozang Road and Temple Road, in houses with gates and flower beds. Perhaps they had always wanted to storm our houses.

I jumped, but it was only the clock striking ten. The chimes, resonant with rich sweetness, sounded discordant in my head. The clock struck ten-fifteen, ten-thirty. The cries of the mob grew louder and more sustained. They seemed so close that I imagined that the mob was at the gate. I thought I could hear voices urging the mob to avenge the blood of their oppressed brethren, to battle the infidels.

"They're coming, they're coming!" the servants shouted, running into the house.

"Oh, my mother! Babuji still hasn't come home!" Mataji wailed. "Ram, save us. Ram, Ram! Save us, save us!"

"House on fire! House on fire!" the servants cried, scurrying to and fro as if they had gone berserk.

"Which house, you mad ones? Which house?" Mataji shouted.

The servants wouldn't say. They just kept running back and forth.

We ran out the side door. The air was filled with smoke, and we all choked, our coughs sounding nerve-rackingly like explosions of firecrackers.

"They've really set a house on fire!" Sister Umi exclaimed. "Look at that glow in the sky!"

Daddyji and Brother Om came running down the outer staircase. "Everyone, all of you, quick, take shelter by the back wall, by Mehta Gulli!" Daddyji exclaimed. Someone grabbed my hand roughly, and we all raced around the lawn to the back wall of the compound, calling to each other and shouting.

"Nimi! Umi!"

"Sureshta, are you there?"

"Gardener, don't just stand there—get a mosquito-net pole and run and help the sahibs on the roof."

"Gardener, hurry, find Babuji!"

We children started to climb over the wall into Mehta Gulli, but Mamaji called us back. "Your daddy said here."

We all cowered by the wall, somehow fitting ourselves into the little area between the tube well, with its pump house, on one side, and the stable and the servants' quarters, on the other. I felt dazed; it seemed suddenly that I couldn't hear anything, that I couldn't smell anything.

"They're going to kill my baby," someone moaned. "They're going to kill the baby in my stomach." It was Auntie Sureshta.

"They'll kill all of us if you don't shut up," someone whispered. Her wailing stopped abruptly, as if a radio had been switched off.

The pump started up, purring and whistling like a giant snoring. Everyone could be killed on the roof and we wouldn't hear it, I thought. I prayed that the pump would stop, that Auntie Sureshta's stomach would be all right, that everyone would stay alive, that we would all be restored to our homes. I prayed for nonviolence and peace; Master Tara Singh's speech seemed a long time ago.

I remembered that at Dadar School, which was run by Christian missionaries, I had thought of myself as a Christian. I wondered what was actually Hindu about me—what had made me want to kill a Muslim when I was listening to Master Tara Singh, and what might make a Muslim kill me that very night. I heard Daddyji's voice in my head: "As Hindus, we are bound by no one god, no prophet, no dogma, no sacred book. We as individuals are therefore free to venerate Muhammad or Christ as a prophet and still remain Hindus. For Hinduism is only a way of life: this is its power and its pride. We Hindus tolerate all religions. We worship thousands of gods, and our beliefs are as various as our geography and our climate. We don't proselytize, because there is nothing to proselytize about. In contrast to us, Muslims are united by their faith in one God, one prophet, one book. For Muslims, religion means complete abandonment of individual personality. Five times a day, Muslims, no matter where they live, turn their faces toward Mecca, kneel, and pray. They all proselytize, and with a sword."

I strained my ears for the sound of the mob, but I heard only the infernal hum of the pump—loud, constant, irritating.

We had been brought up with Hindu and Muslim family friends and Hindu and Muslim servants. We had thought of Muslims as no different from us. But now all that was changed. Our bearer said, "Muslims have a dirty, filthy way of eating. They all eat from the same pot, with the same spoon. They don't care who else has licked the spoon. A Hindu villager never brings his shoes into a house. A Muslim villager will walk around in his shoes all day in the muck and bring the same shoes into the place where he cooks and eats." And Gian Chand said, "Muslims teach cruelty. They teach children to break Hindu idols." And Sohan said, "Most Punjabi Muslims are weavers, cobblers, herdsmen, potters, or blacksmiths. Because they do low-level jobs, they have a low intellect. They live in vice and poverty, which breed more vice and more poverty." I wondered if our bearer had always thought of Muslims as unclean, and if Gian Chand had always considered Muslims cruel, and if Sohan had always thought of them as living in vice and poverty.

I heard a cow moo and cough. So it was dawn, time to milk her, I thought. Just then, Brother Om ran toward us, saying, "All is well."

We staggered to the house. Babuji was on the veranda. We asked him where he'd been, when he'd got back, where he'd spent the night. He was incoherent, and we couldn't even be sure that he had understood our questions. It was as if the happenings of the night had momentarily unhinged him.

"They burned down a Hindu tenement!" he muttered. "The idiots! They burned it down!"

"That must have been the fire we saw," Daddyji said. "But we can be thankful that it was the only fire in our area, and that the mob never crossed Mozang Road."

"The idiots!"

Back in our own house, Daddyji got out a double-barrelled gun that he had bought in Rawalpindi on a whim. For many months, it had stood in a cupboard with some discarded golf clubs. He raised it to one shoulder, then the other, trying to work out how he was supposed to hold it. He had never used a gun, and wondered aloud what happened when you fired it. Did it have a back-thrust? And, if so, did that affect the aim? He loaded it and put it next to his pillow, and warned us and all the servants not to touch it or dust it for fear of setting it off.

News filtered in all day: unprovoked, the police had fired on Hindu college students; Sir Evan Meredith Jenkins, the governor of the Punjab, whom we regarded as partial to the Muslims, had declared martial law; the government had announced a curfew; riots had broken out everywhere; in Gumti Bazaar, Kinari Bazaar, and Kasera Bazaar and in the Rang Mahal area Muslims had killed Hindus and Sikhs and looted and burned their shops; scores of fires were lighting up the sky in the old city; men and women were fleeing their houses and leaving them to the whims of the mob; pedestrians had been stabbed, shops looted. Still no laborers—no door.

A servant brought a letter from Sister Pom. It was for Mamaji, and was in Hindi.

"She says that the baby is due in the third week of April, and that she expects to be in Lahore a month before that," Mamaji said, giving us the gist as she read the letter. "She says that Kakaji and his mother are set against the idea but she's planning to come anyway." Mamaji looked up from the letter. "It's Pom's birthright to come to us. After all, it's her first baby, my first grandchild."

"Of course, it's traditional for a girl to return home for her first confinement, but these are no times for observing such a tradition," Daddyji said. "If anything happened to her, it would be terrible. This is one matter concerning Pom's in-laws on which I can't be mum.

I'm going to write to Kakaji and tell him that Pom shouldn't come."

And by the end of the long day he had written to Kakaji, though Mamaji kept on whispering behind his back that he was making a mistake.

❦

MARCH 6TH: In the morning, Sohan came again. He brought me a knife. "If a Muslim tries to take your sisters or your mother away, or tries to kill you, you have to be ready to kill him," he said. "This knife will be your self-defense and your honor."

I had coveted a Rogers Sheffield knife ever since Daddyji brought one from England for Brother Om, before the war, but Daddyji hadn't been able to obtain one for me locally. Brother Om's knife was small, light, and machine-turned. It had a smooth, bevelled handle and two slim blades, one about three inches long and the other about two inches. The blades were as smooth as Mamaji's full-length looking glass, and their edges were almost as sharp as the Gillette blades Daddyji used in his safety razor. The knife blades had little fingernail recesses for pulling them out, and when they were pulled out they clicked into place, and their strong springs made them seem fixed, like the blades of table knives. The knife that Sohan handed me, however, had a rough wooden handle, like that of a hammer. The handle was big and round, and the wood gave the knife a certain weight and substance. The knife had a switch; a mere touch caused the blade to jump out of the handle. The blade was a foot long and was of rough iron, and it was loose in its socket, but it was curved at the top, like a sword. In all my life, I'd never owned or held anything that excited me or terrified me more than the knife Sohan gave me. Holding it in my hand, I felt I was every bit as powerful as Daddyji or Brother Om, or as the men who took positions on the terraced roofs; I felt whole and strong.

"It will go into a Muslim's stomach like a knife into butter," Sohan was saying. "And the beauty of it is that when you pull it out, if the Muslim isn't already dead that will finish the job."

He showed me how to hold the knife at a tilt when pulling it out of a stomach so that it would slice the Muslim almost in two. I put it under my pillow, and thought that in its way it was as good as Daddyji's double-barrelled gun.

❦

MARCH 11TH: In the evening, the radio reported that in a village named Bewal in Rawalpindi District the Hindu and Sikh women, to escape Muslim raiders, had piled up their beds, clothes, and fuel, made a great bonfire, and hurled themselves into the flames. "They wanted to die with their honor and a pure soul," the radio reported. "A villager, Hatha Singh, said, 'My ladies preferred torturous death by fire to the fury of the mob.' "

"Hare Ram, all those women, for a whole life cycle, cawing and flying around with no place to rest, shunned by everybody," Mamaji said, almost to herself. Any

Hindu who committed suicide was reincarnated as a crow—black, despised, and restless.

❧

MARCH 13TH: It was considered unsafe to leave the security of home even at midday. No one went to school. Except for the servants, no one went shopping. Daddyji alone went daily to his office, in his motorcar, because nothing could be allowed to interfere with his official duties, and every afternoon Gian Chand made the rounds of various relatives to check on them.

Reports of riots continued to arrive from the rest of the western Punjab: in predominantly Muslim villages Muslim marauders had killed villagers, razed entire lanes, destroyed herds and crops; in towns they had abducted women and stabbed people in bazaars in the middle of the day; and on roads they had ambushed lorries and trains.

"Of course, there are reports every day of one Sikh here, another Sikh there slitting a Muslim's stomach or throat with a dagger," Daddyji said. "Those are isolated incidents. But Muslims seem to be killing Hindus and Sikhs in droves. It appears that the Muslim League has got the upper hand. No wonder its leaders are gloating. These disturbances have a pattern. It looks as though the Muslim League were stage-managing these disturbances to prove to the British that, after they leave, Hindus and Muslims can't live together. It must be the Muslim League's plan for getting Pakistan. We must prepare ourselves."

❦

MARCH 14TH: We heard that Pandit Nehru had arrived in Lahore and had been greeted by expectant and excited Hindus and Sikhs.

"They still think that he can bring about a miracle—can halt the destruction of lives and property, can undo the work of the Muslim League," Daddyji said. "But the way it looks to me is that it's too late."

All day, I waited for Sohan, to find out what he thought, but he did not come. There hadn't been a sign of him since the day he brought me the knife. Daddyji thought that he might have gone underground. I insisted that Gian Chand go to Sohan's lodgings, in the old city, and inquire after him. Gian Chand protested, made all kinds of excuses, complained that he might die, but I prevailed. He came back and reported, "Sohan Sahib's door is locked. I could find no one who had seen him." I wondered if Gian Chand had come back a little too soon, and examined him closely on the kind and size of Sohan's lock, which I knew from Sohan's description was an especially secure one; and I was persuaded that Gian Chand was telling the truth. I had a terrible sinking feeling.

❦

MARCH 21ST: My thirteenth birthday. Still no laborers, no door. I waited for Sohan all day. No sign. Under protest, Gian Chand made another trip to Sohan's lodgings. He came back without a scrap of news.

"If the Sahib keeps on forcing me to go to the old

city, I may die, like Sohan Sahib."

I scolded him roundly for having a loose tongue—I was afraid that he would bring about the tragedy by naming it—and went into my room. I felt the knife under the pillow.

❧

MARCH 24TH: Early in the morning, the telephone rang. I ran to get it, but Mamaji had already picked it up.

"Pom!" she exclaimed. "No, we didn't receive any telegram. Nothing is working here. . . . Where did you say you are? . . . At the Lahore station! . . . Sitting on the platform all night! . . . Your Daddy will be right there."

"On the platform all night, with stabbings going on all around the station!" Daddyji exclaimed as we all rushed in the motorcar to get Sister Pom. "It's a wonder that she's safe. How could Kakaji have sent her?"

"Kakaji is living in the United Provinces," Sister Nimi said. "He can't imagine what things are like here."

"But the United Provinces have had their share of Hindu-Muslim riots," Daddyji said. "Don't you remember that last August they had a terrible outbreak in Allahabad, and, last November, terrible riots in Garhmuktesar, in the Meerut district?"

We got to the station in record time. Daddyji ran in and brought Sister Pom out. She was overwrought but safe.

"How different you look, Pom!" Sister Nimi said, laughing.

Mamaji shushed her, and put Pom next to her in the front seat. The two started whispering, as if the rest of us were not in the car.

"You see what marriage does for favoritism," Sister Umi said. "We haven't seen Pom in almost a year, but do we get a chance to talk to her?"

For once, no one took any notice of Sister Umi and her gibes.

❧

MARCH 25TH–26TH: In the morning, we set about sorting the family's prized possessions: the round drawing-room table with carved lions' feet, which the Maharaja of Patiala had given Daddyji; the tall marble statue of a mother and child, which Daddyji had brought from Italy; a camphorwood box that Brother Krishan had brought from Malaya; Mamaji's saris and shawls; lengths of English woollen suiting; and a few pieces of silver and items of jewelry. Then we turned to our ordinary household possessions—rolled up carpets and took down curtains and pictures. We started carrying everything to the storeroom, but there was too much for the storeroom to hold, and a lot of it had to be left where it was, rolled up and bundled—as if waiting to be carried away by the mob. Daddyji had bought some fireproof paint, and we all got ourselves brushes and buckets and worked feverishly slapping the paint on doorframes and window frames, moldings and picture railings—any wood at all.

Just as we were washing up for lunch, Gian Chand announced that the Hindu laborers who were supposed to install the iron door were at the gate. We couldn't believe it. We'd been waiting for them for weeks. We set about unwrapping the door—clanking in its frame—from its tarpaulin shroud and showing the laborers exactly where it was to go. The laborers ran around mixing cement and sand with Sheikh Sahib's water and making an opening in the brick wall, the whole house echoing with the blows of half a dozen hammers against as many chisels. By evening, the overpowering odor of fireproof paint was joined by the odor of damp mortar from the iron door—the new damp odor sadly reminding us of the days of fixing up the house, just a year or so earlier.

"From now on, you must always sleep dressed," Daddyji said when we were having dinner, and his voice sounded very loud in the bare room, as if we were sitting at the bottom of a well. "You girls should all dress simply—you shouldn't take your jewelry or try to carry away your best clothes."

Mamaji protested—jewelry and saris were a woman's only security against ruin—but Daddyji said that now it was a question not of property but of life, and that the less temptation we offered the mob the better.

In the late evening, there were the shouts of a mob in Mozang Chowk, reminiscent of the night of the fourth. We followed a plan worked out with the Hindu and Sikh neighbors on our side of Temple Road—turned off all the lights, bolted the doors and windows, and raced up to our terraced roof. As had been agreed, Daddyji and Brother Om communicated with the neighbors by means of torches, their torch switches sliding and clicking in the still, hot air.

"Look—that's Dr. Mathura Das's torch flashing and flickering," Daddyji said. "He's saying that the mob is not moving. We are safe here for the time being."

I quietly walked all around the parapet, in case I could tell anything from the sound of the shouts.

"Look!" Brother Om cried. "Our Sikh neighbors are signalling to us to abandon ship!"

We deliberately walked down the stairs, Daddyji and Brother Om leading the way with their torches. We joined hands in front of the iron door. With my left hand I held the cold, limp hand of Sister Nimi, and on the right Usha clung to me with both hands. Daddyji counted all of us, including the servants. He stepped through the iron door, carrying his gun under one arm and Ashok on the other—Ashok was just three, and was sleeping—and we followed, being careful not to smirch the wet paint. Then Sister Nimi took Ashok, and Daddyji and Brother Om locked the door behind us. They slipped upstairs to Dr. Mathura Das's roof to keep watch with the men. The rest of us silently walked to the room where the other women and children were gathered.

We had had to run for our lives only once before— the night we all huddled by the back wall of 16 Mozang Road, under the open sky. Then, except for Auntie Sureshta, no one had made a sound, for fear of being discovered, but here in Dr. Mathura Das's house scores of us were crowded into one small room. Women wailed and beat their breasts, as if they were already mourning their husbands and sons, and lamented the jewels and saris they had left behind in their houses.

"I'll never see him again. O Rama, Rama, what did I do in my last birth to deserve this?"

"Who'll take care of the children?"
"Muslims are going to carry me off!"
"A dirty Muslim is going to take me! I am undone!"
Babies shrieked. Little children ran around and were scolded by their mothers for getting underfoot. We Mehta children found a corner and sat quietly on the floor. Sohan's knife bulged in my pocket like something live and dangerous, as if it wanted to betray my secret, and I shifted this way and that way, trying to hide it along my thigh. I wished that I could be upstairs with Daddyji. I wished that I could see, so that I could be upstairs with the men. I wished that I were a man.

It was hot and close and noisy in the little room with the women and the other children—as in an interclass train compartment. Whenever we travelled with Daddyji, we travelled in a motorcar, but whenever we travelled with Mamaji we travelled in a train, and in an interclass compartment—so named because it was between second and third class. As she never tired of repeating, there were so many of us that we couldn't afford to travel in second or first class, and we should consider ourselves lucky that we weren't travelling in third class, which had only wooden benches instead of cushioned berths, like interclass. I hated travelling with Mamaji. The interclass compartment was full of women and children and trunks and bedrolls and baskets, with hardly a place to sit. Nosy women were constantly asking questions about what had happened to my eyes, but they never addressed me, and then they clucked over me, as if because I couldn't see them I must be deaf. How I would long for the familiarity and security of Daddyji's motorcar. And the train journey was endless and frightening. Woman would tell stories of dacoits—dacoits who would stop trains, snatch chains and bangles and rings right off women's bodies, and sometimes carry the women away, leaving their children to weep motherless on the roadside, to die hungry, naked, and neglected.

Ashok jolted me back to the present: he started howling and wouldn't be shushed.

Some time later, Brother Om came down and gave us the word that it was morning and that we were all to return home. Getting out of the crowded room was like getting out of an interclass train compartment, with women shouting and pushing, and calling and scolding their children. Somehow, we managed to find our way to the iron door, and returned to the uncertain safety of our house.

The laborers came back to build us an interfloor room with a concealed door, between the passageway downstairs and the room above it.

"It will take many days, Sahib, to build the interfloor room," the head laborer said.

"Never mind—start," Daddyji said. "My architect brother is arranging for bricks and cement."

Even as he spoke, other laborers arrived carrying bags of cement and loads of bricks, which they dumped in our driveway helter-skelter.

XVIII

APRIL

G RADUALLY, SINCE LAHORE OUTWARDLY RE-
mained calm, we began acting as if everything were back to normal. We children
resumed visiting Bhabiji in her room in Mehta
Gulli and going for walks with her up to the
statue of Queen Victoria on the Mall Road.
Mamaji went to the fashionable Anarkali bazaar and
bought parachute silk, which was being disposed of as
war surplus. She engaged the two family tailors to make
some clothes for the day Sister Nimi and Sister Umi
would get married and need a dowry. She went to the
Mall Road and bought fine Lahore mill cloth and busied herself sewing new quilts and bedspreads for the
sisters' dowries. Daddyji spoke often about how he was
due for compulsory retirement at age fifty-five, in
December, 1950—less than four years away—and how
he would like to go to London to live. He talked about
taking his accumulated leave and retiring a year ear-

lier, so that he would still be young enough to start a new life in London. He and I would go first, by sea. He would put me in school, he said, do some locums, and rent a corner house. He would hang a shingle stating that he was a fully qualified doctor. After all, he was registered with the General Medical Council in England. Once the practice was a going concern, he would send for the rest of the family. When Mamaji protested that she couldn't leave her house and relatives to go and live among foreigners whose tongue and ways she didn't understand, Daddyji would speak about the invigorating English climate and the great opportunities in the West for young and old, men and women. Sometimes, however, he would agree with Mamaji and enumerate the matchless home comforts of Lahore, and talk as if he would like nothing better than to settle down, like Babuji, to the leisurely routine of a retired man, and spend his waning years in Lahore, near his childhood haunts and his clubs.

But just when we were sure that everything had become normal a servant posted on the roof would excitedly report that a neighbor had flashed his torch, and we would have to run to the iron door. It was always a false alarm, but an alarm nonetheless.

❦

ON THE MORNING of April 16th, we were all sitting on the front veranda. Sister Pom was drinking a repulsive concoction—hot milk with ghi and sugar in it. "I'm having pains," she said, abruptly getting up.

Mamaji walked her a few steps into Daddyji's cor-

ner room. "The baby isn't due for a few days," Mamaji
said, almost to herself.

At two-thirty, I heard Daddyji furiously back the
motorcar out of the driveway, with a lot of racing and
screeching. He returned a few minutes later with Auntie Ansuiya Bhagat. She was a doctor and an old family
friend who lived near us on Temple Road. She went
into the corner room, and Daddyji waited with us on
the veranda.

Auntie Ansuiya came out and shouted to Gian
Chand to bring some hot water quickly. "The baby is
on its way," she said, and she rushed back into the
corner room.

Mamaji came out. We had all been talking, but at
once everyone became silent.

"What's happened?" I asked.

"Mamaji is gesturing zero," Usha said.

"It is a son," Mamaji said, gulping, "but without
a voice or life."

Daddyji rushed with her into the corner room.
Mamaji came out to us a few minutes later. She was
laughing. "Did you hear? He made a croaking sound
like a chicken."

She went back and came out and went back and
came out, saying a few words each time—that Daddyji
had bathed the baby in hot and cold water alternately,
that Auntie Ansuiya had given him an injection straight
into his heart and then held him upside down and
slapped him on the back, that the baby had suddenly
uttered a cry and come to life, that he had clearly marked
features but was all bones, that he weighed just four
pounds, that he was white, like an English baby, that

Sister Pom was going to call him Vindoo.

Even though Vindoo was the first grandson, there was no celebration of any kind to mark his arrival. Daddyji and Mamaji couldn't wait to get Sister Pom back to Dehra Dun—back to her own home, with her new family—but medical custom required that for forty days, or, at the very minimum, thirty days, a new mother stay cloistered. Besides, Vindoo was so weak that Mamaji, instead of bathing him, like other babies, would rub some ghi into his skin, wipe it off with a cloth, and dust him with talcum powder. "There, you've had your bath," she would say.

❦

WHEN VINDOO was four days old, we all gathered around the radio for a news broadcast. The music stopped, and the newscaster came on. I heard his words in a blur: Pandit Nehru had said that the Muslim League could have Pakistan only if "they do not take away other parts of India which do not wish to join Pakistan."

We were aghast. For months, we had feared that Pakistan might come, and here was Pandit Nehru conceding it in principle.

"He shouldn't be saying such things," I said. "The Congress leaders should be acting—should be coming to the aid of Hindus and Sikhs in the Punjab and putting down the Muslims."

"Pandit Nehru may be speaking only for himself," Daddyji said. "The Congress leaders have been devoted to the cause of Hindu-Muslim unity too long to abandon it now, and, in a sense, they are right. As Babuji says, history, culture, economics, and logic bind us all together—bind India as one nation." He added, "Nonetheless, I fear for the safety of our home and country. All these centuries, we Hindus have mostly lived by the light of Asoka, Buddha, and Gandhiji and their principles of nonviolence and renunciation. But all that may be over now. We may be walking straight into a religious war."

"You mean Ram Saran and Qasim Ali will fight with each other?" Usha asked.

"For the sake of Ram Saran and Qasim Ali, let's hope not," Daddyji said.

XIX

MAY

D ADDYJI HAD AN ENGLISH FRIEND WHO HAD
his ear near the court of the Viceroy, Lord
Mountbatten. Every day or two, he gave Daddyji a different report. One day, we heard that
Mountbatten was planning to meet Jinnah's
demand for Pakistan and give him the entire
provinces of the Punjab and Bengal and much else
besides. We were horrified. Then we heard that Pandit
Nehru had been told of the plan, and that he had
exploded, saying that the British had ruled India with
the slogan "Divide and rule," and that they proposed
to leave it on a new one—"Fragment and quit." He
had once quipped about Pakistan that "by cutting off
the head we will get rid of the headache," and he now
bitterly complained that the British were proposing to
cut off India's heart, lungs, and stomach along with
its head. Lord Mountbatten had immediately seen
Nehru's point of view and had insisted that only half

of the provinces—the western Punjab and eastern Bengal, in which the Muslims had a majority—should go to Pakistan. We were relieved: for once, an Englishman was siding against the Muslims. But then we heard that Jinnah had threatened to send the country up in flames if he couldn't have the Punjab and Bengal in their entirety. Our spirits plunged. Then we heard that the Congress leaders were holding their ground—with Lord Mountbatten as their support—saying that only the western Punjab and eastern Bengal should go to Pakistan. Our spirits improved.

❧

"IN SPITE of what Babuji says, I'm going over to see if Sheikh Sahib is still interested in buying our house," Daddyji said one evening.

We all cried, "Oh, no!" Ever since we put fireproof paint on the wood, we had been thinking of the house as indestructible, and ever since we heard about Lord Mountbatten's siding with the Congress leaders, we had been thinking of the house as permanently ours.

But Daddyji went to Sheikh Sahib's anyway. He came right back.

"I'd forgotten that Sheikh Sahib can't stand the heat in Lahore, and spends May and June in Dalhousie," he said. "I didn't really want to sell the house anyway."

❧

IT WAS THE MIDDLE of the month. Riots broke out in Lahore with the intensity of the early March days, and for four consecutive nights we had to abandon our house, each night more firmly convinced than the night before that the mob would attack it, if not Dr. Mathura Das's compound—even as, because of our repeated escapes, we all really expected to return home in the morning. Now it was the fifth night. We were all on our roof in the stifling, close air. The Lahore summer was at its full strength: the temperature had been stuck at a hundred and fifteen degrees all day and had hardly come down.

I stood with my big sisters by the parapet. They spoke only to estimate the position of the various fires, some of them seemingly no more than half a mile from our house.

Sister Pom got tired of standing with Vindoo in her arms, and Mamaji pulled out a cot from the rain shelter for her to sit on. Ashok ran now to Sister Pom and now to us. Being the youngest, he had been spoiled by everyone, and he was usually a boisterous fellow, but lately, as if sensing the danger, he had tried to keep himself out of everyone's way. He had even returned to sucking his thumb. He now climbed onto the cot and fell asleep.

At a signal from Daddyji, we all clasped hands and descended the stairs and walked through the iron door, Mamaji carrying Ashok, Sister Pom carrying Vindoo, and Brother Om and Daddyji bringing up the rear.

In Dr. Mathura Das's little room, where once the women had sobbed and moaned, they now made hardly any noise. Where once I alone had had a knife, now practically everyone—Mamaji, my sisters, other women—carried a knife, a vial of poison, or even a pistol. Older women lectured younger women in whispers about the need to preserve their honor and dignity—about the fate of a crow being better than that of a convert to Muhammadanism.

Ashok lay on my lap. I recalled his birth, how he had learned to crawl, how we had nearly lost him to meningitis. Many a time, I had scolded him for sneaking into my room and tinkering with my fan and my electric drill. Now he was lying almost still, sucking his thumb.

A bomb exploded somewhere outside. I started. Ashok sat up, but he didn't cry. I listened, but the men on the roof had not started shooting. I relaxed.

Some time later, Dr. Mathura Das's son came in and told us that it was time to go home, as if we were unwanted guests; and the family passed through the iron door back into our house.

In the morning, the hot, dry winds of a dust storm blasted the house.

Sheikh Sahib's son came. "Your house barely escaped the mob last night," he said, as if he had some firsthand knowledge. "If you won't send your women to my father's house, at least get your daughters out of Lahore."

Daddyji thanked him profusely and walked with him to the gate.

When he returned, he said, "Pom, I'm putting you on the train tonight."

She protested. She wanted to stay with the family. Vindoo was only a month old. There was no time to get proper reservations or to send word to Kakaji.

But Daddyji was adamant. "You leave tonight,"

he said. "And Usha will go with you. Then I can make arrangements for Nimi and Umi to go."

That night, Sister Pom and Usha were on the train, with two big trunks containing Mamaji's saris and jewelry.

X X

JUNE

O N THE THIRD, WE ALL GATHERED AROUND OUR radio to listen to Lord Mountbatten, Pandit Nehru, and Muhammad Ali Jinnah address the nation. Lord Mountbatten had hardly spoken more than a few words when Daddyji said, "It's all over. The British are definitely going to leave, but they're going to leave behind two sovereign nations."

By the time the three men had finished speaking, we knew that what were now officially designated the West Punjab and East Bengal would be Pakistan, but whether Lahore would be in it or out of it, whether Calcutta would be in it or out of it, and so forth, we wouldn't know perhaps until the day of independence. (The problem of boundaries was eventually left up to the Boundary Commission, headed by an Englishman, Sir Cyril Radcliffe, whose awards were final and unappealable.)

"The British are really going to leave," Sister Nimi said. "Isn't that jolly?"

"But what will happen to us after they leave, only God knows," Daddyji said. "If the Congress leaders hope that their concession of Pakistan will end the riots and killings all around us, I think they are sadly mistaken. The Muslims will hail the concession as another sign of Hindu meekness and servility and of Muslim boldness and power, and will spur their mobs on to fresh violence to get Lahore or Calcutta."

"You're just pro-British, Daddyji," Sister Nimi said. "Blood and violence are the price that countries have to pay to get their independence."

"Probably the British will now spread the fear of greater violence," Sister Umi said impulsively. "They think that if they can convince everyone that as soon as they leave we'll all kill each other we will ask them to stay on."

"I think the British will leave, all right," Daddyji said. "There's no question about that now."

"But why did Pandit Nehru ever agree to give Jinnah his Pakistan?" I asked. "Gandhiji repeatedly said that the country would be partitioned only over his dead body."

"The Congress leaders proved to be no match for Jinnah Sahib," Daddyji said. "I knew him personally during my Delhi-Simla posting. He was a member of the Central Legislative Council, which used to meet in Delhi and Simla, and when he was in Delhi he used to stay in the Western Court Hostel, where I also stayed. He is as hard as the Congress leaders are soft. They have spent many years in jail for India's freedom, but

Jinnah Sahib is going to reap the benefits."

"Mountbatten bamboozled them," Sister Umi said. "He just wanted a face-saving way for the British to get out. He said to himself, 'Let the Hindus and Muslims fight it out among themselves.' 'Divide and leave' is the other side of the divide-and-rule coin."

"The Congress leaders couldn't resist the pressure for some kind of action," Sister Nimi said.

"Anyway, Jinnah Sahib's force has won out over Gandhiji's soul force," Daddyji said.

"But Gandhiji can still stop it," I said.

"Gandhiji will say nothing now," Daddyji said. "If he were to hold out for one India now, there would be a worse religious war. You can't take something away once it's been given, and Gandhiji knows it as well as Jinnah."

"I can hardly wait to see the lights glowing on Independence Day," Sister Nimi said. "It will be a real festival of lights, even better than the one we had on V-J Day."

"I'm afraid that Lahore is going to go to Pakistan, that we'll have to flee," Daddyji said, almost to himself, and added, "I think I'll walk over and see Babuji."

I went with him to 16 Mozang Road.

Babuji was, as usual, on his veranda. Yes, he had heard the broadcast. "Jinnah couldn't even speak Urdu on this historic occasion," Babuji said. "What kind of Muslim is he? He drinks and smokes and marries a non-Muslim, and can't even speak the language of his own people."

"But, Babuji, he's won his Pakistan," Daddyji said. "He's made monkeys of the Congress leaders."

"I was talking to Bakshi Tek Chand earlier today," Babuji said. There was hardly anyone he respected more than Bakshi Tek Chand, who was a leading lawyer of the Punjab High Court and, like Babuji, a prominent figure in Arya Samaj. "He assures me that Lahore won't go to Pakistan. How could it? Hindus own ninety per cent of the property in the city. They will have to draw the boundary line at the Ravi River, north of Lahore."

"But, Babuji, what if Lahore should go to Pakistan?"

"We'll stay in Pakistan, then," Babuji said. "Bakshi Tek Chand agrees with me that no Hindu would ever leave his property and go and live in independent India."

"But, Babuji, without Lahore, what will West Pakistan be? It won't have a single important city of the Punjab. As it is, the two halves of Pakistan will be divided by more than a thousand miles."

"But, Amolak Ram, that's why I've always thought Jinnah's idea of Pakistan is nonsense."

"Babuji, if Lahore should go to Pakistan, I believe— knowing the fanaticism of Muslims as I do, both in the service and out of the service—that we may have no choice but to flee."

"Nonsense," Babuji said. "We Hindus will simply have to live in Pakistan. Then, instead of living under British rule, we will be living under Muslim rule. We Hindus will fly Pakistani flags from our gates. What is there in that?"

"But, Babuji, the people of the West Punjab are fifty-five per cent Muslims to our forty-five per cent Hindus. The Muslims could beat us into utter subjection. And remember the history of Muslim conquests. Whenever Muslim conquerors came, they made the Hindu women into their chattels. I have three daughters left to marry."

"But, Amolak Ram, Pakistan is a matter not of conquest but of a change in government."

"But, Babuji, the Muslims say they want Pakistan 'pure Muslim,' and they talk about us Hindus and Sikhs as 'impurities,' to be got rid of like refuse. It's in the Urdu papers every day. And they outnumber us in the West Punjab."

"But, Amolak Ram, can you really imagine us Hindus getting up and leaving? Our people would rather die than quit what is their birthright. Who can throw them out? Where will they go? How could you organize Pakistan completely along religious lines? For hundreds of years, Hindus and Muslims have lived in the same villages and cities, in the same houses and *gullis*. Through the ages, dynasties have changed, governments have changed, one party has gone out and another has come in, but have the people ever left their homes and businesses? Boundaries of countries keep on changing, but people don't leave their homes and investments to go and live penniless somewhere else. Catholics live in Protestant countries. Protestants live in Catholic countries. Jews live everywhere. During the war, there were Japanese living in America and Germans living in England. No doubt some Englishmen were living in Mussolini's Italy and in Vichy France."

"Babuji, who would have thought a year ago that Jinnah would get his Pakistan? I repeat, do not underestimate the fanaticism of the Muslims."

"I'll certainly never leave my house," Babuji said, tapping the floor with his walking stick. "They will have to carry me out. I am a retired man. I have made enough money so that at least three generations of my sons and heirs will never be in want. How can a political change ruin the savings and investments of a lifetime?"

The next morning, Daddyji said, "Nimi and Umi, you must leave tonight by train. I should have sent you when Pom left. I'm going to see Daulat Ram and ask him to send Leil out, too. You'll all go and stay with Dharam Bir in Bombay."

"I'm not going," Sister Umi said. "The whole family should stay together."

After Daddyji left for Mehta Gulli, the sisters tried to persuade Mamaji to take their side. But she was immovable, just as he had been.

When Daddyji returned, he said, "Daulat Ram wants to send Ravi away along with Leil. I think Vedi should go, too."

I cried. I didn't want to be bundled off with the girls. But Daddyji turned a deaf ear to me. He started insisting that everyone except him should go, but Mamaji put her foot down, for once, and refused to leave, and if she stayed Ashok had to stay back with her. So it was arranged that Sisters Nimi and Umi and I, along with Cousins Leil and Ravi, would board the train for Bombay that night, and that in a day or two Brother Om would go by train to Kanpur with Auntie Vimla, who was pregnant and was being sent there to stay with Auntie Pushpa. We argued that the trains were being sporadically stopped by mobs and the passengers robbed and murdered, but in vain.

Before the night was out, we five were all in a train. Once more, I was bound for Bombay.

XXI

REFUGEES

"S OHAN IS DEAD, CLACKETY-CLACK, SOHAN IS dead, *clackety-clack*," the wheels of the train to Bombay repeated like some relentless dirge, and the old woman sitting in the lower berth of the interclass compartment, beneath my dangling legs, kept saying over and over, to no one in particular, "They killed him, killed my daughter-in-law, killed my cows right in front of my eyes."

Sisters Nimi and Umi and Cousin Leil tried to comfort her.

"Here, Mother, put your head on my shoulder."

"In fate, there are good moments and bad."

"Is there anyone with you, Mother? Is there anyone accompanying you?"

"Where are you going, Mother? Are you going to a relative?"

"Which station are you getting off at? Where is your ticket?"

But the old woman wouldn't answer. She just kept on moaning, "They killed him."

Earlier that evening, a stranger had brought me the news that Sohan was dead, and I had not felt very much since. I had thanked him, as if he had come to leave a message for someone else, and had shown him to the gate. Afterward, I had not cried or talked to anyone about it. I had just quickly got ready for the train. I couldn't remember whether, before leaving, I had told Daddyji, or anyone else. I remembered only the guard's whistle and the train pulling out of the station, and remembered thinking that whenever I took the train something died in me: the family I had left behind when I was five years old, on my way to Dadar School, had seemed lost forever, as had the blind school friends there when I was leaving it to go back to my family.

Now the compartment windows were shut securely against the terror of the night, with not even an inch of space at the top for air. Trunks, bedrolls, burlap bags, tins, and baskets, piled up in a jumble, gave the compartment the feeling of a moving barricade against Muslim mobs that prowled the countryside in the night—even as the luggage groaned and shifted and closed us off from one another like a set of partitions. I was squashed up into a corner on a top berth, next to Ravi, who was fast asleep, and my legs dangled just above the old woman's voice and swung with the jolt of the train. I thought of Bhabiji, who was still in Lahore, and how she used to teach us never to swing our legs—in fact, to keep our feet out of sight as much as possible—and fleetingly I felt sad for the mother in the compartment, sad for all of us. A foot or so away from my face, a ceiling fan rattled in its cage, but it hardly threw off any air or stirred the pungent odor of ghi and grain, coconut oil and sweat in the compartment. I wondered if we'd ever be able to go back to our house, if we, too, were refugees, like so many men and women who had been fleeing their homes and shops, farms and orchards, to go and live God knew where.

The train stopped, but there were no compartment doors opening and slamming shut, no clatter of coolies' handcarts, no patter of public taps, no shouts of hawkers and venders. We must be in the middle of nowhere, I thought—the very thing we had been warned against. Mobs would stop trains, would loot whatever little the passengers had managed to flee with, and then would murder them. Trains would pull into stations with half their passengers dead: Muslims dead if the mob had been Hindu and Sikh; Hindus and Sikhs dead if the mob had been Muslim.

There were stirrings below me as people shifted bits of luggage to make the compartment more secure. Then the train lurched and started moving again, at first slowly and then quickly. There were the sounds of cracking joints and regular breathing as everyone settled back.

"They killed him." I wished that I could reach down and say to the old woman that they had killed Sohan, too, that I had lost a friend who was like a brother to me. But I did nothing. I sat on the berth, stunned.

❧

COUSIN DHARAM BIR'S FLAT in Bombay had two small bedrooms, a small hallway, a small balcony, a combination drawing-room-and-dining-room area with a kitchenette, and two little bathrooms. It was on the fourth floor of a five-story building, and he lived there with his wife, Cousin Satya; their three small children, Urvashi, Pradeep, and Sudeep; Cousin Satya's younger brother, Nitya Nand; and their maid and manservant. When we five moved in, Cousin Dharam Bir and Cousin Satya kept their own bedroom, my sisters and Cousin Leil and the maid slept in the children's bedroom, and Cousin Nitya Nand, Ravi, the three children, the manservant, and I slept on the floor in the drawing room. Then more relatives arrived, until there were nineteen of us in the flat, and we had to sleep wherever we could—in the hallway, in the dining area, on the balcony. Some had to double up on cots that were so narrow that their occupants could sleep only with one person pointing toward the head and the other toward the foot. None of us newcomers had lived in a flat before. In Lahore, my sisters and my cousins and I had all had separate rooms, and the congestion of the small flat made us a little irritable.

Bombay apparently had no Hindu-Muslim troubles, and the disturbances of the Punjab seemed very far away. But we had no idea how long we'd be with our cousins. We could make no plans—we didn't know when, or if, Daddyji and Mamaji and our other relatives would be coming out. Cousin Satya, however, was so sweet-natured that she never so much as hinted that we were in any way a burden to her. Cousin Dharam Bir, who was an engineer in the government irrigation service, was mostly at his office or at his club, and we saw little of him. Cousin Satya was unwell. She had stomach trouble, and whenever there was some improvement in that, she would develop a cold. Every evening, Cousin Nitya Nand, who was studying for his M.A. in chemistry, would return with a papaya for her, because he knew that it was her favorite fruit and might help to settle her stomach.

Bombay was very hot and steamy, and we seemed to be constantly sweating. The flat was equipped with a shower and a bathtub; we were not familiar with either of them, because in the Punjab we had bathed under a tap or with a bucket and a dipper. We were always wanting to bathe, but there was a water short-age in Bombay, and each day only some of us could bathe.

One morning, Sister Nimi and Cousin Leil woke up scratching their heads. Cousin Satya took one look at their scalps and said, "We've all got lice."

"How terrible!" Sister Nimi cried.

"You mean Nimi and I have got lice," Cousin Leil said judicially.

"No, Leil," Cousin Satya said. "I also have lice. I think we got them from the maid. She carries Sudeep around all the time, and he got them from her, and I must have got them from him."

Everyone's scalp was duly examined, and a strict regimen was begun of washing the heads of all of us, whether we had any evidence of lice or not, with some foul-smelling medicine. The medicine was so strong that it made me feel that things were perpetually crawling on my scalp. I would slap my head this way and that way, hoping to kill the lice, only to have the sensation intensify—but whether it was actually lice or my nervous pulse or irritation from the medicine or pins and needles of embarrassment, I never found out.

We had barely got rid of the lice (our heads and clothes—the whole flat—reeked of the medicine) when Ravi developed an itching around his chest. In a matter of minutes, he was itching from head to toe. A doctor was called. He took one look at Ravi and said that he had scabies. He prescribed regular baths and an application on the wet body of "scabies medicine." Within a day or two, we all had scabies, and it seemed we were all scratching from head to toe in unison, and were standing all day long in front of the bathrooms for our turn at the bathtub or the shower and the bottle of horrible, slippery medicine.

"Why do we have scabies?" I asked.

"What do you expect?" Sister Umi said. "We are living on top of each other."

"It's the fault of the Bombay washermen," Sister Nimi said. "I hear that you catch scabies from improperly washed clothes."

"Leave it to Nimi to try to excuse our living conditions," Sister Umi said.

I never found out just why we got scabies, but the itch was so pervasive and so unremitting that sometimes I felt I was really on fire. We were cured of the disease as suddenly as we had contracted it.

LETTERS ARRIVED regularly from Mamaji. The letters said that there was a lull in Lahore, and they invariably contained lists of saris and jewelry, cloth and kinds of dinnerware that Mamaji wanted the sisters to buy in Bombay. "Bombay has the best shops," she would write, or "Satya has wonderful taste. You're very lucky to have such a nice person with you to help you choose," or "You won't get another opportunity like this, so make the most of your stay in Bombay."

The letters often came with checks, and after a check arrived the sisters and Cousin Leil would go shopping. They would come home loaded down with rustling packages for the approval of Cousin Satya. I remember that one day they returned with two dinner sets, another day with two tea sets. Every day, all the purchases that were approved would be put away in a trunk that was kept in Cousin Satya's bedroom. In time, there were so many things that the trunk was full and packages were sticking out from under the cots and from on top of the cupboards. The purpose of the shopping was never stated, but we all knew that it was for dowries for the sisters.

Once, the sisters and Cousin Leil came home and said that they had hitchhiked a ride from the Crawford Market with a man.

Cousin Dharam Bir scolded them. "What if the man had taken you where you didn't want to go?" he asked. He had a twinkle in his voice, like Daddyji, but his manner was stern.

"There were three of us," Sister Umi said. "Besides, Daddyji let us do what we liked in Lahore, even though mobs roamed the streets." Sister Umi knew that she had only to mention Daddyji's name to get off the hook, because Cousin Dharam Bir had great respect for him.

Cousin Dharam Bir puffed at his cigarette for a long time—unlike Daddyji, he smoked and drank—but said nothing.

※

ALL DAY, I was left in the company of Ravi, who was two years younger than I was. He was a perfect guide, good-natured and full of curiosity. He seemed to sense that I did not want him to make any allowances for me on account of my blindness. If we were playing hide-and-seek in the *maidan* behind the building and I hit my forehead on the lamppost, he would go on playing as if nothing had happened.

I remember that we liked to get into our waterproofs and gum boots, which we had brought along from Lahore, because Bombay was famous for its monsoon rains, and go for a walk along Marine Drive, on which we lived. On one side of it was a row of multistory buildings like ours, and on the other the Arabian Sea. Between the road and the low breakwater wall, there was a fairly wide footpath. The monsoon rains were late that year, so we would go and sit on the wall and wait to be soaked by the sea. The waves would dash against the wall and drench us—especially when the evening sea breeze was up. We would hoot with delight and compare our waterpoofs to see which one of us had got wetter. Within a matter of days, the salt water had eaten through our waterproofs, so that when there was a monsoon rain we found we had little to protect our clothes. We would nevertheless walk in the pouring rain to a restaurant at the turning of Marine Drive toward Church Gate, and share a plate of potato chips. We would take a double-decker bus to an amusement park in Malabar Hill, where we liked to play around a statue of Mother Hubbard's cow. We would take a tram to Santa Cruz to buy stamps for our stamp albums. (We were just beginning to be aware that India was a country among dozens of other countries.) We would take an electric train to Juhu Beach to bathe in the sea.

On Marine Drive, we would climb onto the narrow breakwater wall and run along the top, while strangers called after us, "You'll fall into the sea and kill yourselves!" When we were out on excursions, we would hang out of the windows of the top deck of a double-decker bus, jump off a tram before it had come to a stop, or jump onto it after it had started up. We would shun the special footbridges over the tracks of the electric trains, and run across the tracks between trains. The more reckless the activity, the more delight we took in it. I remember that in the building we liked to play in the lift. It was a little wire cage with an accordion gate. It went up and down through the building within a latticework wire shaft. All day, we kept busy taking people up and down in the lift or trying to find out what made it work. The building had only one commissionaire. He was a tall, blustering Pathan from Peshawar. He worked twenty-four hours a day, doing double duty as liftman and watchman, and so had little time for either job. He would sometimes threaten us or chase us out of the lift, but for the most part he would leave us alone to play as we liked. Neither Ravi nor I had ever been in a lift before, and we couldn't get over the fact that at the mere touch of a button the lift cage would merrily skip floors or stop at them. If we jiggled the accordion gate even slightly between floors, the lift would stop. But we couldn't get out, because the outer door would open only when the lift cage was level with the floor. Then we discovered a way of opening the outer door manually, by a lever at its top. After that, we could get out of the lift at any point, and either climb onto the top of the cage or perilously hang from the cage floor as the lift shot up or dropped down. Sometimes we would scramble up the cables ahead of the cage right to the motor room on the roof of the building, or scramble down the cables ahead of the cage until we were almost pinned under it in the little well-like space between it and the basement floor.

I don't know how we escaped with our lives, but one thing I do know—though only in retrospect—is that in Lahore we had got so used to living with a sense of danger that in Bombay we couldn't bear to live without it.

🌢

IN THE LATE AFTERNOON, we would all gather in the drawing room. Lieutenant Gautam Singh, who was a young bachelor in the Navy, and who affectionately called Cousin Satya "Sister," would often stop by and join us. By then, Cousin Nitya Nand would also be home. People in the drawing room would laugh and laugh while watching a Sikh gentleman and his English wife, who habitually had tea on a balcony of the next building, but they would seldom explain to me what they were laughing at, and even when they did I couldn't understand what was so funny. They would say, "It's just the way they're sitting," or "It's just the way they're having tea," or "It's just the way he's feeding her pastry." I couldn't get them to be more precise—to explain, for instance, what they meant by "feeding her pastry." Was he passing the pastry on a plate, handing the pastry to her, or putting pastry in her mouth? Perhaps there was nothing to explain. The fun was just in watching a man wait on a woman rather than the other way around, as was usually the case.

None of us drank tea or coffee—we had been brought up to consider them bad habits. In the beginning, Lieutenant Gautam Singh used to arrive with pastries for all of us, but he stopped bringing them when he discovered that Cousin Nitya Nand was a strict vegetarian, who would not eat eggs even disguised in a confection. And then all of us would just sit and laugh—I would join in without knowing why—and run the little children into the bedroom if they became too boisterous, and shoo away the flies that settled on us.

One afternoon, Lieutenant Gautam Singh had the idea of taking us all for ice cream at Parisian Dining, near Church Gate. Cousin Satya wasn't feeling well, and she wouldn't hear of the girls' going unchaperoned with two men, even if Ravi and I were part of the group. So Lieutenant Gautam Singh took only

Cousin Nitya Nand and Ravi and me for ice cream at Parisian Dining.

After that, Ravi and I noticed that whenever Lieutenant Gautam Singh came he would talk mostly to Sister Umi, and Cousin Nitya Nand would talk mostly to Sister Nimi.

"The four are going to have a joint love marriage, like the Sikh gentleman and the English lady," Ravi said. "Right here in this flat. Lieutenant Gautam Singh will wear his naval uniform, stripes and all, and Cousin Nitya Nand will wear his homespun clothes." Cousin Nitya Nand was a nationalist, like Sohan, and though he was planning to study at Cambridge he wore only homespun Indian clothes.

"What about Cousin Leil?" I asked. "Who is it she'll marry?"

"She's not interested just now. She wants to be a lady doctor. It's your sisters who are buying all the stuff for the dowries. Sister Leil hasn't bought a thing."

The girls overheard us. They scolded us roundly and asked us how we dared match them up with anybody, and insisted that they planned to be independent. But we continued to believe that at least one love marriage was in the offing.

❦

"How SURPRISING that no one has ever thought of reading to you!" Cousin Nitya Nand said to me one afternoon. "I suppose everyone left the whole question of your studies to the time you'd go to England and America. I will read to you every morning for an hour or so before I go to my laboratory at college."

"Vedi won't be able to understand what you read," Sister Umi said. "He doesn't know English."

"But I know how to read Hindi," Cousin Nitya Nand said. "I'll get a Hindi book and read that to him."

"He won't be able to understand written Hindi," Ravi said. "It's very difficult. It has all kinds of Sanskrit words."

"I'll get a simple Hindi book," Cousin Nitya Nand said.

"But there's no place to sit and read here," Ravi said.

"Daddyji always told us that you need a good chair to sit in, a good light to read by, and a nice, quiet place," Sister Umi said.

"We'll go outside and sit and read on the breakwater wall," Cousin Nitya Nand said. "After all, our fathers came from villages without electric lights, and they all did their homework sitting by a street light at some roadside." He was soft-spoken but emphatic.

"What will you read to him?" Sister Nimi asked.

"I know a good history of pre-British India in Hindi. I'll get it from the bazaar today."

All day, I worried that Cousin Nitya Nand would forget to buy the book; that if he got it he'd neglect to read it to me; that if he read it to me I wouldn't be able to understand it, and then he would lose patience and interest; that people in the flat would make fun of me for wanting to read a book at all. (I realize now that for them the idea of my reading an ordinary book was as novel as, say, the idea of someone without hands playing the violin.) But as soon as Cousin Nitya Nand walked in that evening he said, "Vedi, I had to look through several shops, but I found the book."

The paper bag containing the book crackled under his arm like monsoon lightning. I felt happy in a surge.

The next morning, even before we'd had our breakfast, he and I went out, crossed the road, and found a perch on the breakwater wall. He started explaining to me what the book was. A little crowd of passersby gathered and started a hubbub. They clicked their tongues and asked nosy questions. Cousin Nitya Nand told them to move along, and then, at his suggestion, he and I turned half around on the wall and, with our backs to the passersby and our faces almost to the sea, continued our conversation. He told me that the book was written by a Communist, and that Communists treated one and all—sighted and blind, rich and poor—alike.

"Are you a Communist, then?" I asked.

"Yes," he said. "But I believe in Communism in its pure form, as it was originally taught by the guru Karl Marx."

His patient way of explaining reminded me of Daddyji, and his independent manner of Sohan.

"The Hindus today think of cows as holy," Cousin Nitya Nand read. "History has a scientific explanation for this." The hubbub of the crowd had died down—most of the passersby had dispersed or moved on—but I had to strain to hear Cousin Nitya Nand's soft voice over the putt-putt of motorcycles and the blast of car horns on one side, the continuous churning of the sea on the other, and the screech of vultures overhead. "All of Northern India was settled by Aryan invaders some thirty-five hundred years ago. They migrated from the Iranian plain over a period of time. They were nomadic people. They lived in harmony with land and animals. They depended for their milk and fuel on their cows. It was only natural, therefore, that in time they should start worshipping cows and thinking of them as Mother Nature. In fact, it is a characteristic of primitive people everywhere to worship life-giving forces. Many other ancient societies display instances of such anthropomorphism."

Cousin Nitya Nand paused to explain to me the meaning of "anthropomorphism." He abruptly asked, "Why are you shaking?"

"Your book is an attack on cows. Sohan and the R.S.S. would hate it."

Under his questioning, I told him about Sohan, and about the R.S.S. meetings that Sohan had introduced me to, where blessings of sacred cows were often invoked.

"The R.S.S. is a chauvinistic, fascist organization," Cousin Nitya Nand said, and then he told me at length what chauvinism and fascism meant, and why the R.S.S. was wrong in many of its "Hindu first" views.

I felt angry at him for attacking the R.S.S., but I didn't want him to think ill of me, because then he might give up reading to me, so I nodded obediently.

He resumed reading: "The horse, the donkey, the mule, and the dog have been better friends to man than the cow, but the cow was believed to be sacred because of its supply of milk. The reader is referred to the place of sheep in other early primitive societies."

I shifted along the wall closer to Cousin Nitya Nand and touched the book in his hand and thought about primitive Aryans coming over vast distances with their cows.

"The Aryans settled along the Ganges River. Practically all early settlements are by rivers. We have records of early settlements along, for instance, the Volga." I had never heard the word Volga before, and it sounded mysterious and far away. "In time, the Aryans began worshipping the Ganges just as they did the cow. We see examples of such personification of rivers in many primitive societies."

We were drenched by a big wave, and our hair, our faces, our clothes, and our shoes were dripping with salt water. We stood up and dried ourselves as best we could. Cousin Nitya Nand more or less mopped the wall and the outside of the book with his handkerchief, and, in our wet clothes, we sat down again.

"The Aryans settled along the Ganges and became dominant throughout North India. They displaced the indigenous Dravidians and made slaves of them. This was the origin of the notorious caste system, which was to become such a ruthless engine of oppression among the Hindus."

In the distance I heard a hawker's cry: "*Bhel-puri! Bhel-puri!*" The cry got louder and louder as the hawker walked toward us along the footpath. I hadn't had the hot, spicy snack since I was in Bombay, at Dadar School, four years earlier. I had no wish ever to visit the school, but I longed for *bhel-puri*. I was afraid to interrupt Cousin Nitya Nand's reading, however, in case he got angry and left off reading.

"What do you think of that idea?"

I had to tell Cousin Nitya Nand that I hadn't been paying attention, and why, but Cousin Nitya Nand, instead of scolding me, laughed and bought me some *bhel-puri*. Then he said, "You're easily distracted, because you're not used to being read to. You'll have to learn how to concentrate."

He resumed reading: "Aryans were tall, martial people, while the indigenous Dravidians were short and pacific. The Aryans imposed their religion and their will on the weaker people and dispossessed them of their homes and land. Such are the ways of conquerors with the conquered, of colonizers with the colonized. We see examples of this phenomenon again in the history of other societies. Ancient wrongs will only be righted when slaves everywhere rebel."

Cousin Nitya Nand looked up from the book and said, "Communism challenges a lot of accepted beliefs, don't you think?"

❧

EVERY MORNING, Cousin Nitya Nand and I would go down to the sea with the book before he left for his laboratory. Sometimes two or three passersby would join us on the wall. If they were quiet, Cousin Nitya Nand would let them sit and listen, too. Every morning, we would be sprayed or soaked by the salt water. Every morning, we would read ten or fifteen pages from the damp book. Every morning, we would have *bhel-puri*. Every morning, Cousin Nitya Nand would walk me back to our building. I remember that over a period of a few weeks I learned a bit about Buddha's teachings, about the Asoka empire, about the Gupta dynasty, about the invasions of Mahmud of Ghazni, about the reigns of Babur, Akbar, Jahangir, Shah Jahan, and Aurangzeb, about the escapades of Clive and Hastings. I couldn't keep all of it straight—the royal good deeds and fratricidal wars, courts and harems would get confused in my head—and sometimes I would switch off and listen to the crashing waves and wonder how old the sea was, how big it was, what caused the waves. All the same, I felt that Cousin Nitya Nand was introducing me to a world much greater than that of Dadar School, of harmonium and tabla, even of the R.S.S. I could not have given a name to that world, but I did one day learn the title of the book; it was "Whither India?"

🌢

A STREAM of letters arrived from Daddyji. One, dated June 10th, read:

You'll be glad to know that the government has sanctioned my request for four months' leave from seventeenth instant. Who knows, I may utilize some of the leave and bring Shanti and Ashok to Bombay. She has always wanted to see Bombay, and Dharam Bir speaks well of the bridge in the Cricket Club of India there.

On the seventeenth of June, he wrote:

Sheikh Sahib has come back from Dalhousie. I ran into him on Temple Road the other day, but he said nothing

about buying our house. I don't think there is a Muslim
alive in Lahore now who would pay a rupee for Hindu property.

And on the fifteenth of July:

Sad to say, my leave has been cancelled and I am back
in harness.

They say that nothing can be allowed to interfere with
official duties. But what duties! All day I am busy dividing
up the assets of the department between the West and East
Punjab, between Pakistan and India, according to the population formula of the Partition—sixty per cent to the West
Punjab and forty per cent to to the East Punjab. We spend
all day counting and haggling over tables, chairs, hat-and-
umbrella stands, typewriters, pencils, and rubbers. We
quibble over operation tables, over X-ray plants, over
microscopes, over the books in the public-health library.
Our Muslim friends also want all the files and records per-
taining to their districts, but many files have common rules
for the whole of the province, so I have to get at least all of
those files retyped. That's a very big job. I am especially
anxious to get one particular file duplicated and completed
before the Partition, on the fifteenth of August. It contains
a hundred years of British standing orders for managing
sanitation during festivals and for controlling cholera,
plague, smallpox, and dysentery during epidemics.

On the eighteenth of July, he wrote:

I think I wrote to you that I have been posted to Simla,
which is to be the new capital of the East Punjab. Yester-

day, we went to the railway station and loaded up our railway wagon—the government has provided each Hindu officer in Lahore with a railway wagon for transporting essential household goods. I told Shanti to treat this like another transfer, and we packed into the wagon our drawing-room carpet, our dining set, half a dozen bedrolls, and four boxes containing your clothes and woollens, and crockery and utensils. The government has guaranteed that the wagon will be attached to the first available train to the East Punjab. Shanti wanted to take the big camphor box containing Krishan's clothes and uniforms, and the clothes of Mysore silk or parachute silk made for you girls, and other things, but they wouldn't fit in the wagon. So we've stored them up in the interfloor room. I've had the door of the interfloor room bricked up and whitewashed to conceal it.

And on the third of August he wrote:

Everyone says that we shouldn't stay here after the tenth, which is being spoken of as the D-Day for Hindus to leave. I hope we can get out by then and go to Amritsar, which is completely under Sikh control. Everyone is playing a guessing game about whether the Radcliffe Boundary Commission will award Lahore to Pakistan or to India. The award may not now come until after Independence. Muslims think that Lahore will go to Pakistan, and Hindus think that it will go to India. In either case, I think the city will go through a terrible period of blood-letting: If the Muslims don't get it, they'll launch a terrible onslaught against Hindus out of resentment. If they do get it, they'll do the same in order to drive out the Hindus and Sikhs, who own most of the property here.

When you left, I thought that Babuji was coming around to my point of view—the February and March disturbances had really started to have their effect—and that he would leave Lahore with us. But he's gone back to his old way of thinking, and he says he won't leave no matter what. He has seen his every confidence in human nature betrayed, yet he continues to put his faith in the sanity of the masses.

Bhaji Ganga Ram, I'm afraid, is just as stubborn as Babuji. He says that if everybody leaves Mehta Gulli he'll stay behind and guard the family houses. I wish he would listen to me, as Bhabiji does—she's prepared to leave whenever we all do.

Of course, if Lahore does go to India we'll all be able to come back and live here as before. But I myself can't believe that Lahore would ever go to India. Without Lahore, Pakistan wouldn't be much.

Mamaji added a long postscript in Hindi, contradicting him:

Your daddy is still busy dividing up the department assets. This responsibility may keep us in Lahore after the Independence Day. Anyway, I don't see how we could leave without Babuji, Mataji, Bhaji Ganga Ram, and Chhoti Bhabiji [his wife] going with us.

Your daddy insists that we leave Lahore with a clean slate, so I've been paying off all our bills and debts. He's even written out a check for his dues to the Cosmopolitan Club three months in advance. I think it's the first time since our marriage that we won't have a single debt.

Your daddy says that we are bound to come back to Lahore to live and that he can't be happy anywhere else.

We'll certainly spend next winter here, because none of you children will be able to stand the winters in Simla. I have such bad memories of the cold in Simla. Either you children were sick or I was sick.

Your daddy says that we should leave the house neat and clean and in such a condition that we can drive down from Simla any time and live in it, so I have been busy laundering the sheets, the blankets, the quilts. I've had them counted, folded, and rolled. I've got all the cupboards lined with fresh shelf paper and arranged everything in them.

The tenth of August came, the eleventh, twelfth, thirteenth, fourteenth. The radio reported that Lahore was ablaze, that the worst riots ever were raging there, and that the fate of the city—whether it would go to India or to Pakistan—would not be announced until after the Independence celebrations on the fifteenth of August. Each day, my sisters and I waited for a letter, a telegram, or a trunk call: for news of Daddyji, Mamaji, and Ashok; of Babuji, Mataji, and our uncles and aunties at 16 Mozang Road; of Bhabiji, Bhaji Ganga Ram, Chhoti Bhabiji, and the rest of our relatives in Mehta Gulli. We tried repeatedly to book a trunk call to Lahore, only to be told that all communication with the West Punjab had been cut. We tried to book a trunk call to several relatives in Amritsar—the first major city definitely on the Indian side of the border— only to be told that the circuits were overloaded with trunk calls booked days in advance. I don't think I ever actually thought, that our parents, or any of our relatives, might be dead, but I thought of the many people who were dying, of the many people who were losing their parents and relatives, and I felt sad and frightened. We all tried to comfort each other, but the words stuck in our throats.

Somewhere outside, on Marine Drive, a drum rolled and an amateur band struck up some martial music. There were the sounds of dancing and singing, of marching and shouting. It was the eve of Independence, and no doubt the celebrations were being led by soldiers—their guns raised, their boots polished. I remembered Sohan, and I wondered what had happened to Mr. Khanna. I fell into a fitful doze, and dreamed that we were back in our house in Lahore. A Muslim mob was chasing us. We escaped through the iron door, but instead of Dr. Mathura Das's house on the other side there was another brick wall.

The ringing of the telephone jolted me awake. We all seemed to jump for the telephone. Sister Umi got it. "It's Daddyji!" she cried. "You're in Amritsar! . . . Daulat Ram Chachaji and Subhadran Chachiji are in Amritsar! They've brought out Bhabiji!"

"What are they saying? What are they saying?" we all demanded.

It seemed that Babuji, Mataji, Uncle Lakshman Das, Bhaji Ganga Ram, and Chhoti Bhabiji were still in Lahore but that all the rest of our relatives had come out safely. We had no chance to say more than a few words before three minutes were up and the trunk call was automatically disconnected.

❧

"EVERYONE SAID that the eleventh of August was the last day for Hindus to get out of Lahore alive,"

Mamaji recalled some months later. "But that morning your daddy drove off to the office as usual, saying
that they hadn't finished dividing up all the department's assets—as if one more chair or table at that
point made any difference. Gian Chand went to the
bazaar and brought back the news that maimed and
wounded Muslim refugees from the East Punjab were
arriving in the city and firing up Muslims—that the
Muslim League was making final lists of Hindu houses
in order to take its revenge that night. When it was
barely twelve, your daddy drove up. I saw one jeep of
official guards in front and one behind. I didn't know
what to think. 'We have to leave this very moment,'
he said. 'The Muslims have already closed the border
to cut off the escape of Hindus and Sikhs.' I barely had
time to call Gian Chand to come with us, and to get a
few changes of clothes and a few things into the car.
'We'd better pick up Sureshta from 16 Mozang Road,'
your daddy said." Sureshta was in the ninth month of
pregnancy. "He told me, 'Lakshman can't leave, because
of Babuji and Mataji, but that's no reason for him to
keep Sureshta back.' I thought that Lakshman would
never let her go. His friend Sundar, Bawa Dinga Singh's
son, had refused to send his wife out, and she was also
very pregnant. But who can contradict your daddy? I
kept mum. At 16 Mozang Road, Lakshman, Sureshta,
and Arun were on the veranda." Arun was their two-
year-old son. "Your daddy ordered Sureshta to take
Arun and get into the car. Lakshman tried to say
something, but he held your daddy in such awe that
he couldn't find his tongue. Lakshman and Sureshta
silently embraced on the veranda steps, and Sureshta
and Arun got in the front seat with Ashok and me.

The poor girl didn't even have time to get a change of saris. Her servant was standing there, and your daddy ordered him to get in the car, too, and he got in the back with Gian Chand. When we were almost out of the gate, your daddy noticed that the servants didn't have much room for their legs. He stopped the car and made Gian Chand put out my Singer sewing machine. I wanted to protest. I'd had it since my wedding day, and what difference did a little discomfort for the servants make? And to leave it right there on the ground by the gate for some Muslim to take! But I didn't dare. All along the Grand Trunk Road were Muslim refugees walking toward Lahore. I didn't see any Hindu or Sikh refugees going in our direction. Probably they were all hiding, afraid to raise their heads for fear the Muslims would chop them off. And you should have seen those Muslim refugees—in dirty clothes, with just a few chipped clay bowls and plates on their heads. They had probably never owned much else. And it was for their sake that all the good Hindu families, like us, were being chased out. The ways of God are mysterious. At the border, you couldn't see the water for the blood in the canal. Men, women, and children were writhing on the road, on the bank, in the ditches, with their arms and legs half cut off, and everywhere there were torsos and heads and limbs. Only God Himself could have told which were Hindus and which were Muslims. The border was barricaded and was being guarded by many Muslim sentries holding guns as casually as if they were sticks. They looked as if they would shoot just for the sport of it. Your daddy motioned to the guards in the jeeps to stay where they were, and walked straight up to the sentries and started talking. I looked at the faces of the sentries and then at Sureshta and recited the Gayatri Mantra. The sentries talked among themselves and looked across at us in a dirty way. I closed my eyes and held my breath. Sureshta nudged me, and I opened my eyes—a higher-up was salaaming your daddy. It seemed years since I had seen a Muslim salaam a Hindu. Your daddy slowly walked to us, with his back to the sentries. His step was so sure that you might have thought he was in his own *gulli*. I don't think I caught my breath until our car had crossed the border. In Amritsar, we went straight to Sureshta's parents' house. We tried repeatedly to telephone or telegraph you, but nothing seemed to work. We camped out there like other refugees. Sureshta's father had given orders that no one who came to the house was to be turned away without food or water, and refugees were arriving all day long—relatives, friends, strangers—with stories that made you think that the world had been turned upside down, that people had become demons."

❧

A FEW DAYS after the trunk call from Daddyji, we heard on the radio that the Radcliffe Boundary Commission had finally awarded Lahore to Pakistan, and, as Cousin Dharam Bir pointed out, this meant that all Hindu property was as good as gone. We couldn't take in the loss of our house and everything in it. Then we got a letter from Daddyji. He wrote that he was sad to inform us that his ancestral village of Nawankote had been razed and that everyone who lived in it had died.

We had never gone to Nawankote, we knew no one who lived in it, but we felt as if part of us had been lost. He said that there was no news from our relatives left in Lahore, but that everyone else from there, including Chhoti Bhabiji's brother Vidya Ratan and Daddyji's first cousin Bahali Ram, had been heard from, and that although all of them had got out, many of them, who had had houses of their own, now did not have so much as a bedroll to their name. They were all camping with in-laws, relatives, or friends. He said that he was writing from Simla, the new capital of the East Punjab, where he, Mamaji, and Ashok had just arrived, and where he was officiating as director of public health. He said that they had been allotted a big, two-story government bungalow on Jakko Hill, but that they had scarcely any bedding, clothes, or utensils. The railway wagon with our few things hadn't arrived. He wanted Sisters Nimi and Umi and me to go to Uncle Dwarka's in Delhi, and Daulat Ram Chachaji wanted Cousins Leil and Ravi to come to Amritsar, Chachaji's new posting. Daddyji said that he was also telling Brother Om, who was still in Kanpur with Auntie Vimla and Auntie Pushpa, to go to Delhi, and telling Usha to go there, too, and that he would come and collect all of us in Delhi as soon as he got some casual leave.

❧

UNCLE DWARKA was one of our few relatives who had settled outside Lahore. He had been living in Delhi for fifteen years or so, and we didn't know him very well—we saw him mostly at weddings. He and his wife, Auntie Santosh, lived in an out-of-the-way rented house on Ram Kishore Road, in Old Delhi. Previously, hardly any relatives had gone and stayed with them, but now they had staying with them almost thirty people, most of them Auntie Santosh's relatives. The house, a dilapidated one-story affair with a little lawn in front and a yard behind, had been put up as a temporary structure to accommodate the guests who had come to attend the Durbar of 1911; it had no plumbing—just an outhouse. When we arrived, it was the monsoon season, and the walls were so damp that if one touched them lime dropped off in chunks. Half a dozen pails were put out to catch the water from leaks in the roof. It seemed that even centipedes had trouble maintaining their hold, for every few hours one of them dropped off the ceiling. The only thing I liked in the house was a tiger skin spread on the floor of the drawing room; it had a furry head, big glass eyes, and big teeth in an open, ferocious jaw.

❧

ONE AFTERNOON, Brother Om arrived by train from Kanpur and Usha from Dehra Dun. We'd hardly had a chance to catch up on their news—Auntie Vimla had given birth to a daughter, and Sister Pom's baby son, Vindoo, had started smiling—when a visitor was announced. He introduced himself as an aide-de-camp to Lord Mountbatten and a friend of Lieutenant Gautam Singh, who had asked him to look us up. "The Muslims from Jaipur are marching toward Delhi," he told us. "They belong to the ferocious Meo tribe, and they say they are going to kill all the Hindus."

"Will they come to Ram Kishore Road?" we asked. "Will they come to Old Delhi?"

"Why not?" he said.

He exuded chilly confidence, and I decided that I didn't like him, even if he was an A.D.C. to the Viceroy. Auntie Santosh's mother started howling, and my big sisters quickly ushered him out. Then I wished we had made him stay and tell us more, but it was too late.

That evening, Muslim shouts erupted in the air. We had not heard such shouts since Lahore, and now there was no iron door, no neighborhood arrangement for escape. We sat up the whole night on the roof, waiting and listening and watching. The only grown man among us was Uncle Dwarka, but his presence was not as reassuring as it might have been, because of a story he used to tell on himself: When, in Lahore, he had failed his B.A. examination on the first try, he had climbed up onto the roof and called down to Mataji, "I'm going to jump! I'm going to kill myself!" Mataji had begged him not to do it, and he had climbed down. He used to add that a passerby had called up to a young man on a roof who was behaving as he had behaved, "Come, jump!" The young man had called down, "What is it to you? I'm just trying to scare my mother." Uncle Dwarka would laugh as he told this story. He was one of our most good-natured relatives, but no match, we felt, for the Meo marchers from Jaipur. Besides, he was extremely distracted, since Babuji, Mataji, and Uncle

Lakshman were still in Lahore and there had been no news of them.

Auntie Santosh's mother, who had taken to her bed, kept up a moan below: "Prepare yourselves for death by Muslims!"

"Everything will be all right, Mother—you'll see, everything will be all right," Auntie Santosh called down to her. "Delhi isn't Lahore. Delhi is our own city, with our own police and our own Congress government. Pandit Nehru is sitting here. Mountbatten is sitting here. No one can touch us."

We all took turns going below and comforting Auntie Santosh's mother—pressing her shoulders and legs, making her cold compresses and taking her glasses of water—but she kept on moaning, "Get ready for death by Muslims!"

"Mother has just had a bad scare in Lahore," Auntie Santosh told us. "She's not been the same since she came out."

Every night, it seemed, there were new eruptions of riots, and we fell into the old Lahore routine of jumping at any unfamiliar noise, of being abruptly awakened, of running outside to look for signs of fire or mobs. But nothing happened, and we got used to the alarms. Auntie Santosh's mother, however, could not be coaxed into leaving her bed.

❧

IT WAS STILL and hot. The garden of Birla House, where Gandhiji was staying in New Delhi, smelled of some flowers I couldn't place. The people around me spoke not the familiar Punjabi but the unfamiliar Delhi Hindi, which sounded stiff and foreign. There was a stir. Then Gandhiji came on the loudspeaker. It was his evening prayer meeting, and Sister Umi, Auntie Santosh, and I had gone to hear what he had to say for himself. His voice had very little volume, and he was hard to understand. He sounded hoarse and toothless. In fact, I caught only every second or third sentence, and got an impression of what he was saying instead of exactly hearing what he was saying. He said he was saddened by what was happening next door, in the East and the West Punjab. He counselled Hindus and Sikhs in the West Punjab not to leave their homes and to stay bravely among Pakistani Muslims at the risk of mass death. He said that if Pakistani Muslims burned down Hindu and Sikh houses the Hindus and Sikhs should rebuild them. If Pakistani Muslims forced their way into the sanctuary of the temple, Hindus and Sikhs were to pray. He counselled the Hindus and Sikhs not to change their religion under any circumstance—he said death was better than surrendering one's religion, one's soul and moral being. He said that Hindus and Sikhs should not lift their hands against their Muslim enemy even if their daughters were raped in front of their eyes, even if their wives were raped in front of their eyes. He counselled Hindus and Sikhs in the East Punjab not to retaliate, not to act like beasts and snakes. He said that violence and hatred led only to more violence and hatred, that violence and hatred could be answered only by nonviolence and love.

A couple of times, people in the audience heckled

him, but for the most part everyone listened to him as
if he knew what he was talking about. I got more and
more angry. I thought that the only reason he could
talk that way was that he didn't have a house, he didn't
have a mother or a sister, he wasn't a refugee and had
no idea how Muslims could behave. He was six times
my age, and I decided that he was wrong about everything. This man whom we had once venerated used to
say they would partition India only over his dead body,
but he had let Partition happen.

"Who does Gandhiji think he is?" I said as we
were driving back. "How dare he say such things?"

"His words can comfort only the Hindu and Sikh
jackals in the East Punjab," Sister Umi said. "They
didn't retaliate until July—when Muslims in the West
Punjab had been killing their Hindu and Sikh brothers
steadily for five months."

"What finally made the Hindus and Sikhs act?" I
asked.

"It was only in July that the Hindus and Sikhs in
the East Punjab started seeing their blood relatives
pouring out of the West Punjab in great numbers as
refugees," Auntie Santosh said. "There is all the difference between hearing about things and actually seeing
them."

When we got back to Ram Kishore Road, I said
to Sister Nimi, who alone among us remained a Gandhi supporter, but who hadn't been able to come with
us, because she wasn't feeling well, "Sohan used to say
that it was not Gandhiji's nonviolent methods but
British decency that won us our independence."

"What rubbish!" she said. "British people decent?

My foot! If they'd been decent, they would have left India long since, but they tried to stay on by every possible means. They imprisoned our leaders, whose only crime was that they didn't like their people to be enslaved. They turned Muslims against Hindus."

"They could have let Gandhiji starve to death during his hunger strikes," I said. "They could have shot him right at the start. Instead, they allowed him to build up his following over decades and become very powerful."

"If they had let him die—never mind killed him—they couldn't have stayed in India for a day. The whole country would have risen up. Then nothing could have saved the raj, and the British knew it."

"Why did they let him become so powerful in the first place?"

"They were stupid," Sister Nimi said. "They just didn't realize how effective his nonviolent methods were being."

"Even if you're right, Gandhiji has done his work now. It's high time that he retired. He's too idealistic to deal with Jinnah and the Muslim League. He must stop interfering with Hindu and Sikh retaliation. We have the right to avenge the Muslim horrors."

"How can you condemn the innocent Muslims in the East Punjab and West Bengal for what Muslims are doing on the other side of the border?" Sister Nimi demanded. "You can't condemn a whole people like that. If we allow fanatics to start taking revenge, where will they stop? There are forty million Muslims in India. What would you have us do—kill them all? Once you let fanatics take over anywhere, they'll carry their war to all of India."

"But if we don't chase out the Muslims, where will we refugees settle? Where will we find space?"

"A province or a country is not like a house, which has a limited space. All of us will simply have to live together. That's what Gandhiji and the Congress leaders, who want India to be a secular, tolerant place for all religions, are saying. If we don't listen to them, they'll be replaced by the hothead Hindu and Sikh fanatics—the R.S.S., the Akali Party, and their ilk, who would have India become a religious state, like Pakistan."

"Well, if we can't get rid of the Muslims we should at least deny them a voice in the government. After all, Hindus and Sikhs have no voice in the Pakistan government. We must make sure that a leader like Jinnah never emerges again."

"But if you deny Muslims a voice in the government you may actually help to produce another Jinnah. We should learn from the British mistakes—that you can't deny people a voice in their government forever. Sooner or later, the people will rebel. Anyway, the question of treating Muslims differently from us doesn't really arise. They are our own kith and kin. That's why an Indian Muslim bears no resemblance to a Muslim anywhere else. Gandhiji's work is far from done."

I repeated some of the Indian history I had learned at the R.S.S. meetings and from Cousin Nitya Nand's reading of "Whither India?" "Buddha taught nonviolence, like Gandhiji, and what happened to India? The Muslims conquered and ruled us for hundreds of years. Then the British conquered and ruled us. The Muslims of Pakistan say they'll come back and rule us again."

"But violence has been a chief cause of the decline of many nations. Nonviolence has never really been tried."

I felt frustrated. I didn't know the history of any other country, and she was a college student. I changed my tack. "Be honest. Have you always thought like this? Have you never doubted your faith in Gandhiji and nonviolence?"

She fell silent, and for some time I couldn't get her to say anything. Then she said, "I sometimes feel very bitter. I feel bitter about the tens of thousands of Hindus and Sikhs who are dying." She broke off.

I felt that she didn't have to say any more. She was the idealist of us all; I recalled that she had turned the balance in favor of Sheikh Sahib's proposal that we pipe in his well water. If she could become bitter, what hope was there for the rest of us?

❦

"THERE IS DADDYJI!" Sister Nimi exclaimed, and she started crying. The moment I felt his large hand on my shoulder, I started crying. It was early in the morning, and he had walked into the house without giving us any notice.

"What is there to cry about?" he asked, and he quoted to us this Urdu couplet:

Those whose plans are stormy, those whose
natures are stormy—
When do they ever turn their boats to the
shore?

"We thought you'd never come," Sister Nimi said.
"I'm here now," he said.

Auntie Santosh pressed him to stay for breakfast,
but he insisted that we had to drive to Simla right
away, so that he could return to the refugee camps in
the plain the following day.

We set off immediately. Daddyji had bought a new
motorcar, and I couldn't get over it. I climbed from
the front seat into the back seat and then into the front
again. I opened and closed the side windows and the
glove compartment. I touched the various knobs and
handles. The car's seats were covered with cloth and
were wide, like a sofa. Instead of a big gear stick on
the floor, which had always got in the way of our legs
in the old car, the new car had a small gearshift tucked
behind the steering wheel. In fact, the car had so much
room that it was almost like a toy house.

"Vedi, the color of the car is black," Daddyji was
saying. "I chose that color because it's less likely to
show dents when it's painted over."

❦

MAMAJI WAS FEVERISH with a Simla cold, and all
she could talk about was the terrible two-story government bungalow they had been living in on Jakko Hill.
"When I first moved into the Jakko Hill bungalow, I

thought I had been put in a tomb, it was so cold—and we didn't have a stitch of warm clothes," she told us. "I borrowed sweaters and blankets from Rasil." Rasil was an old family friend who had summered in Simla for years. "The house was so out of the way that the whole day long all I ever heard was the 'sha-ah-ahn, sha-ah-ahn' of the Simla silence. There were just Gian Chand and Ashok with me, and Muslims were living all around. Without your daddy there, I felt very frightened. One night, I heard some people clambering up the hill. They tried to break into the house. I thought I had escaped Lahore only to die at the hands of Simla Muslims. I called 'Sher Singh! Gian Chand! Ram Saran! Qasim Ali! Raj Kumari! Lakshman Singh!' I must have called the name of practically every servant I'd ever had. They must have thought that I had an army of servants quartered in the house. They ran away. When your daddy came back from tour, I gave him notice that I wasn't going to live in the big house another day. He made inquiries for a more central, safer house and found out that a Muslim officer was just vacating the upper flat of Erneston. Your daddy and I went to see it. We hardly looked at the cottage. We just saw its situation—near the Mall, near your daddy's office. Sardar Swaran Singh's bungalow was one house up from it, and Premier Gopichand Bhargava's was not far." At the time, Sardar Swaran Singh and Gopichand Bhargava were the only two ministers in the East Punjab government, and they divided its main functions between them.

The Muslim officer who had been living in the upper flat had hurried out of the cottage after hearing some rumors about Hindu-Muslim troubles in Simla, and had left everything behind—his crockery, his curtains, his furniture—just as it was. He had gone to stay in the Grand Hotel—considered relatively safe, because the East Punjab government had taken it over. By the time we arrived, Mamaji was living in Erneston. It was a two-story wooden cottage with a tin roof, down a slope from the main road. Its back was mostly blocked by a second hillside. The lower flat was occupied by other tenants, and the upper flat had only three rooms, with a single bathroom. (The kitchen was in a separate little building.) There was a long, narrow dining room, a sitting room with a fireplace, and a bedroom, where Daddyji, Mamaji, Usha, and Ashok slept. There was an open veranda in the front and a glazed back veranda, where the rest of us slept—the sisters at one curtained-off end, I at the other, and Brother Om, when he was around, in the middle. (Brother Om had gone to Ludhiana, down in the plain, to resume his interrupted studies toward his Bachelor of Science degree.) The cottage had little cross-ventilation. Mamaji called it a trap for fever and asthma.

❧

IT WAS ONLY after we started living in Erneston that we began to understand what the loss of Lahore meant to us. Like all Lahore Hindus, we had lost our property to Pakistan—our life savings and the house Daddyji had built, and had paid for after almost twenty-five years of government service. I asked Daddyji once who had taken over our house, and he said, "Some

Muslim or other good at pulling strings," and quoted to me this Urdu couplet:

When the nightingale has abandoned her nest in
the garden,
What does she care who lives there—whether owl
or the auspicious bird.

(In Indian lore, the owl is an accursed, stupid bird.)

The Muslim officer continued to stay at the Grand Hotel while he waited to go to Pakistan in a convoy under military escort. He would visit us daily to look over his belongings and would worry aloud about how he could take them with him. He had exquisite taste and was attached to his belongings. He came one day and said, "Mrs. Mehta, I've got a place in a military convoy, but I can't take anything with me. It's my things or my life." He pleaded with her to buy his things, and was prepared to sell them at any sacrifice price.

But Mamaji wouldn't hear of the idea. She thanked him, and told him that she would help him find a place to store his possessions.

He wouldn't be put off. "You can have my things," he said, "and I'll go and claim your things in Lahore."

"No, thank you," Mamaji said. "Who knows? We may go back to our house in Lahore one day." She treated him to tea.

After he left, we all cried that Mamaji was being foolish.

"Why did you refuse him?" Sister Umi demanded. "Most Hindu refugees who occupy Muslim houses take possession of all their things and don't pay so much as a pice for them."

"A force sale by a Muslim refugee!" Mamaji exclaimed. "Am I so mad that I would risk such a curse? I have been unlucky enough without earning the ill luck of dispossessing a poor Muslim refugee."

Daddyji joined us, and we appealed to him.

"We would be confiscating his things," he said. "It would be wrong to punish one Muslim for the misdeeds of other Muslims."

We argued with both of them, but we couldn't budge them.

The Muslim officer came the next day and had all his things removed for storage. As he was leaving, he saluted Mamaji with the Hindu *"Namaste"* and presented her with a jewelry box. She didn't want to accept it, but there was no way to turn it down, so the jewelry box—which was made of wood, with a lot of decorations, and had individual compartments for bangles, rings, chains, and pendants—became our first new ornamental possession in independent India.

Just about then, we got the news that some Muslims had gone, in turn, to Babuji and Bhaji Ganga Ram and threatened to kill them if they didn't vacate their houses. Babuji, Mataji, Uncle Lakshman, Bhaji Ganga Ram, and Chhoti Bhabiji had all somehow taken shelter in a couple of refugee camps—the last of their kind in Lahore—and been driven with other refugees in lorries, under military escort, right up to the boundary on the Grand Trunk Road, some eighteen miles away, and from there they had gone to relatives, first in Amritsar, and then in Delhi. Mamaji attributed their escape to her honorable dealings with the Muslim officer.

Without the Muslim officer's things, the cottage seemed very bare. We didn't have woollen clothes, and we mostly had to stay indoors, sitting in a huddle on a bed, with Rasil's borrowed quilts and blankets thrown over us, or walking about with blankets around our shoulders like shawls. We inquired every day at the government offices about our railway wagon; it should have arrived in the East Punjab in July, but there was no sign of it. One day, we heard that it was probably lost, because it had been traced to Karachi, where it had somehow got shunted off. Another day, we heard that the Pakistan government had rerouted it to India from Karachi. Then we got a message from Daddyji, from the plain—that the wagon was in Kalka and he had reclaimed it, but that somewhere along the route it had been looted, and all that was left was nine dining chairs, a small chest of drawers, and one carpet. He was having those things sent up to Erneston in a lorry.

❦

DADDYJI WAS HARDLY ever in Simla. Most of the time, he was in the plain, seeing to the sanitary and other health measures of the refugee camps. He said that he had to improvise all the arrangements; Pakistan had reneged on the agreement to divide up the department assets, and everything, including the manuals and standing orders for mass gatherings, had been lost. Even when he was in Simla, he seemed to talk only about refugees: about people arriving or leaving in convoys, in columns, in trains or lorries or bullock carts, on mules or on foot; about trains pulling in or pulling out with massacred or mutilated passengers; about people dying on the roadside, in huts and fields and wells, in scrub and thickets; about fatherless, motherless, sonless, daughterless people without a pice to their name, cast up as if on an unfamiliar shore, with neither prospects nor destination, sitting in some improvised encampment, alternately benumbed and angry, passive and wailing. One week, we heard that the tally of the cross-migration of refugees was five hundred thousand; another week, that it had reached seven hundred and fifty thousand.

The final tally of the refugees in the Punjab was to be ten and a half million, most of them crossing the border within three months of Partition. As many as a million were to die.

❧

ONE MORNING when Daddyji was leaving for the plain, I got in the car with him. "I'm coming with you," I said.

"There's a lot of disease in the plain," he said.

"But you go."

"I am a doctor. All day, I'm out in the open making rounds. Where would I leave you?"

"I'll stay with one of your staff. I have nothing to do all day up here. I want to come."

He gave in, and got Gian Chand to put extra bedding in the car.

We reached a refugee camp near Ambala early in the afternoon. It was dry, dusty, and hot. All around were the stench of filth and the rotting odor of the dying and the sobs and yells of desperate people. Flies droned and settled on the skin; they were very energetic and not easy to swat, and they were so pervasive that they seemed to breed in the air.

Daddyji walked ahead with a couple of inspectors, and I followed with a camp policeman, who held me by the hand. There was no path, and we had to pick our way among men and women huddled on the ground, who didn't stir as we passed. Children followed us, some of them begging for food, most of them as quiet as mice.

"Hare Ram! Hare Ram!" the policeman said. "These brothers and sisters had their own land, were plowing and sowing it through long months and making provisions for their families, and now they can't even move out of the way. You're lucky, Sahib, that you can't see them."

I felt angry at the policeman for talking on as if the refugees couldn't hear him and for referring to my blindness. I felt angry at the people on the ground who wouldn't move out of the way, at the British, at the Muslims, at Partition. I could faintly hear Daddyji talking with his staff about the supplies of vaccine, powdered milk, and powdered eggs, and examining refugees and getting them inoculated. I wished that I could hear them better, but there was no way to walk faster, no way to catch up with them and stay close behind. I called to Daddyji, and he fell back and took my hand. He tried to rouse some of the refugees and get them to talk. Only a couple of them responded. They poured out the stories of their escape and journey in disconnected shouts, as if they thought we were deaf.

There was a commotion ahead. A refugee was tearfully protesting against being inoculated. "I want to die," he was saying. "I want to die."

Daddyji pressed my hand. "His hands have been cut off," he said.

I shuddered. Hands were like eyes to me. On this walk, even more than normally, I had constantly to resist touching anything, for fear of embarrassing others or myself, of drawing attention to my blindness, of encountering something unpleasant or dangerous. No doubt, all around me were refugees with every kind of injury or deformity, but resisting touching them permitted me—just as the wretched policeman had suggested—to avoid knowing about them. Now the refugee without hands was standing so close to me that I could actually have reached out and touched him, and the combined wish and reluctance to touch him was excruciating, because I wanted to make contact. I wanted to learn the extent of his injuries. Did he have arms? Did he have elbows? And I wanted to ask him questions: How had it happened? How did he wash and change his clothes? How did he eat?

"It's in your best interest," the inspector was saying. There was a whiff of alcohol and a childlike exclamation of pain as the refuge without hands was inoculated.

The inspector moved on to the next inoculation.

I tried to speak to the refugee without hands. From his first few halting, softly spoken words in rustic Punjabi, I gathered that he was a Sikh, and knew that because of his beard and long hair he had been a marked man.

"Your eyes, Sahib—where did it happen to you?" he asked.

"We are from Lahore, but it wasn't the Muslims— just a sickness in childhood. Your hands—what happened?"

"In a temple, Sahib. We had taken refuge there with our families. We had been sleeping there for four nights. The fifth night, they came. We expected them. We were ready for them. They told us to come out and become converts. They swore that it was not a trick to disarm us and rape and torture our wives and daughters. They said, 'As Allah is our witness, a mullah is standing outside to perform the ceremony. If you become converts, you can go back to your homes. No one will trouble you.' We cried, 'We would rather die than become filthy Muslims!' We set upon them like a pride of lions. We fought them with guns and knives for two nights and a day. Then our ammunition ran out, our supplies ran out. Still we fought on. The defilers forced their way into the temple. We started killing our women to save them from torture and rape. I cut the throat of my daughter with one stroke. It was the turn of my wife. I hesitated, and I was overpowered by a defiler. I fought back. I think I killed him, but a whole group of them came at me and chopped off my hands and cut off my ears."

I shivered. Daddyji had not told me about the loss of his ears. Perhaps it was too terrible to mention along with the hands.

"Guru Nanak gave me the strength of a lion. I

broke loose and ran after the man who was carrying off my wife. I lost him. I hid and skulked in fields and drains for a week. Then I saw a lorry of Sikh police. They took me to a convoy of refugees."

As he talked, other refugees surrounded us. They chanted and grunted and groaned in assent. They became voluble.

An elderly woman tried to calm them by mentioning the name of Gandhiji.

"Gandhi didn't see his daughter raped!" one of them cried.

"Gandhi didn't lose his wife!"

"He's a coward! He's afraid to come to the Punjab. Let him come here and we'll show him the truth about his nonviolence."

They talked about how they, too, had been maimed, how their relatives had suffered indignities, how the members of their families had died. They wept even as they angrily swore to take revenge on Muslims in India.

❧

It was December. The chill winds blew and the frost set in. We had never spent a winter in Simla. We had been postponing having a fire in Erneston to avoid the expense, but now every evening at six o'clock we huddled around a coal fire in the sitting room, on some office furniture the government had provided us with. Mamaji and my sisters were busy knitting, embroidering, reading—my sisters had resumed their studies in Simla. Even Ashok, who was three and a half, was busy—racing around the cottage, climbing on people's laps, rattling some crayons that a family friend had given him. I alone had nothing to do, and sat at the edge of the semicircle listening to the sound of the knitting needles, of the turning of a page, or of a thread being drawn through a taut piece of cloth on an embroidery frame. The little knitting I had learned at the Emerson Institute was useless—I could scarcely have knitted a panel. Besides, knitting seemed a fit occupation for my sisters and my mother but not for me.

Now and again, I would reach out and touch the knitting in Mamaji's hands to see how far along she was with the sweater, sock, or mitten she was knitting for us, or touch Sister Nimi's book to see how much she had left to read, but their progress only heightened my sense of idleness. Occasionally, Mamaji would ask me to make a knitting ball out of a woollen skein or Sister Umi would ask me to tighten her embroidery frame, but I felt that such tasks were only invented to give me something to do.

I was approaching my fourteenth birthday. At that age, Brother Om had started college. I had spent, all told, three years in school, off and on: two and a half years or so at Dadar School when I was less than nine, and the rest at the Emerson Institute, where I had done little more than learn about the Hira Mandi and its stock of singing and dancing girls. Previously in the years of no schooling, I had been sustained by the dream of going to England or America. Besides, there had been walks with Bhabiji, and her stories; cousins to play with, and kite flying; a music master, and a harmonium and tablas; Ram Saran and Qasim Ali to talk to, and a bicycle to ride; riding on hill ponies with

Usha, who was always there to attend to me; a room of my own at 11 Temple Road, and a sighted friend, Sohan; games, and R.S.S. meetings; Marine Drive, and Cousin Nitya Nand's Hindi reading. The Partition and its aftermath had put an end to all that. And the dreams of going to America were ended, too. Now we had only one servant, Gian Chand, and he was busy from morning to night. Neither he nor anyone else, it seemed, had time even to take me out for a walk so that I could stretch my legs. I felt imprisoned in the cottage, and my hands ached for something to do. The three or four Braille books I had had and my few Braille implements were lost to Pakistan. Daddyji had bought me some made-in-England carpentry tools after he saw me sitting and working with a carpenter at 11 Temple Road, and they, too, were lost.

When I complained to Mamaji that I had nothing to do all day, she would say, "People are dying all around us. We've lost our home, we've lost our old-age security, and you're worrying about having nothing to do. You should thank Ram that you can sit and eat as much as you like and no one can say no to you. When will you get it through your head that your daddy is due to retire in two years, and that after that we won't have his salary, this cottage, our government furniture? Where will we go then? Where will we live? Who will keep us? I can't even run to Babuji and Mataji. They are now poor refugees living off their son's earnings. After retirement, we won't even be able to keep a servant. Who will then wash the pots and pans but me?" Once she got started on the subject of our future penury, she would begin to wheeze and cough and make throat-clearing noises. "We have three daughters to marry off. How will we get together all the dowries? Can you tell me that? And if we can't get them married, then what will they be if not permanent charges? And who's going to rear and educate Ashok, who has barely learned to speak? You? Om? Om is growing up to be an idler. When has anyone ever seen him sitting down and studying? And who's going to take care of you for the rest of your life? And you're complaining. Don't you have any shame or any sense? How was I so unlucky as to have reared such useless children—every last one of them growing up to be a permanent charge." There was no stopping her once she'd got started. I would try to divert her or try to run away from her, but I couldn't. Her tirades always ended in a full-fledged asthma attack, with her collapsing on her bed and asking me to bring her medicine or calling Gian Chand to fetch a doctor for an injection.

The sisters were at their school or their college, or they managed to slip out to their friends, and I was left to bear Mamaji's tongue-lashings alone. When I was older, I realized that she was not so much scolding me as having me share her troubles, but at the time I felt resentful and trapped.

I remember that once I repeated to Daddyji what Mamaji said.

"Don't mind what she says," he said. "She's always had a fear of having no money, because of Babuji's miserliness. But in life money comes and goes. We are lucky to be alive and healthy, and everything will be all right."

"But what will we do when you retire?"

"When I retire, we'll go to the West."

"But where will we get the money?"

"I will get ten per cent compensation for our house in Lahore—the government is going to give every refugee ten per cent compensation. I'll get a provident fund of fifty thousand rupees, and I have a thousand-pound endowment assurance policy in England. The money should be enough to get me across to England to start a new life. Where there's a will, there's a way."

However encouraged I felt when I was with Daddyji, it seemed he was never there to be appealed to when Mamaji started one of her tirades. It was therefore her view of our plight that prevailed with me—with all of us children, I think.

I remember how Mamaji and I used to fight whenever I brought up the subject of the 3A Meccano set—something I did all the time. In Rawalpindi and Lahore, I had played with Meccano Sets 1, 2, and 3, and I had progressed from a set with only strips and screws to a set with wheels, pulleys, angles, and a windup motor—from making a toy bench to making a toy car that sped all around the floor. Now I was ready for the 3A set, which was for sale in a toyshop on the Mall for eleven rupees. I had lost all my Meccano sets to Pakistan, and I couldn't wait to have one in my hands again. The thought was especially tantalizing because I didn't know what new parts the 3A set would contain. I thought about the 3A set all the time—when I was going to sleep or waking up, when I was eating or sitting idle, when I was walking along the Mall. Every day, I would beg Mamaji to buy me the Meccano set. Every day, she would shout at me for being stubborn and provocative. "When will you get it through your head that we are now refugees?" she would bellow. She would start to wheeze and cough. "I'm worrying about how I'll pay school and college fees, how I'll feed you all, and all you can think about is Meccano. Hare Ram! How did I ever give birth to such wastrel children?"

I never got the 3A Meccano set. Once Mamaji had said no, there was no way to get Daddyji to say yes. My big sisters laughed at me for making so much of a mere toy, yet the wish to buy it burned in me for years, like the wish to go to Hira Mandi. Years later, the mention of the number eleven—the number of our lost house, the price of the Meccano set—would fill me with a sadness I couldn't explain. It was years later still before I came to see that perhaps it was because highly emotionally charged adolescent wishes had become fixed on the Meccano set in the toyshop, as on the "gems" in Hira Mandi. But the thought barely diminished the intensity of the feeling, even though by then I was in my late forties.

XXII

LITTLE CIVILIAN

FELLOW

O NE EVENING WHEN I WAS SITTING AT THE EDGE of the fire circle with nothing to do, and not knowing what to do with my hands, Daddyji returned from the plain and said to me, "I have some interesting news for you." There was the sound of people putting down whatever they were doing and turning to Daddyji. "I went to Delhi with Premier Gopichand Bhargava and we stayed at the Viceroy's House as guests of Lady Mountbatten," he said.

Everyone wanted to know what the Viceroy's House was like and what Lady Mountbatten was like, but he continued to talk to me, saying, "I mentioned you to Lady Mountbatten, and she said, 'Then you should meet Sir Clutha, who's also staying here.' She told me that

Lieutenant-Colonel Sir Clutha Mackenzie had been blinded in action in Gallipoli, and that he was here as a representative of St. Dunstan's Hostel for Blinded Soldiers in London, which had been founded during the First World War by Sir Arthur Pearson, who was himself blind."

The idea that Englishmen could be blind was hard for me to grasp. It was like trying to imagine them being servants or sweepers.

"Lady Mountbatten immediately arranged for me to meet Sir Clutha," Daddyji was saying. "I was much impressed by him. He has spent most of his life in welfare work for the blind. He came to India in 1943 at the invitation of the then Viceroy, Lord Wavell. Lord Wavell himself had only one eye, and he wanted Sir Clutha, who had some firsthand knowledge of India from a previous visit, to do something for the blinded Indian soldiers who were returning home from the Japanese front. Sir Clutha eventually established a St. Dunstan's in Dehra Dun—he is its commandant. Everyone says that it is the best training center for the blind in India, but when I told him that I would like you to study with him there he said pointblank, 'That is out of the question, Dr. Mehta. Your son is a civilian, and St. Dunstan's is exclusively for soldiers. Anyway, at St. Dunstan's we don't so much educate the men—most of them are in their thirties or forties and are illiterate—as teach them simple crafts and skills, like spinning, weaving, and caning. We train them to care for themselves, and introduce them to recreational games and music. The idea is merely to rehabilitate them and to save them from a life of idleness in the dirt and poverty of the villages.' I said that there must be some literate blind soldiers, too, and he admitted that there were some and that St. Dunstan's had Braille and typing classes for them. I thought you'd benefit by going there—at least, you would improve your Braille and learn typing—and I asked him if he would use his good offices to get you admitted there as an exception, on compassionate grounds. I told him about my long government service in the Punjab health department—St. Dunstan's comes under the central government's health department. I told him that I had lost a brother who was like a son to me in the Singapore action during the Second World War. I reminded him of Lady Mountbatten's interest in your case. I told him that we were refugees. I told him how you felt shut up in Simla. My words seemed to have no effect, but later on I appealed to Lady Mountbatten, and she talked to Sir Clutha in my presence. He then agreed to take up your case with the government."

In the following days, I went around repeating "Clutha, Clutha" under my breath, the way Mamaji repeated "Ram, Ram"—as if the mere utterance of the name would bring my hands something to do. Within a week or so, we received a letter from Sir Clutha saying that the government had made an exception in my case, and I could attend morning classes in Braille and typing at St. Dunstan's as a special student. He said, however, that it wasn't a good idea to have a young boy stay among war-blinded men who were away from their wives and families, since they might "mislead" me. He therefore asked us to make our own arrangements for my food and accommodations and for getting me to and from St. Dunstan's, which was situated two or three miles outside Dehra Dun proper.

I was very excited at the thought of attending classes again. "I can stay with Sister Pom in Dehra Dun," I said.

Mamaji began to wheeze and cough. "A daughter, once married, belongs to her in-laws—her new family," she said. "Her own family has no claim on her. Usha has already stayed with Pom and Kakaji, and they've refused to take anything from us."

"But why do you have to live with Promila when my own brother Romesh is there?" Daddyji asked. After Partition, Romesh Chachaji had settled in Dehra Dun, where he was trying to establish himself as an architect among refugees who were familiar with his Lahore reputation.

"It's your right to stay with him," Mamaji said. "Your daddy helped to educate him."

Daddyji quoted an Urdu couplet to Mamaji:

> He who does a good deed or a favor,
> Then remembers it, wipes it away.

I insisted that I'd rather stay with Sister Pom, but then Sister Umi butted in and recalled that Bahali Ram Chachaji had taken refuge with Romesh Chachaji after Partition. "Bahali Ram Chachaji's wife has run away, his children have disowned him," she pointed out. "Romesh Chachaji is keeping him as a clerk and a peon only as a family charity case. I'm sure he has nothing to do all day and would be a perfect person to take Vedi to St. Dunstan's and back on a bicycle."

"Umi's perfectly right," Daddyji said. "Besides, Bahali Ram can take you for walks and be a good companion for you. He is a lot of fun."

I protested. I was afraid of growing up to be like Bahali Ram Chachaji—a poor relation, who had failed at everything and never amounted to anything. He had a double thumb and had always been a figure of fun among us children. I didn't want to be associated with him. But there was no getting around Daddyji, and Romesh Chachaji was informed of the plan.

I was made ready for Dehra Dun. I had not been completely separated from my family since I left Dadar School, around my ninth birthday, and Mamaji remarked that I seemed only too happy to leave. She was right—I couldn't wait to go.

❦

I HAD BEEN to Dehra Dun—it was in the United Provinces, two hundred miles or so from Simla—only once, when we were driving up to the hill station of Mussoorie. Then Dehra Dun had felt open, cool, and uncrowded, but now, as I climbed the staircase to Romesh Chachaji's flat, it felt tight and close. The flat was in Ashley Hall—the town shopping center—over Bombay Boot House and Romesh Chachaji's office. Romesh Chachaji was on the terrace of his flat, playing with his three children: Vijay, a son, and his twin sister, Usha—they were about eight—and Naresh, a son of about five. They all embraced me, and I noticed immediately that Usha sounded as mellifluous and vibrant as ever but that Vijay slurred his words and stuttered, as he always had.

Savitri Chachiji called out from inside, "Who is it?" I scarcely recognized her voice, because she was having an asthma attack.

Romesh Chachaji took me in to her, whispering on the way, "Be sure to say to your *chachi,* 'I fall at your feet.' " I stiffened. It was a greeting we children used only for Bhabiji, not for an aunt. Romesh Chachaji pressed me against him affectionately. "Do it for my sake, youngster."

I went up to Savitri Chachiji, who was lying on a cot. "I fall at your feet," I said.

Instead of blessing me, as Bhabiji would have done, she muttered to Romesh Chachaji, as she tried to catch her breath, "Why don't your people understand that we are refugees ourselves? Isn't one of your Bahali Rams enough? We have only three small rooms, and Vedi has his own blood sister here with a big house. Why has he come to eat our heads?"

Savitri Chachiji had always been one of my favorite relatives. She was from Bombay; I'd gone to Dadar School there. She was born a Christian; as a child, I'd thought of myself as a Christian. She was our only *chachi* who spoke English and had made a love marriage. I couldn't understand why she was talking to me like that. Years later, I learned that her son Vijay was mentally backward. She had hidden from the fact in Lahore, where Romesh Chachaji had position and wealth, but in Dehra Dun she was almost unhinged by it.

Presently, Romesh Chachaji took me out onto the

terrace. "Vedji, let God keep you happy and cheerful," Bahali Ram Chachaji said, shuffling out of a room. His voice was thin and pathetic, like a mosquito's whine.

"Bahali Ram, the youngster will stay with you," Romesh Chachaji said.

"Then where will the servant sleep?" Bahali Ram Chachaji whined. "The room is too small for three cots."

"The servant will have to set up his cot on the terrace," Romesh Chachaji said.

Bahali Ram Chachaji made little grumbling noises. "The servant's cot will be in the way. Savitri won't like that. She'll push me out of the house to make space for the servant. Then where will I go?"

Romesh Chachaji told him that there was no danger of that, because he now had a new duty—to take me to and from St. Dunstan's on his bicycle.

"Thank you, thank you," Bahali Ram Chachaji said, with audible relief.

Romesh Chachaji went downstairs to his office.

"Romesh is a good gentleman," Bahali Ram Chachaji said, taking me into his room. "Partition has been good."

"What's good about it?" I asked, taken aback.

"In Lahore, Romesh had a big office, with draftsmen and clerks and peons, and he didn't know what was being done under his nose in his name. Now, here, he has to do everything himself. In Lahore, I never got to see him in the office. Now he and I pull together like two bullocks under the same yoke." He added, as if he had transgressed, "But I am nobody and he is somebody." He was nearly Daddyji's age, but he talked to me as if we were the same age. He abruptly asked,

"Would you like to hear the story about the Nihala guard?"

I had heard the story countless times from him— in fact, I had grown up hearing it—yet I never tired of it, perhaps because he took such pleasure in telling the story that it was hard not to share his enjoyment. It was like a joke he told on himself: it was in pink English—a funny, Jabberwocky Punjabi and English, which was the best he himself could do in English.

I nodded, and Bahali Ram Chachaji started telling the story as if I had never heard it before. "There was a guard in Nihala. There was trouble on the train. It was his official duty to send an English telegram to the guard ahead in the next station. He tried and tried, and then sent this telegram: 'HANAIRI CHULLULLING LAMPING BHUJUDGING. IF THERE IS ANY HERGING MERGING, NIHALA GUARD WON'T BE JIMAYWAR.' " The message meant "Storm is blowing. Lamps are going out. If there is any turmoil and trouble, the Nihala guard won't be responsible."

❧

RAJPUR ROAD rumbled with the noise of big lorries ferrying between Mussoorie, about fifteen miles above, and the plain. The bicycle was old and rattly. The front bar, on which I sat, was bent. My legs were too long for me to sit on it comfortably—there was no way to support my feet. I sat with my knees half raised, being careful not to get in the way of Bahali Ram Cha- chaji's pedalling and not to scrape my feet on the ground.

"We are going to be run over and killed," Bahali

Ram Chachaji kept muttering, recklessly weaving in and out of the traffic. "These lorry drivers are all hot-head Sikhs who don't know a lorry from a bicycle."

There was a crash ahead. Bahali Ram Chachaji veered the bicycle to the side so fast that it tipped over. We picked ourselves up. Neither one of us was hurt.

It seemed that a lorry had been precariously stacked with steel girders and beams, so that they were sticking out on both sides. A beam had caught on a lamp-post and fallen off. No one was injured, but all traffic was stopped.

It was some time before we could go on.

❧

MAJOR JONES, who was an assistant to Sir Clutha and was called the After Care Officer, held me by the shoulder as he showed me around St. Dunstan's, pushing me forward and pulling me backward, turning me this way and that way—making me feel that I was a toy soldier in his hand. His breath smelled like cow dung. It made me shrink away. (Years later, when I smelled stale whiskey on a friend's breath, I recalled Major Jones, and realized that he must have been drinking, even though it was morning.)

"This compound used to be the Governor General's Bodyguard Lines," he said. "You see, his Bodyguard Force was quartered here, and they used this estate for their exercises on horseback." He spoke an Englishman's bad Hindustani; instead of saying *gorda* ("horse"), he said *gora* ("white man"). The more he talked, the funnier he sounded. "It was a big force and they had dozens of white men [horses] on the grounds in stables. St. Dunstan's has open grounds all around it. There are fifty or sixty ex-servicemen in residence—most of them were privates in the infantry. There are a couple of government bungalows here—Sir Clutha lives in one, I live in the other—but the classes are all held in the old stables, and the old barracks are used for the hostel. Most of them have tin roofs and are nice and noisy in the rain." He abruptly asked, "What's the matter?"

From all around came clacking and clanging sounds, as if dozens of men were teasing cotton with carding bows. "That sound!"

"Oh, that!" Major Jones said, with a hearty laugh. "That's blind soldiers making war on the steel posts and guide wires with their walking sticks. Newly blind people have great difficulty getting around without a full-time attendant or a guide, so the compound has been strung with guide wires that go along both sides of the path from the hostel to the latrines, from the hostel to the workshop, from the workshop to the kitchen, from the workshop to the recreational room. The soldiers find their way around by following the guide wires with their hands or their sticks and counting the steel posts along the way. You can get along without them, eh?"

I said I thought I could.

"I don't know what spell your father cast on the higher-ups, but this is no place for a civilian, and a young boy at that," Major Jones said. He laughed. "These are embittered, isolated men. They are not fit company for any boy, but, as my commanding officer used to say, 'a good soldier follows orders.' "

🌸

MY FIRST CLASS was in typing, and for it I went to the workshop, where I was greeted by a partially sighted Australian teacher, Mr. Cameron. He introduced me to the only other pupil in the class, a Muslim named Ghulam Quadar.

I put out my hand and almost screamed—what I touched was not a hand but a metallic claw.

"Come closer and touch," Ghulam Quadar said, in a high-pitched, shaky voice. He pulled me closer with his claw. The claw was actually an angular hook attached to metal tubing. "The Japanese blinded me and cut off my arms," he said in a chillingly matter-of-fact way. "I was transferred here directly from the hospital."

He is worse off than the refugee without hands, I thought, and the Japanese must be worse than the Muslims. I asked, "How do you type?"

"I'm learning to type with this mechanical arm," he said. He insisted that I see for myself. Both his arms were cut off at the elbow. His left arm ended in a smooth, elbow-like projection—it felt naked and exposed under his short-sleeved shirt. The section of tubing was attached loosely to his right upper arm with a canvas strap. His typewriter, instead of having rows of keys, had metal steps with a hole where each key would normally be.

"It is an ordinary typewriter keyboard with a special plate," Mr. Cameron said.

"I've memorized the keyboard," Ghulam Quadar said. "I can type by counting off the holes with my hand. I'm going to type 'Ghulam Quadar' for you."

He counted under his breath and cursed under his breath as he searched with his hook for "g," the hook's end clattering over the plate's holes and steps much as the sticks of the soldiers clattered along the wires and the steel posts outside. His fumbling—the slides, the jumps, the clinks of metal against metal—set my teeth on edge. Then there was the sound of the thrusting of his hook into a hole and of its striking a key. "There she is!" he exclaimed. I feared that he would never finish with the word, but he doggedly carried on with "h" and "u" and "l" while Mr. Cameron and I stood over his typewriter like two education inspectors. He had no sooner finished typing "Ghulam Quadar" than he started typing a sentence, which he said aloud, letter by letter, word by word. "N-o-w, now . . . i-s, is . . . t-h-e, the . . . t-i-m-e, time," and so on.

"When Ghulam Quadar came to my class, he had never been near a typewriter," Mr. Cameron was saying. "Now he can type like anyone else, and he has a speed of five words a minute." Ghulam Quadar couldn't return the carriage and start the next line; Mr. Cameron had to do that. He couldn't read what he typed; Mr. Cameron seemed to check the typing by listening to the sound of his hook marking off the holes in the plate. His English was worse than mine; Mr. Cameron helped him with the spelling. But there was no stopping him.

Mr. Cameron sat me down beside Ghulam Quadar, at a typewriter on the same table. It was an ordinary typewriter, the kind that Daddyji's clerks used to type on. I remember thinking that there was an unexpected boon in having Mr. Cameron for a teacher. Because he spoke only English, and Ghulam Quadar and I were the only pupils, I would get plenty of chance to practice my English with him.

In subsequent days, sitting at the table beside Ghulam Quadar, I learned how to position my fingers on the home row. I learned that "s" was next to "a," and "d" next to "s," and that I had to stretch my forefingers to strike "g" or "t" or "b," and that there was no key for number one—that the letter "l" was used instead. In my head, I tried to redesign the keyboard, simplifying it by putting "a" next to "b" and "b" next to "c," even as I redoubled my efforts to master the intractable typewriter I had. I remember once asking Mr. Cameron why the keyboard was so strangely ordered. He said he didn't know—typewriters just came that way.

❧

EVERY DAY, I spent an hour in the typing class with Ghulam Quadar. When his stump slipped out of the hollow of his mechanical arm, he would ask me to set it right. He would try out on me his dolorous and biting Urdu verses, which came to him spontaneously and were always about unfeeling women with hearts of stone. Outside class, he had an attendant, who had to help him with everything. At lunchtime, if his attendant was late in coming to get him he would ask me to unscrew his hook and screw on a spoon, and when the attendant arrived he would go off to have his meal, his metal arm clanking against the guide wires. Once, he fell sick, and I went to visit him in Double Disability Ward, where he lived with another armless man, Ali Ahmed, who had been a cook in the infantry. It was one of the strangest places I'd ever been in, and for days afterward I couldn't get it out of my head. By his bed was a tap in the cement floor which shot water straight up, so that he could wash himself, and in the middle of the ward was a pillar wrapped with a Turkish towel, so that he could rub against it and dry himself. He had applied to the government for a second arm, and every week or so he would type a follow-up letter with the help of Mr. Cameron, always closing it, "Thanking you in anticipation." Every day, he waited eagerly for some news about his second arm. I found that I waited with him, sharing his anticipation. But he never heard anything.

❧

SOMETIMES I was given a Braille lesson by Mr. Cameron, but more often by Mr. Advani, a friendly Hindu teacher, blind himself, who taught in an adjacent classroom. He was only about ten years older than I was, and, like me, he had gone blind when he was a child. After learning Braille in the School for the Blind in Karachi, he had attended a school for the sighted, but he used to say, "Blind people can only be taught in a blind school."

During one of my first lessons, he asked me, in

familiar Hindi, "Can you read Grade 2 Braille?"

"I don't know what that is."

"How old are you?"

"Fourteen."

"And you don't know Grade 2 Braille?" Mr. Advani explained to me that Grade 1 Braille had no contraction signs or abbreviations, and that Grade 2 Braille had many contraction signs and abbreviations.

"Do you know any contractions?" he asked.

"I know three—those for 'and,' 'of,' and 'for.' "

Before the hour was up, he had taught me many contraction signs: dot five before "p" for "part," dots five and six and "t" for "meant," dots four and six and "n" for "sion," dots five and six and "n" for "tion." He had also taught me abbreviations: "b" for "but," "f" for "from," and "abv" for "above."

"What do 'sion' and 'tion' mean?" I asked.

"They don't mean anything, but many English words end with them."

"Why are there any contractions at all?"

"Because reading Braille is so much slower than reading print. There are blind soldiers here who can hardly read four Braille words a minute."

Over a period of time, I became adept at reading Grade 2 Braille, in which most books for children over nine were embossed. St. Dunstan's had a little library of Braille magazines, such as *Reader's Digest,* and books, such as Agatha Christie's "Murder on the Orient Express" and "Simple Shakespeare for Children," and I read everything in it avidly. The magazines and books were all in English, of course, and my English vocabulary was so small that I wasn't always able to understand what I read, but I read on, turning page after page, until I got the gist of the story. The reading—and listening to Mr. Cameron talk—helped my English vocabulary. For the first time, I felt that I was making real progress.

❦

THE ST. DUNSTAN'S compound was large, and the buildings were few and far apart. Most of the walks were in open space, and the men, clacking and clanging their sticks on the steel posts and guide wires, stumbled along them like infants learning to walk. Feeling at once sorry for them and superior to them, I refused to walk like them, with my hands on the metal guide wires—never mind carrying a stick. Without the sounds of walls to guide me, I would sometimes bump my head on a steel post. Many of the posts were tall, because they had lamps at the top, and they were so slender that they would have been hard to detect with facial vision even without the noise all around me. The bumps on my forehead and eyebrows, my nose and lips only made me more defiant, and I ran instead of walking. The men soon knew my step, and in my hearing they would say things like "He's so active," "He walks straight, without guide wires," "He's a mere boy."

One morning, by the commandant's bungalow, I met Sir Clutha out walking with Captain A. H. Mortimer, who had recently arrived and replaced Major Jones. I hadn't met Sir Clutha before—he was mostly away in New Delhi or shut up in the commandant's bungalow. In fact, I had heard that he didn't much like us Indians and stayed away from us—didn't trust any "native chap" even to interpret for him. The government had therefore found him Captain Mortimer, who, though an Englishman, had been born and bred in India and spoke perfect Urdu.

"Who goes there?" Sir Clutha asked, in English.

"It's the little civilian fellow," Captain Mortimer said. "He doesn't use a stick or the guide wires."

"Halt!" Sir Clutha said.

I was already standing still.

"Why don't you carry a stick or use the guide wires?" Sir Clutha asked, through Captain Mortimer.

"I don't need to," I said, my heart racing under my shirt.

"You'll crack your head open, and then you'll learn," he said.

I was about to say that though I had hurt myself frequently I would never carry a stick or use the guide wires, but I bit my tongue and kept mum, as Bhabiji had taught us to do when we had the impulse to talk back to our elders or betters.

"I know well who you are," Sir Clutha was saying. "Your father is a persistent bloke."

I didn't know what "bloke" meant—Captain Mortimer used the English word "bloke" in his translation—but I detected a certain irritation in Sir Clutha's voice and was glad when he hurried away.

I couldn't believe my ears: Sir Clutha walked clanging his stick on the guide wire, just like a recently blinded Indian soldier. Yet he was attended by Captain Mortimer. I made a mental note to tell Daddyji that though Sir Clutha was a New Zealander and a "sir," who hobnobbed with personages no less than Lord and Lady Mountbatten, he had much worse mobility than I had.

❦

ONE DAY, Bahali Ram Chachaji arrived at St. Dunstan's on foot.

"Where is the bicycle?" I cried.

"It's broken," he said. "I have no money to get it repaired. We will have to foot it now, coming and going."

"But that will take a lot of time!"

"What to do?" Bahali Ram Chachaji said.

"I'll borrow some money from Sister Pom, and we'll just get the bicycle repaired," I said.

"It costs a lot of money," he said. "Pomji won't like it."

"She won't mind—it's a necessity."

We walked out onto Rajpur Road. "The question is, how do we get home now?" I said, and I added, "I have an idea. Raise your hand, Chachaji. Some car will stop and we will get a lift back."

"We don't have anyone of our acquaintance with a car here."

"You don't have to know anyone to get a lift. Raise your hand."

He wouldn't do it. I would have done it myself, but I didn't know exactly how it was done. I thought he must know, so I ordered him, as if I were his superior.

"All right, all right," he said.

Immediately, a car stopped. An authoritative-sounding man said, in English, "Where are you going?"
Bahali Ram Chachaji started stuttering.
"Will you please help us reach R. C. Mehta's house in Ashley Hall?" I said.
"Jump in," the man said.

❧

ONE AFTERNOON, after the bicycle had been repaired, I was very thirsty when I came back from St. Dunstan's, so while Bahali Ram Chachaji was bringing the bicycle up the stairs I raced ahead of him onto the terrace. I felt something crunchy and gritty underfoot. I stepped back. I thought I had broken Savitri Chachiji's glass bangles; when she washed clothes on the terrace she often took off her glass bangles and put them on the floor by her side.
"Ill-begotten son of an owl!" Savitri Chachiji shouted, running out onto the terrace. "Putting your filthy boots on my kernels of wheat before they're dry! I'm not your mother. I don't have to take care of you." I thought that she would calm down, but she turned her tirade onto Bahali Ram Chachaji. "He can't see, but what's the matter with your eyes?"
"Savitriji, I was bicycle-minding," Bahali Ram Chachaji stuttered.
"Dolt! What will we eat tonight—your shoes? A dolt and a blind boy are going to be my ruin."
One or two neighbors' windows rattled open. Romesh Chachaji came running up the stairs. "Take your blind nephew," Savitri Chachiji said. "Take your

dolt of a cousin. I am leaving."

Romesh Chachaji said nothing. He was afraid of Savitri Chachiji's temper.

"Let it be," Bahali Ram Chachaji was saying. "Vedji just stepped on a few grains of wheat. Here, I'll just wash them."

"Don't talk back to me!" Savitri Chachiji shouted. She had two voices—the gentle voice of a well-bred Bombay girl and the sharp, strident voice of a *gulli* woman who regularly fought with her neighbors. She went on shouting like a *gulli* woman.

I remembered in a flash hearing that Bhabiji had taken Savitri Chachiji for a witch upon first seeing her, after Romesh Chachaji's elopement. In fact, Bhabiji had got ill with the shock of the elopement and had almost died. I had fallen ill at the same time with meningitis. Bhabiji had rallied, but I had been left blind, and Mamaji had drawn a connection between the two illnesses.

I heard Sister Pom's voice from behind, from the staircase, as in a dream.

"I don't want to stay here another day!" I cried.

"I'm taking him home with me," Sister Pom said. "It's settled. I'll inform Daddyji."

Within minutes, Sister Pom had swept up my few belongings and packed them in a suitcase—crying the whole time. She took me down the stairs, with Romesh Chachaji close behind, whispering apologies: "She was a queen in Lahore, but here she is struggling in three small rooms over Bombay Boot House, like a shop-keeper's wife. . . . She isn't in good health. . . . She has been embittered—your *chachis* have treated her as an outcast, because she's an Indian Christian. . . .

Her asthma has really got worse since Partition. . . .
Bahali Ram is always complaining. He keeps her riled
up."

In the tonga, Sister Pom said to me, "You know
how loving and wonderful to me Biji is." Biji, as Sister
Pom called her mother-in-law, spent six months a year
in Allahabad with her elder son, Kelly, and the other
six in Dehra Dun with Kakaji. She had just arrived for
her Dehra Dun stay. "But she has very high blood
pressure and a very finicky temperament, and she has
trouble sleeping. You mustn't make any noise. You
must promise to live in the house so that she won't
know you're there." She asked, "How did you wash
yourself at Romesh Chachaji's?"

"Bahali Ram Chachaji would heat me some water
when he was heating water for his tea," I said.

"Now you'll have to do without Bahali Ram Chachaji," she said. She stopped the tonga and bought me
an electric immersion heater for three and a half rupees,
so that in the mornings I could heat the water for
washing my hands and face without troubling the servants.

Kakaji's bungalow couldn't have been more different from Romesh Chachaji's walkup flat. It was on Old
Survey Road, where old Dehra Dun families lived. It
had a compound of its own, with clumps of litchi and
mango trees, and separate servants' quarters. It had
both a front veranda and a portico, and was almost
level with the ground, seemingly having no plinth. It
was cavernous and run down, without plumbing, and
consisted of a few big rooms that opened into one
another.

That evening, before we sat down to dinner, Sister

Pom arranged for her Indian Christian manservant, Massey, to take me on a bicycle to St. Dunstan's and bring me back. She wrote to Daddyji and told him that she had brought me away from Savitri Chachiji's. She installed me in a big room. I hadn't had a room to myself since Lahore, and I felt like a prince.

❧

MY CLASSES AT St. Dunstan's occupied only a couple of hours in the morning. At Romesh Chachaji's, I had kept busy in one way or another—by playing with the children, reading my Braille books and magazines (I had been able to get my own free subscription to *Reader's Digest*), or sitting in the office with Bahali Ram Chachaji and listening to his jokes and stories. Every day, too, I had looked forward to a visit from Sister Pom, who would often stop by at four o'clock on her way to Kakaji's dental surgery, which was just fifty yards away. I would go there with her. In the surgery, I would examine dentures and casts of mouths, and try to imagine what the patients were like, while Kakaji finished up. Then the three of us would walk over to the Siwalik Club, named after the surrounding hills. While Kakaji played tennis, I would sit at the edge of the grass court with Sister Pom and whichever of her friends happened to be around. After tennis, we would go into the club—just a big bungalow—for lemon or orange squash. Back at the flat, Bahali Ram Chachaji and I would play gin rummy with my Braille cards in our room late into the night.

But at Kakaji's, except for walks to the surgery and

the club with Sister Pom, I had nothing to do all day. I had finished all the magazines and books I could read at the St. Dunstan's library, and Sister Pom and the servants were completely occupied with Vindoo or with Biji. Then, to make things worse, Sister Pom got a letter from Daddyji saying that now that Vindoo was a year old everyone was eager to see him, and she should come with him to Simla. She immediately left, with Vindoo and his ayah.

One day, I was running from room to room, sitting now in this chair and now in another chair, going out to the veranda and coming back into the bungalow, cracking my knuckles and worrying the buttons on my shirt, when Biji called me to her. "Child," she said hazily. As usual, she was taking snuff and chewing *pan,* and had a preoccupied air. "You seem lost without Pom. There's a harmonium in the house. Why don't you amuse yourself with it?"

"It'll make noise."

"No, it'll make music."

After that, for an hour or so a day, when I had made sure that Biji was not having a nap, I would sit on the carpet in the drawing room and play a few tunes and ragas on the harmonium. Kakaji even arranged for Massey to take me on a bicycle every second day to a music master who lived near Kakaji's surgery, for private tutoring.

✿

WHEN SISTER POM had been gone scarcely a fortnight, Kakaji developed a high fever. A doctor was called, and his diagnosis was that Kakaji had typhoid. I was quite frightened. At home, we children often got sick, but Daddyji hardly ever got sick.

I urged Biji to inform Sister Pom, but she said, with a sniff, "There's no need to alarm her. Kakaji will get better with the medicine."

But the fever did not go down for four or five days, and then I overheard the doctor saying to Biji, "Kakaji may have smallpox." I got Massey to rush me to the post office—it had the nearest telephone—and I booked a trunk call to Sister Pom.

"Hello," I said, and she started crying, sensing that something was wrong.

"Kakaji has smallpox!" I shouted into the phone.

"I'm coming right back," she said through her tears.

❦

ONE AFTERNOON, I was walking with Sister Pom to the surgery. (Kakaji had completely recovered from what turned out to be a severe case of chicken pox.) Usually, she walked briskly, but that afternoon she was a little slow of step. Usually, her arm under my hand felt steady—when we walked together she would have her hand thrust in her coat pocket and I would have my hand looped through her arm—but that afternoon her arm was fidgety, as if she were worrying something in her pocket. "You know how badly off Biji is," she said. She was a very direct person, and I couldn't understand why she was talking in such a roundabout manner. "Well, I overheard Biji talking to Kakaji last night. She said that your harmonium playing gives her headaches and sends her blood pressure up."

I caught my breath. "The harmonium was her idea."

"It's not just the harmonium—it's everything," she said vaguely. "You know, I'm going back to Simla"— she had left Vindoo behind and was returning to Erneston to spend some more time there—"and I don't want anything to go wrong when I'm not here. I think it would be best if you shifted to the hostel." She added, "You could have been killed in the bicycle accident."

When Massey was taking me to St. Dunstan's one morning in her absence, the front bar of his bicycle had broken off, and I had fallen onto the road. Even though I had to have a bandage on my head and spend a few days in bed, bicycle accidents were common, and in themselves, I felt, would not have made Sister Pom decide to push me out of her house.

"I'll go there tomorrow and talk to Captain Mortimer," Sister Pom was saying. In March, he had succeeded Sir Clutha as commandant.

I recalled that Sir Clutha, in his original letter to Daddyji, had been adamant that I should not stay at the hostel, among isolated men two or three times my age. Anyway, I didn't think the government would ever allow me to live in Army barracks and eat Army rations. But there was something in Sister Pom's voice that stopped me from saying anything.

❧

SISTER POM TOOK me to St. Dunstan's, with my luggage, in a tonga, and Massey followed us on a bicycle. Sister Pom had somehow persuaded Captain Mortimer to let me stay at the hostel, though I was to be segregated by having a room of my own. Captain Mortimer had arranged for me to stay in a corner room in the Madras Barracks, one of the hostel buildings. The room had no bathroom; the hostel had only communal latrines and communal taps. Captain Mortimer had a small tin tub placed on the veranda to one side of my room, and a commode set up under a tarpaulin tent in a corner of the veranda.

I complained that the tub was out in the open.

"You can take a bath when it's dark," Sister Pom said.

I wanted to protest, but there was an edge to her voice, as if she were angry or tearful.

She turned to Massey and told him that he would have to stay in the hostel and daily cook my food, clean my room, and bring my bathwater.

"I want Massey to sleep in my room," I said.

"He'll have to stay with the other hostel servants," she said.

"But I can't sleep in my room alone," I said.

"Why not?" she asked.

"I'm afraid," I said.

"Afraid of what?"

She started unpacking my suitcase and arranging the things in a small wall cupboard. There was a sudden whirr in the room, and I jumped. Then I realized that it was only the sound of a table fan—Sister Pom had brought one along, and Massey had plugged it in—and that its whirr sounded very loud because, except for a cot, the room was bare. I ordered Massey to unplug the fan, but Sister Pom told him to leave it alone, because it was very hot.

"I want somebody to be on duty at night," I said. "But what are you afraid of?"

I couldn't reply, because what I was afraid of was ghosts. Even at Old Survey Road, if I was a bad boy at night a ghost ticked me off like an ill-tempered teacher. For instance, if I slept with a sheet over my head, as Daddyji had told me not to do, because I needed oxygen, the night-ghost would shake me by the shoulder and wouldn't leave me alone until I had pushed back the sheet. If I slept all curled up, with my knees against my stomach, as Sister Pom had told me not to do, because it would keep me from growing, the ghost would tug at my feet until I had stretched my legs down to the foot of the bed. If I snored, as Sister Umi had told me not to do, because it kept her awake, the ghost would pinch my nose until I woke up. The day-ghost was no less vigilant. If I put my finger in my ear to stop an itch—when Mamaji caught me doing that, she would slap my hand—the ghost would put a crick in my neck. If I swung my legs while I was sitting on a bench or a cot, as Bhabiji had told us children not to do, because it disturbed whoever was sitting alongside, I was sure to be punished. Just the day before, I had been sitting on a bench with Ghulam Quadar. I had my legs crossed and had been gently swinging my free leg. Although it was making the bench shake, Ghulam Quadar hadn't seemed to mind. But when I got up, the ghost had created a terrific wind and practically obliterated my facial vision:

I had walked straight into a lamppost. When I first came home from Dadar School, I hadn't been able to sleep at all for fear of the ghosts. When I told Daddyji about them, he had laughed and said, "If there were ghosts, the British could surely get them to fight on their side and win the war." I had said, "But they might fight on the German side." He had said, "But the Germans haven't won the war. Have you ever heard of any ghost fighting on any side?" I'd had to admit that I hadn't. The subject had been dropped, because I couldn't think of anything else to say. In time, staying at home had made me forget about the ghosts, but now that I was to sleep in a hostel I knew that they would reappear in full force.

"What are you afraid of?" Sister Pom repeated.

"The hornets," I said. St. Dunstan's had no screens or chicks, and somewhere in the room a hornet was buzzing. It was a very big hornet, I thought, because I could hear it over the whirr of the fan.

"Where?" Sister Pom asked.

"There, Mistress," Massey said. "Up on the ceiling."

Sister Pom and I stepped out of the room, and Massey jumped around with his duster. He managed to shoo the hornet out the window, and we went back into the room.

"I'm afraid of hornets and ghosts," I said.

Sister Pom pretended she hadn't heard the word "ghosts," and that made me think that she herself must be afraid of them. She patted me on the head.

"I don't like the tub outside," I said. "I could never take a bath there, dark or not. It would make noise.

Everyone would know. I don't like the tent outside. It sticks out. I could never go to the bathroom there. I'll go and stay with Romesh Chachaji."

"But Savitri Chachiji won't have you."

"Let me stay at Old Survey Road. I won't ever play the harmonium."

Sister Pom started crying.

"Let me come back with you at least for one night."

"I can't do anything," she said, between her sobs.

She was my sister, I thought, but now she belonged to another family. I became lost in thought. I scarcely noticed her hustle and bustle as she finished unpacking my suitcase, pushed it under my cot, and said that we would meet the next day—either she would come to see me or Massey would take me to visit her.

"Don't worry," I said, gulping. "I'll be all right." Then I realized that I was speaking to an empty room she had already left.

There was an eerie sound of somebody snapping a towel outside my window. I shouted "Massey! Massey!" I went out and shouted some more. He didn't come. I stood outside my room listening. All I heard was the sound of my heart. I walked slowly into the room.

I slammed the door and the window shut and bolted them. I listened. Everything was still, as before a monsoon rain. Then I heard the ghost up on the tin roof, pounding his heels, as if he were getting ready for a classical dance. I sat on my cot; he crossed the roof and began pounding just above my head. I went and stood near the window; he began pounding there. He seemed to be able to see me through the tin roof. I was afraid to stay in, in case he dropped down and attacked me. I was afraid to go out, in case he chased me and caught me. I felt utterly trapped.

I lay down on the cot. He started pounding above my chest in rhythm with my heartbeat. I turned onto my stomach.

I must have fallen asleep, because I was awakened by someone screaming outside. He's found another game, I thought. I'm spared for one more night.

❦

THE MEN in the hostel wouldn't leave me alone. They would stop by my room at any time of the day without invitation or warning, and when I was outside walking they would call to me; they recognized my fast walk. They would catch me by the hand or put an arm around my shoulder. They seemed only half-clothed—they wore undershirts and shorts. They had pungent breath and were inept. They spoke languages I didn't understand (they were from different parts of India)—languages that sounded harsh and guttural and very foreign. I had difficulty listening to them—I would hear and not hear. They were big, and I was small. They were old—a couple of them older than Dad-dyji—and I was a boy. They were from poor homes, and I was, as they never stopped reminding me, from a "good family." Many of them had wives and children, but, like Ghulam Quadar, they had apparently been brought to the hostel straight from the hospital, and had not been with their families since being blinded. Most of them had never learned to read or write; they could correspond with their wives, if at all, by paying a postal clerk to write and read their letters. Most of them had already been at St. Dunstan's for a year or longer and had begun to despair of ever being able to walk again without assistance or guide wires. While they had made some progress in learning to weave, to cane, or to sing, few of them thought that they would ever be able to earn their living. Even fewer believed that they would ever be able to go home and live with their families. Men who had "double disabilities," like Ghulam Quadar, spoke openly about being permanent wards of St. Dunstan's.

❧

ONE MORNING, people along the veranda outside Mr. Advani's class shouted, "Her Excellency Lady Mountbatten is coming! Inspection! Inspection!"

Mr. Advani cleared his throat and told me, "Get ready for a demonstration."

I sat up in my chair, with my hands on the Braille book in front of me.

I heard the voices of Captain Mortimer and Sir Clutha and a rustle of women's clothes. There was a whiff of scent—a kind I had never smelled before. My heart raced under my shirt as the heart of my pet myna used to race under my fingers.

"Read, Ved Sahib," Mr. Advani said.

I had no idea what book was under my fingers or what words I read. I wanted to tell Lady Mountbatten that Daddyji knew her, but before I had finished reading a couple of lines the rustling clothes and the scent were gone—the party had moved on to Mr. Cameron's room.

That evening, I was alone in my room. I was fiddling with the fan, trying to see if I could stop the rotating blades by sticking my fingers through the wire guard. I was careful to keep my fingers near the center of the assembly, where the blades were close together and so were not very dangerous. I don't know why I was doing it. Perhaps I was mesmerized by the clicking sound that the blades made against my fingernails. Perhaps I simply had nothing better to do with my ever restless hands.

Suddenly, I thought I heard Daddyji's footsteps on the veranda. Ghosts, I thought. They're coming to punish me for being naughty with the fan.

Just as I was about to get up and slam the door shut to scare the ghosts away before they scared me, I heard Daddyji's voice say, "How are you, Son?"

If Lord Mountbatten himself had walked into my room, I couldn't have been more surprised.

"I just happened to meet Sir Clutha on the way here," Daddyji was saying. "He told me that Lady Mountbatten was here today and that you read for her. He said that she was much impressed."

"I don't like living in the hostel," I said.

"Why not? It's a nice, open, cool place, with litchi trees all around. It's like being in the hills. I understand that Pom has made good arrangements for your food and water. What don't you like about the place?"

I wanted to tell him that I didn't like men catching hold of me and breathing on me, that I could never find Massey when I needed someone even to swat the

Mountbatten tea party, Simla, 1948.
Left to right: Umi, Lord Mountbatten, Pamela Mountbatten,
Nimi, Daddyji, Lady Mountbatten.

flies, that hornets flew in and out of the room, that centipdedes and spiders fell on my pillow in the middle of the night and left me trembling hours after I had brushed them off, that at night I was afraid to put my feet on the floor or to go to the bathroom outside. I wanted to tell him about the ghosts. But I didn't tell him anything. For some reason, I felt afraid of him, the way I did of people in authority—even friendly ones, like Captain Mortimer. I felt unworthy—just the way I remembered feeling when I was at Dadar School. More than anything, I was afraid that Daddyji might take me out of St. Dunstan's and stop my typing and Braille classes, and that I might find myself back in Simla, sitting at the edge of the fire circle and not knowing what to do with my hands.

"The place is too alone," I said.

"But you're much safer here than at Romesh's or Pom's. Rajpur Road is no place for bicycles. In fact, I was surprised at how many lorries there were on that road. I can't imagine how Bahali Ram, with his poor coördination, got you back and forth on the bicycle."

❧

WHENEVER I COULD, I would slip into Mr. Cameron's classroom and type letters—to Daddyji, to Mamaji, to my sisters in Simla, to Brother Om, at his college in Ludhiana, and to Cousin Nitya Nand, in Bombay—and pretend that I was among familiar voices, not at St. Dunstan's at all. I complained about the food that Massey cooked, and I asked for more money to buy food supplements from the officers' canteen—a discount shop in St. Dunstan's which I was permitted to use. I wrote at length about the trouble I had in meeting my expenses. I had to pay not only Massey and the music master but also a sweeper, who came to sweep my room and clean the commode every day, and a washerman, who came for my clothes every week. In one letter, I told them that I had dismissed Massey and hired another servant. In another, I asked permission to stop going to the music master, because his place was too difficult to get to on a bicycle from the hostel. In practically every letter, I asked for a typewriter, a 3A Meccano set, a radio, and an extra bucket for bathing—I wanted the servant to fetch the water for the tub two buckets at a time. (In retrospect, I realize that I must have looked to things to take the place of people I missed, to take up the slack in days and nights when I had nothing to do and had no idea how long I'd slept or been awake. St. Dunstan's had neither a bell nor a striking clock. I had just heard about the Cyma Braille pocket watch, made in Switzerland, but it cost almost as much as a typewriter, and I didn't allow myself even to think about it.) Although I never got a typewriter of my own that worked, or the right Meccano set (never mind a Braille watch), I did eventually get a radio, and I would spend hours tuning it to get a clearer shortwave signal or the sound of BBC news broadcasts, or taking it apart and putting it together—and pretending that the people singing or speaking over the set were my friends.

The replies to my letters were read to me by one or two partially sighted, literate soldiers, who would wonder aloud about my family—about how we could find so much to say to each other. But I had just discovered correspondence, and the soldiers' remarks—

like much else—only went back into the letters.

As it happens, most of my letters from 1948 are lost; hardly anyone kept them. The letters I received in reply I saved.

On April 4th, Cousin Nitya Nand wrote:

Bombay

My dear Vedi,

Received your letter of the 18th March. I have got my typewriter repaired and now it is working very well. I will send it to you when I find somebody going to Dehra Dun. I don't want to send it by post because again it might be spoiled on the way, and it was quite difficult to get it repaired this time. If you come to know of somebody who might be coming to Bombay from Dehra Dun, you please let me know. I will send it with him. If you like I could send it up to Delhi and then you try to get it from Delhi. Anyway you let me know what ever is to be done and I will do accordingly. I could probably send it to Simla even. You shouldn't worry about it and in due course of time we are bound to find somebody who could take it up to Dehra Dun.

I am glad to know that you have learnt your type writing so well and are learning music also. What more is taught in the school?

Do you like to collect coins also? I have got some coins lying with me. If you want them I could send those to you.

If you want anything else from Bombay, you let me know.

With love,

Yours aff'y

From Cousin Nitya Nand, on May 7th:

c/o H. K. Thakkar Esq.
2 Flag Staff Road
Civil
Delhi

MY DEAR VEDI,

It is a long time back since I wrote to you last—and received your reply. I am extremely sorry that I didn't write to you earlier. You see, Vedi, I have had too much of work for the last few months, because the work is nearing completion, and I had to do the lab work as well as write up all that I had done. I had literally had no time at all to do anything, and I didn't want to write to you unless I had done what you had asked me to do. I used to go to the lab at 7 in the morning and come back at about 8-30 at night. So I hope such a nice little brother as you would excuse me for this delay.

I have taken about fifteen days leave and have come to Delhi. I shall stay on here for about ten days more. I have got that 3A Meccano set and have brought it here along with the typewriter. I will send both these things to Dehra Dun with a relative of mine who is going to Dehra Dun in a day or two. I shall let you know in my next letter about his definite programme, so that either he could deliver the things at your place or you could get them from his place.

I hope you are going on well with your studies. Please let me know all that you are studying & learning these days. If you want anything from Delhi, let me know. Where is Sister Pom nowadays?

With love, yours aff'y

P.S. I will send the coins also along with.

From Cousin Nitya Nand, on May 23rd:

MY DEAR VEDI,

It is long since I have heard from you. I sent the typewriter & Meccano set through your Uncle R. C. Mehta.
Even before I received your letter I had contacted your Uncle
and had decided to send the things through him. I am very
eager to know whether you have received the things in a
proper condition. Please let me know at once about it. I
hope the typewriter is working properly, and the Meccano
set is the one that you wanted. Inside the box of the typewriter I had put an envelope containing some coins. I hope
those have not been misplaced while opening the typewriter
and you have received those too. . . .

Please write to me about how you spend your whole
day. I hope you do like your St. Dunstan's life and you
should start liking your food too.

More later.

With Love
Your aff'y

The typewriter did arrive, but it was damaged,
and the Meccano set turned out to be No. 3, from
which I had long since graduated, instead of No. 3A.
The coins, however, were very nice to touch and show
off.

From Sister Umi, on May 24th:

Erneston
Simla

My dearest Ved,

Daddy got your last letter day before yesterday. We were all pleased to know that you were hale & hearty. Every one here is in good spirits and best of health. Nimi and I went for a picnic to the Wild Flower Hall on cycles. Gurmeet and Balijeet Malhotra & Uma Vasudev were with us too. We had great fun. On our way back one cycle punctured. Half the time we had to walk but besides that coming down a hill on a cycle was divinely. The weather here is getting very warm. It must be terrible down on the plains. I do hope you are working hard. We got a letter from Om. He is perfectly alright. Daddy will write to you himself about the radio set.

With fondest love from all

Your affectionate

Sister

From Sister Umi, on June 9th:

Erneston

Simla

My dearest Ved,

Thanks very much for your letter which I got a few days back. I could not write to you earlier as my exams have started. [Umi was taking her B.A. finals: Nimi had already finished.] Today is a holiday so I am writing to you. Yesterday it was Gurmeet Malhotra's birthday. We went for tea and had great fun. I do hope you have made some friends in Dehra. How is your music getting on? Enjoy as much as you can. This is the only time in life to have fun. How I'd like to be in school again!! I haven't done very well in my papers but they were quite tolerable. Nimi goes for her tennis regularly. Vindoo can stand now. Ashok has bought a new mouth organ for five rupees. Usha is doing pretty well too but her rudeness cannot leave her. Anyway she is improving in her work too. Pom and Billoo are doing fine. [When Pom returned to Simla after Kakaji's illness, she took Billoo, her sister-in-law, with her.] I have become quite friendly with Billoo. I do think she is enjoying her stay here. Mummy and Daddy are enjoying themselves. Every second day they are out for lunch or tea or dinner. Every day we all think of you and Om and talk about you. We all miss your pleasant company in the house. Any way such is life, Dear. Hope to meet soon. My holidays for 10 days will start from 12th June.

With fondest love from all

Yours

From Sister Pom, not dated:

Simla

MY DEAR VED,

Billoo and I reached Simla safely. Daddy had come to the motor stand, so we had no difficulty in getting home. Vindoo refused to recognise me at first. But now again he has become fond of me.

Daddyji sent Biji 200 rupees for you. You can pay off your Board & Lodging, Massey and Masterji. Mama says for the time being you can take a bucket from Biji and then she'll send you a new one with Billoo.

I hope you go to see Biji every alternate day. Do you ever meet Kakaji? Usha remembers you a lot.

With love from all of us.

Yours,

From Sister Pom, on June 9th:

Erneston

MY DEAR VED,

I was so pleased to get your letter. But I was sorry to learn that you have turned out your servant [Massey]. I am sure you are having a lot of difficulty. . . .

Are you having good food? We are all having a nice time here. Om is expected here on the 10th. Billoo is still here. She'll go back when Kakaji comes.

Is it very hot there? You must be having a good time with litchis and mangoes.

Mama will send you the clothes with Billoo. I hope you brought the bucket from Biji.

You must keep on writing to us. We all feel so happy when we get a letter from you. . . . Nimi has a fine time, with tennis and shorthand. Vindoo has started standing up.

More in my next letter. With love from all of us.

Your loving sister

From Sister Pom, on June 28th:

MY DEAR VED,

I was glad to know that you have kept another servant. Is he as good as Massey was? Can he take you for your music lessons on a cycle? What are you paying him?

I hope you go to Biji quite often. If you want anything ask Billoo for it. Mama also sent you some money. I hope you won't need any more till I come back. . . .

Om came to Simla for a fortnight but unfortunately he was ill for most of the time. . . . Ashok is becoming more sensible every day. He remembers you a lot.

With lots of love,

Your loving sister

From Usha, on July 1st:

Erneston

MY DEAR BROTHER VED

How are you? I am quite well. You did not reply to any of my letters. You must bring me a doll when you come, because Ashok has broken that one which you gave me. Vediji, I miss you a lot because you were the one who used to take me out for walks, nowadays nobody does. Allright, bye-bye.

Your loving sister

From Mamaji, in Hindi, on July 1st:

Simla

MY LOVING VED, LOTS AND LOTS AND LOTS OF LOVE,

Ved, your daddy has gone on tour. Perhaps he'll return on the 3rd. Son, he's very busy in his work. That's why his letters to you get delayed. Do not worry when his letters are delayed.

I will send you more rupees. Don't be anxious about it. I have written down all your accounts. Youngster, your payment to your sweeper and washerman is high.

When your daddy comes, I'll discuss your accounts with him and get him to write you a letter.

Nirmila has gone off to the physical-training college at Tara Devi. She's going there to get training in sports and games. It seems half the family has gone away and left home.

Well, trust God keep you all happy in your respective efforts. Let God make you all excel in your efforts. My prayer to God is only this: that He give you all health and you become successful in your lifework.

Everyone's love,

Your mama

From Mamaji, in Hindi, written over July 10th, 11th, 12th:

MY LOVING SON VED, LOTS AND LOTS AND LOTS OF LOVE,

Ved, your loving letter received. After reading it, I got to know all the news.

Whatever you get to eat, please eat it. You should learn to eat everything.

Ved, you should also practice your singing.

Your daddy has made an arrangement to get a radio for you in Ambala. He will try to send it to you quickly.

Spend money carefully. Please buy from the officers' canteen and send one dozen boxes of condensed milk, of cornflakes, or Lux flakes, of Ovaltine, of Sunlight soap—or whatever else you think is cheap. Also, buy six underwears, those with legs. Please send that home, too. Everybody's

love. Ved, please make arrangements for getting milk. You
definitely must drink milk every day.

Your Mama

From Sister Pom, on July 14th:

MY DEAR VED,

You will be glad to know that Daddy has bought a
radio for you. I'll bring it when I come to Dehra in the end
of this month.

Yes, we have seen the account you sent of 250 rupees.
I hear you want some more. You can take another 100 rupees
from Kakaji, but be very careful in spending it. You should
not waste a penny. You are big enough to realise Mama's
condition as far as money is concerned. Now Nimi has gone
to Tara Devi for her physical training course. So her expenditure is also 100 rupees per month. Om is also spending
about 150 rupees.

Now, what about your music? I am sure you will be
very good by the time I come back. Do go and see Biji.

Write to us by the return of post your account and the
money you have taken from Kakaji.

With lots of love
Your loving sister

From Daddyji, on July 22nd:

Simla

MY DEAR VED,

I have received all your 3 letters and I quite appreciate
your difficult position with your Music Master. Under the

circumstances, you may discontinue going to his place till such time that Promila goes back to Dehra Dun. Thereafter in consultation with her, you may start taking music lessons at Promila's place and not at the Master's house.

I am glad that you are going to read and write in Braille system before Her Excellency Mrs. Sarojini Naidu. [After Lady Mountbatten's visit, a succession of Indian dignitaries came to visit St. Dunstan's.]

I have read your composition with great interest and am well satisfied with the progress you have made in English language, but I would advise you to write short sentences and also learn the use of punctuation and spellings.

I have seen the details of your expenditure and will send more money through Promila who shall settle your accounts every month.

I have purchased a new Philips radio set for you. It is lying in Ambala and will be sent with Promila.

Vindoo has just started to learn how to walk. Sheila with her son, Mohinder, and Leila [Cousin Leil] are with us and Ashok and Mohinder are good friends and play together.

Lakshman, Sureshta, and their two sons, Arun and the baby, are coming tomorrow with Babuji to stay with us here, so we shall have good company.

I shall be going out on tour on the 29th inst. to Delhi and shall return to Simla on the 7/8th Aug.

Om Prakash is doing well at Ludhiana and everybody else here and in Amritsar are fit and well.

You should not worry about your music lessons if no arrangements can be made at Dehra Dun. You can on your own practice from records.

With best wishes from us all.

Yours affectionately

Surprisingly, the letter was signed "Amolak Ram Mehta." It made me feel very grown-up.

From Sister Nimi, without a date:

> c/o Miss M. Alfred
> The Homestead
> Tara Devi
> Simla Hills

MY DEAREST VED,

Thanks ever so much for your affectionate letter which I received some days ago. Vedi, Pom is thinking of going to Dehra Dun with Dad on the 29th July. So she will take your radio along with her, otherwise Daddy shall give the radio to Uncle Romesh in Delhi so when he goes to Dehra Dun he will take it along with him and give it to you. I know how lonely one feels without a radio especially on rainy days. Vedi, how about your music? You must have improved a lot by now. When do you intend coming up to Simla? Won't you have any holidays? My course will finish in Dec. Have you made any friends there? If you have how do you like them? So far I have not made any real friends here—I talk to all the girls. More over I remain so busy the whole day long that I don't even get time to talk. . . .

Really Vedi, Radio gram is an excellent thing. We have bought some nice new records. When you come here, we shall have great fun. Om, too will be coming to Simla in September as he is not keeping fit. He shall appear from Simla. [Om was to appear for his F.Sc., an examination leading to his B.Sc.] All are doing fine. Reply soon.

With fondest love, yours aff'y

From Babuji, on August 7th:

> 11 Ram Kishore Road
> Delhi 1948

MY DEAR VED,

It is long time since I have seen you. [We hadn't met since before the Partition, in Lahore.]

While leaving Simla day before yesterday, I was sorry to learn that you had a cycle accident & received injuries. [I was on the bicycle of my new servant, and we were knocked over by a lorry that was coming very fast.] Thank God it was not worse. I hope you are out of bed by this time & attending to your wounds and work.

> With love & blessings

From Sister Umi, on the same day.

> "Erneston"
> Simla

MY DEAREST VED,

We were very sorry to learn about your accident and are still worried about you. I do hope the wound is not very serious and Pom has seen you after that. She must have taken you to the doctor. Please do let us know all about yourself. [Sister Pom had to take me to the doctor several times, because the wounds were bad and required a lot of attention. Besides, I was pulled down because of bad food and lack of sleep.]

With fondest love from all

> Yours,

From Mamaji, in Hindi, on August 14th, 16th, 17th:

My loving son, Ved, lots and lots and lots of love,

Ved, got your letter. Reading it gave me a lot of joy.

Ved, some clothes I've sent to you with your Daddy, but the cloth for your knickers got left behind. That I will send with Malhotra.

Ved, don't waste money. Please spend with care.

> Lots and lots of love,

> Your Mama

From Sister Umi, on August 19th:

> "Erneston"

> Simla

My dear brother Ved,

Ashok is persuading me to write to you. It is 9 P.M. now and he is yawning away but he will not listen to anything but tell me to write to his Vedi Bhapa [Brother]. He is getting very naughty and bosses over Arun unnecessarily. Poor Arun is so frightened of him. Now Ashok has started climbing trees. This evening he was on the swing with Googi & Padi [nicknames of Uncle Lakshman's sons]. He gives one push to them & gets two in return even then he does

464

not care and carries on. Now he wants me to stop for he can't wait any longer. After this he will doze off.

With love from all.

Yours,

From Ram Gopal Khanna, the ex-principal of the Emerson Institute, without a date:

> Government Industrial School
> Rewari, East Punjab

MY DEAR VEDI,

I am pleased to see that you are put up in a good school. Take the best advantage of it. I am glad you have learnt Type. May I expect a letter from you in Type written script.

I am Transferred to a school where I have to supervise leather work. Do you want a good shoe. Let me know per return. Luck has made me a *mochi* [Untouchable cobbler]!

No blind school has so far been started in East Punjab.

I want a detailed letter from you. I met your Daddy at Jullundur. He was all hale and hearty.

Yours affectionately

❧

ONE MORNING in September, 1948, when I had been at St. Dunstan's for about eight months, I was walking by the workshop area, and Captain Mortimer called to me: "Ved Sahib!" He often talked to me in Urdu and so used the polite form of address. "Stop for a moment. I've written to Doctor Sahib that you must try for education elsewhere, that you've learned all St. Dunstan's can teach you."

I felt I must have done something wrong. I felt like crying. I wanted to tell him that I didn't want to leave, didn't want to go and sit at the edge of the fire circle; but I didn't know how. "I have no place to go," I said. "I'm making good progress in typing and Braille. You can ask Cameron Sahib and Advani Sahib."

"I know," he said. "Cameron Sahib tells me you're typing your own letters, Advani Sahib tells me that you are fluent now in reading Grade 2 Braille, that you've sometimes even taught Braille classes for him. But the men here are bitter men, without their wives and children close by. You're a happy boy of fourteen. It's best that you get out. I've written to Doctor Sahib that the company of resentful, lonely, discouraged men is not good for an impressionable boy."

"But I have nowhere else to go to school."

"But, thanks to St. Dunstan's, you can now read and write and speak English. You also know from the example of Sir Clutha how well a blind person can do. It's time you went to the West."

XXIII

THANKING YOU
IN ANTICIPATION

T HE FORMER PRINCIPAL OF MY FIRST SCHOOL
wrote to the director of the Perkins Institution, in Massachusetts:

🌱🌱🌱
🌱🌱🌱
🌱🌱🌱

> New Delhi
> June 30, 1948

DEAR DR. FARRELL:

I am now writing to you on behalf of a blind boy about
whom I wrote to you when he was a student in my school
at Bombay about the year 1943. I am giving below his
details:

Name: VED PARKASH MEHTA
Date of Birth: March 21, 1934

Blinded in January 1938 from an attack of Cerebro-spinal-Meningitis.

Health: Good
Father's name: DR. A. R. MEHTA, M.B., B.S., D.T.M. (London), Director of Public Health, East Punjab.
He is a refugee from West Pakistan. His services are being continued in the Union of India.

I wrote to you in 1941 and again in 1943 to enquire whether you could kindly grant the boy a maintenance scholarship at Perkins and admit him as a special student as you do in the case of students from other schools in the U.S.A., Japan, and China. You were then of the opinion that the boy was too small to leave his parents. He is now 14 and is attending St. Dunstan's at Dehra Dun as a day scholar. I am told that he has shown special aptitude for music and he and his parents are anxious that he should specialize in Western music. The boy can speak and understand English. I am now writing to request whether you can kindly consider him for a maintenance scholarship in Perkins Institution.

If you gave him a scholarship, his father would send him to the institute in company of an American missionary who may be going to the States. I had a very frank talk with Dr. Mehta and he has agreed to the following terms, if you could accept the blind boy as a scholar in your institute.

I. Dr. Mehta would arrange for his passage and stand responsible for all the financial obligations in this respect.

II. He would deposit with you an amount varying from $100 to $200 immediately.

III. He would stand responsible for his ward's pocket money, as we say it in India, meaning additional personal expenses.

IV. He would be responsible for the payment of his boarding fees for holidays in a *rural area,* so that Dr. Mehta may find it easy to pay the bills for the holiday months.

He would also, if necessary, find out a local guardian for the boy in Boston.

I do not know whether I have done the right thing in making this request to you at this moment when Perkins is probably passing through a period of financial readjustment, but I have done this in full faith that due consideration will be given. I shall personally remain grateful if you consider this case sympathetically.

Yours sincerely,

Ras Mohun

The Rev. Dr. Gabriel Farrell, B.Sc., B.D., D.D.,
Director,
The Perkins Institution,
Watertown, Mass., U.S.A.

The head of my third school wrote to my father:

Phone 606
St. Dunstan's Hostel for
Indian War-Blinded
Governor General's
Bodyguard Lines,
Dehra Dun, U.P.
July 26th, 1948

Dear Dr. Mehta:

I feel I should give you a little advice regarding Ved Parkash's future. As you know this place is primarily a centre where we teach handicrafts. Braille and typing etc., are really secondary considerations and are only taught to such of our men as were literate before becoming blinded. We do not aim at a very high standard of education but merely at enabling the men to read Braille and be able to type. Ved, of course, could read Braille before he came here and is a very excellent reader. He can now type quite satisfactorily and I feel that you should consider the possibility of placing Ved in circumstances where his education can now progress beyond the standard which we have here. I feel certain that your ambition for Ved is that he should ultimately get a university degree and enter one of the higher callings open to a really capable blind man.

I also feel that Ved would be much better off in the society of boys of his own age. This constant association with mature men who have recently become blinded and who tend to regard their blindness as a terrible blow upon their fate and as perhaps visited upon them by the gods for some misdoing, may I feel tend to warp Ved's outlook. The child who has been blind since early childhood, regards blindness as normal and it does not have a very serious psychological effect upon him, but should he become imbued with the somewhat depressed outlook of one or two of our blinded men, it might give him some sort of complex.

Ved is a charming youth, most respectful and obedient and he has been very helpful on occasions in conducting the Braille classes when the actual Braille master, for some reason or other, has been away, and I should be only too glad for him to be here as long as he wishes to stay. However, having the interest of all blind persons at heart and not only those of our blinded ex-servicemen, I feel that you should very seriously consider the next step in Ved's progress—a step over which, I fear, we are not competent to help him for the reasons I have quoted above.

Yours very sincerely,

Sd/-A.H. Mortimer
Commandant
St. Dunstan's Hostel

A. R. Mehta, Esqr.,
Director of Public Health
East Punjab
Simla

The reply from Perkins:

Perkins Institution and
Massachusetts School for the Blind
Watertown 72, Massachusetts
July 29, 1948

Mr. Ras Mohun
Assistant Educational Advisor (Blindness)
Government of India
Ministry of Education
New Delhi 3, India

DEAR MR. RAS MOHUN:

I have your letter regarding Ved Parkash Mehta, and recall our previous correspondence about him. I am sorry to have to say that I am still of the opinion that it would be inadvisable for this boy at the age of 14 to come to this country with the long course of instruction that the completion of his education would require. There are, as you know, many problems involved as to his personal care, provision for the holidays and so forth. I note your suggestion regarding the boarding fees for the holidays, but at the present time it is practically impossible to secure boarding homes of that type.

These, however, are factors that you and the father will have to weigh. Then, too, I must make the statement that we are not in a position to grant a scholarship at this time. Our funds are much more restricted than they were when you were at Perkins. We have already committed ourselves to two girls from China, entering this fall, and that is about the extent of scholarship aid for the regular school program. As you know, we have a larger opportunity to give scholarship aid to those who are qualified for the Harvard Class.

It is always nice to hear from you, and I hope that your work is going along in a good way.

With all good wishes,

Sincerely yours,

Gabriel Farrell,
Director

Mr. Ras Mohun forwarded Dr. Farrell's letter to Daddyji, and Daddyji forwarded it to Captain Mortimer, but Captain Mortimer was convinced that I must leave St. Dunstan's—and the company of "mature men"—for my own good. That September, Daddyji brought me back to Simla, and I once again began living with the family in our rented upper flat of Erneston.

❧

"IT LOOKS LIKE a rotter of a day!" Brother Om exclaimed. "The balloon would have been up by now if it was going to be."

"What time is it?" I asked, stretching my legs to the bottom of the bed.

"Six o'clock," he said. "Go back to sleep."

He was leaning over my bed in the glazed veranda and looking out the window, which alone afforded a view of the balloon that the authorities would send up to signal that there would be ice-skating—that in the night it had been cold enough to freeze the water in the tennis court turned ice-skating rink. Ice-skating was the main sport in Simla in winter, as tennis was in summer. It seemed that my big brother and big sisters were always rushing off, morning and evening, for ice-skating or tennis, and that I alone was left behind. In Simla, I had no teachers, no friends. Usha was away at boarding school in Dalhousie, and Sat Dev, Daddyji's peon, who was assigned the duty of taking me out for walks, was kept so busy at the office that he often didn't show up. Most of the day, I was shut up in the cottage with little to do.

I so much wanted to go ice-skating with everyone else, but Sister Nimi had told me, "Ice-skating is one thing you can't possibly do. The rink is very crowded, and you have to see to avoid the other skaters. The skate blades are so thin that if you stood still to listen to where other skaters were, your feet would fly out from under you, and you would hurt yourself and everyone around you."

I had carefully examined her skate blades, and they really were as thin as she said they were. Indeed, I had difficulty imagining how anyone could stand on them without holding on to something. Then I remembered that bicycles didn't stay up unless one was moving. "But I learned to bicycle," I had said.

She had rejoined, "That was because you could practice by yourself in our empty compound for hours at a time."

Now Sisters Nimi and Umi joined Brother Om on my bed, pinning me under my bedclothes, as if I weren't there.

"Look! The window is wet with frost," Sister Umi said. "It must have frozen last night."

"Look! Look!"

"The balloon is up! The balloon is up!"

The three started bustling about, looking for their skates and boots, caps, mufflers, and mittens. Soon they were all dressed and were off—talking with balls of sweets in their mouths.

I stood shivering at the open door, listening to their retreating voices as they hurried up the slope.

Once, I had made them take me along. I had stood alone at the edge of the rink and listened to the happy shouts of the skaters as they went round and round to the tunes of popular film songs. Now and again, someone had skated up to me and asked "You're Om's little brother?" or "Why are you up so early if you can't skate?" or "Enjoying the music?" or "Cold enough for you?" I had hated the attention and had felt stiff with cold. After that, I'd stayed back in the cottage.

I quickly shut the door. The cottage felt bitter.

Jets of icy air blew in through the cracks around the windows and swept through the glazed veranda. I went back to bed—the only place where I could stay warm—but I couldn't go back to sleep. I waited for Mamaji or Ashok to wake up—Daddyji was on tour—but for a long time neither of them stirred.

It was that day, I remember, that Sat Dev told me about roller skates—that they required no rink of any kind, and that if one was good at balancing, as I was, one could learn to skate quickly on any wooden floor. I took all my pocket money, went with Sat Dev to the Mall Road, and bought myself a pair of roller skates. Like ice skates, the roller skates had tiny lips for attaching them to the soles of the shoes. Like ice skates, they had little nuts under the lips for adjusting the lips to fit the shoes snugly.

I fitted the skates onto my shoes with a little skate key that came with them, and started practicing standing on them on the wooden floor of our front veranda—pretending that they were ice skates and that the veranda was my private ice-skating rink. Holding the railing, I went up and down the veranda, half walking, half sliding. Now I would roll on one foot and bump along with the other, now roll on both feet. Sometimes the skates would shoot out from under me, and I would land on my back, but before the wheels had stopped whirring I would be back on the skates. In time, I discovered that by half sitting in a crouch with my weight forward I could skate without holding on to the railing. After that, it was only a matter of days before I was standing upright and skating unaided.

Whenever any other people were in the cottage—
the lower-flat tenants or Mamaji—they would complain about my skating. *"Grr-rrr-rrr* all day long,"
Mamaji scolded. "My head hurts. I don't know what
tortures you will think up next." I learned almost to
enjoy the deafening noise of the skates, and sometimes
even wished I could make more noise, so that I could
take revenge for not being able to go ice-skating.

The veranda was no more than fifteen feet long and
four or five feet wide. Sometimes I would get so dizzy
from skating back and forth, back and forth, turning
and turning, that I would have to lie down to stop my
head from skating, as it were.

One morning, I took my roller skates and went up
the slope to the road. It was after everyone had gone
to school or to college, to the office or to the bazaar,
and the road felt empty. I sat down at the roadside and
put on my skates and made them fast with the skate
key. And I was skating on the road. The road was open
and unconfined. The air was bracing. I felt giddy. I'll
skate down to the next house, I thought. I was gaining
speed. I heard a rickshaw coming. I tried to slow down.
But I realized in a panic that skating on tarmac was
not at all like skating on a wooden floor: the skates
seemed to be racing ahead on their own momentum. I
swerved to avoid the rickshaw. I missed it but smashed
into a lamppost.

I returned to the cottage with my lips swollen and
blood trickling down my face, with my roller skates
and half of a broken upper front tooth in my hands,
barely able to enunciate words to explain what had
happened. Even when the swelling in my lips went

down, I had trouble preventing words with "th" sounds in them from coming out in a hiss. I had to retrain myself to pronounce such words by placing my tongue a little higher, above the broken tooth.

❧

ONE COLD SUNDAY morning, Daddyji and I left our cottage for Clarke's Hotel, at the foot of the Mall. We were going to see a Mr. Baldwin, a representative of a large American corporation. The corporation's business in India was growing, and it wanted to do something for the country, so it was considering giving scholarships to deserving Indian boys for study in America.

We were walking along with our hands scarcely touching—as if I were normal and the road belonged to us. But I hadn't slept all night. One moment, I had felt excited, thinking that Mr. Baldwin would finally get me to America, and the next moment frightened, thinking that Mr. Baldwin's corporation could not possibly be interested in me, because my formal education had stopped with the fourth standard.

"Americans as a rule are easygoing people," Daddyji was saying. "They're very understanding. Even if you make a mistake in reading, it won't matter." I had brought along the latest Braille issue of the *Reader's Digest* so that I could do a reading demonstration for Mr. Baldwin. "Americans put a great deal of stock in personal impressions, and we Mehtas always make a good impression."

At Clarke's Hotel, Daddyji sent up his visiting card,

and we were directed to Mr. Baldwin's room, upstairs.

"So this is the young fellow, Doctor," Mr. Baldwin said, taking my hand. His hand was stiff and unfriendly. "Come on in and take a seat, son." He led me to a chair with a folding table in front of it.

Mr. Baldwin chatted for a time with Daddyji. Daddyji's British friends spoke English in a crisp, relaxed way that never failed to delight me, even though I didn't understand much, but Mr. Baldwin spoke fast in a nasal voice that I didn't like.

Then Mr. Baldwin came and stood beside my chair.

"Why does he cover his mouth that way?" he asked.

"I broke my tooth roller-skating," I said, putting my hand down. I don't like him, I thought. He should have directed the question to me.

"You must learn to be careful," he said, and he added very slowly, as if he were making an effort to speak to a child, "I understand you want to go to America. What education have you received so far?"

I told him in my little English, feeling ashamed and nervous.

"All told, four years, and you say the boy is over fourteen," Mr. Baldwin muttered. Then he said to me, in a brisk, businesslike manner, "Your dad says you have a *Reader's Digest* there—what month is it?"

I didn't know. I found the date and read it out.

He riffled through magazines on a table and announced, "As it happens, I have a print copy of the same month—we are in business."

Thinking that he would ask me to read an article of my choice, I had rehearsed "The Most Unforgettable

Character I've Met," and had learned all the difficult words in it. But, to my horror, he said, "There's a good article here about American youth and the effect of comic books on them. I think you'll find that interesting. Could you turn to it?"

I ran through the table of contents, painfully feeling that he was watching my hands—he had returned to the place beside my chair. I missed the article the first time around, and had to go through the table of contents again. Finally, I found the article and started reading it, holding my arms close to my sides and pressing down hard on the dots, in order to steady my fingers. I stumbled in the very first sentence, but Mr. Baldwin did not come to my rescue. Daddyji also said nothing. I read on, without paying attention to punctuation, the words coming out as isolated sounds, and "th" as "s."

Mr. Baldwin stopped me. "The sentence you just read—what does it mean?"

"I don't know." The sentence had unfamiliar big words, like "manifested," "juvenile," "delinquency."

He set up a portable typewriter on the folding table and started dictating to me from the same *Reader's Digest* article. If I can only steady my fingers, I thought, I'll be able to type it. I've just read the words, so I should know how to spell them.

I typed the first sentence of dictation fast, feeling excited, but then I realized that I was using the third row instead of the second one as the home row. I never did get my bearings after that. I typed and back-spaced, then typed over again.

Some time later, Mr. Baldwin was saying, "Doctor, your son's language handicap"—he again talked to Daddyji as if I were not in the room—"and the very sketchy quality of his educational foundation would put him in a poor situation in America, where he would have to compete with boys and girls who have been in school continuously from age six."

Daddyji protested. He said that I was quick to learn.

"Doctor, I'll write to a friend in my company back home, acquaint him with your circumstances, and try to find out what can be done," Mr. Baldwin said.

I didn't follow all the exchanges between Mr. Baldwin and Daddyji at the door, but I did catch one sentence: "I want to be frank, Doctor—I think this boy should stay here."

The door shut behind us, and Daddyji and I descended the staircase. "Success depends on determination and perseverance, and hard knocks are the best school for learning them," Daddyji was saying. His voice was confident, as usual. "It doesn't matter about the scholarship. Remember, I am always there. I will stand by you, and you will go to England or America. We'll manage somehow. I'll get leave and take you across."

"But I don't want you to pay. We are refugees. Mamaji says you have too many responsibilities."

"But if my children aren't my responsibility, then what is? From the very day you lost your sight, I set my heart on giving you as good an education as the other children. You have waited a long time."

A phrase from Daddyji's old diary which he had

quoted to Cousin Dharam Bir, and Cousin Dharam Bir had once repeated to me, came back now: "I'd sell my soul to give Ved an education."

"But when I lost my sight you had no idea about Partition and how it would change everything."

"Remember Lalaji's circumstances." Lalaji was Daddyji's father. "He used to say, 'I've come into the world to donate education.' No man in his position even dreamed of having an England-returned son, and yet both Daulat Ram and I studied in England. The sacrifices I have had to make to send you children to school are nothing compared to the sacrifices he made. I tell you, Son, education is in our blood."

"But I'll never get admission anywhere."

"Once you're in England or America, some school will be bound to take you. They won't send you back. I myself went to England without having an admission. Once I got there, doors fell open. We Mehtas carry our luck with us." He quoted an Urdu couplet:

Raise yourself to such heights that the Almighty,
Before deciding your fate, asks you, "What do you desire?"

I laughed right out, and forgot to cover my broken tooth.

❦

COUSIN NITYA NAND, who had gone to Cambridge for his postgraduate studies, wrote temptingly but confusingly:

St. John's Road
Cambridge

10 October, 1948

MY DEAR VEDI,

I got your loving letter just before I left Bombay; I have after all reached this place, and was glad to know that you are coming here too. I am looking forward to meeting you here.

I was sorry to know that the typewriter which was repaired at Bombay is not working well. I wish you had got it sent to Bombay, and I would have got it repaired again from the same man. Vedi, wait until you come here to get the typewriter repaired. It will be extra wastage of money to send a new one from here and it might even get damaged on the way. In the mean time you can get the old typewriter repaired, which you might have even got done by now, and use it for the next few months. I shall write to the National Institute for the Blind, and get one reserved for you, so that you get it as soon as you reach this place. Anyway you can discuss it with Daddyji and let me know, and I shall do accordingly. I am writing to Sister Nimi also about it. So write to me soon about it.

I had a very good journey and am now very comfortably settled in England.

With love,

Yours affy,
Nitya Nand

St. John's Road
Cambridge
7 December, 1948

MY DEAR VEDI,

I received your nice letter of the 6th Nov. just two days back. Certainly I shall try my best to get you admission in one of the schools here. I shall be going to London monthly and will personally go and try to get your admission done. I shall let you know about it in due course of time. You don't worry about it at all.

With love,

Yours affy,

Nitya Nand

Mr. Cameron, one of my teachers at St. Dunstan's, and my newfound correspondent, wrote:

Sarabjee's Flats,
The Mall
Ranikhet, U.P.
29th January, 1949

MY DEAR VED,

Thank you for your letter of the 22nd ultimo, duly to hand, and for your kindness in offering me "We're Here." If you don't mind, I will send it on to St. Dunstan's after I have read it, as it will be of no use to me once I have done so.

I must also thank you for offering to present me with

other books from your library; the only other book I would like to have is "Certified School Composition Writing," in 2 volumes, which you got out from Edinburgh last year, also any other educational books you would like to give away.

I am returning herewith, under separate cover, all the magazines which you so kindly let me have to read, except the magazine *Deepavali,* which has some very interesting articles on blind welfare in India, which I shall return later on if you wish.

I shall be glad to receive another bundle of magazines as soon as you send them, as I have read every article in those you sent.

I will give you my opinion on the book which you have promised to send me after I have read it. I certainly do not think "We're Here" a masterpiece, but it makes very pleasant reading while it lasts.

So you were determined to get "Sons," by Pearl Buck, in spite of my telling you that it was not a fit book for you to read!

No doubt you would like to know what sort of place Ranikhet is! I will tell you. It is a very pleasant hill station and a cantonment. We have the Kumoun Regiment here, in fact it is the centre for these troops. Ranikhet is about 6000 feet above sea level, and about fifty miles from the railhead. There is a very fine car road all the way, in fact it goes right on to Almora, and even further. It must have been a lovely place when the British were here and very crowded, but now most of the houses are lying empty. There are some very fine walks and forests of pine trees. One can also motor here, for miles around. Its climate is also very fine, not too cold; I wear a cotton suit all day, with a pullover all day. There is also a very fine station club, with a library

and plenty of tennis and billiards for those who are able to
play.

I have just received "The One Who Looked On." Many
thanks for same.

I will close now, as I have no more for the present.
With best wishes.

Yours sincerely,

H. L. Cameron

Although my typewriter was broken—the carriage
jumped, the left margin didn't hold, the bell often
didn't work—I typed on it from morning to night,
sitting at the dining table or in my bed, my fingers
stiff with cold. I wrote to Cousin Nitya Nand urging
him to make personal representations to English schools,
to Mr. Cameron about my impressions of what I read,
to Dr. Farrell urging him to reconsider, to Mr. Ras
Mohun and Captain Mortimer asking for letters of ref-
erence. I wrote off for books and magazines from Braille
printing presses abroad. (There was no Braille printing
press in India.) After I had read whatever material I
received, I sent it on to Mr. Cameron, who had lost
his job and could not afford to get material from abroad
himself.

Through my reading, I came to know the names
of many schools for the blind in England and America.
I read that the American Printing House for the Blind
put into Braille many of the publications of American
schools for the blind. I got hold of the catalogue of
these publications and learned the names of many more
schools, in states I had never heard of. I started sys-
tematically writing to all of them, giving my particu-

lars, saying diplomatically that that school was my first choice, and closing, "Thanking you in anticipation, Yours faithfully."

Whenever the postman brought a crinkly airmail envelope, I would race with it to get it read—generally to Sister Nimi. The letters, though they were answers to mine, would often turn out to be addressed not to me but to Daddyji, as if the authorities did not wish to enter into serious correspondence with a semieducated blind adolescent. Sister Nimi would open them anyway and read them to me. They were invariably letters of rejection, voicing more or less the same opinions: "Bringing these boys to England appears not altogether to be doing them a kindness." "It is essential that he not be too subjected to Western influence too early in life." "He's much too old for our school. It would be five or six years before he could finish our high school. Besides, what would he do for his holidays? Where would he go?" The principal of the Royal Normal College for the Blind, in England, referred us to the Secretary-General of the National Institute for the Blind. The Secretary-General explained that his institute was a welfare organization, and referred us to the headmaster of the Worcester School for the Blind. And the headmaster wrote to Daddyji that he had discussed my case with the Secretary-General, and that "we both agree that it would be a mistake to bring your son over to England during the most formative years of his life." To our surprise, he added, "We have had two Indian students at our secondary school for blind boys in Worcester and both of them on their return have found themselves ill-adjusted to Indian life, and out of touch with the interests of their people."

The director of a school in Paris inquired in French about the level of my proficiency in that language. (We had to get his letter translated.) The principal of a school in Edinburgh wrote that his was not a school at all but an asylum, and referred us to his friend the superintendent of the New York Institute for the Education of the Blind. "What does he want to do with his education?" the superintendent wrote. "Does he want to specialize in anything?"

"Shall I write to him that you would like to specialize in Western music?" Daddyji asked when he saw the letter. "If you could master Western music and fuse it with Indian music, you might have a great future in our cinema. Our film songs have started using Western harmony, and this has really enhanced their popular appeal."

"I don't want to go in for music," I said. "I want to study."

"What about going into work for the blind, then?"

"I have no interest in that. I just want a normal education, like everyone else."

Daddyji sent a rigmarole of an answer to the New York school, and we heard nothing more from it.

It was around that time, I think, that I typed out a letter to Prime Minister Nehru asking him to help me get to England or America, and telling him about Daddyji's long government service and about our all being refugees.

"Little Sahib, Pandit Nehru has the problems of millions of refugees on his mind and the weight of the entire country on his shoulders," Daddyji's clerk said when I took the letter to him to be checked for typing mistakes and stamped and posted. "He doesn't have time to worry about Little Sahib."

"Never you bother. Just post the letter. Register it, and bring me the receipt. I must have the receipt."

I got the receipt and, two weeks later, a perfunctory acknowledgment from the Ministry of Education, telling me that nothing could be done. I kept a brave face in front of Sister Nimi while she read it, but then I went back to my corner of the glazed veranda and broke down.

❧

COUSIN DHARAM BIR came to visit us in Simla. A great fuss was made over him. He was so close to Daddyji that if anything had happened to our parents during the Partition troubles he would probably have become our guardian.

"So what do you think, Dharam Bir, about Ved's going to America?" Daddyji asked.

Cousin Dharam Bir had just returned from there. He blew some smoke out slowly—he was about the only one of our relatives who dared to smoke in front of Daddyji. "It's a sick, immoral society," he said. "No place for any young boy. He's bound to go astray there."

"I don't know, Dharam Bir. I've always thought of America as God's own country, the land of opportunity," Daddyji said.

Cousin Dharam Bir blew out some more smoke. "In truth, I don't think Ved ought to go abroad at all. Suppose he did get all the education he wants and you want for him. What would he do with it? You know how many young people there are in this country today walking around with B.A.s and M.A.s. They can't get jobs—and they can see. Suppose he got sick there. Who would take care of him? Who would pay the doctor and hospital bills? Who has ever heard of a blind boy of fourteen going alone halfway round the world, to a place where he knows nobody—with neither family nor friend, neighbor nor relative to turn to in case of need? I think he would have a happier life if he stayed at home and concentrated on his music. That way, he would be close to us, and if he needed help we could all take care of him."

Later on, when Daddyji and I were alone, he said to me, "I wonder if Dharam Bir isn't talking sense. We do not know how your small education compares with that of boys and girls there. You may have to start at an elementary-school level. Whatever money I'd spend on sending you to the West could be used for you here to study music and perhaps one day to teach it. We could even open a small shop for selling musical instruments. What do you think?"

I asked myself yet again if I could ever be happy teaching music. I recalled my visit to the refugee camps. I remembered the refugee without hands. People had lost their limbs and lives, homes and land. What was the sacrifice of my ambition to go to the West compared with their loss? "Whatever you think best," I said, swallowing hard. "But can I still go on writing to schools in England and America?"

"Of course," Daddyji said. He put his hand on my shoulder. "Who knows? Something may still work out."

WEEKS PASSED. I continued writing letters to schools, appealing to one to reconsider, asking another to send me its admission forms. I now typed out this letter:

Simla

31st January, 1949

To

The Manager,

Arkansas School for the Blind,

Little Rock, Ark.

DEAR SIR,

Unfortunately I am a Blind boy of nearly 15 years of age. I beg to state that I would like to come over to America for my further studies. I know the following subjects.

English

Mathematics.

I can read Braille and can write Braille and I know sighted Typing with touch system. I know contraction and brivations. I have colified from the following Institution:

1. Dadar School for the Blind.

2. Emerson Institution for the Blind. Lahore Pakistan.

3. St. Dunstan's for the War Blinded. Dehra dun. India.

I have been studying in Dadar Blind School Bombay for nearly four years. I learnt Braille reading and Writing and English. I was sent there by my father when I was only five and a half [actually, a month short of five]. I got Blind when I was Four Years old, I lost eyesight with Manigitis. I studied in Emerson Institution For the Blind Lahore for one year [actually, six months], where learnt only Mathematics. And little bit of my Country Language. Then I was sent over to St. Dunstan's for the War Blinded. As this Institution was only ment for War Blind Soldiers then even as I was Civilian I had to come across many difficulties before I could get myself admitted in St. Dunstan's. I was taken there as a extra ordinary case. I stayed there for only one year [eight months] since I must confess that I made very good progress in St. Dunstan's. I stayed in St. Dunstan's Hostel for months and rest with my relation. I am herewith enclosing a copy of a Certificate from St. Dunstan's from which I think that you will be able to judge that what is my position at present. St. Dunstan's is the biggest Institution going in India. And there is no more scope in India for my studies as I have gained from St. Dunstan's what they could teach me. However, I shall feel obliged if you could send me your Application Form & Particulars. Anyhow I would like to possess your form & Particulars even if you do not think [I am suitable] or if such question arises that with which you would like to know some information. As this matter has been already been extremely delayed I won't like the matter to be more delayed. I am very sure that you will help me in this matter. I am typing this letter myself. The typing and Braille gr 2 was taught me in st. Dunstan's. My Father won't mind spending any thing as far I can be admitted in your School. I would like to complete your full course. I am herewith enclosing a Picture of mine I hope you will appreciate it. Do you have university Examination?

I do hope to get a reply in affirmative.

An early reply is requested.

Thanking you in anticipation,

Yours faithfully

V. P. Mehta c / o Dr. A. R. Mehta,
Director of Health services,
Erneston (Upper Flat)
Simla, East.
East Punjab (India)

February 16, 1949

Mr. V. P. Mehta
c / o Dr. A. R. Mehta
Director of Health Services
Erneston,
Simla-E
East Punjab, India

DEAR MR. MEHTA:

I have your letter of January 31, in which you state you
would like to attend the Arkansas School for the Blind.

In reply, I will say that we shall be happy to have you
if details can be arranged. By this I mean, entrance into the
United States, which I presume can be arranged on a student basis, financial details, length of time you will want
to stay, course, or courses you will want to pursue and perhaps other details.

The usual fee charged for out of state pupils is $600.00
per school year of nine months. I am not sure that $600.00
would be the fee charged you, but certainly no more than
that.

We offer an academic course which prepares you for
University entrance. This consists of the usual courses offered
in most American public schools. In addition we offer broad
courses in music, many vocations and athletics.

I am not enclosing an application form, but will send one later if you are still interested. We are sending you a Braille copy of the *Arkansas Braille News* so that you may read for yourself something of our educational programme here.

May we hear from you again, if you are still interested in our school.

Sincerely yours,

J. M. Woolly, Superintendent.

"Happy to have me!" I shouted. "It's an acceptance!"

"What do you know about the school?" Sister Nimi asked.

"All schools are the same."

"I think you'd better show the letter to Daddyji and see what he says."

That evening, I handed the letter to Daddyji. "That's encouraging, all right," he said. "But the school is in the South. That's a very poor part of the country. It may not have more than two or three classrooms. For all we know, it may be a school for Negroes. All the same, I'll follow the lead. But don't bank on it too much."

I could tell from his warm voice that in spite of his reservations he was happy for me.

"Is Arkansas near Johns Hopkins?" I asked. He had studied at Johns Hopkins.

"Not at all," he said. "By the way, I remember reading somewhere that the name of the state is not pronounced 'Arkan*sas*' but 'Arkan*saw*.'"

"Why is that?"

"I don't know. Perhaps people who live in that state have an odd accent."

"I don't care whether it's a school for Negroes or not, or what kind of accent they have—I'll just go there."

"That may be just as well. There may be no way to find out from here what the place is like."

Daddyji wrote to Mr. Woolly:

Registered Air Mail

Director of Health Services
East Punjab
Simla, dated the 9th March, 1949

DEAR MR. WOOLLY,

I acknowledge with many many thanks your kind letter to my son Ved Parkash Mehta, dated the 16th February.

Both my son and I are grateful to you for the hopes given therein to admit him into your institute. . . . Since [his blindness] over eleven years ago, I have left no stone unturned to give him as best an education as was possible in India, but as you know the facilities in my country are very limited indeed. . . . Ved regularly receives "Reader's Digest" every month and reads the same and he can read, understand and talk in the English language fairly fluently. He was presented with a small radio set a few years ago which has helped him a great deal to increase his knowledge of English as well as of the world. He has also a very good ear for music and if given proper facilities to develop the same he should do extremely well in this line.

He is a fairly tall boy for his age being 5′ and 5½″ in height with straight nose, straight hair and a fair complexion like that of an Italian or a Spaniard. In fact he may be called a handsome youth of the pure Aryan type as we all are from the north of this country.

I enclose a letter from Captain Mortimer, the Commandant St. Dunstan's Hostel, Dehra Dun. The letter is self explanatory and it was as a result of this advice from the Commandant that my son has been making efforts to get admission into an institute where he can have a fuller scope for his ability and ambition. The opinion of Captain Mortimer with regard to his ability and chances of making his life a success will I am sure interest you all the more in the boy and one day it may give you satisfaction in the fact that a really deserving case received support and due consideration from you.

In the absence of a proper form I hope the information given may enable you to kindly confirm his admission.

I have noted the usual fee charged and in case no special reduction can be given in the case of this deserving child, I shall be prepared to meet these expenses as well as to arrange for his board and lodging during Christmas and summer vacations; even though I may have to beg or borrow (being incapable of stealing!). Perhaps you are aware that there is rather a strict control on foreign currency particularly the dollars which are considered to be hard currency. But I am sure, as soon as I receive a certificate of admission for my son to your institute, I shall be able to arrange with the Reserve Bank of India to allow the requisite amount for his education. May I add here that you will very kindly recommend the amount including his expenses during the vacations so that the full demand is made in the very first instance.

Thanking you once again for your very kind letter and the interest shown in my handicapped son.

With kindest regards, I remain,

Yours sincerely,

A. R. Mehta

J. M. Woolly Esqr., Superintendent,
Arkansas School for the Blind,
Little Rock, Arkansas.

P.S. Reply per return of post shall be greatly appreciated.

March came and went, and April came and went—still there was no reply. I grew despondent. I supposed that perhaps Mr. Woolly had spoken to authorities in other schools and thought better of accepting me. Then, in the middle of May, Daddyji returned from the office with this letter from Mr. Woolly:

May 6, 1949

Dr. A. R. MEHTA
Director of Health Services
East Punjab,
Simla, India

DEAR DR. MEHTA:

I am happy to tell you that my Board of Trustees will permit me to admit your son to School at the beginning of the next school year, which will be about September 5, 1949. We will advise you later of the exact date.

I have located a place here in the City where he can spend his Christmas vacation, and also his summer vacations. We have an Agency which is concerned with the rehabilitation of newly blinded adults, which will be happy to take him during these vacations. Board and room there, will be in the neighborhood of $40.00 per month. It is a nice place and I can tell you he will be very well cared for, but of course, will receive no educational benefits at those times.

His tuition here will be $600.00 per school year. That, plus summer board and room, travel expenses, clothing and other incidentals, will make it necessary to have $1000.00 to $1200.00 available for the first year, I believe. Prices are on the decline in this country and perhaps he might do on somewhat less in subsequent years.

I am enclosing the usual application form required of State pupils, and would appreciate your completing and returning it to me.

Sincerely yours,

J. M. Woolly, Superintendent

The application form was very simple. Daddyji filled it out by hand, reading aloud some of the questions and his answers as he went along: "Color? Fair, like an Italian or a Greek. Was the child born blind? No. Is the child subject to epilepsy? No. Is there any physical deformity? No. Is it addicted to the use of tobacco or spirituous liquor? No. Is it of sound mind? Yes, highly intelligent. Has it had smallpox? No. Measles? Yes.

Whooping cough? Yes. Mumps? No. Has it now any contagious disease? No. Any offensive disease? No. Is it subject to fits? No. Were any of the relatives blind, deaf, and dumb, insane or afflicted with any infirmity of body, especially syphilis or tuberculosis? No. Give railroad station: Simla. Bus: Simla. Is this the nearest point of communication? Yes. Certificate to be signed by the parents or guardian: 'We hereby agree to furnish suitable clothing for the above applicant at the time of his entrance into the school and during his continuance there, and to provide for his travelling expenses to and from the institution, not only at the time of the first entrance and final departure but at any other time when his removal is requested by the Superintendent of the School.' "

"Why do they want to know about the railroad and the bus?" I asked as Daddyji was signing the form. "Why do they want to know about travelling expenses?"

"The application must be for local residents. They've probably never had an out-of-state student, never mind a foreign one. But you'll find all that out for yourself when you get there."

Daddyji sent off the application with a letter thanking Mr. Woolly ("The whole family is happy to learn that Ved has been admitted to your School and I can assure you that in due course you will find him a credit to his Alma Mater") and asking him what clothes I would need ("Ved is in a growing age and every few months we find that his clothes have either to be altered or discarded. . . . If you would kindly give me an idea of the present-day prices of woollen and cotton suits, shirts, blankets, cotton sheets, etc., I shall be able to compare the prices ruling here in India and arrange accordingly") but tactfully omitting to ask whether it was in fact a school for Negroes.

A day or two after Mr. Woolly's first letter arrived, I received copies of the *Arkansas Braille News.* I couldn't take my fingers off them. They told of how the blind students went around the town with just a white cane. They told of the school's course of study and of the social-adjustment program, of band music and athletics. I didn't know how a cane could take the place of the hand of, say, Usha or Sat Dev. But the *News* made the school sound like the best one in the world, and I couldn't wait to get there.

❧

"THE AGENT is my personal friend," Daddyji said as we walked into the office of Thomas Cook & Son on the Mall Road. "He may be able to get us a passage on a ship. Anyway, Mr. Woolly's letter can be used to get you a passport, an American visa, and dollar exchange. I have four months' accumulated leave, and we can go as far as England together. There I can look into the possibility of starting a medical practice in London in a year and a half, after my retirement. I can also try to arrange to get you into a school in England. If I can't, you can fly on to Arkansas and try your luck there. And I'll come back home for the final year of my service."

Daddyji introduced me to the agent: "This is my son who will be going to America."

"Congratulations, young man," the agent said.

499

I was five feet five and a half inches and weighed ninety-one pounds, but I felt that I was as tall and broad as the Aga Khan and was being presented with my weight in gold. I felt that I was already in "God's own country, the land of opportunity."

"Ships going to England are very full these days," the agent said, shuffling the pages of a register. "There's a long waiting list for every ship." He stopped shuffling and drummed his pen on the register, as if he were considering something. "But, as it happens, I have a cancellation of a small cabin with two berths on the S.S. Corfu—I have not informed our office in Delhi yet—and I can give it to you and your son, no questions asked. The ship is sailing in June. It will dock in Tilbury on the eleventh of July."

"Done, my friend," Daddyji said, his voice wide with a smile. He immediately began writing out a check for a deposit.

Daddyji thanked the agent, and we shook hands with him and walked out.

I had never been near a ship, and I couldn't imagine how a huge building with bedrooms and bathrooms, drawing rooms and kitchens, stairs and parapets could move on water without wheels or legs, coolies or animals. I couldn't imagine why waves didn't pitch it over or how people could stand on it, walk on it, eat on it. And S.S. Corfu sounded like such a tiny name for such a vast conveyance.

"We should have a good few weeks on the Corfu together," Daddyji was saying. "It will give you a chance to practice your English with me."

"And you will teach me how to eat with a knife

and fork." I had never learned to eat with a knife and fork; Indian food required only a spoon. Once or twice, I had tried to eat a poached egg on toast with a knife and fork, and it had slid off the plate and ended up in my lap. I used to stay awake wondering if I could ever learn to master a knife and fork.

"A knife and fork—oh, that you'll learn in no time on the Corfu. It's just a matter of being served English food and having to use them."

"And tying a necktie?"

"That, too. We'll have plenty of time on the Corfu."

We were in front of Clarke's Hotel, and I hurried Daddyji along.

❧

IMMEDIATELY AFTER our visit to Thomas Cook & Son, Daddyji went to New Delhi for a few days. When he returned, he said, "I have been posted to the capital. I am going to the central government as deputy director-general of health services."

We all spoke at once:

"Daddyji promoted!"

"Where is a little hill station and where is the capital of independent India? What is the comparison?"

"Yes, where is the Punjab government and where is the central government?"

"We'll be living in the same city as Babuji and Mataji—just as we did in Lahore."

"I have been trying for this post for some time," Daddyji said. "It enables me to stay on in service another year after my compulsory retirement at fifty-five." He turned to me. "But this means, Ved, that I won't be able to take my accumulated leave this summer, and we'll have to postpone our going to England for a year or so. But the year will pass very quickly."

"But we're already booked on the S.S. Corfu!" I cried. "You can't back out now!"

"We'll have to cancel our passage."

I protested, I pleaded, I sulked. I argued that I had nothing to do all day, that I couldn't live in the confines of Erneston another day. I said that I would go on the S.S. Corfu alone.

"A year will go very quickly," Daddyji said again.

"Daddyji has a duty not only to you but also to the rest of us," Sister Umi said.

"If we don't all make sacrifices, the country will go to the dogs, just as the British said it would when they left," Sister Nimi said.

"If you can wait a year, I'll take you," Daddyji said. "But if you insist on going this summer you'll have to go alone. It's up to you."

"I'll go alone," I said, without hesitation.

"Come to think of it, the shipping company won't allow you to travel alone," Daddyji said. "It would be liable if you fell down or hurt yourself. We know you won't but they will still take that view. We'll have to try to find someone to travel with you."

❦

IN THE MORNING, Daddyji left for New Delhi, saying that he would send for us the moment he was able to arrange for accommodations, and promising to look for a travelling companion for me.

44 Western Court
New Delhi
4-6-49

My dear Ved,

I am very glad to receive your affectionate letter of the
28th May. Though I still feel that the best plan will be that
I take you myself to U.S.A. even if we have to postpone
your studies by a year, still I have contacted Govan Brothers, Christian Medical Association and have asked Mr. Ras
Mohun to contact American Mission people to find a suitable companion for you by S.S. Corfu, which will reach on
11th July Tilbury London (please note the correct spelling).
As desired by you an advertisement will also be put in the
Statesman and let us hope for the best.

Please ask Thomas Cook & Son, Simla to send your file
to their Delhi office where I shall deal with the case on the
spot. I have also made an appointment with the Reserve
Bank people to get dollars. Your passport application also
needs completion for USA which can only be done after
dollars are sanctioned.

Namaste to you all.

Daddy

Erneston,
Simla East, E. P.
6th June 1949

My dear Daddyjee,

I was very pleased to have your affectionate letter of 4th
June which I received yesterday. I have also received a letter

from Mr. Cameron, who was Braille/typing teacher in St. Dunstan's and for whom we tried to get a job. He can see partially and he is very good in English. Now we have got a spare berth and I have written him to offer it on payment of course. He is a very nice person and once we thought of calling him up to Simla if I could learn something from him. But however the proposal was dropped if you remember. But I still think that if he could travel with me in the same cabin I think it will be very good company and as he won't be able to do any thing else that he will be able to devote all the time to teaching me. I bet that I shall be able to learn a lot from him. I would also like you to write to Mr. Cameron. He can see his way and has got so much sight. I also hope that he shall be able to assist me on the board to move about as desired by Thomas Cook people. However, you are the best judge. If this plan of mine is valid to your point of view, please call me down to Delhi so that I could get my clothes and visa etc. made or done. The time is very short and I would like you not to delay this matter at all. The things which I need I shall bring along, for instance, my type writer, Braille writer, books which I would like to read in the ship. Please ring me up or wire me to come. I shall be waiting eagerly. Regarding going a year after, I believe that the thing you want to do to-morrow that should be done to-day and the thing which you want to do to-day that should be done, the very minute. I am of course follower of Great Man Gandhi in this. Now I have got no English teacher. I have packed my books and am absolutely ready to leave Simla whenever I receive instructions from you for which I am waiting very patiently.

I am using office typewriter and it has got a defect which is that it makes spaces when I do not even press the space lever. It also misses some letters and the people who have some idea of this say that it is due to rains.

Sat Dev the peon is transferred. The Finance Secretary Mr. K. S. Malhotra told him that he would come and take up his work at his office immediately. He refused many times but then Mr. Malhotra passed Official orders and told the present deputy director of health services to send him immediately. At the same time, Mr. Malhotra also told him that as soon as Dr. Mehta asks for you you shall be sent to him without any delay and you need not worry. Sister Umi told me to convey this message to you. She also says that if you want to keep him call him at once as Sat Dev says that even if he has to leave his Government Job here and become a private servant of yours he shall do so without any hesitation.

With respects to you and love from all.

Yours

Ved

New Delhi
7th June, 1949

MY DEAR VED,

I have carefully considered your letters and I have made effort to contact certain people who are going to United Kingdom by S.S. Corfu. I have been able to contact through Mr. Ras Mohun, Reverend G. Ross Thomas, whose daughter Patsy with two other friends is travelling by the same ship. [Patsy Thomas's mother had been the superintendent of Dadar School, and Mr. Ras Mohun had intended to send me on a ship to America with her in 1942. The coincidence made me remember all over again the years of waiting.] I have also been able to secure 600 dollars for the first six months of your education in U. S. A.; there was some difficulty in obtaining the same as the name of your school does not appear in the institutions recognized by the Reserve Bank for teaching purposes in U.S.A.

I have very carefully discussed the question of your proceeding either by this boat or by air. Everyone of the friends and those dealing in passages have stressed the point that the best course for you is to travel in the last week of August directly from Delhi to Little Rock. The 'plane will leave at 1:30 in the afternoon reaching London next day in the evening and a day after will reach New York and on the fourth day you will be in Little Rock. The stewardess on board the aeroplane shall look after you during these three or four days which will certainly pass like a pleasant dream. I have come to the definite conclusion that you will have to go by this means, whether you like it or not; you must have trust and confidence in my decision. As regards the expenses, it is not for you to worry and even here the saving is not worth the trouble of the long voyage and break of journey in England.

I do not consider it fair either to ask Miss Thomas to look after you on the voyage, where perhaps your cabin may be at one end of the ship and theirs at the other, or, even on a different deck. Although Nitya Nand will do all to make your stay in United Kingdom fairly comfortable, I am worried that it will affect his studies and it will be perhaps hard for you to pass as long as six weeks in England doing nothing, and from England, in any case, you will have to fly as no passage from England to New York can be arranged by any shipping company till about the middle of

October, when the Atlantic Ocean becomes really rough and I have an experience of such a weather, which, to say the least, is not congenial by any means.

Please consider the matter carefully keeping in view the experience of your father and friend, as against your youth and your enthusiasm, and write to me definitely tomorrow. Day after tomorrow, I shall send a telegram to Bombay cancelling our passages by S.S. Corfu.

I quite appreciate your point of view that you have no teachers to teach you and how difficult you find the time to pass, but I have taken everything into consideration before coming to the decision that you must fly and get to Little Rock within the shortest period from India which will be as little as three to four days only and very comfortably you shall reach your destination.

Lastly, I would like you not to fret at all to have trust in God who does the very best for us.

With my very best wishes for you all, I am,

Yours affectionately,

Daddy

Erneston,
Simla East, E.P.
15th June, 1949

My dearest Cousin Nitya Nand,

Taking every thing in consideration I have decided to go by air to U.S.A. via U.K., where probably I shall be lucky enough to see you. I shall be flying from India in the third week of August. I shall be in the place where I want to go on the fourth day. I shall reach the next evening in

507

U.K. the day I start at one 30 P.M. Daddyji being in Delhi even consulted Mr. Ras Mohun and he also advised Daddyji that I should go by Air because, being not big enough, I may get ill or such like things may happen in the voyage. Although I would have loved to go in the Ship than by air, it could not be helped. What was decided by Daddyji I thought there was not use grumbling on it and I have not taken it to heart at all.

Please do see me when I shall reach England, for an hour or so. I shall write to you later about the name of the aeroline and the name of the aero drome where it will land.

Please do let me have your opinion that does one feels lost when one is out of ones own Mother Country and is so far from their parents. Specially I being in U.S.A. shall be very far from my parents and I always ask how will I manage to pull on. But for the sake of my future I think that it is very necessary for me to study very hard, wherever I may be, as I think that is my duty towards my parents who will take so much pains to send me out and then give me so much money. Please also let me know if there is any way for a Blind boy like myself to earn little bit in U.S.A. As you being in U.K. must be knowing Blind students who partly support themselves to Educate themselves. I do not want any person in our family or relatives to feel that if I could have been a sighted Boy I could earn partly if not whole to educate myself as others do in abroad who are foreigners. I am that sort of a person who would like not even one person to feel that I should have been sighted as I do not feel that myself. I think that I am better off than others. I would like to know if or how the Blind students in U.K. are earning to educate themselves partly and are less nuisance to their parents as I want to be.

It is very certain that I must give you a nice present

while passing through England. But for a person like you who is very simple I cannot decide at all.

Do write to me something about foreign countries and how the people there are and how to deal with them because now when I reach U.K. I won't have enough time to talk or take lessons from you very long. I do not know about any thing of the people there and how to live with them and how to manage or pull on with them with keeping your dignity.

Now there is one more thing which is worrying me, that is, that if there is war between Russia and United States before I leave for U.S.A. my father may not send me at all or the U.S.A. people may not accept me. Please let me know that will there be any war so soon as all that. If there be, then My future will be ruined absolutely and my ambitions will remain where they should not.

Do write to me something about your self and of your college.

May I closing hoping that I shall have a letter from you very soon and shall have answers to the questions which I have raised in this letter.

With respect,

Ved

Erneston,

Simla East, E.P.

15th June, 1949

My dearest Daddyjee,

Brother Om collected my typewriter from Captain Puri yesterday. But I regret that there are yet three defects in

the typewriter though I am typing on it now. I can type on
it alright. Without the typewriter I feel lost. It types well
no doubt. There are three defects which are that the tabu-
lator does not work, at times the back spacer fails, and there
is a little defect in margin releaser that is, that once the
carriage reaches the end it does not come back unless you
press the margin releaser. I am writing also to the Under-
wood people and explaining the defects and telling them
that when I come down to Delhi on my way to the U.S.A.
I shall have to get the defects removed.

I am writing to National Institute for the Blind as you
directed in your telephone call to Sister Nimi saying that I
shall be travelling by air and that I thank them for all they
did to help with the sea passage.

I feel very dull whole day long as we have been trying
our level best to find an English teacher who could give me
accelerated lessons for Little Rock, but so far we have been
very unsuccessful. I went over to C. L. Chopra's place but
he refused absolutely to come and teach me. I also asked
Principal Mr. A. R. Khana of Bharagawa Municipal College but could not get a satisfactory reply. I wish I could
get a proper teacher who could correct my pronounciation
and my English. But where there is will there is way and
so I am pulling on.

I hope that you are in your best health and do not have
to work more than you should.

The weather here is quite nice but I hear in Delhi it is
very hot. Therefore I think it must be difficult for you to
go about in the sun. Please do let me know about the visa
if you have been able to do something about it and which
injections are necessary in order to obtain it. I shall get
those injections here and shall obtain medical certificates

and on your instructions I shall dispatch them on to you.

Please also do let me know whether there is any possibility of getting some fare concessions by air. I wrote to one of my friends in England of course pen friend and he told me that he thinks that through the blind welfare officer by which he meant Mr. Ras Mohun I should be able to get some concession. However, you being in Delhi I think you will be able to get some concession. Please do not take the ticket unless you are very sure that there is no such rule as that blind people are entitled to get concessions. Have you heard anything about securing a government scholarship for me?

With respects.

Yours affectionately,

Ved

Arkansas School for the Blind
Little Rock, Arkansas
June 1, 1949

Dr. A. R. Mehta
Director of Health Services
East Pb.
"Erneston," Upper Flat, Simla East,
India

DEAR DR. MEHTA:

Ved will not need much wool clothing as our winters are rather mild. He will need one or two wool suits for dress wear, three or four cotton or wool pants for school wear and perhaps a few pair of light cotton pants for summer wear. I should say a dozen cotton shirts would suffice for a year. He should have a jacket of some sort for school wear during the winter. If you want to buy a light overcoat he could use it. However, it is not essential. Light weight underwear and socks are sufficient since our building is steam heated. You will not need to send sheets, blankets, towels or pillow cases since we supply those.

Shirts may be bought wholesale through the School at around $2.00 each. A wool suit of good quality will cost $35.00 to $45.00. We can buy everything he needs at wholesale, except suits, overcoats, hats and such, and I believe save you some money.

I am enclosing a list of clothing which we recommend for the usual nine months school term, however your situation will be somewhat different.

We have found a place for vacation periods that will be happy to have Ved at any time you may send him. However, I would suggest he try to arrive not later than September 1st.

As you probably know, our school system is composed of eight grades in elementary school and four years of high school. From your correspondence, I judge Ved is ready for either the last grade of elementary school or the first year of high school. Will you please give us your thought as to where he should be placed. We, of course, want to put him where he should be and will administer some tests on his arrival to try to determine his placement. However, we would appreciate your thought on the matter.

Sincerely yours,

J. M. Woolly, Superintendent

Dty. Director General of Health Services,
Government of India
New Delhi
20th June, 1949

DEAR MR. WOOLLY,

I am very grateful to you for your letter dated the 1st instant, in which you have given the details of the clothes etc. required by Ved. Your directions will be complied with.

Ved and myself were to come via sea but as my leave has been cancelled and I have been appointed Deputy Director General of Health Services with the Government of India at New Delhi, Ved will now have to come alone. I have decided to send him by air. It is proposed to send him in the middle of August. He will reach New York in three days' time and may spend a week or 10 days with a niece of a friend of mine—she is married to a blind musician and they, being both Europeans [by which he means Americans], are settled in New York. Ved shall fly from New York to Little Rock and will inform you of the exact time and date of his arrival.

As regards standard of his education, Ved may be fit for the last grade in elementary school. I do not think he is fit for the first year of high school. You may, however, judge for yourself. All I can say is that he is exceptionally intelligent and quick to grasp and has an excellent application. In fact he is exceptionally brilliant as compared with my other six children and I have every hope that you will find him so. Moreover, his outlook on life is very responsive and he is a happy child.

513

With kindest regards, I remain,

Yours sincerely,

A. R. Mehta

To

J. M. Woolly Esqr.,
Superintendent,
Arkansas School for The Blind,
Little Rock, Arkansas

June 28, 1949

Dr. A. R. Mehta
Dty. Director General Health Services
Government of India
New Delhi

DEAR DR. MEHTA:

We shall expect Ved the latter part of August, will meet him at the Airport and immediately provide for him.

Formal class work will begin around September 12, and I am sure he can use the time prior to then in making acquaintances, seeing the City and perhaps we can administer some tests to determine his grade placement.

If questions arise regarding his trip, please write me.

Congratulations on your promotion.

Sincerely yours,

J. M. Woolly, Superintendent

Erneston,

Simla 2,

3rd July, 1949

MY DEAREST DADDYJEE,

With great difficulties I have been able to get hold of C. L. Chopra again. But as now the rainy season has started here C. L. Chopra says it will be difficult for him to come regularly. He says that when the day is good only then he shall be able to come.

I went to shop yesterday and gave two pants and one suit to be made. I also gave one dressing gown to be made and I shall get all these above mentioned clothes by the tenth of this month. I shall be also able to obtain all the inoculation and vaccination certificates by the tenth. You need not worry at all. I asked the health officer if I could take only half dose of cholera and if he would certify that I had taken full dose. But he refused to do so. I shall take first dose of cholera in my life to-morrow and the other on the seventh day as stated in the form.

Lieutenant Gautam Singh is visiting here. He says that it shall be necessary for me to take over coat with me. He also says that I shall not have to get my over coat weighed and I shall be able to put my small things in the pockets of it and that I should fill them up. Please do let me know whether I shall need an overcoat or not. In the list also it was stated which was sent by Arkansas that I should bring a light overcoat with me.

With due respects.

Yours affectionately

Ved

❦

WE ALL MOVED to New Delhi and started living in one big room in a government hostel for officers called Western Court, sleeping on the floor among trunks, utensils, and plates. (The room had a back veranda, where the servants set up a little kitchen.) Mamaji found herself a pandit, and he fixed the fourteenth of August—the day before her forty-first birthday and the day before the second anniversary of Indian independence—as the most propitious day for me to fly. Since Partition, Daddyji had begun giving in to Mamaji in such matters. He said that although he didn't believe in such things he would not gainsay the pandit. He got me reservations for that date.

Mamaji busied herself in getting my clothes sewn. Sister Umi started knitting me a sweater. Sister Nimi bought me records of love songs of Saigal and Noor Jehan to remind me of home. Sister Pom came from Dehra Dun to be with me. Ashok painted me a picture. Every time America was mentioned, Usha would become quiet or start to cry. Brother Om started avoiding me, as if my going were a matter of indifference to him. I mostly stayed in bed, feverish with inoculations: cholera, more cholera, typhoid. (I had not been able to take the inoculations in Simla.) Then I was down with malaria for a few days.

❦

ONE MORNING, Daddyji came home from the office and said, "I've succeeded in getting an appointment for you to see Prime Minister Nehru tomorrow. It seems you're the first Indian blind boy ever to go to America for education, and you'll be going off with his blessings."

The most venerated man in India, the leader of three hundred and fifty million people, and he was going to see me. "What will we talk about?" I asked.

"Well, you'll bring your typewriter and the *Arkansas Braille News* and give a demonstration. Om will come along and bring his camera and take a couple of snaps of us."

The next day, I got into my newly sewn long trousers and proper jacket, and Daddyji, Brother Om, and I drove to the Prime Minister's house.

We were a few minutes early, and we drove around the streets, which seemed unusually quiet. The air, heavy with August heat and Delhi dust, blew in through the open windows, messing up my hair and my new clothes and covering the seat with grit.

We pulled up in front of the Prime Minister's house exactly at the appointed time, twelve, and were asked to wait in a room just beyond the front veranda.

I opened and set up my typewriter (now repaired), inserted a page, and double-checked the home row. One flubbed interview was enough, I thought.

"I hope Pandit Nehru won't object to my taking a picture," Brother Om said, fidgeting with the camera.

"Why should he?" Daddyji said. "He's probably one of the most photographed men in the world."

There were gentle but deliberate footsteps, and we all stood up. "This is my son Ved, about whom I spoke to you, Panditji," Daddyji said, putting his arm around my waist. "And this is my eldest son, Om."

We did our *"Namaste"*'s and sat down, I with Pandit Nehru on a sofa, and Daddyji and Brother Om across from us.

I wanted to tell Pandit Nehru that I had kept my faith in him all through the cruel days of Partition, that I loved him like Daddyji, that I was prepared even to forgo ever going to America if I could serve him in any way. But my tongue felt like a wedge of ice in my mouth.

"Panditji, he can type. You can dictate to him," Daddyji said.

"Oh!" he exclaimed.

I waited, my fingers poised over the keys, to do his bidding.

Prime Minister Nehru seemed to be lost in thought, but then he dictated this slowly, as if he were thinking it out as he went along: "I shall be an unofficial ambassador of my country. Wherever I go, I will behave in a manner that will bring honour to my homeland."

I took out the page and handed it to him. The cheep-cheep of a sparrow on the veranda sounded very loud in the silence.

"Panditji, would you autograph it?" Daddyji said.

"Oh!" he exclaimed. "Oh! If you like."

Daddyji gave Pandit Nehru his fountain pen, and he signed it.

Daddyji asked me to read aloud a few sentences from the *Arkansas Braille News*.

"That's not necessary," the Prime Minister said. There was a little rustling at my side, as if he were gesturing. "What happened?"

Pandit Nehru, Ved, Daddyji, New Delhi, 1949.

"Meningitis," Daddyji said. "He was very small."

"Oh!" he said, again with surprise in his voice. He added, to me, "I was almost your age when I went to England. But that was a very long time ago."

I had often heard him speak on the radio, but I was not prepared for how youthful he sounded. He could be a student, I thought—an older student, but still a student. I felt very close to him.

Pandit Nehru stood up.

"My eldest son would like to take your picture with Ved, Panditji," Daddyji said. "The light on the veranda is good."

We walked out onto the veranda, and Brother Om took two pictures—one of Pandit Nehru and me, the other of Pandit Nehru, Daddyji, and me.

As I was taking leave of him, Pandit Nehru abruptly said, "I think your father told me you were going to Arkansas. Why Arkansas?"

I felt blood rushing to my cheeks. I didn't want him to know about all the rejection letters I had received. (I destroyed most of them one day when I was seventeen, because I thought of them as constituting a record of my shame.)

"It is Arkansas, isn't it?" he asked.

"Yes," I said, my voice barely audible to me. "That's the only place that would have me."

✤

BESIDES MY PARENTS and my brothers and sisters, Bhabiji, Mataji, Bhua Parmeshwari Devi and Bhaya Mukand Lal, Chachas Daulat Ram and Balwant and

Raj Kanwar and Romesh, Chachis Subhadran and Sheila and Janki and Savitri, Uncles Dwarka and Lakshman, Aunties Pushpa and Vimla, Cousins Vidya and Shanti and Dharam Bir and Satya and Prakash and Dev and Nishchint and Sheila and Leil and Yog and Ravi and Swaran and Rani and Rajinder and Asha and Satinder and Usha and Vijay and Naresh and Arun and Anil and Dimpi were all coming to see me off at the airport. But Mamaji said that Babuji's health was indifferent and he might not be able to come.

With Daddyji, I went to visit him at Uncle Dwarka's, in Old Delhi, where he was then living. He was sitting on the veranda and reading a newspaper.

"I don't know when we'll meet again," he said. "People who go to America nowadays never come back."

"Babuji, he'll come back," Daddyji said. "But it may be ten years or more, because he'll have to do his high-school graduation and then go to the university. Who knows? Then he may want to go in for a Ph.D."

"Your daddy is a very ambitious man," Babuji said.

"I'm certainly ambitious for him," Daddyji said.

"I would like to give you something to remember your grandfather by," Babuji said. He got up and went into his room, which was just to one side of the veranda.

I sat on a wicker chair drumming my fingers and wondering what Babuji could possibly have to give me. He had lost everything. He had been able to bring just his walking stick from Lahore.

Babuji returned and put in my hand some thin papers held together with an ordinary shoelace type of tape. "Just some papers," he said. "Family papers."

I held them on my lap as he blessed me and gave me the customary sweetmeat to sweeten my mouth.

In the car, I asked Daddyji what the papers were.

He glanced over them and said, "They look like some fragments he's copied out for you from his diary about Partition."

I thought no more about them until years later, when I was trying to recall my departure. Then, when I had read them, I asked myself: What could Babuji have had in mind? (By then, he was dead.) How could he have given me something so staggeringly apt—especially since at the time Babuji believed that I was destined for the life of a music master, and that my going to the West was a whim of Daddyji's and mine which had to be humored?

The diary fragments read:

20 June / 1947 A daughter named Renu born to Vimla in Lahore. Second son of L. {Lakshman} Das born 24 / 8 at 10.30 pm at Amritsar. Trouble started in the Punjab in Feb-March. Massacre & destruction of property by Muslims created a record. The mischief spread to Amritsar, Lahore, and other places in June and by end of August conflagration was in full swing—Had to leave Lahore on 27 / 8 as a refugee. Stay in Lahore having become most risky. Came to Amritsar where Bhagwan Das was working as addl. [additional] Sessions Judge. I was accompanied by wife & Son Lakshman Das. His wife had left earlier with Shanti & family on 11 / 8. Knew that Lahore was to go to Pakistan but believed that this would bring calm & peace and that Muslims will stop their nefarious activities. As a fact the situation grew worse and Hindus & Sikhs were forced to run

away for their lives. Immigration from both sides was in full force. Men, women & children were ruthlessly attacked in trains, trucks, & on foot, on both sides of the border & both Govts. failed to stop this carnage. This continued till end of Sept.—This continued in October, too. Convoys of Refugees from both sides continued their journeys by foot, by truck, & by rail—Left Amritsar for Delhi on 25/10 with Lakshman Das & his wife & boys & my wife in his Car—Refugees met us on the road which had been destroyed by floods of Sutlij & Beas Rivers. Reached here at 8.30 p.m. Delhi was full of refugees from Pakistan, rich & poor, old & young. All had suffered immense losses & were depressed.

At Delhi, too, the atmosphere was far from calm. Mahatma Gandhi did heroic work to restore peace—His daily speeches at his evening prayer meetings proved most effective in this connection. This created a sort of opposition & revolt in certain type of Hindus who were for retaliation against Muslims. This culminated in a most brutal act by a Hindu Mahratha young man who shot M. Gandhi dead at his prayer meeting on evening of 30/1/1948. What a tragedy. A Preacher of Ahimsa and a Saint thus assassinated by most violent act of a Hindu. God's ways are mysterious. There was a universal revulsion & general condemnation of this tragedy not in whole of India but in the whole world—Lakshman Das left for Lahore on 6/2 to work in his Bank there. He remained in Lahore for a fortnight.

On 27/2 full 6 months after our exit from our home, 16 Mozang Road, Lakshman Das went there to bring out our goods left there. But it was found that everything valuable had been stolen by the occupants!! What a sad commentary upon Muslim mentality. Highest to lowest have become callous & feel no scruple in robbing Hindus by all possible means.

Lakshman Das arrived in Delhi on 1.3 by air—He had fever due to Jaundice. His stay in Lahore nervousness, worry, & anxiety led to breakdown of his health, which needs rest, physical & mental.

Lakshman Das transferred to Lucknow. Reached there on 6 / 5. Wife went to stay with Pushpa, who was ill—I spent a fortnight in Simla in May.

4 / 6 / 1948—Sister Durga Devi died in Delhi at 4 p.m. after prolonged illness.

His will be done. A link with past snapped-

19 /5 / 1948—Daughter born to Santosh at Delhi-8 a.m. Named ——— [She was named Munakshi, or Minna.]

PRESCRIPTION OF HAIR OIL

Soak half a seer [a *seer* is two pounds] Emblica Officinalis in water overnight. In the morning add to this half a seer of pure mustard oil. Put the mixture on fire and heat till water evaporates. Remove it from fire. Cool. (Strain to remove emblica officinalis and) keep oil in bottle. It should be applied on wet hair. Hair will grow and baldness will disappear. . . .

BHAIRON RAS PILL

Piper Longum	1 Tola [11.75 gms.]
Piper Nigrum	″
Zingiber Officinale	″
Sulphuatum Hydragyrium	″
Rome variety	
Soda Biberas	″
Sulphur treated with Emblica	″
Officinalis	

Anacyclus Pyrethrum	"
Anaqua Sodii Chloridum	"
Cannabis Indica	"
Sweet Flagroot-superior quality	60 Mashas [one fifth of a *tola*]
Milk	½ seer
Water	½ seer

The last three are to be boiled together till the needles of Sweet Flagroot can be removed easily.

All the other ingredients are to be pounded fine and mixed with the boiled product and made into pills the size of a gram.

It is efficacious in the treatment of Cholera, Diarrhoea, vomiting, stomach-ache.

Babuji's concerns, many of them now incomprehensible, were also fragments of my life, for his diary fragments, painstakingly copied out by hand, crystallized my past of exertion and depression, of waiting and impatience, of births and deaths, of sickness and superstition, of loss and exile—right down to his home remedies for many of the afflictions I left behind when I left India that August.